A2 FILM STUDIES
The Essential Introduction

 KT-195-827

A2 Film Studies: The Essential Introduction gives students the confidence to tackle every part of the WJEC A2 level Film Studies course. The authors, who have wide-ranging experience as teachers, examiners and authors, introduce students step by step to the skills involved in the study of film. The second edition has been redesigned and rewritten to follow the new WJEC A2 syllabus for 2009 teaching onward, and is supported by a companion website at **www.alevelfilm studies.co.uk** offering further advice and activities.

There is a chapter for each exam topic including:

- The small-scale research project
- The creative project
- Aspects of a national cinema – Bollywood; Iranian; Japanese; and Mexican
- International film styles – German and/or Soviet; Surrealism; Neo-realism; and New Wave
- Specialist studies – urban stories and empowering women
- Spectatorship topics – early cinema before 1917; documentary; experimental and expanded film/video; and popular film and emotional responses
- The single film critical study – every film covered

Specifically designed to be user friendly, the second edition of *A2 Film Studies: The Essential Introduction* has a new text design to make the book easy to follow, includes more than 60 colour images and is packed with features such as:

- Case studies relevant to the 2009 specification
- Activities on films like *All About My Mother*, *10*, *Vertigo* and *City of God*
- Key terms
- Sample exam questions
- Suggestions for further reading and website resources

Matched to the new WJEC specification, *A2 Film Studies: The Essential Introduction* covers everything students need to study as part of the course.

Sarah Casey Benyahia is a teacher of Film and Media Studies. She is the author of *Teaching Contemporary British Cinema* (2005) and co-author of *AS Film Studies: The Essential Introduction* (2nd edn, 2008).

Freddie Gaffney is Chief Moderator for Film Studies with the WJEC. He is also a screenwriter, filmmaker and Senior Lecturer in Location and Studio Production at Ravensbourne College of Design and Communication. He is co-author of *AS Film Studies: The Essential Introduction* (2nd edn, 2008).

John White is an A level examiner for Film Studies with the WJEC and a lecturer in Film, English and Media at Anglia Ruskin University in Cambridge. He is co-author of *AS Film Studies: The Essential Introduction* (2nd edn, 2008), co-editor of *50 Key British Films* (2008) and also of *50 Key American Films* (2009).

247 350

The *Essentials* Series

This series of textbooks, resource books and revision guides covers everything you could need to know about taking exams in Media Studies, Film Studies or Communication and Culture. Working together the series offers everything you need to move from AS level through to a degree. Written by experts in their subjects, the series is clearly presented to aid understanding with the textbooks updated regularly to keep examples current.

Series Editor: Peter Wall

AS Communication and Culture: The Essential Introduction, Third Edition
Peter Bennett and Jerry Slater

A2 Communication and Culture: The Essential Introduction
Peter Bennett and Jerry Slater

Communication Studies: The Essential Resource
Andrew Beck, Peter Bennett and Peter Wall

AS Film Studies: The Essential Introduction, Second Edition
Sarah Casey Benyahia, Freddie Gaffney and John White

A2 Film Studies: The Essential Introduction, Second Edition
Sarah Casey Benyahia, Freddie Gaffney and John White

Film Studies: The Essential Resource
Peter Bennett, Andrew Hickman and Peter Wall

AS Media Studies: The Essential Introduction for AQA, Third Edition
Philip Rayner and Peter Wall

A2 Media Studies: The Essential Introduction, Second Edition
Peter Bennett, Jerry Slater and Peter Wall

AS Media Studies: The Essential Revision Guide for AQA
Jo Barker and Peter Wall

Media Studies: The Essential Resource
Philip Rayner, Peter Wall and Stephen Kruger

A2 FILM STUDIES
The Essential Introduction

Second edition

**Sarah Casey Benyahia,
Freddie Gaffney and John White**

Routledge
Taylor & Francis Group

LONDON AND NEW YORK

NORWICH CITY COLLEGE		
Stock No.	247350	
Class	791.43 BEN	
Cat.	BZ	Proc	3UL

First published 2006 by Routledge

This edition published 2009
by Routledge
2 Park Square, Milton Park, Abingdon, Oxon, OX14 4RN

Simultaneously published in the USA and Canada
by Routledge
270 Madison Avenue, New York, NY 10016

Routledge is an imprint of the Taylor & Francis Group, an informa business

© 2006, 2009 Sarah Casey Benyahia, Freddie Gaffney and John White

Reprinted 2010

Typeset in Novarese and Bell Gothic by Keystroke, 28 High Street, Tettenhall,
Wolverhampton
Printed and bound in Great Britain by Bell & Bain Ltd, Glasgow

All rights reserved. No part of this book may be reprinted or reproduced
or utilised in any form or by any electronic, mechanical, or other means,
now known or hereafter invented, including photocopying and recording,
or in any information storage or retrieval system, without permission in
writing from the publishers.

British Library Cataloguing in Publication Data
A catalogue record for this book is available from the British Library

Library of Congress Cataloging in Publication Data
Benyahia, Sarah Casey.
   A2 film studies: the essential introduction / Sarah Casey Benyahia,
   Freddie Gaffney and John White. — 2nd ed.
      p. cm. — (The essentials series)
   Includes bibliographical references and index.
   1. Motion pictures. I. Gaffney, Freddie, 1964- II. White, John. III. Title.
   PN1994.B4334 2009
   791.43—dc22 2008044827

ISBN10: 0–415–45436–0 (pbk)
ISBN13: 978–0–415–45436–0 (pbk)

CONTENTS

Figure acknowledgements   vii
Preface   xi

Introduction   1

PART 1   FILM RESEARCH AND CREATIVE PROJECTS (FM3)   21

1   Introduction to FM3   23
2   The Small Scale Research Project   28
3   Creative Projects   47

PART 2   VARIETIES OF FILM EXPERIENCE – ISSUES AND DEBATES (FM4)   69

4   Introduction to FM4   71
5   Bollywood 1990 to the present   79
6   Iranian cinema 1990 to the present   99
7   Japanese cinema 1950 to 1970   124
8   Mexican cinema 1990 to the present   144
9   German and Soviet cinemas of the 1920s   162
10   Surrealism   184
11   Neo-realism   201
12   New Waves   229
13   Specialist Study 1: Urban stories – power, poverty and conflict   250
14   Specialist Study 2: Empowering women   268

PART 3 VARIETIES OF FILM EXPERIENCE (FM4): SPECTATORSHIP TOPICS 287

15 Spectatorship and early cinema before 1917   289
16 Spectatorship and documentary   315
17 Experimental and expanded film/video   344
18 Popular film and emotional response   364

PART 4 VARIETIES OF FILM EXPERIENCE (FM4): SINGLE FILM – CRITICAL STUDY 383

19 Introduction to single film – critical studies   385

    Modern Times (Chaplin, US, 1936)   386

    Les Enfants du Paradis (Carné, France, 1945)   392

    Vertigo (Hitchcock, US, 1958)   394

    The Battle of Algiers (Pontecorvo, Algeria/
      Italy, 1966)   399

    Sweet Sweetback's Baadasssss Song
      (van Peebles, US, 1971)   401

    Solaris (Tarkovsky, USSR, 1972)   406

    Happy Together (Wong Kar Wai, Hong Kong, 1997)   409

    Fight Club (Fincher, US, 1999)   413

    Talk to Her (Almodovar, Spain, 2002)   419

    Morvern Callar (Ramsey, UK, 2002)   423

    Glossary   426
    Web resources   435
    Bibliography   437
    Index   441

FIGURE ACKNOWLEDGEMENTS

i   Electric Theatre, *circa* 1900. Photo by Keystone/Getty Images   3

ii   *Arrivée d'un Train en Gare de la Ciotat* (Lumière, 1895)
© Lumière/The Kobal Collection   6

iii   *10,000 Years BC* (Emmerich, 2008) © Warner Bros Pictures/
The Kobal Collection   11

iv   *Moulin Rouge* (Luhrman, 2001) © Twentieth Century Fox/
The Kobal Collection/Ellen Von Unwerth   18

2.1   *Munich* (Spielberg, 2005) © Dreamworks SKG/Universal/
The Kobal Collection/Karen Ballard   32

2.2   *Im Lauf Der Zeit/Kings of the Road* (Wenders, 1975)
© Filmverlag Der Autoren/The Kobal Collection   37

3.1a   *The Cabinet of Dr. Caligari* (Wiene, 1919) © BFI   51

3.1b   *Casino Royale* (Campbell, 2006) © MGM/United Artists/
Sony/The Kobal Collection/Jay Maidment   51

3.2   *Pirates of the Caribbean: The Dead Man's Chest* (Verbinski, 2006)
© Walt Disney/The Kobal Collection   58

5.1   The notorious slum colony of Dharavi in Mumbai. Photo by AFP/
Getty Images   81

5.2   Indira Gandhi photographed in 1981. Photo by RDA/Central
Press/Getty Images   87

5.3   Publicity shot for *Dil to Pagal Hai/The Heart is Crazy* (Chopra,
1997) © Yash Raj Films   89

5.4   Advertising for *Dil Chahta Hai/The Heart Desires* (Akhtar, 2001)
© Excel Entertainment   94

6.1   Young Iranians out shopping in Tehran. Photo by Scott Peterson/
Getty Images   104

6.2   *Persepolis* (Paronnaud and Satrapi, 2007) © 2.4.7. Films/
The Kobal Collection   108

6.3   Mania Akbari in *10* (Kiarostami, 2002) © MK2/Abbas Kiarostami
Productions/The Kobal Collection   109

6.4   *Offside* (Panahi, 2005) © Jafar Panahi Film Productions/
The Kobal Collection   118

7.1   *Rashomon* (Kurosawa, 1950) © Daiei/The Kobal Collection   127

7.2   *Tokyo Nagaremono/Tokyo Drifter* (Suzuki, 1966) © BFI   131

7.3   *Nihon no yuro to kiri/Night and Fog in Japan* (Oshima, 1960)
      © BFI   135
7.4   *Saikaku Ichidai Onna/The Life of Oharu* (Oshima, 1952)
      © BFI   137
7.5   *Tokyo Monogatari/Tokyo Story* (1953, dir: Ozu) © Shochiko/
      The Kobal Collection   138
7.6   *Shinju ten no Amijima/Double Suicide* (Shinoda, 1969)
      © BFI   139
8.1   Poster for *Sólo con tu pareja/Love in the Time of Hysteria*
      (Cuarón, 1991) © Fondo de Fomento a la Calidad
      Cinematográfica   148
8.2   *Batalla en el Cielo/Battle in Heaven* (Reygadas, 2005) © BFI   153
8.3   *Babel* (González Iñárritu, 2006) © Anonymous Content/Dune
      Films/The Kobal Collection/Murray Close.   157
8.4   *Arráncame la Vida/Tear This Heart Out* (Sneider, 2008)
      © Altavista Films   160
9.1   First World War losses. Reproduced by kind permission of
      Matthew White   163
9.2   *Strike* (Eisenstein, 1924) © Goskino/The Kobal Collection   167
9.3   *The Cabinet of Dr Caligari* (Wiene, 1919) © BFI   176
10.1 *L'Age d'Or* (Buñuel/Dali, 1928) © Vicomte Charles De
      Noailles/The Kobal Collection   187
10.2 *The Phantom of Liberty* (Buñuel, 1974) © BFI   192
10.3 *Alice* (Jan Svankmajer, 1988) © BFI   199
11.1 *The Bicycle Thieves* (de Sica, 1948) © BFI   205
11.2 *L'albero degli zoccoli/The Tree of Wooden Clogs* (Olmi, 1978)
      © RAI/IC/GPC/The Kobal Collection   210
11.3 *Ossessione* (Visconti, 1943) © Industria Cinematografica
      Italiana/The Kobal Collection   214
11.4 *Roma, Citta Aperta/Rome, Open City* (Rousellini, 1945)
      © Excelsa/Mayer-Burstyn/The Kobal Collection   222
12.1 *Au Bout de Souffle/Breathless* (Godard, 1959) © Films Around
      the World, Inc.   233
12.2 Humphrey Bogart © The Kobal Collection   240
12.3 *Chungking Express* (Wong Kar Wai, 1994) © Jet Tones
      Productions/RGA   244
13.1 *La Haine* (Kassovitz, 1995) © Lazennec/Canal+/La Sept/
      The Kobal Collection   254
13.2 *City of God* (Meirelles, 2002) © Globo Films/The Kobal
      Collection   260
13.3 *Tropa de Elite/Elite Squad* (Padilha, 2008) © Zazen Producoes/
      The Kobal Collection   266
14.1 A cinema audience watching Ginger Rogers © The Kobal
      Collection   272
14.2 *Todo Sobre mi Madre/All About My Mother* (Almodovar, 1999)
      © El Deseo/Renn/France 2/The Kobal Collection   275

14.3 *Roozi ke zan shodam/The Day I Became a Woman*
(Marziyeh Meshkini, Iran, 2000) © Makhmalbaf Productions 282
15.1 An interior view of the kinetoscope 292
15.2 *Arrivee d'un Train en Gare de la Ciotat* (Lumière, 1895)
© Lumière/The Kobal Collection 295
15.3 *Le Voyage à travers l'impossible* (Méliès, 1904) © BFI 299
15.4 The front of Comique movie theatre, a nickelodeon theatre in
Toronto, Canada, circa 1910 304
15.5 Florence Lawrence – the Biograph Girl circa 1918 © IMP/
The Kobal Collection 306
15.6 *Intolerance* (Griffith, 1916) © Wark Producing Company/
The Kobal Collection 309
16.1 *La Sortie des Ouvriers de l'Usine Lumière/Workers Leaving a
Factory* (Lumière, 1895) 317
16.2 *Drifters* (Empire Marketing Board, UK 1929) © COI/The Kobal
Collection 320
16.3 Filming *Night Mail* (Watt/Wright, 1936). Reproduced by
permission of Frenchpix.com 322
16.4 A poster advertising *Triumph des Willens/Triumph of the Will*
(Leni Riefenstahl/Nazi Party, 1935) © NSDAP/The Kobal
Collection 325
16.5 *Notebook on Cities and Clothes* (Wenders, 1989)
© Road Movies/The Kobal Collection 334
16.6 *Bowling for Columbine* (Moore, 2002) © Alliance Atlantis/
Dog Eat Dog/United Broadcasting/The Kobal Collection 340
17.1 *Metropolis* (Lang, 1926) © UFA/The Kobal Collection 347
17.2 *Meshes of the Afternoon* (Deren, 1943) © BFI 353
17.3 *Man with a Movie Camera* (Vertov, 1929) © BFI 355
17.4 *Tout va bien* (Godard, 1972) © Anouchka/Vicco/Empire/
The Kobal Collection 359
18.1 A cinema audience watching in the dark 366
18.2 *Un Chien Andalou* (Buñuel/Dali, 1928) © Bunuel-Dali/
The Kobal Collection 370
18.3 Dietrich in *Morocco* (Sternberg, 1930) © Paramount/
The Kobal Collection 374
19.1 *Modern Times* (Chaplin, 1936) © Chaplin/United Artists/
The Kobal Collection 386
19.2 *Les Enfants du Paradis* (Carné, 1945) © Pathé/The Kobal
Collection 392
19.3 *Vertigo* (Hitchcock, 1958) © Paramount/The Kobal Collection 394
19.4 *The Battle of Algiers* (Pontecorvo, 1966) © Casbah/Igor/
The Kobal Collection 399
19.5 *Sweet Sweetback's Baadasssss Song* (van Peebles, 1971)
© Yeah/The Kobal Collection 404
19.6 *Solaris* (Tarkovsky, 1972) © Mosfilm/The Kobal Collection 406
19.7 *Happy Together* (Wong Kar Wai, 1997) © Block 2 Pics/
The Kobal Collection 409

19.8 *Fight Club* (Fincher, 1999) © Twentieth Century Fox/The Kobal
Collection   414
19.9 *Talk to Her* (Almodovar, 2002) © El Deseo/The Kobal
Collection/Miguel Bracho   419
19.10 *Morvern Callar* (Ramsey, 2002) © Company Pictures/The Kobal
Collection   423

X FIGURE ACKNOWLEDGEMENTS

PREFACE

A2 Film Studies: The Essential Introduction is designed to be used as a follow-on volume from *AS Film Studies*. It uses the same framework of case studies, summaries and activities to introduce a range of topic areas and help students to develop their ideas independently. As with the previous volume, the aim is to aid a clearer understanding of the link between theory and film, and to suggest models for future work. The move from AS to A2 can be recognised initially in two ways: the wider range of films studied and the development of critical approaches.

AS Film Studies emphasises the popular, mainstream forms of film familiar to students through cinema, DVD and TV. The higher level of study at A2 is founded on that knowledge but extends the scope of the films analysed – introducing film from different countries and cultures as well as different historical periods. The interest in and willingness to engage with different forms of film styles is at the heart of A2 film studies and can be expressed in a variety of ways. The Small Scale Research Project (FM3) allows you to follow an interest or passion arising out of your studies or from your personal engagement with film, and encourages exploration of the widest possible avenues of film-related study. The Studies in World Cinema (FM4) section covers a great variety of cinematic contexts, themes, styles and periods including new wave films, surrealist film, Japanese and Mexican cinema. While the film texts are likely to be unfamiliar, the approach to study is based on the skills introduced at AS: textual analysis of film language, institutional context and the spectator experience.

In addition to the extended range of film styles covered, the development from AS to A2 is apparent in the greater emphasis on critical and theoretical approaches to film, some of which – spectatorship, representation, messages and values – were introduced at AS. The specification for film studies describes the application of critical approaches at this level as taking students to the 'threshold of theory' and this is central to the approach here. While many of the ideas explored in this area are complex and – at times – abstract, the use of specific examples and case studies seeks to introduce them practically with integration into the areas previously covered. Rather than reinforcing a canon of theories and theorists, students are encouraged to try out and test ideas as they work through their own examples and to evaluate the usefulness of such approaches. Some of the critical concepts studied are also indicative of the development of film studies as an academic discipline; 'Empowering Women' replaces feminist and gender approaches and there is a greater emphasis on the role of the audience – beyond the traditional concept of the film spectator.

Ultimately it is hoped that this book will encourage students to seek out new film experiences and question the role of film and film institutions in the wider society – while enhancing the enthusiasm for watching films which brought them to this subject in the first place.

We would like to express our thanks to Aileen Storry (Associate Editor, Routledge), Andrew Watts (Production Manager) and Ann King (Copy Editor) for their help in the preparation of this book. Thanks are also due to those colleagues and family members who provided invaluable support and understanding throughout; and to the staff and students of the Media and Film Departments at Colchester Sixth Form College and Cambridge Regional College for their helpful contributions.

INTRODUCTION

What are the underlying issues we should begin to consider as we develop our study of films? This chapter considers:

- the fundamental nature of film as a medium
- the complexity of the concept of realism and the 'real'
- one way of dividing film into four major types
- the relationship of ideology to filmmaking and viewing

INFORMATION BOX   *i*

This chapter will introduce a range of ideas that will be important for the second year of the WJEC's A level in film studies. At this stage in your studies you will be asked to think more deeply about the nature of film and the experience of watching films. You will also be expected to consider a broader range of films including foreign films and films made in deliberate opposition to mainstream cinema.

Film technology

To begin with, let us reconsider the nature of films. Normally we simply take them for granted as a form of entertainment; but, as you know, film studies demands that we should be somewhat more questioning and analytical.

Bringing films to the screen involves quite complex technology, first, to record, and second, to replay images that often pose as real life but are, in fact, fictional constructions. (Even documentaries are in some sense false and unreal, and might be considered 'fictional constructions'.) Various machines, and machine operatives and overseers, are used in an attempt to capture some aspect of human life and experience.

ACTIVITY

In what ways might documentaries be considered to be 'false and unreal'? You might think about, for example, setting, performance, use of the camera, editing and sound, as well as ideas connected to character, storytelling and narrative structure.

INFORMATION BOX

Films obviously cannot be real life because they are 'staged', with actors pretending to be something they are not within a constructed space that again purports to be something it is not. One of the traps we need to be careful to avoid is the urge to talk about filmed situations as if they were real. (This is equally important for anyone working within related fields such as the study of literature.) The key to our understanding has to be to see these 'fictions' as precisely that: constructed fabrications (or narratives) that have been made by a particular cast and crew engaged for that task.

(If you have completed the first year of a film studies A level, this should amount to nothing more than a formal statement of the position at which you have already arrived in your understanding.)

In films, a series of still photographs are put together and shown one after the other at a certain speed in order to create the illusion of movement. Effectively we have a mechanical version of that exercise whereby you draw a character in a series of developmental poses on the corner of a notepad and then by flicking quickly through the pages make that character appear to come to life. (Often, of course, when you watch older films, some, or all, of the cast will be dead. The camera has captured something of them (or of them pretending to be a character in a fictional narrative) and this has been preserved in such a way that they are able to continue to communicate with us.)

This highlights an important idea for film studies, namely that film is an 'illusion', a term which implies both 'pretence' and 'contrivance'. Throughout its 100-plus-year history the film experience has often been sold to the public in terms of the 'magic' of cinema, and Hollywood films themselves have often been referred to as creating the 'illusion of reality'. You should now begin to think more deeply about the nature of this 'illusion'.

ACTIVITY

- In groups, if possible, research the origins of cinema and the development of early cinema technology. What are the forms of entertainment that are generally seen as pre-dating and leading towards the cinema experience? Where and when did filmmaking first begin? Where and when did the cinema originate? In basic technical terms, how do cameras and projectors work?
- Decide on an area to research as a group and prepare a short five-minute presentation.

Figure i Electric Theatre, circa 1900: an early cinema in America advertises 'moral and refined' moving pictures, 'pleasing to ladies, gentlemen and children' (Photo by Keystone/Getty Images).

What you should recognise time and again, as you complete the tasks set in this book, is that there are no simple answers to the sorts of questions you are being asked. The response to every question is invariably much more complex than you might initially have anticipated. For example, in considering where and when cinema originated, do you include early 'peephole' devices where only one person at a time could use the device to view the images, or 'magic lantern' shows that did not actually employ film? You might consider that the first impulse towards cinema came from the moment people began to tell each other stories, or from the moment a role and place was found within the community for the storyteller – an individual valued not for his or her productivity but for some other non-material contribution to the group.

REALISM: A cinematic style that attempts both to use filmmaking techniques to create the 'illusion of reality' (and thereby allows an audience to engage with the on-screen subject as 'real') and to shoot narratives that are representative of 'the real' without attempting to 'fix' a meaning on them (allowing the audience to 'read' a film's reality in a variety of ways according to their own view on the subject, and to what they see on screen).

Generally, we associate this term with the effort to accurately reproduce some aspect of the day-to-day world in which we live. Whether this is possible, and if possible, to what degree and in what ways, are points that have been endlessly discussed. Use the term with care, thinking about exactly what you mean each time you employ it. In one sense, for example, film is obviously not realistic: it is a two-dimensional representation of a three-dimensional experience.

Originally 'realism' was the term used to describe a nineteenth-century movement in art and literature that aimed to represent people and places as they were rather than as classical art had portrayed them. The focus was on the contemporary social life of the lower classes which had not usually been represented in 'art'.

André Bazin, a French film critic, argued that the mechanical photographic approach offered by cinema made it an objective medium ideal for representing 'the real'. However, if film does bear some relationship to 'the real' (whatever that might be) it is clearly a highly constructed version of 'the real' arising from a particular perspective and involving choice, selection and contrived performance (what should be filmed, from what angle, what should happen, how it should be lit and so on).

- How would you define the concept of 'the real', or 'the real world'?
- What difficulties can you see with any definitions you might arrive at?
- Compare your ideas with those of others, if possible.

Real/unreal

Films are edited in such a way as to seemingly present, if not the real world then at least some possible real world; while all the time we are in fact being offered completely unreal (if not downright surreal) sequences. Consider: this is a medium in which instantaneous movement through time and space, time-travel, is an accepted norm. We can at one moment be in a certain place at a certain point in history only to be transported in the next instant either backwards or forwards through time to a totally new, totally different location. What relation does this have to our everyday experience of the world? Surely it is a very strange, unreal experience when seen like this? You can remember your life, or tell the story of your life, in this fashion; but you cannot live the day-to-day, moment-to-moment fact of your existence in this way. (This is, of course, a trait shared with all other forms of storytelling, the novel, for instance.)

ACTIVITY

- List the locations and time-periods used in any film you have seen recently.
- How frequently were you 'transported' through time and space by the film?
- Could you map out diagrammatically the movements that occurred?

Film language

We no longer cower as objects appear about to move out of the screen towards us – as early audiences apparently did for one of the Lumière brothers' early screenings in Paris of a train arriving at a station (although the physical sensation of shock or surprise is still very much a valued part of the cinema experience). The reason we no longer duck is that we know what to expect, we know how film 'works', we have learnt the language of film and the relationship of film to our physical experience of the real world.

Figure ii *Arrivée d'un Train en Gare de la Ciotat* (Lumière, 1895). Early cinema goers did not know the language of film.

More correctly, each of us is socialised into an understanding of film mechanics from an early age. The debate may continue about the educational value of young children watching TV, but what is certain is that this is the start of a process which means that by the time they go to the cinema they are already familiar with the basis of the film experience.

The language of film, as with all living languages, continues to evolve. Early silent cinema clearly has basic similarities to our experience of film today but at the same time there are also differences. As film students you will now be expected to show some interest in how film has changed and developed over time, and how your experience today is similar to, and different from, that of audiences in other periods.

ACTIVITY

Briefly research the names of other filmmakers who were working around the same time as the Lumière brothers and who could also be considered to be contenders for starting the whole idea of cinema. Which countries did they come from? When were they working? Were the technologies they were using different from those employed by the Lumière brothers or broadly similar?

ACTIVITY

If you know any young children, try to observe the way in which they interact with things they see on the TV screen and/or how they react when they are taken to the cinema for the first time.

Film as an illusion

In studying film it is vital never to lose sight of the fact that films are an illusion being created in specific ways and for particular reasons, and that the whole process is open to assessment and analysis by the viewer, or spectator. Stories involving exciting characters, intriguing plots, pace, action, surprise and suspense are so enticing and the technology being used in the cinema is so mesmerising that the tendency is for the force of the narrative to take over, preventing us from achieving the critical detachment necessary for analytical investigation.

SPECTATOR: Technically this term is most correctly associated with a psychoanalytical approach to film which focuses on the relationship of the individual to film. The approach suggests that in following the narrative, certain subject positions are constructed for the viewer to occupy; men, for example, might identify with the male hero and women

continued

with the female protagonist hoping to achieve marriage. It was brought to prominence by feminist film theory in the 1970s which saw the dominant positions offered for the viewer by Classical Hollywood films as being essentially 'masculine'.

ACTIVITY

Consider the last film you saw: was there a character with whom you felt you were being asked to identify and was the film constructed in such a way as to encourage you to achieve that identification?

Different types of film

You are already familiar with the concept of genre which enables us to group films as being, for example, science fiction, horror or romantic comedy; but there is a further way of dividing film into rather broader categories. 'Sci-fi', horror, 'rom-com' and similar genre categorisations all refer to narrative realist film of one sort or another, but there are forms of film that do not rely on using actors to tell a story within a recognisable (even if sometimes fantastical) world.

ACTIVITY

What are these broader categories or types of film? Make a note of the different sorts you have seen, or can think of.

(Note that, as stated above, for the purposes of this exercise, sci-fi films, noir films, romances, dramas, comedies, thrillers, horror films and so on should all be seen as subsections of one particular type that is 'narrative film' in which imagined stories are told to the audience using a variety of styles and approaches. This will therefore be the first broad category on your list, 'narrative film'; but can you think of any others? One type has in recent years made a comeback into the cinema with films such as *Fahrenheit 9/11* (Moore, 2004) and *Super Size Me* (Spurlock, 2004). A further type is used by Quentin Tarantino for certain chapters within *Kill*

Bill, Vol. 1 (2003). Yet another type moves away from stories and realistic photographic representations of the real world to use film in an altogether different way. Furthermore, if you take a look at cinema and TV advertising you will find all four types in regular use.)

Compare your list with others, if possible, and discuss any differences.

four types of film

There are four major types of film.

- The first is the *fictional narrative film* telling stories about people with whom an audience can identify: this is clearly the dominant form of cinema. It is the form that as we said above is often itself split into a series of different genres – romantic comedy, psychological thriller, action, science fiction and so on.
- The second is the non-fictional *documentary film*, which in general terms could be seen as the straightforward effort to record on film some aspect of contemporary human society (with perhaps an attempt in the process to reveal some 'truth' about the real world).

INFORMATION BOX

i

The documenting of reality was really what the Lumière brothers started with, what they called 'actualities' (for example, workers coming out of a factory, or a train coming into a station). However, the issue of where fact and the documenting of real life ends and fiction starts is a tricky one. The simple presence of the camera may clearly change not only people's actions but also what they have to say and how they say it, perhaps encouraging them to 'play' certain roles they feel are expected of them. If this is the case, maybe anybody taking part in a documentary becomes in a sense an actor.

- Watch a scene from a Ken Loach film that uses ordinary people (or 'non-actors') and consider how effective you think this has been as a filmmaking technique.
  (A scene that could be used for this exercise would be the one in *Raining Stones* (1993) in which the central character, Bob, and his mate are in the working men's club trying to sell mutton.)
- Why has Loach chosen to use people who are not professional actors? Can you tell they are not trained as actors; and if so, how? (You should consider issues such as body language, delivery of lines and interaction with the camera.) Is the scene effective? In what ways could it be considered to be effective, or ineffective?

- The third film type is the *animated film*, which makes drawn or sculpted figures look as though they are moving and speaking. This form of film can now, through the use of computer-generated images, overlap into mainstream fictional films, becoming such a successfully integrated feature that we are barely able to see the join between one acted illusion of reality and the other computer-generated illusion of reality. Just as excitingly, animation can be mixed with a traditional fictional narrative, as in Quentin Tarantino's *Kill Bill, Vol.1* (2003).

INFORMATION BOX

You should notice how both documentaries and animations still employ storytelling. Perhaps this is another point at which you should consider once again the place, role and importance of storytelling in human society.

CGI [COMPUTER-GENERATED IMAGES]: This is obviously an interesting technological development in itself, but the most important aspect of these images for the industry is probably the way in which they have made animation a much cheaper, and therefore more profitable, possibility. Traditional animation involving the production of thousands of individual drawings was both time-consuming and expensive, and as a result few feature-length animations were made. From *Toy Story* (Lasseter, 1995) onward, full-length animations have become an important part of the commercial film business.

Figure iii *10,000 Years BC* – one of the many films released in 2008 that rely on CGI.

■ The final type of film is *experimental film*, which exploits film's ability to create a purely abstract, non-realistic world. (As suggested earlier, one area where this type of film is now being used is in TV and cinema advertising – large cinema screens in particular lend themselves to the almost hypnotic abstract patterning of light and colour.) Old-fashioned children's kaleidoscopes and various styles of abstract painting serve to remind us of just how fascinated we are by colour, shape, light and combined patterns of these elements. Film clearly offers excellent possibilities for such abstract patterning allied (importantly) to movement. Even within our most usual experience of film (i.e. fictional narratives), it seems likely that this fundamental aspect of cinema, the flashing of shapes and colours before our eyes, is probably an important part of the attraction.

The purpose of advertising is obviously to sell products to potential purchasers. What you will notice if you study advertising is the way in which the full range of film styles and types are used in the effort to engage us as consumers. Fictional narratives, animation and (spoof) documentary are all used along with abstract experimental work involving a variety of shapes, colour and movement as a means of attempting to persuade us to identify with manufactured goods or services, or perhaps to encourage us to simply 'buy into' an idea or concept that is linked to a particular product (e.g. the rugged outdoor life and '4-x-4' vehicles).

In what ways could commercial films made for the cinema be seen to be similar to and/or different from advertising 'shorts'? Make a list of your ideas and discuss them with others, if possible. (Noticing that the advertising 'short' could be seen to be 'a film' is part of the process of broadening your understanding of exactly what constitutes film.)

Popular usage of the term 'film'

Without wishing to undermine the value of other types of film it remains the case that owing to the mainstream dominance of narrative realist film we will need to continue to pay particular attention to it. Films involving narrative and a realistic setting almost totally dominate the marketplace; so much so that whenever 'films' are discussed it is normal to take the term as shorthand for these sorts of movies. However, you should now begin to become more aware of other possibilities for film.

Neither documentaries nor experimental films are usually even thought of as being part of the broad sweep of 'film', and animation is predominantly seen as being subsumed within the general term. Furthermore, the term 'film' is also generally viewed within popular consciousness as being shorthand for 'Hollywood films', so that when people talk of 'film' they are often in fact referring to 'Hollywood narrative film'. This raises the issue of where British films and films from other national cinemas from across the world (and indeed, American films made outside of the big Hollywood studios) might fit into our understanding of the term 'film'. Certainly you will now be expected to become increasingly aware of other national cinemas and the relationship of those cinemas to Hollywood. What appears to be our simplistic, perhaps lazy, use of the word 'film' may to some extent reflect the successful marketing of one form of film over a long period of time by massively powerful global organisations.

ACTIVITY

How do you use the term 'film' in general discussions with friends? Consider your usage in the light of the comments above. Do you ever discuss animated film? Do you ever discuss documentaries, or experimental film? Do you ever talk about foreign language films; if so, which ones, and why is it that you are aware of these and not others?

(In film studies you will be asked to use the term with much more critical awareness than might be the case in everyday discussions.)

The intermingling of film types

Naturally, the neat classification approach that sees four basic types of film is something of an over-simplification, as the points made above on animations and documentaries will already have suggested. Within actual films the four types outlined here often overlap, or intermingle. To make the point clearer you could consider surreal film: surrealism attempts to explore the nature of the subconscious mind and would be difficult to pigeon-hole into any of the four major types of film used above, probably being seen to straddle the first and last categories. Surrealism tries to delve beneath the surface reality of human experience to some deeper level where 'normal' logic and time constraints no longer exist, and so quite naturally it is likely to try to disrupt the normalcy of film experience. (As an example of a surrealist film, you could watch *Un Chien Andalou* (Bunuel/Dali, 1928).)

In the past it was filmmakers working outside of the mainstream who were given (or gave themselves) the space to be more adventurous in combining types, forms and styles of filmmaking. However, increasingly in recent years, filmmakers working within the commercial film world have looked to playfully combine types of film or elements of filmmaking style. Some viewers enjoy this experience, happily accepting the playfulness with which the fictional narrative employing naturalistic sets that they have been watching might abruptly take on an animated comic-book style, or the way in which a film that has been signalling that it is a road movie might suddenly turn into a vampire movie. Other viewers feel themselves profoundly cheated and disturbed by this disruption to the parameters of the fantasy in which they have invested time and imaginative energy.

VAMPIRE FILMS: These movies stretch back at least to the silent *Nosferatu* (Murnau, 1922) and feature female as well as male vampires. The most interesting discussions around these films involve issues to do

continued

with gender, sexuality and power. It is possible to see both male and female vampires as reflecting male desire and/or being connected to misogynistic attitudes. On the other hand, female vampires do put the woman in a position of power.

How would you interpret these sorts of films? Do you believe such interpretations might be valid? Do you know any vampire films to which you could try to apply these ideas? Discuss all of this with other people if at all possible. (Increasingly you will be encouraged to consider such theoretical approaches to films.)

Time-machine technology

One of the central connecting features of all four types of film (and surreal film) is that they involve the intentional manipulation of both space and time. As we have already said, we as spectators can be transported through space in an instant whether it is from one room to another or from one country to another; and we are able to travel through time whether it is back into the past or forward into the future. These are two dimensions to life that are obviously of very basic interest to us as human beings, and both may be seen to be intimately connected to the concept of memory. In memory (as in dreams, which are often said to offer experiences similar to those explored in surrealism) we are freed from the limitations of time and space; we travel at will through the usually entrapping confines of human experience.

ACTIVITY

What is your view on this? Had you, for instance, ever thought of film as rather strange, or magical, in the way in which it transports us through time and space?

Film theory

The distinctive and defining relationship that film has to space and time has given rise to two conflicting fundamental theories about film. Some theorists, following Dziga Vertov,[1] have argued that film should concentrate not on telling stories but on investigating the nature of time and space in a consciously abstract way. This tendency moves us towards the fourth type of film looked at previously, that of experimental film, and away from the fictional narratives that have in fact formed the predominant tendency throughout film history. Others, such as André Bazin,[2] have maintained that the strength of film is its photographic ability to realistically portray the natural world, and have suggested that filmmakers should focus on this possibility in order to show human events in such a way as to reveal something of the nature of the human experience. This approach emphasises the potential qualities of film that are the very opposite of experimental.

NATURALISM: The idea that through the close observation and realistic recording of human interaction we are able to get nearer to understanding the complexities of individual characters and the wider society. This began as a late nineteenth-century movement in theatre and the novel but has had a profound influence on film where, for instance, acting has often been judged on the ability to reproduce the fine detail of human behaviour. This could be seen as an extreme form of realism.

INFORMATION BOX

As usual our first instinct should perhaps be to recognise that these two possibilities, the experimental and the photographic, may not necessarily exclude each other. As we have already seen and our own experience tells us, in practice various film types can often be (effectively) combined.

ACTIVITY

In terms of use of the camera and editing, how do you think these two theorists, Vertov and Bazin, might advocate that films should be made? What sorts of camera shots might each want to see used? And how would they each expect shots to be edited together? Which approach, for instance, do you think might advocate the use of the long take as opposed to a lot of editing? Which approach might be especially interested in eye-level camera shots as opposed to high-angle and low-angle shots, and why? Discuss your thoughts on this with others if possible.

ACTIVITY

Do you feel that film should be either one thing or the other; that is to say, either a fictional narrative, or a documentary, or an animation, or an experimental film? Or do you think it is acceptable and effective under the right circumstances to combine these types of film? Can you give any examples of films you think have successfully combined these basic types? Discuss your response with others.

A starting point

Whatever type of film we may be watching and whatever approach the filmmakers have adopted towards filmmaking, it is true that all films can give the viewer sensual pleasure and an emotional experience. However, it is also the case that careful analysis of a film can release a series of potential meanings that may not have been at first fully appreciated. This approach will make the intellectual experience offered by film more apparent.

A film has been constructed, put together in certain ways for certain reasons and in order to attempt to achieve certain effects. And, since it has been 'put together' in this sense, we can work on it to take it apart and better understand its workings. In the process we may be able to deepen our appreciation and understanding of the ideas and concerns that lie behind it. This much will already be familiar to you.

However, as we begin to deepen our analysis of film we need to be particularly aware of one overriding factor in the creation of meaning, and that is that films inevitably exist within an ideological context. They are made by producers with particular (essentially political) outlooks and received by audiences who similarly have their own distinctive perspectives on the world. In this sense films (and the media in general) are part of the ongoing, and for the most part unrecognised and unacknowledged, debate about how society should be seen and understood. Should women be seen as slyly seductive, manipulative and potentially deadly as they tend to be in films noir from the 1940s and 1950s? Or should they be seen as desiring the achievement of marriage above all else as they have tended to be seen in romantic comedies? Or should the two be seen in tandem in order that we come to understand that there are essentially two types of women in the world? Filmmakers may use such representations of the world in the construction of their films: audiences then have the choice to accept or reject these ideological perspectives.

IDEOLOGY: A set of beliefs and values by which an individual, a group or a whole society orders its understanding of the world. Each of us views the world in a particular way, we have beliefs about how society should be organised and what values should underpin everything that happens in society, but not everybody shares our view of the world; that is to say, they have a different ideological perspective on things.

ACTIVITY

- List the beliefs you feel should be fundamental to society and to the ways in which people live. For instance, you might end up with:

  - democracy
  - freedom of speech
  - freedom of sexual orientation
  - gender equality
  - multiculturalism
  - racial integration
  - abolition of the monarchy
  - housing according to social need
  - free health care.

- You might, of course, end up with a very different list. But whatever points you finally decide upon, these loosely described ideas (in an admittedly simplistic way) will be the component elements defining your particular ideological take on the world. How do you think you have arrived at the position where you hold these beliefs? Assuming we agree that you were not born with them, where do these beliefs come from? Compare your list with those arrived at by others if possible, discussing differences and similarities. (In these discussions there is a key ground rule: you are free to discuss any ideas but with respect for the other person.)

Social, historical and cultural context

To make sense of any film we need to be aware of one further factor, which is that every film is made within a particular social, historical and cultural context, and is likely to explore a further social, historical and cultural context within which the story is set.

Figure iv *Moulin Rouge* (Luhrman, 2001).

You could think about any film you like to make sure you understand what is being suggested here, but as an example consider *Moulin Rouge* (Luhrman, 2001).

Knowledge of the historical context within which the film is set and awareness of the cultural significance of the Moulin Rouge within French society of the period will enhance our understanding of the film. At the same time the choice of this subject matter as a source for a film will say something about the period and society within which the film has been made. What is it about contemporary society and perhaps the filmmakers' understanding of that society that has meant they have seen this subject as being of interest to modern audiences?

As a further example, consider sci-fi films in general. These form part of the genre convention set in the future, but the most interesting thing about them is the way in which they deal with issues perhaps to do with war, or environmental pollution, or race that are actually of powerful current concern. Placing these films in the future does not prevent them from actually relating to, and often commenting strongly upon, contemporary society.

Producers and audiences and ideology

So, we need to be aware that films are made by people with a particular ideological understanding of the world and viewed by audiences with perhaps different or similar ideological outlooks. As a result, films will always contain perspectives on issues such as gender, sexuality, race and class; perspectives that will contain within them implied social values.

In our readings of films we need to be aware that any film will be offering a very particular view of the world, and that as such it may be seen to be potentially influencing the ways in which we, the audience, see that world. Its perspective may gel with our own view, clash with our outlook, or fall somewhere in between. The film will have a political dimension; a presence and potential influence within the contemporary world.

ACTIVITY

- In groups, compare the lists of key factors in their personal ideology that people have come up with. Is there any broad agreement or are there a wide range of perspectives? If there is broad agreement in quite a few areas, why do you think this is the case?
- If people are willing to do this, you could try to get two people with quite different ideological perspectives to run through their lists, explaining their positions to the whole group.

(Do try to be sensitive at all times in this exercise: remember you are potentially going to be dealing with people's most deeply held beliefs. Constantly bear in mind the key ground rule of showing respect for the individual while being prepared to challenge and debate any views being put forward: confront the idea and not the person.)

Overview: the importance of narrative

If we were to return to consider three of our four broad types of film – fictional narrative, documentary and animation – we might say they were all connected by the fact that they each tell a story. So, isn't all film (with the exception of some purely abstract experimental work) fictional narrative? If so, does this mean that the difference between animation, documentary and fictional narrative comes down to whether they are using animated figures, non-professional actors playing 'themselves' or professional actors taking roles?

CONCLUSION

Film:

- can be divided into various types but these categories are problematic and not always clear cut;
- almost always depends in some fundamental way upon storytelling, employing narratives that revolve around the use of particular characters and settings;
- is always working on us to get us to respond in some way;
- may be used to encourage us to respond in different ways according to the ideological outlook of the filmmakers.

Notes

1 A Russian filmmaker and theorist working in Soviet cinema in the 1920s.
2 A French film critic of seminal importance to the French new wave directors of the 1960s.

Further Reading

Bordwell, D. and Thompson K. (2000) *Film Art: An Introduction*. New York: McGraw Hill (ch. 2)

Parkinson, D. (1995) *History of Film*. London and New York: Thames and Hudson

Phillips, P. (2000) 'Story' and 'Character' in *Understanding Film Texts: Meaning and Experience*. London: BFI

Phillips, P. (2003) 'The film spectator' in J. Nelmes (ed.) *An Introduction to Film Studies* (3rd edn). London: Routledge

Thompson, K. and Bordwell, D. (2003) *Film History: An Introduction*. New York: McGraw Hill

part 1

FILM RESEARCH AND CREATIVE PROJECTS (FM3)

INTRODUCTION TO FM3

THE SMALL SCALE RESEARCH PROJECT

CREATIVE PROJECTS

1 INTRODUCTION TO FM3

In this section we look at:

- the concept behind film research and creative projects
- what is required from each section of FM3
- why the small-scale research project is structured around set frameworks and how these help contextualise learning
- what is different about the creative projects at A2
- how to apply learning from other units

SYNTHESISING LEARNING: At AS level there was a clear and strong focus on the construction of meaning and emotion, and on the relationship between producers and audiences. This was defined through the application of *macro* and *micro* techniques, and dealt with issues of how spectators made meaning from an extract, and from the examination of British and American film through their producers, audiences and broader contexts.

At A2, the learning developed across two units and a range of topics is brought together and synthesised to approach a research project (that may have been stimulated by study of AS level units) and a practical, creative project where meaning and emotion can be explored within a 'live' context of producer and audience.

The significant factor here is in focusing learning undertaken down to these two projects, applying knowledge and skills in a practical research or constructional way.

FM3 has been designed to build on the AS Units FM1 Exploring Film Form, and FM2 British and American Cinema, to give students the opportunity to apply learning from other areas of study within the course, and to develop work based around either a pre-existing interest or one that has developed from studies in film. Essential here is the drive that comes from having passion about a topic, or from the desire to create a piece of work that will affect an audience and have an influence over spectator responses. It is this level of personal engagement that will deliver success in this unit, and which can be shaped and directed through considering how other elements that have already been encountered can have a use in the areas of project work for this unit.

The FM3 structure

FM3 is divided into two separate sections, though there can be a relationship between the two:

- Small Scale Research Project
- Creative Project – which has three options: film production, screenwriting, documentary step outline.

It is entirely possible (or for the step outline, compulsory) that an area studied for the Small Scale Research Project may lead to further developments in the Creative Project, or could have a more direct connection (such as a project investigating Blockbuster films leading to a Creative Project that deals with the Blockbuster through a screenplay, a video sequence, or directly through the step outline).

INFORMATION BOX   *i*

Small Scale Research Project

This is designed to allow students to develop research skills within a contained and manageable structure (that does not encourage unwieldy or unfocused approaches), through reference to one of the following contexts:

- *Star/performer* – focusing on an individual or group of individuals. It is envisaged that this will allow 'star study' but will also engage with historical developments, cultural features, fandom, issues of performance and so on.
- *Genre* – this may focus on a single genre or a range of genres and is designed to develop investigations that consider film as a

---

structured product that is designed to relate to other, similar films. Approaches here may include genre study (codes, conventions, stars), genre as a tool of industry, evolution in genres, genre as national cinema, and genre as a cultural product.

- *Auteur* – focusing on the auteur (in the broadest sense), either individual, collaborative or any less conventional approaches.
- *Social, political and cultural studies* – focusing either on the social, political or cultural contexts of production (such as McCarthy-era films), or on the commentary offered by films on particular social, political and cultural contexts (such as the Iraq War).
- *Gender issues* – focusing on the exploration of film from a gendered perspective (such as feminist film or gay cinema), or of film-language in constructing a gender-based 'look', or even from specific individual perspectives of those involved in filmmaking and how gender has a bearing on their critical reception. This is a framework that presents clear variety of opportunity
- *Ethnicity* – this may focus on films or bodies of work that concern themselves directly with issues of ethnicity, or may focus on a body of film produced by a particular ethnic group or individual. Ethnicity is considered in a broad, encompassing sense.
- *Institution* – a focus on cinema's industrial context – its institutions – is the driving force behind this framework. This is likely to include studios, regulation and censorship, government support for indigenous cinemas, and national cinemas.
- *Technology* – focusing on the impact or development of a particular technology. This will include direct approaches such as the development of CGI, the coming of 'the talkies' or the attempts at realising the world through colour, and indirect approaches such as tracing early cinema's use of the close-up, following the impact of bullet-time editing, or the adoption by Hollywood of wire-flying techniques.

Research skills are widely valued both in higher education and in the world of employment, and the Small Scale Research Project is designed to encourage the development of these skills and of an understanding of how differing research tools may be used to investigate or analyse a topic area. The Small Scale Research Project uses the area of investigation as a means of developing research skills, and as such the research should be to the fore. The approaches to, and techniques of, research, the research material, and the application of this research material are of far more significance than any 'answer' that may be offered. It is intended that the research begins with one key film and broadens out from there, taking in at least two other related films, and a variety of sources of material.

Creative Projects

The Creative Projects are designed to either build on creative skills first developed in the AS level FM1 Creative Project, or to develop new film-related skills. Within the Creative Project the work undertaken is contextualised by an active engagement with topics and issues raised by AS level study, such as film form, star study, genre study, issues of representation and so on. It is sectioned as a choice from three diverse opportunities to carry out practical work and produce a 'product':

- *Production* – at A2 this develops the scene-specific constructional skills from the production option in the FM1 Unit, towards a longer piece of work (either a key sequence from an imagined feature or a complete short film) that emulates professional practice within the chosen form. The focus here is on an individual contribution to making meaning, and so production roles and decisions within those roles are major contributors to assessment.
- *Screenwriting* – at A2 this develops the sequencing skills learned through the extended step outline found at AS level in the FM1 Unit, and allows a more sophisticated scripted approach to either a key sequence from an imagined feature, or a complete short film. Whereas at AS level the related option was very much about investigating visual storytelling, screenwriting at A2 is much more about a professional engagement and so is concerned with using the conventions of screenplay layout, and with the application of a range of cinematic techniques that reflect a deeper understanding of how stories are constructed for the film medium.
- *Documentary step outline* – this builds directly on the skills learned through the extended step outline in the FM1 Unit through the development of a step outline (in an industry recognised form) for a 30-minute-long documentary intended for broadcast or as an additional feature for a DVD. The topic of the documentary must arise from the area of investigation for the Small Scale Research Project.

The Creative Projects at A2 involve a far more structured approach to practical project work than at AS, and the key important difference is in the need to demonstrate engagement with topics and issues arising from study at AS or A level in the production work, and in doing so to give it a foregrounded context, and to afford the surrounding paperwork a focal point of reference. The 'topics and issues' should not only be evident in the surrounding paperwork, but should be identifiable from the 'product' made (it should leap from the page of a script or step outline, and should be 'on-screen' in a video production).

The Creative Projects offer the opportunity to spring from investigating and analysing film and film-related products, to being involved in the complex decision-making processes of making a film or film-related product. This gives ample opportunity to evidence what has been learned in other areas of the course by signposting its application to the practical task (either in the supporting paperwork or more directly by 'adopting' the style of a particular director, writer or move-ment), and offers the opportunity to adopt a 'hands-on' approach to learning.

Applying learning

As this unit is about synthesising and applying learning in new contexts, it is important to approach it having both assessed what has so far been learned about film (both in and out of the classroom), and reflected on what has stimulated, intrigued or excited in this learning. Since both elements of FM3 are practical in nature and will demand a significant investment of time, success in them will be aided by starting from a point of interest, as opposed to adopting the suggestion of someone else (or, worse, trying to second-guess someone else's interests in order to impress them).

In the Small Scale Research Project, learning may be applied by beginning with a film that is familiar (though perhaps not in the context it is about to be explored in), and examining it from one of the AS approaches adopted in FM1 or FM2 (see *AS Film Studies: the Essential Introduction*). There may be material that was collected together in one or more of these units that would be useful to the research and may even end up in the catalogue. There may also have been references given out (books, magazines, websites) that could equally be a useful starting point to the research process.

Similarly, when it comes to the Creative Projects, it is worth reflecting on the *micro* analysis and the Creative Project undertaken in FM1, where meaning will have been identified from the practical construction of a film sequence, or the *macro* aspects considered in FM2. In reflecting on these, it is essential to identify what practical devices were used to make meaning and how effective they were in doing so – then to apply the effective devices to the current or planned production. It is worth remembering that the wide body of films watched both in and outside the classroom also contributes to the practical application of learning in the Creative Projects.

2 THE SMALL SCALE RESEARCH PROJECT

Creating the project

This chapter looks at:

- the components of the project including the annotated catalogue, and the presentation script
- how to define an *area of investigation* to ensure that the project stays focused
- working closely from a single film, using it as the basis of researching other films, and as the basis for broader research
- selecting research material for inclusion in the catalogue, and calculating its relative worth to the project
- compiling an annotated catalogue, commenting on the items included and identified for deselelction
- Constructing a presentation, using audio-visual material, and referencing the research material

What needs to be produced for the Small Scale Research Project?

The Small Scale Research Project is likely to begin with an idea based around a topic (such as Hong Kong martial arts movies), or arising out of a single film (such as *RocknRolla* (Dark Castle Entertainment, UK 2008, *Dir*: Guy Ritchie) as an example of contemporary gangster film), and should very much arise out of student interest, excitement and a sense of involvement, as it will need to be driven by passion and enthusiasm. Once the first idea has been considered, it needs to be fleshed out to see if research in this area is feasible, and if it is seen as so then the project formally begins with the Project Proposal Form – a document that is sent to a moderator for approval.

INFORMATION BOX

The *Project Proposal Form* asks you to fill in the following:

- *Area of investigation* – this is the subject of your research and may be written as a statement (Guy Ritchie's representation of the gangster) or, if it helps focus your work, as a question (How does *RocknRolla* develop Guy Ritchie's interest in the representation of the gangster?), though questions tend to direct a project to predetermined answers, whereas statements tend to lead to findings.
- *Project context* – the research project is carried out in relation to one of a predetermined set of contexts: star/performer, genre, auteur, social, political and cultural studies, gender issues, ethnicity, institution or technology.
- *Focus film and related films* – you are expected to anchor the project on one film that will be the focus of the research, and in doing so make extensive reference to it. You should also list at least two other films you expect to reference as part of the project.
- *Research resources* – not necessarily the research itself (as this form should begin your project), but a range of places you will go to obtain research (e.g. specific named libraries, books, magazines, archives, websites, people).
- *Tutor comment* – which is where your tutor has the opportunity to identify his or her thoughts on and support for your project. It is possible that a tutor may identify issues of concern that you have discussed with him or her in order to seek moderator advice.

Once the moderator has approved the project (and has perhaps offered some advice to ensure it does not run into later problems) you can begin your research. As you build a body of research, and near the end of this phase, you should be thinking about selecting items from it in order to begin building the Catalogue of Research.

INFORMATION BOX

The *Catalogue of Research* is a list of selected research items designed to demonstrate research ability, through a range of research that offers breadth and depth. Items should include material chosen from the total

continued

primary research undertaken (including the focus film and the other supporting films), and material chosen from the total secondary research undertaken. A *Commentary* should be offered on each item selected, with a brief summary of key material that did not make it into the Catalogue, offering reasons for its rejection.

The Catalogue is the document that underpins the principal component of the project, the Presentation Script, and it is essential that material selected for the Catalogue is chosen with the intention of using it to shape the Presentation Script itself.

INFORMATION BOX

The *Presentation Script* is a structured script that is written to support an audio-visual presentation of the project and its findings, and as such may be written in short form using headings, bullets and notes. It is important to conceive of this as a presentation (even if it is never presented) and to include appropriate reference to the catalogue items through appropriate presentational tools (e.g. screening film extracts, PowerPoint slides, playing audio material, passing out handouts).

ACTIVITY

Look at the period you have for the Small Scale Research Project from the date it is introduced through to the hand-in date. How much time do you think needs to be given over to each section of the project?

Draw up a timeline across the project period and enter the dates by which you would like to have finished the sections of the project. Aim to complete the project ahead of the deadline so that revisions can be made prior to the final hand-in.

Ask your tutor if there is an opportunity to obtain some feedback on the sections of the project prior to the final deadline, so that you have the opportunity to maximise your marks by responding to the feedback.

Choosing an area of investigation

As the primary motivating force behind the Small Scale Research Project is the 'excitement' generated by the opportunity to investigate a particular area, it follows that there should be as few restrictions on the choice of subject as possible. Therefore, the area of investigation may be chosen from any type of cinema, mainstream or 'art house', of any period (contemporary, historic, or a mix of both), and from any national cinema (it is possible to take a comparative approach also, pitching work from one type of cinema, period or national cinema against another). There is no restriction on work outside feature production, and so film documentary, animation, experimental film and short film production are all suitable areas for consideration.

It should be noted that the focus film must not be one that is identified in any other area of the Specification (either at AS or A2) as a topic or Single Film Critical Study focus film, though such films may be included as 'related films'.

The area of investigation should be placed within the context of an issue chosen from one of the following:

- *Star/performer* – this context allows the consideration of the star/performer or performance as a significant element of making-meaning, and as such the investigation may centre on a particular star or group of performers, or style of performance (an investigation into the Stanislavsky technique, for example).
- *Genre* – this context sees genre as a structuring and encoding device that positions the audience expectation of a film text. Multiple approaches can be made here, from the simple (a particular film exemplifying a genre) through to the complex (the discussion of whether a film has mutated the genre into another genre).
- *The auteur* – allows a film or body of films to be seen in the context of an authorial voice. It is intended that this context be as broadly interpreted as possible, and so the traditional view of an auteur as a single person (usually the director) is extended to include any individual who leaves a 'signature' of control (over the production and/or over meaning) on a film, be they the screenwriter, the cinematographer, the composer, or even an actor. Indeed, this is taken further still by considering the collaborative auteur (two or more individuals who when they come together on a project leave an unmistakable signature – Scorsese and DeNiro, for example), and the institutional auteur (where an institution, be it a studio, a government agency or a collective, leaves a signature on a film irrespective of who actually worked on it – the comedies produced at Ealing demonstrate this well).
- *Social, political, and cultural studies* – allows the investigation of the context of production/reception and could also consider a comparative approach (e.g. researching audience response to Leni Riefenstahl's *Triumph of the Will* (Leni Riefenstahl/Nazi Party, Germany, 1935) on its release, in other countries, and more contemporary responses). Also included here would be the investigation of the social/political/cultural impact of a film on a culture or cultures (the

Figure 2.1 *Munich* (Spielberg, 2005), an example of a film that had a social/political/cultural impact.

furore around Stephen Spielberg's *Munich* (Dreamworks/Universal/Amblin, USA, 2005) is a good example of this).

■ *Gender issues* – encourages an approach that allows the study of gendered films or gendered filmmaking, but also one that allows the study of gendered spectatorship. Issues of sexuality, of gender, of representation, and of other related contexts can be explored either singly or through a comparative approach (such as comparing male and female directorial approaches to the crime movie genre).

■ *Ethnicity* – may be explored through diverse approaches including analysing the representations within a film, and issues around those making a film. It should be viewed as a broad church approach that can include more traditional topics (such as Blaxploitation movies, or the representation of the American Indian in the Western genre), but can also include a much more localised ethnic focus (such as the role of Sami directors within Finnish film culture).

■ *Institution* – engages with issues of industry that may have been stimulated from concepts engaged with in FM2 British and American film. Most obvious will be the industrialised production contexts for film production (the studios, the production companies, and even the established methods of production), but issues around film finance, producing, law, regulation, distribution, exhibition and governmental influence over filmmaking are all valuable areas through which to contextualise a research project.

■ *Technology* – this context is one that encompasses all the constructional devices in cinema, from production through to distribution and exhibition methods. A wide range of investigations can be contextualised by technology from an historic approach dealing with a production development such as the introduction of surround sound, through to the impact of video on the industry, or the implication of digital exhibition (most importantly with the broader areas of investigation is the need to anchor them to a particular focus film).

Whatever the chosen area of investigation, the starting point of the research should be to identify what is specific and distinctive about the focus film and about any other supporting film texts as a group of films (although it is perfectly acceptable to include films that offer an alternative to the chosen focus film in order to highlight the differences). When placed against the contextualising issue, it should be clear how the distinctiveness of the focus film makes meaning, and how it foregrounds the area of investigation. In doing this you will ensure you are working from film text to broaden out the context, thereby giving your research a solid foundation.

> **FOCUS FILM:** A film that forms the central focus of research or investigation. Such films should offer significant qualities in relation to an area of investigation, and it should be relatively easy to select key scenes from them to illustrate points relating to a particular context. It is worth not only considering the film as a text (the film itself) but also the film's context (the specific production context as well as the broader social/historic/political context). A focus film may be considered as a catalyst for an event or movement, and may be considered as a symptom of an industrial or social/political condition. Such films should form the basis of consideration of other related films – either ones that share common elements, or those which offer clear contrast.

The range of areas of investigation is deliberately broad to ensure that most students are able to feel that their interests and passions can be incorporated into the project. Examples of such areas of investigation include the following.

Star/performer

■ Area of investigation: the characteristics of Rhys Ifans' performance across different directors and production contexts
■ Focus film: *Enduring Love* (Film Four/Film Council/Pathe/Free Range/Inside Track/Ridgeway, UK, 2004, *Dir*: Roger Michell)

- Related films: *Twin Town* (Polygram/Figment/Agenda/Animimage, UK, 1997, *Dir*: Kevin Allen), *Notting Hill* (Polygram/Working Title, US/UK, 1999, *Dir*. Roger Michell), *The Shipping News* (Buena Vista/Miramax, US, 2001, *Dir*: Lasse Hallström)
- Area of investigation: meaning brought to a film by Juliet Binoche
- Focus film: *The Unbearable Lightness of Being* (Saul Zaenetz, US, 1987, *Dir*: Philip Kaufman)
- Related films: *Les Amants du Pont Neuf* (Artificial Eye/Christian Fechner, France, 1991, *Dir*: Leos Carax), *The English Patient* (Buena Vista/Tiger Moth/Miramax, US, 1996, *Dir*: Anthony Minghella), *Chocolat* (Brown/Golden/Holleran, US, 2000, *Dir*: Lasse Hallström)

Genre

- Area of investigation: the shaping of the gangster genre by the films of Martin Scorcese
- Focus film: *Mean Streets* (Taplin-Perry-Scorcese, US, 1973, *Dir*: Martin Scorcese)
- Related films: *Goodfellas* (Warner, US, 1990, *Dir*: Martin Scorcese), *Casino* (Universal/Sylalis/Legende/De Fina/Cappa, US, 1995, *Dir*: Martin Scorcese)
- Area of investigation: the perceived communist threat and the rise of the American science fiction film
- Focus film: *The Day the Earth Stood Still* (TCF, US, 1951, *Dir*: Robert Wise)
- Related films: *Plan 9 from Outer Space* (Wade Williams Productions, US, 1958, *Dir*: Ed Wood), *On the Beach* (UA/Stanley Kramer, US, 1959, *Dir*: Stanley Kramer

The auteur

- Area of investigation: Luc Besson's move from French film to Americanised movies and the impact on his cinematic style
- Focus film: *Leon* (Buena Vista/Gaumont/Dauphin, France, 1994, *Dir*: Luc Besson)
- Related films: *Subway* (Gaumont/Films du Loup/TSF/TFI, France, 1985, *Dir*: Luc Besson), *Nikita* (Palace/Gaumont/Cecci/Tiger, France/Italy, 1990, *Dir*: Luc Besson), *The Fifth Element* (Columbia/Gaumont, France, 1997, *Dir*: Luc Besson)
- Area of investigation: Ealing Studios' 'signature'
- Focus film: *Kind Hearts and Coronets* (Ealing, UK, 1949, *Dir*: Robert Hamer)
- Related films: *The Man in the White Suit* (Ealing, UK, 1951, *Dir*: Alexander Mackendrick), *The Lavender Hill Mob* (Ealing, UK, 1951, *Dir*: Charles Crichton)

Social, political and cultural studies

- Area of investigation: German film's reflection of Germany before and after reunification
- Focus film: *Kings of the Road* (*Im Lauf der Zeit*) (Wim Wenders Prod, W. Germany, 1975, *Dir*: Wim Wenders)
- Related films: *Run Lola Run* (*Lola Rennet*) (Columbia TriStar/Bavaria/German Independents/X Filme, Germany, 1998, *Dir*: Tom Tykwer), *Downfall* (Momentum/Constantin/Bernd Eichinger, Germany/Austria/Italy, 2004, *Dir*: Oliver Hirshbiegel)
- Area of investigation: films dealing with the Vietnam War as a symptom of modern America
- Focus film: *Platoon* (Hemdale/Arnold Kopelson, US, 1986, *Dir*: Oliver Stone)
- Related films: *Forrest Gump* (Panavision, US, 1994, *Dir*: Robert Zemeckis), *Hamburger Hill* (Paramount/RKO, US, 1987, *Dir*: John Irvin), *The Deer Hunter* (Universal/EMI, US, 1978, *Dir*: Michael Cimino)

Gender issues

- Area of investigation: Kathryn Bigelow's approach to the contemporary horror film
- Focus film: *Near Dark* (F/M, US, 1987, *Dir*: Kathryn Bigelow)
- Related films: *From Dusk Till Dawn* (A Band Apart, US, 1996, *Dir*: Robert Rodriguez), *The Forsaken* (Sandstorm Films, US, 2001, *Dir*: J. S. Cardone)
- Area of investigation: American New Queer Cinema and identity
- Focus film: *Go Fish* (Can I Watch, US, 1994, *Dir*: Rose Troche)
- Related films: *Paris is Burning* (Off White Productions, US, 1990, *Dir*: Jennie Livingstone), *All Over Me* (Baldini Pictures, US, 1997, *Dir*: Alex Sichel)

Ethnicity

- Area of investigation: British-Indian cinema coming of age
- Focus film: *Bend it Like Beckham* (Kintop Pictures, UK, 2002, *Dir*; Gurinder Chadha)
- Related films: *My Son the Fanatic* (Arts Council of England, UK/France, 1997, *Dir*; Udayan Prasad), *Bhaji on the Beach* (Channel Four Films, UK, 1993, *Dir*: Gurinder Chadha)
- Area of investigation: the changing representation of young black men in British film
- Focus film: *Bullet Boy* (BBC Films, UK, 2004, *Dir*: Saul Dibb)
- Related films: *Pressure* (BFI Production, UK, 1975, *Dir*: Horace Ové), *Babylon* (Diversity Music/National Film Finance Corporation, UK/Italy, 1980, *Dir*: Franco Rosso)

Institution

- Area of investigation: the impact of the Hays Code
- Focus film: *Ecstasy* (Elektafilm, Czechoslovakia/Austria, 1933, *Dir*: Gustav Machaty)
- Related films: *Tarzan and His Mate* (MGM, US, 1933, *Dir*: Cedric Gibbons), *The Outlaw* (Howard Hughes Productions, US, 1943, *Dir*: Howard Hughes)
- Area of investigation: American Zoetrope – independence and success
- Focus film: *Apocalypse Now* (Zoetrope Studios, US, 1979, *Dir*: Francis Ford Coppola)
- Related films: *The Good Shepherd* (American Zoetrope, US, 2006, *Dir*: Robert DeNiro), *Sleepy Hollow* (American Zoetrope, US/Germany, 1999, *Dir*: Tim Burton)

Technology

- Area of investigation: development of CGI in animation and its impact on audiences
- Focus film: *Toy Story* (Buena Vista/Walt Disney/Pixar, US, 1995, *Dir*: Jerry Hopper)
- Related films: *Toy Story 2* (Buena Vista/Walt Disney/Pixar, US, 1999, *Dir*: John Lasseter/Pete Docter/Ash Brannon), *Shrek* (DreamWorks/PDI, US, 2001, *Dir*: Andrew Adamson/Vicky Jenson)
- Area of investigation: the development of colour film techniques
- Focus film: *Gone with the Wind* (MGM/Selznick International, US, 1939, *Dir*: Victor Flemming)
- Related films: *The Black Pirate* (Technicolor, US, 1926, *Dir*: Albert Parker), *Flowers and Trees* (Walt Disney, US, 1932, *Dir*: Burt Gillet), *The Sheltering Sky* (Palace/Sahara/TAO/RPC/Aldrich Group, UK/Italy, 1990, *Dir*: Bernardo Bertolucci)

ACTIVITY

Choose one of your favourite films and see how many of the five categories you can get it to fit into. Are there any that it suits better than others?

Next pick one of the categories and list all the films you can think of that would fit into it. Are any of these films ones that you are excited by?

Lastly, devise an area of investigation for one of the films that you are interested in researching. Does this fit with more than one of the five contexts? If so, which one does it fit best, and why? What would you have to do to it to make it fit the other context(s) better?

Working from a film text

It is essential that the research project is firmly centred on a single filmic text in order to ensure it remains 'small scale' (as befits the percentage of the overall A level marks allocated to it), and to ensure that it is focused and has depth, rather than the superficiality that can come with a more generalist study. With this in mind it is therefore of the utmost importance that the focus film is carefully chosen in order to guarantee that it affords the opportunity to refer not only to the area of investigation, but also to one of the eight project frameworks.

Figure 2.2 *Kings of the Road* (Wenders, 1975).

Thus, Wenders' *Kings of the Road* is a better choice for looking at the area of investigation on 'German film's reflection of Germany before and after reunification', as it directly addresses what it is like to be German in a divided Germany, and directly portrays the divided Germany through the constant images of the Berlin Wall and the border fences. It also directly addresses the social, political and cultural context through the story itself and the images and representations placed on screen. *Run Lola Run* may address social, political and cultural issues, but the reflection on 'Germany before and after reunification' is less directly addressed. Similarly, *Downfall* looks back to the last days of the previously unified Germany from a perspective of a reunified Germany, so while it fits both the area of investigation and the project framework, it would require more effort to tie the text closely into both.

Initially the film text can address the area of investigation and the project framework through looking at the *macro* and *micro* issues that present themselves from it. Close examination will reveal sequences, characters, dialogue, images, and even cinematic technique which may be used to illustrate an argument, or embed the area of investigation within the project context. Closely referencing the text offers the best support there is in an investigation, since there is nothing as strong, as primary, as a source focus film.

In order to make a focus film work for the project you could approach it by:

- Identifying key scenes within it – ones that are powerful, provoke emotion or are essential for moving the plot forward.
- Identifying the narrative structure of the film, and any significant narrative devices used to tell the story.
- Listing the key characters and their relationship to the area of investigation.
- Listing an important scene against each of these characters in which the area of investigation is prominent.
- Identifying the significant *micro* elements (cinematography, *mise-en-scène*, performance, editing and sound) that have some bearing on the area of investigation.
- Listing any messages and values that are expressed in or by the film (you may want to identify where these appear).

In this way you build up useful in-depth knowledge of the film with which to compare other related films, and with which to illustrate any significant points arising from your research.

ACTIVITY

Taking the focus film you chose in the last activity, carry out the above tasks. Does this deepen your knowledge and understanding of the focus film? As you carried out the tasks did you develop any ideas for lines of research, or make links to other films or existing research?

The Catalogue

The Catalogue is simply a list of research material, which ideally contains a mix of both primary and secondary research, and offers evidence of diversity in sourcing the material. It is important that each item is referenced appropriately, and that each is accompanied by a short commentary on why it was selected, what use it has, and what its relative value is.

In compiling the Catalogue you should not simply be placing in it every piece of research that you uncovered, but rather judging each piece on its merits, and making a selection of the best items for inclusion. Ideally you should be looking at between ten and fifteen items for a relatively mainstream topic, and as few as seven or eight for a more challenging or unusual topic (these numbers include the focus film and the minimum of two related films).

INFORMATION BOX

i

Selecting Catalogue items

Selecting items for inclusion in the Catalogue is sometimes more difficult than it would at first seem, but some simple logic and the weighing of items against each other tends to simplify the process.

Internet Movie Database references are sometimes merely listings, offering little more insight than that offered in something like *Halliwell's Film Guide*, and as such do not weigh as heavily as websites that offer in-depth analysis.

Similarly, magazine reviews have a level of currency determined by the publication, with a review from *Sight and Sound* most likely weighing more heavily than a review from a local newspaper.

Equally, with books, titles that relate specifically to the area of investigation should make it into the Catalogue before more generalist texts (unless there is a specific chapter that is more relevant – in this case the chapter should be identified in the Catalogue referencing).

Primary research – interviews, phone conversations, e-mail responses, questionnaires – should almost always appear in the Catalogue, though, where there is a significant amount of primary material, some should make way for secondary research to ensure you display a balanced representation of your research.

When commenting on each item you should try (in five lines or fewer) to identify the following:

- How the item relates to the area of investigation.
- What value the item has offered the project.
- The nature and reliability of its source.
- How it compares to other items.
- The basis for its inclusion.

At the end of the Catalogue you should offer a brief paragraph identifying some items that were not selected for inclusion, and a rationale as to why this deselection occurred.

A Catalogue for a project that addresses genre through an area of investigation that considers 'the emergence of a "gothic" genre in American film' may well look something like this:

CATALOGUE

FILMS

Item 1: *Edward Scissorhands* (Fox, US, 1990, *Dir*: Tim Burton). Very useful, as it has all the markers of the new gothic genre on display, and also has a clear relationship with Burton's early films and his later ones.

Item 2: *The Crow* (Entertainment/Most/Pressman, US, 1994, *Dir*: Alex Proyas). The genre was still in cult territory here, and this shows in the comic-book feel. Development of genre markers and influence of Burton is clear. Useful, but could have easily been one of several other films in this place.

Item 3: *The Craft* (Columbia, US, 1996, *Dir*: Andrew Flemming). This is the film that was the turning point for the genre, where it suddenly not only got mainstream acceptance but also spawned similar films. Very much a teen movie, this shows the changing focus towards a new audience. Invaluable.

BOOKS

Item 4: Baiss, B. *The Crow: The Story Behind the Film* (Titan, 2004). This was a very good piece of research, as it not only told the story of making the film but also gave a broad overview of what makes a gothic film. This is possibly the most useful piece in the catalogue.

Item 5: Smith, J. and Matthews, C. *Tim Burton* (Virgin, 2002). This gives a clear sense of what Burton's work is all about, and how he practically defined the new American gothic genre. Detailed information on all of his films, and on the thoughts behind them, this led me to some of the other material in the Catalogue and some deselected from it.

MAGAZINES

Item 6: *Tim Burton: Cinema's Prince of Darkness*, supplement in *SFX Magazine*, March 2005

Details on Burton with a clear emphasis on the gothic elements. Could not miss being included.

Item 7: Travers, P. 'Auteur in Angora' in *Rolling Stone Magazine*, July 1995

An interesting article that looks at Burton as an auteur – some good references to his film and some discussion of his 'burtonesque' genre.

INTERNET

Item 8: *http://www.thetimburtoncollective.com* The Tim Burton Collective is a fan-based site that offers a considerable range of articles, biographical information, and links for Tim Burton. This was the best of the Tim Burton related sites, as it seemed authoritative and was also recommended by many other sources.

Item 9: *http://www.sensesofcinema.com/contents/04/31/lost in translation.html*. 'Neon Gothic: Lost in Translation' by Wendy Halsem – this is a great article by a university lecturer that served to widen my view of the gothic. Full of film references, it took my research in several unexpected directions (some not so fruitful).

Item 10: *http://minadream.com/timburton/EdwardScissorHands.htm*. This is quite a sophisticated site, but I sense it is still a fan site. Full of information about Burton and the gothic, this was particularly useful for looking at *Edward Scissorhands*.

Item 11: *http://www.darklinks.com/dmovies.html*. Dark Side of the Net – this was a little bit strange (particularly the movie forum) but it did clue me in to a whole range of American gothic films that I hadn't even considered before. Not as relevant to the focus films as the other sites, but good for a general overview.

CONFERENCE

Item 12: *Deviance and Defiance*: The seventh Biannual Conference of the International Gothic Association – Panel 1.3 Gothic Cinema (11 August 2005). As I was on holiday in Canada this summer I stumbled across this University of Montreal event. This was perfect research (although there were parts where I simply didn't understand the panellists!), particularly when I got to talk to John Hogland from University of Kalmar afterwards about American gothic films.

DESELECTED MATERIAL

Vampress.net (*http://www.vampress.net/forum*) had some useful fan

continued

comment on the three films, but it never really got beyond the superficial. The Crow's Loft (*http://www.thecrowsloft.com*) was quite detailed and authoritative on the film, but never got into the gothic or genre that much. There were a few film reviews from *Empire*, *Total Film* and *Sight and Sound* that were useful background reading but had no direct relationship with the investigation, and similarly Mark Salisbury's *Burton on Burton* (Faber, 1995) was good to see Burton's own words, but there was so much that was outside the project that it really didn't fit.

ACTIVITY

Take your research material and colour code it (a mark on top, or in the margin, or a coloured sticker) with four colours representing:

- focused on area of investigation
- focused on project context
- useful background
- interesting but not well related.

Take the research and compile it in colour groupings. For each group, number the research with 1 representing the most useful in that group.

Finally, go through the material by number and colour to select or deselect for the catalogue.

Constructing the Presentation Script

The Presentation Script is where you present the findings from your research, and it is important to note that this does not necessarily mean presenting an 'answer'. Research does not always lead to an answer – rather it offers a range of information (the findings) from a number of sources that may provide 'answers' but equally may remain simply material gathered around an area of investigation. The key to a successful presentation script is being able to clearly think through what it is you have found out in relation to the area of investigation and the project framework.

All presentations have defined audiences, and it is useful for you if you can clearly define who it is you will be presenting to (even if you have no intention of actually presenting your findings – though I would urge doing a presentation if time allows, as this is a valuable way of testing whether the presentation script works, and getting audience feedback both on the presentation itself and on the project as a whole). By defining the audience you can tailor the presentation to them, making you think about potential responses, and about what you can do to make the presentation more inviting and interesting for them.

It is worth considering what kinds of stimulus material you can use in the presentation to keep the interest levels up in the audience, and at what points they should be inserted for maximum effect.

ACTIVITY

Consider what material you would like to use in your presentation. Showing clips from the focus film and related films is obviously a good idea, and this can lead you to briefly discuss them.

Perhaps a still image or a sequence from a documentary would be useful too? You may have some audio material that you could insert either as an opening or closing device or as an illustrative example.

If you have carried out some primary research you could convert any data gathered into charts or graphs and display them to your audience. Alternatively you may have comments from interviewees that you could enlarge and display.

Think carefully about why you are including this material, and what you hope to achieve from it. Remember: if it is not stimulating the audience, it should not be in the presentation.

The Presentation Script should be in a format suited to a presentation, and may:

- be in note form
- be bulleted or numbered
- be short pieces of prose with reference to presentation material connecting them
- use headings and subheadings.

It will clearly indicate where a piece of material will be inserted and will make attempts to ensure that the material used in the presentation is referenced and addressed by the script. Catalogue items referenced or used in the presentation should be indicated by Catalogue Item number. An essay format is not appropriate to this task, and will not attract the rewards that more innovative approaches will benefit from.

A Presentation Script may look something like this:

PRESENTATION SCRIPT

CITIZEN CAINE – THE PERFORMANCE OF MICHAEL CAINE

Run audio: Theme music from *The Italian Job* (Item 3) – 30 seconds then fade out.

Projector: BCU Image of Michael Caine's face from *Alfie* (Item 9) – fade for video.

Presenter: Michael Caine exploded on to 1960s British cinema with his first starring role in *Zulu* (Item 2) in 1964, and immediately marked himself out as a charismatic and dynamic performer.

Video clip: Battle scene from *Zulu* (Item 2) – 1'14".

Presenter: My research project looks at the development of Michael Caine's performance across a number of films focusing on the 1960s and 1970s, and making clear reference to his more recent work. Two films central to this examination that I will make reference to throughout this presentation are *The Quiet American* (Item 4) *and The Ipcress File* (Item 1).

Projector: Split screen freeze frame of Caine in *The Ipcress File* (Item 1) as a young man, and freeze frame of Caine in *The Quiet American* (Item 4) as an older man.

Presenter: In this presentation I will cover:

- Caine's acting style
- Caine's approach to acting
- The meanings produced by Caine's work
- Critical opinion of Caine's acting
- Caine's British and American work
- Caine's own musings on his films.

Flip chart: Display bullet points for duration of presentation.

Projector: Poster of Caine in *The Ipcress File* (Item 12).

Presenter: At this point I would like to quote Caine himself speaking on the Southbank Show (Item 6): 'People are always asking me about. . . .'

What you should be able to see from this example is a clear sense of the Presentation Script as being for presentation, with regular breaks in the spoken delivery to introduce stimulus material from the Catalogue. This extract is approximately 250 words long, and covers approximately 2 minutes and 45 seconds of time. If I use all of my allotted 1500 words then I can expect my presentation to last somewhere in the region of 12–18 minutes (assuming I show five or six clips of between 60 to 90 seconds' duration).

You will notice that the presentation begins with music, then has a visual, followed by the presenter, and then a video extract, before returning to the presenter. What I am hoping to do here is demonstrate my understanding not only of the tools available to me in a presentation, but also of the rhythm of a presentation. In doing this I am also showing awareness of the audience and its needs both for stimulus and for regular changes in activity to ensure it keeps focused and alert to the information presented. A range of props are used, all of which are in the Catalogue, and so I am not only showing a diversity of approach; I am also showing a confident knowledge of my Catalogue and that I can use the items I have selected in discussing my subject, thereby demonstrating their value in being included in the Catalogue.

A good presentation outlines what will be in the presentation at the beginning, delivers what it has promised and then recaps on what has been presented at the end. In this presentation the points to be covered are clearly identified for the audience and are reinforced by the flip chart. The points also focus on the area of investigation and the project context, and as such are a reminder to the marker and moderator of how well the presentation is designed to deliver focused information on my chosen subject.

At the end of the Presentation Script it is wise to offer the audience the opportunity to ask questions, and this can be written in (without writing the questions and answers) as a time-limited slot. This again shows excellent presentation skills and consideration of the audience. If you are actually presenting this material it is also worth considering offering the audience the opportunity to comment on their experience of your presentation (either as verbal feedback or perhaps by getting them to complete a short questionnaire), as this will enable you to make adjustments and revisions before the final project hand-in date.

ACTIVITY

Take the clips you have selected from your focus film and other related films, and show them to some friends without trying to contextualise them.

Ask them what they understood from the clips, and what they remember of the clips. Their responses are likely to be similar to your audience, and as such will highlight points of focus in your selection which you may not have thought of, but which could distract your audience away from the message you want to get across.

Top tips for a successful project:

1 Clearly define your area of investigation from the start
2 Carefully choose your project framework
3 Choose an appropriate focus film
4 Don't select more than three or four related films
5 Start working on the project sooner rather than later
6 Seek advice from tutors
7 Prepare a project timetable and stick to it
8 Plan where you are going to research and how long for
9 Ensure you get a mix of sources and a variety of kinds of material
10 Know when to stop researching
11 Collate and order the material before cataloguing
12 Only put your best material in the Catalogue
13 Have a good reason for each selection and write it in the commentary
14 Carefully choose which de-selected material to identify
15 Have a good reason for each de-selection – write it down
16 Make sure the Presentation Script is lively and busy: not an essay
17 Choose audio-visual material carefully to illustrate your points
18 Allow space for an audience to ask questions
19 Reflect on process and product before evaluating
20 Identify what you have learned.

3 CREATIVE PROJECTS

In this chapter we will consider:

- the choices on offer in the Creative Projects
- approaches to applying learning
- creating the 'aims and context' for the Creative Projects
- constructional decisions in making the creative product
- the reflective analysis and the forms it can take

One of the best ways of understanding the processes involved in the film industry is to attempt some form of production yourself. The production of a script, a piece of moving image, or a documentary step outline brings with it an awareness of the complex tensions involved in making meaning, and gives the opportunity to apply all the filmic study you have carried out up to this point.

The FM3 Creative Project offers three directions for you to engage in practical work, with each contextualised by the need to address a specific identified audience and by reflecting active engagement with issues arising from previous study in the work. You can develop a script sequence from a feature, or create a complete short film; you could engage with moving image production through a sequence or complete short; or you could produce a documentary step outline arising from the area of investigation for the Small Scale Research Project.

The Creative Projects in FM3 build on the initial skills developed in the FM1 Creative Projects at AS Level (see *AS Film Studies: the Essential Introduction*), and introduce new skills and knowledge, and new areas of study. The significant difference between the two levels comes in the expectation of the emulation of professional practice, and in the demonstration of active engagement with issues arising from previous study through which the Creative Projects are contextualised.

The FM3 Creative Projects again offer three distinct options for making meaning through the creation of practical work, with each option designed to develop and strengthen the understanding of a particular skills and knowledge base, through the attempt to replicate professional forms and professional practice. Each option is equal in value to another, and each offers the opportunity for a range of levels to be achieved. The options are:

- *Film/video production*: offers the opportunity to develop an extended sequence from an imagined feature (fiction or non-fiction, mainstream or non-mainstream), or a complete short film of between 3 and 5 minutes (and possibly build on production skills developed at AS).

   While it is possible to undertake a film/video production as an individual (and many individuals successfully undertake such tasks) it is equally possible that the production will be made by a small group of no more than four people. In this instance each member will need to select and carry out a specific production role (e.g. director, cinematographer, sound, editor), though this excludes acting. The finished production should clearly show evidence of the individual roles, and while group members may 'try out' various production roles they should take responsibility for and analyse the role they have chosen as their primary role.

- *Screenplay*: at A2 it is a requirement that candidates use an accepted industrial form for the screenplay, and utilise the conventions of the master scene script – where camera direction is virtually non-existent and the script deals primarily with screen direction and dialogue. The balance between dialogue and direction is important, and it is suggested that dialogue never pass beyond 50 per cent of the total script. The important aspect here is that the script has the potential to be filmically treated, offering a director the sense of the visual, the cinematic 'feel', and as such it should clearly lend itself to moving image production.

   The screenplay option encourages the production of either an extended sequence or a completed short film script, with a total word limit of approximately 1800 words, and should clearly demonstrate active engagement with issues arising from previous study.

- *Documentary step outline*: candidates should use an industry standard approach to creating a step outline for a 30-minute documentary that is intended to be broadcast on a suitable television channel or as a DVD 'extra'. The step outline should 'walk' the reader through the proposed documentary, and should be approximately 1800 words long.

   For this option it is essential that the documentary idea arises from the area of investigation from the Small Scale Research Project. It does not have to have a direct correlation and can be loosely (though clearly) connected.

On either side of the chosen practical option sits a piece of written work that provides a context for the practical option and reflects on the processes of production and the finished work. The *Aims and context* is a relatively short piece of prose that details the intentions that underpin the production, explicitly identifying the intended audience for the work. It should also identify any individual roles (where appropriate) and the issues underpinning the creation of the project. The *Reflective analysis* completes the project and reflects not only on the practical work, but also on its relationship to the Aims and context, and in doing so allows the opportunity to assess whether the work reached its audience and its relative success. The Reflective analysis can be presented in a number of forms: as a piece of prose (this may include illustrations), in digital form such as a web-based blog, or as a DVD commentary.

INFORMATION BOX ⓘ

Replicating professional practice

While the intention at A2 is to replicate professional practice it is not intended to restrict or limit the range of potential approaches that may be adopted in relation to a piece of practical work. There is no imperative to fit into a particular way of working or style of production other than the one you choose for yourself. Thus, it is likely that if your issue arising from previous study is connected to Soviet formalism, then your working practice and the end product would be very different to that which would develop if your issue was connected to the Hollywood Studio system.

Similarly, the professional practice of a Hollywood scriptwriter contracted to a Studio is very different to the professional practice of the British screenwriter who is often writing speculatively, in isolation, and in the hope of selling a script.

The professional practice of a documentary maker differs from the UK to Europe, and from Europe to Hollywood, and so there may be a number of common industrial models to be adopted.

Professional practice is related not to a particular style of practical work, but to the context of its production, and so if you identify your intention in production as producing a surrealist piece of work then the professional practice should replicate that of the surrealists.

Write a list of possible issues arising from your previous study, then number them according to which you feel most and least comfortable with (with 1 being most comfortable). Consider which you would use for each of the three practical options.

Swap these issues for each practical option. How does this affect the potential production work? Does it open up possibilities you had not thought of, or does it close down the options?

Aims and context

This piece of paperwork is the founding document of your project work in the FM3 Creative Projects, and as such it should be carefully constructed to allow the Creative Product and the Reflective analysis to be adequately assessed. As well as defining which of the three practical options you have chosen, you should also identify:

- A defined and recognisable audience – consider this well, as this will define the success of the product, and as such the project as a whole. You should aim to be as specific as possible about the audience, considering age, gender, class, occupation, outlook, interests and so on. Identifying an audience of students is not specific enough – are they mature or at secondary school, all one gender or mixed, all of a similar intellectual level or of mixed ability? You can see the difference a defined audience makes. Having a defined audience also allows you to focus more easily on ensuring that their needs are met by your product.
- Stylistic/formal influences that inform the work and structure it. A piece structured by the conventions of Hollywood is very different in nature from one informed by German Expressionism. The more effort you make in defining these, the easier the construction of the product becomes, since they define the model you will then have to work within.
- The issue arising from previous study that has been adopted in relation to the work, and how you intend to let it shape the work. Marking out how you see the issue's role means that you have control over how it is perceived by the marker, and this means that you can structure the marker's view and therefore tailor your product towards the marks.
- The role you are going to undertake and what you hope to learn from the production opportunity. This is probably more important when working in a group production, since clarifying your intended contribution again shapes the marker's view of your role and makes it easier to work to the marks. If you are working in a group it may be worth identifying how you see the contributions of others.

(a)   **(b)**

Figure 3.1 The conventions of a Hollywood film like *Casino Royale* (b) are very different to those of a German Expressionist film like *The Cabinet of Dr. Caligari* (a).

- Your intentions, both in terms of physical construction and approach, and in terms of time scale and processes. This shows that you have considered and mapped out the project, and even if it does not follow to plan you still have the advantage of having planned it in the first place. Considering the way you would like an audience to react would be a beneficial approach, especially if you can also identify any techniques you are considering using to provoke a reaction.
- The application of learning – what previous learning are you going to apply in this project and what new learning do you hope to develop? You should consider all the units you have engaged with both at A2 and AS level, and identify which units the learning is being applied from. It is worth trying to identify how and where this learning will be applied and how it will assist in making-meaning.

ACTIVITY

Make a list of all the previous learning you could apply to your chosen practical option. Make sure you note which unit it all comes from, and where you think it will be applied in your project.

Note down beside each identified element of learning how it will assist in making meaning in your project. Can you see how this helps structure the work for you by mapping in how it will be used?

INFORMATION BOX   *i*

Example aims and rationale – film/video production
Farewell my Maltese Lady from Shanghai

A short film in the style of a film noir but using elements of comedy to appeal to my target audience of 18-year-old middle-class males with an intellectual leaning and a clear knowledge of film history.

My aim will be to introduce the learning about cinematography gained from FM1 studies to explore the generic codes and conventions of film noir.

As this is a film noir I will be using a genre-based approach, and have been reading some interesting material (e.g. Steve Neale, Pam Cook) around this.

I intend to direct the piece and as such I have been reading up on directing (Michael Rabinger's works are particularly interesting). I would like to try using an improvisational style like Mike Leigh's – we saw some of his work in FM2 and it really impressed me for its 'real' qualities. Although this is not really a noir technique I think it will stretch the form, and as such is beneficial in developing new learning.

Getting into the mindset

The biggest part of any production work is persuading yourself that you are capable of making a practical piece of work that has value, and ensuring that you are thinking like someone who works in the particular field (e.g. a screenwriter, a filmmaker, a documentary-maker). To ensure that you are able to engage with a piece of practical work through a workable professional approach it is essential that you understand the mindset of practitioners in each option.

■ **The filmmaker**: filmmakers are all about passion, vision and single-mindedness. They become obsessed with a script and envision it, developing it and making it their own. They have a knack of being able to 'see' a script play out in front of them, almost as if the words are forming images on their eyes, and it is this idea of images that is central to what a filmmaker does. They tell stories by making images that multi-layer the narrative, adding sounds and effects either to provide emphasis or to make the construction invisible and seamless, and move characters around within their world in order to reflect issues in our world.

The filmmaker is also entirely about compromise: compromising when the impossible cannot be done; compromising parts of the script when a shoot overruns; compromising in the face of a producer's or studio's criticisms. The skill of the filmmaker is in making the right compromises – knowing which battles are necessary to fight for the sake of the story, and which are just about ego. For the filmmaker, finishing the film well comes above everything, and it is not uncommon for filmmakers to consider achieving between eight and ten shots in a day as a very successful day's shooting: precision, craft, passion, determination and compromise are the tools behind this approach.

- **The screenwriter**: screenwriters, contrary to popular opinion, do not find writing easy, and most have stories about the range of activities they will undertake in order to avoid actually having to sit down at the word processor and face a blank page. The screenwriter is plagued by stories: stories demanding to be told, characters that will not keep quiet, plots that unfold with the opening of every kitchen cupboard door. As such the only way screenwriters can find rest is to work, wrenching the story from their fingers, and wrestling with the need to sleep and the desire to be rid of the screenplay.

However, simultaneously they are driven individuals who care passionately about structure and about the way a turn of phrase can position a director into believing he or she thought up a shot that the writer subtly indicated in the screenplay. Every word is carefully selected for the power it has, and every character that is created is given a destiny to fulfil.

- **The documentary-maker**: documentary-makers are often fascinated by the small, inconsequential detail that others would not even notice. They are storytellers, like the scriptwriters, but theirs is a craft of fact and of potential. Assembling facts that will support the direction they wish to travel in, they then make connections between these facts, between locations, between interviewees and between shots, seeing the constructional potential and weaving a polished product from a myriad of source material. They will craft and recraft their step outlines, recognising them as the blueprints for the finished documentary, and will add a sequence here, swap a sequence there, often changing things right up to the moment of shooting, and then reorganising everything once more in editing.

Documentary-makers probably have the closest connection with their audience, since their documentaries are most often connected directly to their audience by being about them or their concerns. As such, they are conscious of the weight of responsibility their chosen path has rewarded them with.

ACTIVITY

Look at the descriptions above. Which description suits you best? Does it match your production interest? If not, do you think there are alternative approaches to your production interest that work just as well?

continued

Compare your results with your friends. Can you come up with descriptions for these three roles as students? What similarities are there? What is different?

Film/video-making

The task in the A2 FM3 Creative Projects is to adopt a key role in a production, investigate the responsibilities of that role, and apply your learning to that role within a production context. It is envisaged that likely roles include:

- **Director**: responsible for the meaning and quality of the finished production, the director works with writers, cast, crew and post-production teams to ensure that their 'visualisation' is shared and applied consistently by everyone. For directors to be able to work effectively they must know the script well and understand the nature of a visual medium. They should also have a general awareness of the techniques of particular key crew roles so that approaches can be discussed with knowledge on both sides.
- **The cinematographer**: responsible for the 'look' of the film and the most important person on set after the director. In collaboration with the director, the cinematographer will make all the decisions about lighting and camera matters (e.g. what equipment is selected, how it is used, where it is placed and for what effect).

  It is likely on a small shoot that the cinematographer will also be the camera operator, and will physically control the camera. Two key skills of the cinematographer are composition and camera movement, both in relation to how meaning is generated.
- **The sound recordist**: responsible for capturing 'live' sound, 'atmos' sound (background noise for particular locations), wildtracks (the sound of a location without action or dialogue over it), for creating sound effects, for 'dubbing' sound on (perhaps re-voicing badly recorded dialogue, for example), and for recording the soundtrack. Sound is almost always a weakness in student productions, and it is often because it is badly recorded in the first place, or because no one is allocated this vital job from the start. The sound recordist is one of the most creative people in the production process, particularly when it comes to creating sounds, and will usually work closely with the editor in post-production.
- **Editor**: responsible for cutting together the shot footage, and making sense of the story according to the director's vision. The editor perhaps has the most opportunity to experiment, and can often produce work which strays from the original intention, but which is far superior to that originally discussed. It is an absolute necessity (due to the duration of post-production) that the editor is completely familiar with the editing system that is being used; otherwise there can be a significant delay, and more importantly the potential for failure.

The film/video production process can be split into three parts (pre-production, production and post-production) which are described in considerable detail in Chapter 3 on the Creative Project (FM1) in *AS Film Studies: The Essential Introduction*.

PRE-PRODUCTION: the vital period of planning a production where casting, location scouting, budgeting, scheduling and rehearsing are all carried out.

PRODUCTION: the intensive period when the director and crew are in the studio or on location and are shooting the film/video. This is where the effort in pre-production pays off, and where all of the extensive planning comes into play.

POST-PRODUCTION: the period when the finished film/video 'rushes' are viewed and then edited. This is the time when all post-production sound activities happen and get dubbed on to the final edit. Any special effects, narration and titles are added to the finished film at this stage.

ACTIVITY

For your imagined film, create a production timeline that has allocated periods of pre-production, production and post-production. You would be wise to over-estimate the amount of time needed and to add a couple of weeks on to the end to allow for run-overs. It may be equally wise to work back from a deadline date.

On the timeline, mark the points of activity for each of the principal crew members. What do you notice about the workload? Is there anything you can do to even out any imbalances of workload?

The screenplay

All screenplays – feature dramas, documentaries, short films – are structured in order to obey some inherent 'rules' of telling stories. Many books are sold every year that claim a particular structure is the only correct way of writing a screenplay, but the essential truth is that there are many ways to structure a screenplay, each with its own merits in relation to the story it is telling. It is the relationship between story and structure that is the important thing in the telling.

If I dim the lights, gather my audience close, speak in hushed tones, and punctuate my opening with lengthy pauses and fearful glances around the room you would be right in thinking I am about to tell a ghost story. If I then launch into a love story you would feel pretty cheated: the opening structure positioned you as audience in relation to the story, and when it turned out the story was not the one you were positioned for you were made to feel uncomfortable (this is called narrative dissonance).

If I do tell you a ghost story you will have an expectation of how it should be delivered: the opening will set the scene and introduce the principal characters, there will be a complication that sets the events in motion, and the story will be resolved either positively or negatively. A good storyteller will lead you on an emotional roller-coaster ride, building you up and bringing you screaming down before building you up even higher, ready for the next descent. This structure is represented in film by the relationship between scenes, sequences and acts.

SCENE: a single unit of action within a film, usually defined by location. When a character moves out of one location and appears in another it is usually seen as a scene change (unless there is continuous on-screen movement between the scenes in which case it is seen as a sectionalised scene, numbered 1a, 1b and so on). Scenes can be seconds long (a single shot of an eye at the sights of a rifle, for example) or can be lengthy, with conversations, entrances, exits and action dominating them.

SEQUENCE: a set of related scenes will build into a sequence, where they become a larger unit of story. Sequences may follow a task or an action (such as defusing a bomb or a chase) intercut with some related scenes (the bomb-maker travelling to the airport, or a freight train heading towards a level crossing), or may be structured around a set of scenes with a common element running through them.

ACT: a larger unit of action that usually segments the story into beginning, middle and end (or a variant on this providing five acts, seven acts and so on). The act is often defined by a change of fortune, either for the better or for the worse, and this is a change that signifies the end of one part of the story and the beginning of another.

PLOTTING: a story is 'plotted' by taking out the key elements, the parts of the story that have dramatic effect and can be visualised. This can be

---

approached by writing down a single short sentence that sums up an element (which will become a scene) on a small card. These cards may then be laid out, reorganised, removed or added to, until a skeleton of the plotted narrative emerges.

ACTIVITY

Take a story you are interested in visualising, and 'card' each important element. Lay out the cards in the order you feel is 'right' for them. Now take away every third card at random. Does the story still make sense? If not, how many cards do you need to replace to get it to make sense? Discard any cards you do not replace – they represent unnecessary scenes.

■ **Action**: all scenes involve action – even if it is of a character sitting still, there will be lots of action to describe. Action can be broken down into background action (the action in the background of the scene) and key action (the action that is important to move the story forward, and the actions of the principal characters). Action should be central to the description of the scenes, and should not ignore the tiny but important actions – the twitch of an eye, the flare of a nostril, the dilation of pupils, the match touching the fuse. There is an old adage of the film industry that still holds true: *Show, don't tell*.

It is important to remember that since the script is the blueprint for a film, everything you want to appear on screen must be written in. If it is not in the screenplay there is every chance it will never end up in the film.

ACTIVITY

View a key scene from one of your favourite films several times. Now write out the scene using a standard script layout, paying particular attention to capturing the detail of the action. View the scene again if you need to.

continued

Are you surprised at the amount of detail that has to be described? Is there anything you have included that you could cut without affecting the meaning of the scene?

Figure 3.2 *Pirates of the Caribbean: The Dead Man's Chest* (2006) – even in scenes when characters are motionless, there is still action to describe.

■ **Characters**: you will most likely be writing stories about characters who are active in the pursuit of something (freedom, money, love, a lost treasure), and the design of these characters is essential to a successful screenplay. Many screenwriting texts go into considerable depth with characters' backstories in order for them to seem like real, three-dimensional people, with a history, a present and a future. However, there are two elements that are essential to character development:

■ the character's attitude
■ their behaviour that demonstrates their attitude.

A character's attitude will always be manifested in their actions and behaviour, even when a character is created with conflicting attitudes and behaviours. Thus, an evil genius may be given a pet to care for, or be fond of flower arranging, but his true character will eventually manifest itself in his behaviour, and he will harm the pet or destroy the flowers.

A character's attitude may also manifest itself in 'ticks' of behaviour – they may charge into situations before thinking, or become edgy when placed under stress. These 'ticks' could also be in the dialogue – the society gentleman whose lower-class roots come out in his language when faced with a threat, the shy, retiring schoolteacher who trips over her tongue and curses when faced with Mr Right.

ACTIVITY

Identify your favourite character from a film. What would you describe as his or her dominant attitude?

Think about the way this attitude is manifested in the character's behaviour. Now list five behavioural traits he or she displays.

The character may well have a goal in the film (something he or she is seeking). Does the character's language change in any way whenever he or she is connected to this goal? If so, why do you think this is?

What ticks of behaviour and language does your character display? How does this help the audience to understand the character?

- **Dialogue**: Good dialogue is written to sound like the kind of speech we hear in everyday life, and is far removed from the lengthy, pointed speeches of stage dramatists. However, if you listen carefully to well-written dialogue, it sounds like the kind of 'everyday' speech, except it flows and has a point, where so much of the speech around us is interrupted, unstructured and without point. Good dialogue is more than just having an 'ear' for speech, it is about selecting the right phrases, the right words, which when set against another character create tensions and subtexts, and which, when played in total, move the story forward.

  When writing dialogue it is important to develop each character's voice – their way of speech – so that they become individuals rather than all sounding like the screenwriter. This is difficult to achieve at first, and sometimes it is best just to write down what they need to say, and worry about editing in their 'voice' later.

Find a well-populated location (a café, a bus, a sports event) and position yourself so that you can clearly hear some of the conversations going on. Is it easy to pick out individual voices not only by tone but by what they say?

Listen to the rhythms of speech – how some people speak fast, others slowly. How does this affect your view of the speaker?

Note down key phrases, or snatches of dialogue that you hear. See if you can rework this dialogue into script dialogue – what do you have to do to make it play for the screen?

It is vital that you use conventional industry-recognised film script layouts, to ensure you are demonstrating an awareness of industry conventions and professional practices. While there are a number of variations of film script layouts (as opposed to television script layouts), they all largely conform to the master scene layout that is recommended as a model for scripting at A2.

MASTER SCENE LAYOUT

39. EXT. PRIVATE LONDON GARDENS. DAWN.   39.

Autumn is setting in and the gardens are turning to the rusts of a changing season. Were it not for the distant RUMBLE of London traffic and the SCREAM of airliners making their way over tower blocks down the flight path, this could be in the country.

Daniel sits on a bench, head hanging in his hands, suited but dishevelled – the events of the previous night now taking their toll on him. An empty bottle of champagne lies on the bench beside him.

A DOG WALKER walks past, but is stopped in her tracks as the dog stops to sniff at Daniel. He does not notice. The dog walker pulls the reluctant dog on.

An ELDERLY WOMAN meanders her way to the bench and pauses, panting a little, before sitting down at the opposite end to Daniel. They sit together quietly for a moment, Daniel with his head in his hands and the Elderly Woman looking him up and down. She reaches into her bag and pulls out a Tupperware tub. Opening it she reveals a packet of oatmeal cookies.

ELDERLY WOMAN
(to Daniel)

Fancy a cookie?

Daniel looks up slowly and glances first at the outstretched cookie, and then up to the Elderly Woman's face.

ELDERLY WOMAN

A cookie. Always helps me sober up after a night out.

DANIEL

Who said I was . . .

ELDERLY WOMAN
(interrupting)

Drunk? Well look at yourself, and look where we are. No one except a drunk would sit in this toilet at this time of the morning. Did she dump you?

Scenes in a professional screenplay are numbered consecutively starting from Scene 1, although if a character moves on-screen from one location to another the two scenes are considered as one and labelled 1a and 1b.

The scene number sits at the start of the 'slug line', and is followed by either INT (Interior) or EXT (Exterior), a specific location, and if it is day or night (in the case above, DAWN is identified, as this may require a specific kind of lighting). All of this information appears in upper case.

Underneath this is the 'action descriptor', which is written to 'set the scene' in terms of *mise-en-scène*, lighting and mood. You will notice that both background action and key action are identified. When characters are introduced for the first time their names are capitalised, but appear in lower case subsequently. You will notice that sounds are also capitalised so that the sound crew can note on the screenplay that they will have to dub in some sound.

It should be obvious that the script does not offer anything that cannot be visualised (no thoughts or inner monologues), but does capture small details that 'speak' to the audience (Daniel not noticing a dog sniffing at him, for example, suggests a level of preoccupation). If it cannot be expressed visually or in dialogue, then it probably does not belong in the screenplay.

Dialogue is always set in from the margins at each end, and separated from any 'action descriptors' by a double space. The character speaking has his or her name centred (and capitalised) above the speech and if a particular tone is needed this is described under the name in italics.

As a director 'visualises' a script there is no need to write in specific camera instructions or suggestions as to shots – these are the decisions that belong to the director and the DoP (director of photography, or cinematographer). At A2 level only a master scene script is acceptable. In this you should try to 'infer' camera instructions through the descriptions you offer. The line 'his feet shuffle on the tinder-dry ground' would, with any half-decent director, lead to a close-up of feet shuffling – you got 'your' shot, while the director can congratulate himself on the brilliant interpretation of your script.

ACTIVITY

In the screenplay extract above, where would you place your close-ups, and why? Do you think the screenwriter planned this? What shot would you use to open this scene? Compare your opening shot with those of others.

In a group, discuss how the scene could be shot, and, when it comes to the dialogue section, who the camera will favour. Why is this?

Consider the timing of each shot. What happens to the 'flow' of the piece if you alter the timings for each shot?

Documentary step outline

A documentary-maker's role is essentially about communicating an issue or concept to an audience in order to raise their awareness and offer them information with which they can engage with the viewpoint being expressed. There are a variety of documentary approaches that can be adopted and these are explored in Chapter 16, 'Spectatorship and documentary'.

In all documentary-making there are two key elements that documentary-makers need to keep at the forefront of their minds:

1   the audience – their level of existing knowledge and interest in the subject
2   the form or style being adopted and its relationship to the subject.

These two elements should shape every content and stylistic decision the documentary-maker makes, and as such are primary to the success of the documentary.

Once the subject and the audience are identified, the documentary-maker begins ordering his or her thoughts through a planning system called a step outline. This is a brief note-form activity that sketches out the structure of the documentary sequence by sequence, and is often written out on small 6″ × 4″ cards so that they can be physically laid out in a line and then rearranged to make the finished piece flow appropriately.

A difficulty that novices have with such an activity is connected to the belief that documentary is either 'truth' or at best should be unmediated. This belief means it is impossible to sketch out the content of an interview until after the interview has occurred, and so impossible to insert such an interview into a relationship with sequences either side of it. However, documentary is like any other form of filmmaking – it is a construct. As a construct it is fairly easy to work out what a potential response in an interview will be, based on who is being interviewed and what questions are asked. It is a safe bet that the Conservative Party leader, David Cameron, will answer in the negative if asked if he believes in nationalisation. Similarly, it is a safe bet that a Catholic priest will speak out against euthanasia. It is not only possible to estimate the kind of material an interview is likely to contain, but it is equally possible to ask the questions that will elicit such desired responses. Thus, in accepting documentary as a construct, the planning of this construct becomes possible.

ACTIVITY

Devise a set of questions for an interviewee that will elicit a desired response.

Next, devise a second set of questions that either elicit an opposite response, or direct the interviewee away from their natural response.

How predictable are the responses? How easy do you find such manipulation?

TYPICAL STEP OUTLINE

A typical step outline may run like this one for *Things Can Only Get Better – British Film after the Tories*:

Scene no.	1	Page no.	1
Slugline	Int. Studio. Day		
Endpoint of last scene	n/a		
Characters in scene	Narrator + key politicians on rear screen footage of Labour's 1 May election victory		
Point of scene	To show the jubilation at the defeat of the Tories and to give a context for the narrator's discussion of the state of UK film		
Conflict	Tension between scenes of jubilation and expectation and audience's knowledge of subsequent history		
Ending/central question	Can things only get better for British film?		

Scene description (without dialogue)

Narrator sits in front of rear projection of news footage from Labour's landslide victory over the Tory government. Speaks directly to camera

Scene no.	2	Page no.	2
Slugline	Int. Film Council Offices. Day		
Endpoint of last scene	Narrator introduces Wilf Stephenson		
Characters in scene	Wilf Stephenson		
Point of scene	For ex-head of BFI to give a view of the position of British film at the end of the period of Conservative government		
Conflict	Bitterness at wasted years		
Ending/central question	What would the incoming government do for British Film?		

Scene description (without dialogue)

Wilf Stephenson sits in a darkened office with film paraphernalia (steenbeck, posters) behind him. He is suited and speaks confidently, including questions in his answers.

You should be able to see that there is a formulaic approach to noting down the scenes in a step outline, and you should also see that this form allows for each scene to be interchangeable. The scenes are described briefly, as they are designed to sketch out the documentary, not to be the definitive script for it. Accordingly, only key information is recorded, and there is a succinct nature to the step outline's construction.

Reflective analysis

The Reflective analysis is an analysis of the creative product within the context of the aims and context (to a maximum of 1,000 words), and as such it should consider the following elements:

- reflection on aims and rationale
- the identified issue
- the decisions underpinning construction
- consideration of audience and their response to the product
- what prior learning was practically applied
- what new learning/knowledge/skills have been developed.

With so much to do it needs careful attention and drafting, in the same way that the Aims and context did, and in the same way that the projects themselves have been treated. The Reflective analysis carries a significant proportion of marks with it, and these should not be thrown away just because they sit at the end of a project.

It is essential to refer to the identified issue, and the Aims and Context and the audience, as these ingredients tie the three elements of the project together. These lead to talking about the creative project, and in arriving at this point it should be easy to comment on process, product and application of learning. Ending with identifying what new learning has taken place is a good way of highlighting your efforts to the marker, and to demonstrate that it has been a learning process.

INFORMATION BOX

Example of Reflective analysis – Film/video production *Farewell my Maltese Lady from Shanghai*

Using Steve Neale's and Nick Lacey's work along with watching a lot of old black and white movies, I was able to identify the key ingredients of film noir and went to a lot of trouble to replicate them. The 'twist' with

continued

this is that this film was aimed at a modern cine-literate 18-year-old target audience, and so it needed bringing up to date, and needed to address the market's desire for humour (which I think the title reflects). Audience response was quite positive, and at its first screening the scene of the dead narrator in the pool (who kept coming up for air) at the start got a huge laugh. Many of my film studies group expressed surprise at the lengths I had gone to for the noir look.

I was very lucky with the actors as they all worked very well. After reading Michael Rabiger's *Directing* I abandoned the idea of the impro-visational approach, and instead worked in rehearsals with the actors to really push their performances. Maggie (who plays Velma La Tour, the nightclub singer) was very demanding and needy, and I was getting quite fed up with her until she got on set, when she was no longer Maggie but Velma. Tom (Dick Private, the PI) was an absolute star and as he is a big noir fan he was able to make really valuable contributions. I learned a lot about my own directing skills and confidence from directing these two actors. In the scene where Velma tries to seduce Dick I made sure that the team members responsible for camera and lighting were aware of the look I was going for on a micro level, with shafts of light highlighted by smoke from cigarettes. The lighting was a big element here and I was insistent we get some Venetian blinds to shine a light through in order to get that noir 'slatted' look. Beth wasn't quite sure of where I was going with this, but once she saw what we could do, she really went into overdrive and every shot was dripping with noir lighting and tight framing. Her close-ups exceeded my expectations and she made a point of taking as many 'pick-up' shots as possible in order to give Dave some room for manoeuvre in editing. I had hoped to do one silhouetted shot, and Beth developed such a stylistic flair for this that we took several other unplanned shots that all ended up in the finished film. I think they lend a certain level of creepiness to the piece and this balances out the comedy elements that could otherwise have overtaken the piece.

As a team I think we worked really well. I did much of the ground work and acted as a kind of producer. The majority of the *mise-en-scène* came from the efforts I turned in, from the three-quarters-drunk bottle of scotch, through the 1940s costumes, to the vibrant red lipstick that Velma was wearing (I got this idea from the neo-noir *The Last Seduction*, and although it was more modern than I originally planned, when we tried it, it worked, so it stayed in). Beth turned in a great performance on camera and really worked hard to achieve the look we both wanted. Her idea to use joss-sticks to create a smoky atmosphere in the club really makes the scene. I was really pleased with her lighting in the pool hall, and I think she quite liked my idea of spinning a fan in front of the light to get a flickering shadow (very noir). Pete did a good job on location sound and created a 'cool' soundtrack to reflect the noir theme. Dave's editing was really sharp and his suggestion to bleach out the daylight scene gives it a real *Sunset Boulevard* look. Trying to get the whole thing shot in two days was a bit of a push and I think that's a decision I'd revise if doing it again. Generally the time scale worked, and I think the result shows that, though more time to perfect the titles would have been good as they let it down quite a bit – I guess that this was my fault, as I got caught up in the production and didn't really consider the titles until it was too late to do anything about it.

The final scene with the guy in the fez was difficult to get right because of his performance. I was looking for a Peter Lorre sinister kind of thing, but the actor didn't know who Peter Lorre was and so came over as far more aggressive than I wanted. We spent more time shooting his scene than any other and it was frustrating. I had tried to employ some of the techniques I read about in Michael Rabiger's *Directing*, but in the end I resorted to walking it through for him to copy. Not the best technique, but it meant I eventually got close to what I wanted.

It was really good to finally get a chance to apply the mise-en-scène, cinematography, performance, sound and editing theory I learned in FS1, and I enjoyed learning more about film noir. Most of all, I have learned more about film on those two days of making film than I have in the rest of the course (sort of), as it brought all the theory into focus.

(approximately 900 words)

The Reflective analysis does not have to be presented as a piece of written work, but instead may be presented online as a web-based product, or read over the creative project itself as a DVD commentary track. There is little to discriminate between these approaches, and the key questions should be: Does the approach suit the creative product, and is it an approach that is manageable for you in the time available?

Top tips for a successful creative project

1 Consider carefully the issue arising from previous study and make sure it is evident.
2 Be realistic about what can be achieved within the time scale (particularly if working in film/video production).

3 Consider and work to your audience.
4 Identify what learning you want to apply and how you will evidence its application.
5 Set a timetable and stick rigidly to it.
6 Carry out research (into the subject, but also into your role).
7 Be creative – but try not to get carried away; remember the point of the exercise.
8 Compare your approach and the result against a professional approach and result.
9 Actively seek out constructive criticism.
10 Revise, edit and perfect.

Recommended reading

Scriptwriting

Gaffney, F. (2008) *Screenwriting*, Auteur
Hunter, L. (1994) *Screenwriting*, Hale
Owen, A. (2003) *Story and Character: Interviews with British Screenwriters*, Bloomsbury pbk

Production

Block, B. (2001) *The Visual Story*, Focal
Katz, S. (1991) *Film Directing Shot by Shot*, Wiese
Rabiger, M. (2007) *Directing: Film Techniques and Aesthetics*, Focal

Documentary

Rabiger, M. (2004) *Directing the Documentary*, Focal
Swain, D. (1998) *Film Scriptwriting: A Practical Manual*, Focal

Internet sites

http://www.script-o-rama.com Drew's Scriptorama: Script and screenwriting site
http://www.cyberfilmschool.com Cyber Film School: Pro-end DV filmmaking site

part 2

VARIETIES OF FILM EXPERIENCE – ISSUES AND DEBATES (FM4)

INTRODUCTION TO FM4

BOLLYWOOD 1990 TO PRESENT

IRANIAN CINEMA 1990 TO PRESENT

JAPANESE CINEMA 1950 TO 1970

MEXICAN CINEMA 1990 TO PRESENT

GERMAN AND SOVIET CINEMA OF THE 1920s

SURREALISM

NEO-REALISM

NEW WAVES

URBAN STORIES

EMPOWERING WOMEN

4 INTRODUCTION TO FM4

In this section we look at:

- the concept of a *synoptic* dimension to exploring varieties of film experience
- what is required for each section of FM4
- identifying issues and debates in analysing film texts and in the broader social and economic contexts of cinema
- how to synthesise learning from other units
- how to reflect critically

The *Synoptic* dimension

SYNOPTIC: this word is related to the word *synopsis*, and literally means 'of, or relating to a summary'. In this instance it is used to point towards the nature of the FM4 Varieties of Film Experience as bringing relevant elements of the learning from the other units at AS and A2 to bear on a single film, and to suggest that this earlier learning has a clear place here.

FM4 has been designed as a synoptic unit, in which learning from other units of the course (both at A2 and AS) is revisited, and in which it is applied to new areas of study. Skills developed in FM1 Exploring Film Form, for example, where textual analysis skills are used to explore individual sequences, will be invaluable when approaching study at FM4, as would the knowledge of an industrial context gained from FM2 British and American Film. This synoptic approach is one that further develops previously attained skills, and one that develops confidence in existing knowledge and skills, through encouraging their broader application.

While there is still 'new' learning to be engaged with in this unit, it is vital that any new area encountered has (as a background or context) previous learning applied to it. This not only means that a higher level of connection is made between the units, but that there is a great opportunity to deepen the knowledge gained in previous units through application in FM4.

The structure of FM4

FM4 is divided into three distinct sections:

- Section A – World Cinema
- Section B – Spectatorship Topics
- Section C – Single Film – Critical Study

As may be seen from the titles, the intention is to work from the general to the particular, while allowing the application of broader knowledge of the film industry and of film theory gained in each of the AS level units. Of course, there is also significant new learning taking place here through the engagement of new areas of study, and with particular individual film texts.

INFORMATION BOX

Section A – World Cinema

This section is focused on an engagement with a prescribed World Cinema topic, both in terms of exploring relevant films and also in terms of the broader production, social and historical contexts underpinning them. There are four options to choose from in this section:

Aspects of a national cinema

- Bollywood 1990 to present
- Iranian cinema 1990 to present
- Japanese cinema 1950 to 1970
- Mexican cinema 1990 to present

One of the above topics should be explored through the study of two principal films (each by a different director) and through one or two supplemental films that can be studied in less detail. Study does not have to cover the whole period, so long as the period decided upon and the films chosen are indicative of the chosen national cinema's

---

characteristics. Significant stress should be placed on gaining an understanding of the value to the spectator of studying film within a context of a national cinema.

International film styles

- German and/or Soviet cinema of the 1920s
- Surrealism
- Neo-realism
- New waves

The topics in this option are designed to explore a film style that may have begun within a national cinema, but which has subsequently developed international influence and significance. It is advisable to study the original context that produced the movement through at least two key films studied in depth. A broader awareness of the development of the movement should be inculcated through the study of at least one other film. An alternative approach would be to look at parallel developments within a movement, possibly within different national contexts. Whatever approach is adopted, it is important to consider spectator response, and furthermore to consider both the responses of the original spectators and the responses of contemporary spectators engaging with these films and film movements for the first time in new contexts.

Specialist study 1: Urban stories – power, poverty and conflict

Study should revolve around the examination of two key, self-selected films that represent life in challenging urban environments from the fractured society of a defeated Berlin in *Germannia anno zero* (*Germany Year Zero*) (Produzione Salvo D'Angelo, Italy, 1949, *Dir*: Roberto Rossellini), to the desperate, impoverished ghettos of Brazil in *Linah De Passe* (*Line of Passage*) (Double Helix Entertainment, Brazil, 2008, *Dir*: Walter Salles and Daniela Thomas), or from the futuristic sci-fi landscape of *Metropolis* (UFA, Germany, 1927, *Dir*: Fritz Lang) to the terrorist context of Nablus and Tel Aviv in *Paradise Now* (Augustus Film, Palestine/France/Germany/Netherlands/Israel, 2005, *Dir*: Hany Abu-Assad). The key focus films should be supplemented by two other films that can be studied in less detail. Whichever films are selected for study, it is the connections between films that may come from very different periods and contexts that are important.

continued

Specialist study 2: Empowering women

This topic encourages the study of how film engages with empowering women, and this may be done through a variety of geographical approaches, perhaps looking at individual continents, or by comparing approaches from differing continental cinemas. The important consideration in this topic is to explore films that come from contrasting social and cultural contexts. It is expected that this topic will be studied through two principal films and two supplementary films that may be studied more broadly.

Section A is very much about working with specific film texts and exploring how film form and the film language within them is used both to create meanings and to affect spectator response. While there are no prescribed films, it is important to select key films that link accessibly to the chosen topic, as films that connect obliquely may prove difficult to apply the broad-based examination questions to.

INFORMATION BOX

Section B – Spectatorship Topics

Work here focuses on an area of specialist study, which should be supplemented by watching as many films as possible from the area of study, broad reading around the subject, and by visiting relevant websites. The emphasis across all of the options is on the interaction of film form with the spectator, and as such it offers direct development from studies in FM1: Exploring Film Form. The four optional areas of specialist study are:

- **Spectatorship and early cinema before 1917**: focusing on how and why film form, film language and spectatorship developed in the way they did between 1895 and the first recognisably full-length feature films (up until 1917). Study can be approached through the exploration of a number of short films from 1895 to 1905, on two feature-length films from 1913 to 1917, or on a mix of early shorts and one later feature-length film.
- **Spectatorship and documentary**: an examination of a wide range of film (and video/television) documentary and the

relationship of its form and film language to the spectator and representations of the 'real'. An historical or contemporary approach may be adopted, and shaped around traditional film work and that produced on video or digitally. While short documentaries may form a significant part of the study, a minimum of two feature-length documentaries should be engaged with.

- **Spectatorship: Experimental and expanded film/video**: a focus on alternatives to the mainstream, and often radical departures from the conventions of film form and representations to which we are most commonly exposed. The key to this is to also explore the challenges such work creates for the spectator and the subsequent spectator response. Study in this unit should encompass a number of short films, a number of works installed within the context of specific locations and spaces, two feature-length films, or a combination of any of these. Where possible, study should include visits to galleries and video installations to facilitate a broader understanding of the area and the possibilities for experimental film/video.

- **Spectatorship: Popular film and emotional response**: exploring how popular mainstream film can provoke a powerful emotional response in the spectator, one that is often sensory in nature. A variety of emotional responses can be considered from shock caused by horror films, through the emotional distress caused by melodramas, to the awe of sheer spectacle as caused by large-scale action fillms. The focus in whatever emotional response or type of film explored is one that considers how films create the emotional response that they do, and how context may change or shape such a response. As such it is essential that issues of spectatorship are brought to the fore. At least two feature-length films should be studied for this option.

Section B offers the opportunity to comment directly on issues and debates through well-supported examples and well-constructed case studies. It is not a place simply to repeat orthodox opinion, but is instead a place to explore and to challenge these opinions, and in doing so develop a clear, personal response that is built on study across several units, a deep engagement with the Section B study area, and personal experience as a spectator.

i

INFORMATION BOX

Section C – Single Film – Critical Study

Work here is a truly synoptic application of accumulated knowledge, centred on a single text from a list of prescribed films:

Modern Times (Charles Chaplin Productions, US, 1936, *Dir*: Charlie Chaplin)

Les Enfants du Paradis (Pathé Cinéma, France, 1945, *Dir*: Marcel Carné)

Vertigo (Alfred J. Hitchcock Productions, US, 1958, *Dir*: Alfred Hitchcock)

The Battle of Algiers (Casbah/Igor, Algeria/Italy, 1965, *Dir*: Gillo Pontecorvo)

Sweet Sweetback's Baadasssss Song (Yeah, US, 1971, *Dir*: Melvin Van Peebles)

Solaris (Creative Unit of Writers and Cinema Workers, USSR, 1972, *Dir*: Andrei Tarkovsky)

Happy Together (Block 2 Pictures, Hong Kong, 1997, *Dir*: Won Kar Wai)

Fight Club (Art Linson Productions, US, 1999, *Dir*: David Fincher)

Talk to Her (El Deseo SA, Spain, 2002, *Dir*: Pedro Almodovar)

Morvern Callar (Momentum/Alliance Atlantis/BBC/Company, UK, 2002, *Dir*: Lynne Ramsay)

Study should engage with text, context and critical reception of the chosen film, and should contextualise this engagement within a relevant critical approach. Critical approaches may include the contexts described in the FM3 research project, or those engaged with in other sections of the AS or A2 units.

Section C demands a broader engagement with critical approaches to the chosen film and to the study of film in a wider sense. It would be valuable to study critical responses to the chosen film in order to consider wider issues of spectatorship that the film may engender. It is advisable to look not only at responses from 'respected' sources but also at those produced on the more dynamic, but perhaps less well versed in film theory, fan sites and film message boards.

Approaching FM4

This unit is different to the other units across the AS and A2 specifications, as it expects much of the learning and filmic references to come from studies in previous units, and as such is more about extracting that learning and those references, and supplementing them with additional material. Key to study in this unit is to constantly consider a film within the social and economic contexts in which it was produced, and equally importantly, the social and economic context in which it is screened. This latter point impacts directly upon personal response, and is a 'trigger' that shapes the way a spectator engages with either a contemporary film or one that is from an earlier period (or alternative national cinema).

Before commencing study on this unit it is worth undertaking a *skills and knowledge audit* where the skills and knowledge learned and developed in other areas of the course are considered and evaluated. Only by recognising what learning and filmic references exist to be drawn upon and applied can a synoptic approach to this unit be successfully engaged with.

ACTIVITY

In order to approach a synoptic unit it is essential for you to undertake a skills and knowledge audit. Create and complete a table like the one below and list against each unit the skills and knowledge you have developed.

FM1: Exploring Film Form	Knowledge
	Skills
FM2: British and American Film	Knowledge
	Skills
FM3: Film Research and Creative Projects	Knowledge
	Skills

FM4 expects an engagement with 'critical reflection' from the perspective of spectatorship, and it is in this area that the key skill for this unit is developed. Critical reflection requires not a simple acceptance of theories, of commonly agreed views and of the opinions of 'authorities', but rather the careful weighing of these against the experience of film as spectator. A theory, view or opinion may carry with it significant academic value, and may be offered as an indisputable 'fact', but if it does not match the experience of a spectatorship it should at least be investigated and challenged. It is the consideration of this issue that this unit champions, as it is in measuring theory, views and opinions against experience that either an understanding of these is developed, or that they are challenged and revised, or that original thought (through personal response) is expressed. Any of these are desirable outcomes of study in this unit.

5 BOLLYWOOD 1990 TO THE PRESENT

This chapter:

- offers a general indicative approach to studying popular film from India since 1990
- gives a brief overview of the history of Indian cinema prior to 1990 in order to supply a background against which to see more recent developments
- suggests ways of approaching two case study films

INFORMATION BOX

i

This chapter will be relevant to the section 'FM4 – World Cinema' in the WJEC's A level in Film Studies. It will be directly applicable to questions relating to 'Bollywood: 1990 to the present' but you should note the particular requirements of this section of the syllabus which suggests that students should work on two films in depth supplemented by a further two films studied less rigorously.

Films mentioned

As you work your way through this chapter you need to watch both *Dil to Pagal Hai/The Heart is Crazy* (Yash Chopra, 1997) and *Dil Chahta Hai/The*

continued

Heart Desires (Akhtar, 2001) several times. You may like to apply the sorts of approaches suggested here to other Bollywood films made since 1990, such as *Hum Aapke Hain Koun!/What Do I Mean to You?* (Barjatya, 1994), *Dilwale Dulhaniya Le Jayenge/DDLJ/The One With a True Heart Will Win the Bride* (Aditya Chopra, 1995), or *Kuch Kuch Hota Hai/Something Happens* (Johar, 1998); or, perhaps, two rather different films such as the historical dramas *Asoka* (Sivan, 2001) and *Jodhaa Akbar* (Gowariker, 2008).

'Bollywood'

This term is used to refer to popular Hindi language films produced in Mumbai (still widely recognised as Bombay and officially known by this name until 1995). The films combine a distinctive approach to filmmaking with traditional elements of Indian culture and a Hollywood-like attempt to appeal to the mass market. In more recent years conventional Indian perspectives on issues surrounding the family and individual duty have been increasingly matched by aspects of a more Western outlook. The style of the films has, however, remained noticeably different to Hollywood:

- prominence is given to song-and-dance routines with high production values
- narratives focus on family relationships and use elements of heavy melodrama
- a mixed genre is employed with intermingled scenes of action, comedy and intense romance
- the stars are displayed as highly attractive heroes and heroines to be admired and emulated in their moral values.

> **BOLLYWOOD:** this term is a pun on the word 'Hollywood'; and, as with 'Hollywood', it refers not only to a place of film production (Mumbai, formerly Bombay) but also to a style of filmmaking.

Somewhere between 150 and 200 films a year are currently made in Hindi by Bombay-based filmmakers, but in most years this amounts to less than 25 per cent of the total made in India as a whole, since films are made in a range of other languages in this huge country. With a population of a billion people and eighteen recognised languages, there are several other important filmmaking centres in the country, such as Madras and Hyderabad. Madras, for example, actually produces more films in a year than Bombay but these are in the regional languages of Tamil and Telugu.

Hindi is India's official language and is spoken (with distinct regional variations) by about 40 per cent of the population. It therefore offers the possibility of larger audiences. By not using the main regional languages found in Bombay (Gujarati and Marathi) the industry based here was able to appeal to a wider national audience. In addition, in recent years, the widely spread diasporic Hindi-speaking Asian market has been seen as increasingly important to the Indian film industry, with Bollywood productions beginning to feature in box-office charts in the United States and Britain.

Approaching 'Bollywood' films

To somebody born and bred in the West and on their first visit to the country, India operates as a forceful assault on both the mind and the senses. What visitors remember and tell you on their return is just how different it is in every imaginable way. Utter destitution and poverty exist alongside lavish displays of individual and corporate wealth. Some people will be wearing the most immaculately tailored clothes and expensive jewellery, while others in the same street will display amputated limbs in an attempt to beg. Shanty towns of recycled plastic, wood and metal exist next door to glass-fronted twenty-first-century office blocks owned by multinational corporations.

Figure 5.1 The notorious slum colony of Dharavi in Mumbai is towered over by nearby office blocks and residential buildings. The plans to redevelop Dharavi – known as Asia's largest slum – have met with strong protests from the residents.

ACTIVITY

Research the Indian caste system and draw up a list of the categories within this rigid social hierarchy. Consider the ways in which this system is linked to both the religious and social contexts of India. How is the system related to Hinduism? How does it affect social outlooks and expectations? Try to find time to discuss your findings with others.

However, it is more than just the sights that are different; the sounds, tastes and smells are also entirely different from anything the European traveller is likely to have encountered. This is a vast country with a range of intermingling cultural traditions, an array of religious beliefs, and a political diversity that spans the left-wing to right-wing possibilities from extreme to extreme.

ACTIVITY

Prepare brief outlines (no longer than one side of typed A4 paper) of the key aspects of the main religions to be found in India. Work with others if possible and divide the task carefully among yourselves. You should definitely cover Hinduism, Islam and Sikhism, but you could add others if you wish.

When you come to watch Bollywood films you will be told to prepare for an experience that is entirely different from anything you have previously experienced. And yet, just as the visitor to India must hold on to some sense of commonality existing beneath the new and strange social and cultural surface, so too must the student coming to Indian films. There is difference but there is also a great deal of similarity. Indian films deal with themes of love and romance, use narratives that rely on heroes and villains, and integrate aspects of genres such as comedy and action. So, what is so different?

The greatest difficulty may be the language and the subtitles but that is no different from dealing with French or German films. In both cases cultural, historical and political references can be missed because of a lack of familiarity with the country. But actually we can often miss these sorts of references in British films if we don't know enough about history or politics, or more importantly if we haven't been prepared to put in the work to find out crucial background information.

Tips from Ruchi, a student in Delhi:

1   To enjoy these films you will need to be open to a new kind of cinema.
2   In many Bollywood films, the storyline isn't great but it's the way the films have been made that makes all the difference.
3   In most of the films it's the music, cast and dialogue that create the film's popularity. For example, *Dilwale Dulhaniya Le Jayenge/DDLJ/The One With a True Heart Will Win the Bride* is the most typical Bollywood film you will find, and it became really popular largely because of the music.
4   Many of the films have perfect casting: for example, in most of his films no one else would be able to carry off the role played by Shahrukh Khan. We also have some brilliant dancers like Hrithik Roshan, Shahid Kapoor and Madhuri Dixit.
5   It is mainly the music that makes Bollywood films unique and yet, although the storylines are more often than not copied from Hollywood you do come across some quite original ideas sometimes. Recent examples would be *Iqbal* (Kukunoor, 2005), *Rang De Basanti/Paint It Saffron* (Mehra, 2006), *Swades/ Homeland* (Gowariker, 2004), *Taare Zameen Par/Stars on Earth* (Khan, 2007), and *Chak De India/Go For It, India!* (Amin, 2007).

Indian filmmakers can only use cameras to film performances given within certain chosen locations or settings, employ sound equipment to record dialogue, edit these actions together into filmed sequences, and add sound effects and a musical soundtrack. In other words, they cannot do anything any differently to any other filmmaker. The actors will only be using their bodies and voices to perform. They might be talking, singing, walking or dancing, but they won't be doing anything we have not seen before. They might be performing comedy sequences, or tragic scenes, or emotionally charged scenes, or singing about love or death, but they won't be doing anything we have not seen on screen before. The overall combination of events, themes, genres and techniques may be in some limited sense uniquely Indian but it will only be a slight re-formulation of everything we have seen and analysed as film students before.

So, when coming to Bollywood films, expect to find some difference and be prepared to consider carefully social, cultural, historical and political contexts that may be new to you. But, as always, be excited by difference in film as an expression of both human and filmic diversity.

Research the concept of 'arranged marriages'. How important is this as an aspect of Indian society? Are there different interpretations of how 'arranged marriages' should be organised? To what extent is this concept related to particular religious beliefs and to what extent would you see the term as being related to socio-economic considerations?

Research the term 'forced marriage'. Is this related to the notion of 'arranged marriages' and, if so, in what ways. How is it different? How would you define 'force' in relation to this concept? (Should we consider the role played by aspects of 'force' that might be at work within society other than physical force – psychological force, the force of social expectation or cultural tradition, or economic forces, for example – or are these sorts of 'forces', or what we might describe as expressions of power in society, simply not relevant?)

The development of Indian cinema and 'Bollywood'

A Lumière film screening was given in Bombay in 1896, less than a year after the new technology was first used in Paris. The hotel in which this occurred operated an apartheid system that refused entry to Indians, but by the early 1900s filmed 'shorts' were being shown to Indian audiences in Bombay, Calcutta and Madras. Still photography had been taken up equally quickly in the 1850s in each of these cities as well as elsewhere, clearly indicating an enthusiasm for new technologies in general and for photographic images in particular.

Bombay had been established by the British as the main export-import centre for the country and so new technologies were always likely to emerge and establish themselves here. The first Indian feature film, *Raja Harishchandra* (*King Harishchandra*), was shown in Bombay in 1913. This film was based on a story from the Indian epic the *Mahabharata*, demonstrating the way in which connections between the new technology and the longer cultural tradition of the country were quickly established by filmmakers. This may have been new technology but it could be used to tell old stories, thereby helping to make cinema accessible to the masses. By the 1930s Bombay was responsible for more than 60 per cent of the country's film output.

The music, song and dance associated with Bollywood was introduced with the coming of sound in the 1930s. This was a further aspect of Indian films that appealed to the mass audience, and once again this appeal was achieved by building upon earlier cultural (in this case, musical) traditions. This awareness of audience expectations among local filmmakers meant that by the end of the decade the percentage of foreign films being shown in India had fallen below 10 per cent. Films were being made in Calcutta, Madras, Lahore and Pune, as well as in Bombay. However, Bombay was the only centre to choose to employ a form of Hindi (Hindustani) as the spoken language in its films and this was to prove crucial in enabling Bombay-made films to appeal to a more widespread nationwide audience.

'Playback singing' in which songs are pre-recorded and the actor lip-synchs the lyrics was introduced in the mid-1930s, enabling the actor to engage in more highly choreographed and energetic dance sequences. By the late 1940s not only had the profession of the unseen 'playback singer' become an acclaimed film profession but the technique had become a key feature of the production process.

PLAYBACK SINGING: a technique under which songs are pre-recorded by specialist singers allowing the actor to lip-synch the lyrics. Playback singers have an acclaimed role in the Bollywood film industry.

Tips from Milu, a student in Delhi:

1   Don't take the song-and-dance routines as useless distractions; sometimes Hindi films communicate powerfully through their songs.
2   Watch out for the villains; sometimes these parts are enacted by some of the greatest actors (for example, Amjad Khan as Gabbar Singh in *Sholay* (Sippy, 1975)).
3   The punchline of the villain is often funny but it may be difficult to fully appreciate if you don't know Hindi.
4   These films are pure entertainment; they will not follow the rules of real life. You should watch out for the music (A.R. Rehman), acting (Aamir Khan, Naseeruddin Shah, Pankaj Kapoor, Shabana Aazmi), the dialogue which is often hilarious (*Munna Bhai* (Hirani, 2003)), and the increasingly tight storyline (*Johnny Gaddar/Johnny Traitor* (Raghavan, 2007)).
5   Some other good actors to watch out for are Konkona Sen Sharma, Irfan Khan, Rahul Bose and Kirron Kher.
6   Stars like Shahrukh Khan, Amitabh Bachchan and Akshay Kumar may not be brilliant actors but they are incredibly famous as stars here.
7   You need to be open to a new kind of cinema. My cousin's friend who's not Indian cried through the whole of *Veer-Zaara* (Chopra, 2004), so it is possible!

During the 1930s powerful studios emerged such as New Theatres in Calcutta, Prabhat Studios in Pune and Bombay Talkies. But there were also a raft of many smaller production companies offering competition and the larger studios never succeeded in integrating production, distribution and exhibition in the style of the big Hollywood studios. They therefore always remained vulnerable and liable to go out of business during periods of economic downturn.

As the demands for Indian independence from British rule increased during the 1930s and as the Second World War placed further pressure on the British Empire, so the censorship of films became tighter; anything that called into question the authority of the British was banned. Famously, *Kismet (Fate)* (Mukerjee, 1943) managed to circumvent this by incorporating a song that although explicitly attacking Germany and Japan could equally be read by the audience as anti-British.

In 1947 India won its independence but with immediate disastrous results brought on by the final act of British rule, which was to suddenly partition the country into India and Pakistan. Pakistan was designated as Muslim homeland in an attempt to safeguard this religious minority, but the actual result of Partition was to unleash a wave of vicious sectarian attacks between Hindus, Muslims and Sikhs. More than ten million people were forced to uproot themselves from communities in which they had lived for generations in a period of only two months. Their aim was to escape the violence and find safety either on the Hindu or the Muslim side of the border, but it is estimated that more than one million people were killed as the convoys of migrants were attacked.

Punjabi Hindi filmmakers moved from Lahore (in Pakistan) to Bombay, strengthening filmmaking in the city; while the key competitor city of Calcutta lost much of its Bengali audience as East Bengal became part of East Pakistan (later Bangladesh). With this loss of audience, Bengali film-workers also moved from Calcutta to Bombay, further improving the city's position as the premier filmmaking centre.

After Independence, with ethnic violence and food shortages needing to be addressed and pressing demands for improved health care and education, the film industry was understandably not seen as a priority by the government. Any government attention cinema did receive was not geared towards supporting Hindi popular film production. Cinema that appealed to the masses, it was believed, should be educational rather than escapist and a heavy entertainment tax was imposed on the industry. Censorship also became increasingly restrictive and musical dance sequences were criticised by both politicians and intellectuals as offering a 'low' form of entertainment without any potential for 'improving' the audience. Filmmakers who were encouraged were those who, influenced by Italian neo-realism, tried to show the poverty and deprivation of ordinary people's everyday lives, or those who attempted to promote the concept of the new Indian nation.

Severe political problems began to emerge in the early 1970s. There was increased tension and eventually war with Pakistan, droughts leading to food shortages, and difficulties with the economy led to social unrest. Confrontations on the streets between the police and left-wing students and union members increased. In 1975 there were calls for the prime minister, Indira Gandhi, to resign after she was found

Figure 5.2 Indiri Gandhi pictured in 1981.

guilty of contravening election rules. She responded by declaring a 'state of emergency' under which more than 100,000 politicians, journalists and political activists were arrested and held without trial. Gandhi portrayed herself as the saviour of India, but when elections were held again in 1977 she was heavily defeated.

A new type of film emerged to reflect this period of political uncertainty with the hero (most famously India's biggest star, Amitabh Bachchan) as the 'angry young man' bringing vigilante justice to a corrupt society. Clean-cut heroes in musical romances dealing with family issues were replaced by cynical heroes operating on the streets. By the 1980s rather than just corrupt businessmen being seen as the problem, politicians were also being portrayed as a source of corruption.

ACTIVITY

Research the 1980s in more depth. Find out in particular what happened to Gandhi after she became prime minister again in 1980 and list key events under her son's (Rajiv Gandhi) period of government from late 1984. Your final set of notes should not extend to more than one side of A4 paper.

The past and the present historical moment

The title of this chapter gives a clear sense of the type of film and very limited time period we are being asked to consider – popular films made in India since 1990. However, if we are to give ourselves a fair chance of coming to terms with these films we need to have some grasp of the key features of Indian society, and this will only come from spending a little time considering the longer historical perspective. For example, in *Dil to Pagal Hai/The Heart is Crazy*, God is continually referred to as the instigator of love between couples, but the very general way in which the term is used leaves the 'He' as open and therefore capable of being interpreted as the God of any religion. Apart from the fact that there is in Hinduism a willingness to accept the gods of other religions, the effort underpinning this in the film is to draw the various religions of India together – this is the 'God' who unites all rather than a specifically Hindu or Muslim or Sikh god. Whether the film is successful in this may be open to debate, but the implicit attempt to unite rather than divide has to be appreciated in the light of the violent religious conflict found in the history of India since 1947. Similarly, moving from content to style, if we are to begin to appreciate the specific use that is made of genre in popular Indian film we need to view these films in relation to both the historical development of film in India (the coming of sound and 'playback singing', for example) and the wider context of a culture that has historically prioritised displays of music and dance.

Case study

DIL TO PAGAL HAI/THE HEART IS CRAZY (1997)

(Director: Yash Chopra. Cast: Shahrukh Khan (Rahul), Madhuri Dixit (Pooja), Karisma Kapoor (Nisha), Akshay Kumar (Ajay). Lyricist: Anand Bakshi. Music: Uttam Singh. Cinematography: Manmohan Singh. Choreography:

Figure 5.3
Publicity shot for *Dil to Pagal Hai/The Heart is Crazy* (1997)

Farah Khan and Shiamak Davar. Screenplay: Aditya Chopra, Tanuja Chandra, Pamela Chopra and Yash Chopra.)

Storyline and plot

This is a straightforward romantic comedy. The audience knows from early on in the film that this will be about the bringing together of Rahul and Pooja; the key interest for the viewer is in seeing how this will be achieved. The central pleasure is a feeling of being complicit in, and part of, this bringing together of the central characters.

As in Western 'rom coms' there is a barrier, or series of connected barriers, to the union of the central pair of lovers. And, again as in the Hollywood-style genre, the problems preventing the lovers coming together will usually be both personally and socially created. The difference between Hollywood and Bollywood is that social prohibitions and expectations relating to marriage and particularly to the woman's role are that much stronger in conventional Indian society than in the West.

continued

ACTIVITY

- What are the barriers to Rahul and Pooja's love? To what extent are these personal and to what extent socially constructed?
- How does this film attempt to straddle Western outlooks and more traditional Indian perspectives on love and marriage?
- Identify specific scenes in which it is possible to see tensions between conventional and changing (more Westernised) values.
- What is the significance in this respect of the shot at the end of the film in which Pooja's aunt and uncle join the rest of the audience in standing and applauding?
- When you have considered these things fully for yourself discuss your ideas with others, if possible. Make sure that you do this by reference to specific scenes that show the issues you are attempting to debate.

Narrative structure is often seen to revolve around the conflict between good and evil with a villain coming between the hero and his goal. If there is a villain in this film it may be said to be embodied in a malevolent God who makes love and male–female pairing such an impossibly difficult process to understand. The darkest moments come in Nisha's and later Rahul's reactions to their experiences of unrequited love. Rahul is determined to turn his stage-show comedy into a tragedy because this, it seems, is the truth of human experience. When Nisha says she must be 'bad' for feeling so jealous of Pooja, Rahul replies: 'He is bad: the one who plays around with us humans.'

ACTIVITY

- Find the scene in which Nisha and Rahul sit beside a lake and discuss this notion of a malevolent god (about 150 minutes into the film). How does this scene relate to the scene that precedes it and the one that follows it?
- Is this a fantasy scene, or are we supposed to see it as actually happening within the 'reality' of the narrative?

■ In what ways is it similar to song-and-dance sequences in the film? (How is it different from these scenes?) Why has it been filmed in this way?

Duty, responsibility and family

The themes of duty and responsibility are most fully explored through the character of Pooja. However, it is noticeable that her sense of duty to family and awareness of her social responsibility as a woman are not abstract concepts to be maintained in order to satisfy some traditional sense of honour or to acknowledge her as being subject to male authority. Pooja's sense of duty and responsibility is towards deeply loved family members who have gained her love as a result of years of family warmth. (See the flashback showing Pooja arriving at her aunt's house as an orphan.) Significantly, it is her 'teacher' who stresses an alternative form of responsibility, towards herself and her 'dreams'. Remember: all of this occurs against the backdrop of the early discussion about arranged marriages between Pooja and her friend Anjali, and the statement by Pooja after Ajay has asked to marry her that: 'Love will happen in due course. And we are Indian girls: we can't choose our life partners.'

ACTIVITY

From what you have found out about Indian society do you believe audiences in that country would be satisfied by Pooja's efforts to follow her traditional duties? Might different audience members react in different ways? If possible, discuss these questions with others.

How significant do you believe Ajay's actions to be in the resolution phase of the film? How would various potential audience members respond to his role at this point?

Melodrama

Although exaggerated emotion is often cited as a key feature of Bollywood films this is clearly nothing new to audiences more used to Hollywood

continued

products. Melodramas follow intense trials relating to love and family experienced by a central female character.

> **MELODRAMA:** intense, heavily emphasised, if not exaggerated emotional drama often revolving around the family-related trials and tribulations experienced by a central female character.

ACTIVITY

Identify what you see as the four or five key emotional moments in the film.

If possible, compare your list with those arrived at by other people. Have the same moments been chosen? Discuss reasons for your choices.

Decide on the top four moments from the group and analyse how elements of film construction and narrative structure have combined in these scenes to create strong emotional responses from the audience.

Fantasy and reality

Most mainstream Hollywood films could not be further from reality than they are, and yet sometimes when viewers come to Bollywood films they suddenly become concerned about a lack of realism. All films are fabrications, illusions, constructions created through the trickery of directors, cinematographers and editors (and more recently, CGI experts). And yet, however much films might be seen (and be constructed) as escapist fantasies, they all relate in a range of ways to the everyday reality of the individual viewer's life. Audiences are elaborately and intricately aware of the fantastic nature of films and enter into a creative partnership with the sounds and images put before them.

ACTIVITY

Find the scene in which Pooja mimics Rahul without knowing he is watching her (about 112 minutes into the film). There is a moment here in which Rahul moves closer and closer to Pooja, as if they are about to kiss.

What is happening at this point in the relationship between the filmmakers and the audience? To what extent does it depend upon mutual acknowledgement between filmmakers and audience of the partnership that exists between them?

What is the relationship between fantasy and reality at this point?

(Remember that this final question might depend upon whether we are talking about the 'reality' within the narrative or the knowing 'reality' of the filmmakers and audience's shared understanding over, above and beyond this constructed interior reality of the film.)

Stars

From the outset the audience is left in no doubt about the type of film they can expect to see. The question 'What is love?' is immediately announced and the two central characters who will need to be brought together are shown (although significantly, especially in relation to the couples that follow, not within the same shot). Just as importantly, the main stars are attractively displayed for the viewer.

There is a further 'reality' that is always present within Bollywood films (as there is within Hollywood films) – the (again, highly constructed) 'reality' of the star system. Indian stars are high-profile media celebrities and the fandom that attaches to them is intense and passionate.

ACTIVITY

Research the careers of Shahrukh Khan (Rahul) and Madhuri Dixit (Pooja). Prepare handouts on each (no longer than one side of A4). Exchange these with other people who have undertaken the same task and compare your findings.

continued

To what extent do you believe the audience is watching characters (Pooja and Rahul) in this film, and to what extent do you think the audience would consider they are watching Dixit and Khan? In other words, what is the relationship between the stars and the characters they play?

Case study
DIL CHAHTA HAI/THE HEART DESIRES (2001)

(Director: Farhan Akhtar. Cast: Aamir Khan (Akash), Preity Zinta (Shalini), Akshaye Khanna (Siddharth), Dimple Kapadia (Tara), Saif Ali Khan (Sameer), Sonali Kulkarni (Pooja). Music: Shnkar Mahadevan, Ehsaan Noorani and Loy Mendonsa (Shankar-Ehsaan-Loy). Cinematography: Ravi K. Chandran. Screenplay: Akhtar and Kassim Jagmagia.)

Figure 5.4 Advertising for *Dil Chahta Hai/The Heart Desires* (2001)

Storyline and plot

The story follows the enduring friendship between three middle-class young men living in Mumbai as they adopt the usual (socially expected) trajectory of moving away from each other to find female partners. They are perhaps rather stereotypical characters: the romantic (Sameer), the somewhat intro-spective artist (Sid) and the self-confident extrovert (Akash). Although we follow several plotlines particularly between each of the three male leads and their female love interests, the crucial plot relationship is between Akash and Sid. The heart of the film is the breakdown and final restoration of this relationship. More than any of the others, it is Akash who is taken on a journey that enables him to learn about himself and the world and eventually to return to his friendship with Sid.

ACTIVITY

What is the Hindu festival of Holi? How might an understanding of this festival be relevant to the opening section of this film?

(What you should recognise after this exercise is the way in which we can understand a scene quite happily in an Indian film without certain background cultural awareness, but how that little extra knowledge can add to our depth of understanding.)

Song (and dance)

The opening song is strongly connected to the theme of the energy and unbounded optimism of youth. However, it could equally refer to the style of this film that uses the traditional Bollywood form but in new ways that perhaps move it away from sections of the conventional audience towards increasing identification with an emerging global middle class.

> We are today: why should our style be old?
> The earth and sky are created for us.

In terms of the songs, the most obvious departure from normal Bollywood fare lies in the absence of dance routines. (Only in the song 'Woh Ladki Hai Kaha' that gently parodies the older style do we see dancing and sudden changes of exotic location and costume.)

continued

For much of the time there is an intense seriousness to the music and lyrics that often counterpoints the colourful images we are being shown, allowing the audience to respond to the usual (expected) pleasure of the spectacle but also to consider issues on a more thoughtful level than perhaps Bollywood usually demands. As we see the 'boys' enjoying themselves in Goa, for example, we are asked to contemplate, 'How strange is this journey', that is to say, the journey of life.

Comedy (and melodrama)

Comedy is clearly present, as in Akash's attempt to dance with Shalini without knowing she is engaged to Rohit, or Sameer's clumsy introductions when his family attempt to instigate an arranged marriage with Pooja. But the more usual melodrama sometimes takes on a cutting edge of tragic realism in this film: Tara's pain at being denied the chance to see her daughter on her birthday, for example, becomes tragic rather than melodramatic.

ACTIVITY

Choose a section of the film where the mood seems to change from comedy to something more dramatic. Analyse this section carefully to see how the change is achieved. You should make sure you consider not only each aspect of the performance of the actors but also location, lighting, camerawork, editing and sound.

This is not to deny that melodrama is an important part of the genre mix in this film and you may like to identify where and when we experience this most intensely. You could start by considering, first, the relationship between Akash and Sid, and second, the nature of the resolution phase.

Duty, responsibility and family

In contrast to *Dil to Pagal Hai*, which looks particularly at the pressures on women, this film focuses on the sense of duty and responsibility faced by young men, especially those who might be inclined towards a more Western outlook on the world. Sameer's mother tells him as she tries to introduce the idea of an arranged marriage with Pooja: 'Your father and I had an arranged marriage. Listen to me: we are not forcing you to get married. We have known them for years and we thought we would turn friendship into a marriage alliance, that's all.'

Even among young, quite Westernised friends Sid's transgression of social norms and expectations in loving an older woman who has a daughter and has been married (initially at least) seems to be too much of a departure from tradition. Akash cannot comprehend such behaviour.

At the heart of this film is the challenge to traditional values currently being offered by an increasingly Westernised Indian middle-class youth. As Sid's mother tells him:

'This is the problem with your generation: you think anything goes. But that is not so, Siddharth.'

Dil Chahta Hai was a critical success (winning the National Film Award for Best Feature Film in Hindi in 2001, for example). It was also commercially successful but its main audience tended to be from the urban middle classes. The challenge to traditional values offered by the film was perhaps too much for more conservative parts of the Bollywood audience. After several moments when the audience has been teased into expecting Akash to profess his love for Shalini he eventually does so in such a way as to challenge the whole concept of arranged marriages in the most dramatic fashion possible. And, as in *Dil to Pagal Hai*, the arranged marriage is again made to concede to the concept of destined love between soulmates.

ACTIVITY

Working in groups if possible, produce a list of as many differences and similarities as you can between *Dil to Pagal Hai* and this film. Try to refer to specific scenes in order to illustrate each of the points you make.

Presence and absence in Bollywood films

Bollywood films are filled with spectacular visual images and intense melo-dramatic moments designed to engulf the senses. The locations are often scenically spectatacular, the sets and costumes lavish (the opera scene in *Dil Chahta Hai* was specially commissioned for the film), and the drama emotionally overwhelming. But while recognising the special presence of

continued

Bollywood films it may also be worth considering the absences. Primarily, there is no indication of the poverty that is to be found everywhere in India. In *Dil Chahta Hai* the only sign of these sorts of social issues comes when we see a down-and-out on the Sydney underground!

EXAM QUESTIONS ?

- To what extent are spectacle and escapism the key features of Bollywood films, and are these features particularly important within Indian film?

- With reference to the films you have studied, what role do song-and-dance sequences play within Indian films?

- How important is comedy within the Indian films you have studied?

- To what extent are traditional gender stereotypes challenged (and to what extent are they simply reconfirmed) in the films you have seen?

Further Reading

Banker, A. (2001) *The Pocket Essential Bollywood*, Pocket Essentials
Ganti, T. (2004) *Bollywood: A Guidebook to Popular Hindi Cinema*, Routledge
Kabir, N.M. (2001) *Bollywood: The Indian Cinema Story*, Channel Four Books
Kasbekar, A. (2003) 'An introduction to Indian cinema', in Nelmes, J. (ed.) *An Introduction to Film Studies*, Routledge.
Mishra, V. (2002) *Bollywood Cinema: Temples of Desire*, Routledge
Raheja, D. and Kolhari, J. (2004) *Indian Cinema: The Bollywood Saga*, Aurum
Rajadhyaksha, A. (2000) 'Indian cinema', in Hill, J. and Church Gibson, P. *World Cinema: Critical Approaches*, Oxford University Press (pp 151–156)
Rajadhyaksha, A. and Willeemen, P. (1994) *Encyclopaedia of Indian Cinema*, BFI
Thomas, R. (2000) 'Popular Hindi cinema', in Hill, J. and Church Gibson, P. *World Cinema: Critical Approaches*, Oxford University Press (pp 157–158)
www.filmindia.com
www.cinemedia.net/NLA/indin.html

6 IRANIAN CINEMA 1990 TO THE PRESENT

In studying this topic area you will consider the following:

- The problems of defining national cinema
- The wider contexts of Iranian society (past and present)
- The effect of censorship on filmmakers
- Definitions of realism
- The relationship between film and audience

Films mentioned

The principal films discussed in this section are *10* (Abbas Kiarostami, 2002) and *Offside* (Jafar Panahi, 2006). Along with the principal films you will also need to study one or two further films but in less depth.

Some suggestions for supplemental films:

- *Through the Olive Groves* (Abbas Kiarostami, 1994) which follows the problems a film crew face making a film in rural Iran. It has been described as postmodern in its references to filming and filmmaking and focuses on the distinction between film and reality, as does *10*. (As this is not an auteur study the two principal films must be by different directors.)
- *Blackboards* (Samira Makhmalbaf, 2000) focuses on a group of itinerant teachers in northern Iran who look for students in order to exchange education for food. Written and edited by one of the key figures of Iranian cinema – Moshen Makhmalbaf – and directed by his daughter.
- *Persepolis* (Mariane Satrapi, 2008) A French-Iranian animation – please see below for further discussion.

Iranian cinema and empowering women

The principal films in this topic would also be relevant for study in the empowering women topic area, where another Iranian film *The Day I Became a Woman* (Marziyeh Meshkini, 2000) is used as a case study. (Please remember however that the same film cannot be used to answer two topic areas in the exam.)

The study of Iranian cinema challenges conventional ideas about the definition and function of a national cinema; it also provides an insight into a culture and country which is often negatively represented in the West.

In this topic you will consider:

■ How can we define a national cinema? Who defines it? The audience? Filmmakers? The state? Academics?

■ How do definitions change when films from a national cinema are made outside of the nation? Many of the filmmakers associated with Iranian cinema actually work abroad, creating what has been referred to as a 'cinema of exile'.

■ The relationship between the state (government, legal and religious authorities) and cinema: From the beginning of cinema in Iran the different state authorities have attempted to control film production and mould films to their own aims. This has included control of funding, distribution and regulation (often censorship) of films, both indigenous and imported.

■ The audience for national cinema: Iranian films seen – and celebrated – in the West (US and Europe) as national cinema are often not released in Iran due to state censorship, while Iranian films exhibited in Iran are rarely exported, creating a gap between the West's and Iran's perception of Iranian national cinema.

■ The role of new technology: There is a thriving pirate DVD market in Iran which allows people to see films (Iranian and foreign) that are otherwise banned. This is also true in the take-up of satellite television which gives access to channels that are technically outlawed in Iran. Iranian filmmakers – such as Abbas Kiarostami – are in the vanguard of experimenting with new technology (e.g. filming with digital cameras and experimenting with form).

Iranian cinema: pure cinema?

Iranian cinema – particularly the work of those directors celebrated as auteurs – is also experimental and non-mainstream. The films often provoke questions about the role of the filmmaker and the spectator; what do we expect from a film – even, what is cinema? In this context Iranian cinema links with some of the ideas approached in the New Waves topic area – indeed, Iran had its own New Wave in the 1960s which was influential on the French New Wave.

Iranian cinema: context

This study of Iranian cinema is not designed to be an historical overview but it is important to have some understanding of the background and contemporary situation in Iran in order to understand the content of the films and the position of the filmmakers.

i

The following is a brief overview; for a more detailed historical background go to the BBC news website at: http://news.bbc.co.uk/1/hi/world/middle_east/806268.stm.

Political history	Film history

1906 Constitutional monarchy founded with the Shah as head of state (ends in 1979).

1935 Persia is renamed Iran.

1900–1930 Early film production in Iran is non-fiction.

The Iranian film industry is largely private, with films sponsored and viewed by the Iranian royal family; commercial cinemas show foreign imports.

1930 First non-fiction feature film made in Iran (*Abi and Rabi*, d. Avanes Ohanian) (like today, during this period many Iranian films were being made outside Iran by a Western educated elite).

1941 – Muhammad Reza Pahlavi installed as Shah (with British backing), rules until the revolution in 1979.

1948 First sound film made in Iran; national cinema becomes increasingly popular, partly due to the increased censorship of foreign imports.

1951 Iran is a wealthy country due to oil. Parliament votes to nationalise the oil industry, removing control from British oil companies.

Britain imposes an embargo on Iran which damages the economy and leads to a power struggle: the Shah flees the country.

1953 The Shah is reinstated after a coup and is backed by British and US intelligence agencies – this reliance on Western power will have great implications for the future of Iran.

1950s US government aids Iranian film production for propaganda purposes (Iran is a key territory in the Cold War).

Socially conscious Iranian films censored or banned.

1960s The 'White Revolution' is the move to modernise and Westernise the country, a movement which becomes tyrannical; reliant on the secret police to quell dissent.

1960s As part of the Westernisation project private TV networks were set up with the backing of US TV companies – showing imported NBC TV shows and MGM films.

continued

Political history	Film history
	Popular Iranian cinema of the time is dominated by melodramas, comedy and *luti* (tough guy or gangster) films.
	1969 Iranian New Wave: *Gav* (*The Cow*) d. Dariush Mehrjui and *Qaisar* (*Caesar*) d. Masoud Kimiai represented a new style of filmmaking which dealt with contemporary and controversial issues in Iran.
1970s The Shah's policies alienate the clergy and his authoritarian rule leads to riots, strikes and mass demonstrations. Martial law is imposed.	Development of a complex film culture; film festivals and student film societies, founding of the Ministry of Culture and Arts (MCA) which sponsored (but also banned) Iranian films.
1979 The Islamic fundamentalist, Ayatollah Ruhollah Khomeini, returns to Iran following exile in Iraq and France to take up his position as the Spiritual Leader, or *wali faqih*, making the country a theocracy. Iran is declared an Islamic Republic	Cinema (Iranian and foreign) seen as supporting the Shah and therefore an 'agent of cultural colonisation'. The burning of cinemas was part of the strategy of dismantling the Shah's regime – by 1979 180 cinemas had been destroyed. Islamic revolution meant many film makers went into exile, creating an 'exile genre' of cinema. 'Purification' of cinema led to women being absent from the screen.
1980–1988 Iran–Iraq War.	**1982** Clerics drew up a series of regulations to ensure that cinema was used 'properly'. **1983–1986** Film production increased with fifty-seven films produced in 1986. These were high-quality films with key people such as Makhmalbaf emerging as controversial figures.
1989 Ayatollah Khomeini issues a religious edict (fatwa) ordering Muslims to kill Salman Rushdie for his novel, *The Satanic Verses*, considered blasphemous to Islam.	Women film directors emerged and more women were represented on screen.
1990 Earthquake strikes Iran, killing approximately 40,000 people.	Abbas Kiarostami awarded Palme d'or for *Close Up*.

Political history	Film history
1990 Iraq invades Kuwait – Iran remains neutral in the first Gulf War.	*A Time to Love* (Moshen Makhmalbaf, 1991) is indicative of a new openness in Iranian cinema as it dealt with the forbidden subject of a love triangle (the film was not shown in public in Iran but was debated in the press).
1997 Mohammad Khatami, a reforming, liberal politician, wins the presidential election with 70 per cent of the vote, beating the conservative ruling elite.	
1999 Pro-democracy students at Tehran University demonstrate. Clashes with security forces lead to six days of rioting and the arrest of more than 1,000 students.	*Life and Art: The New Iranian Cinema* showcases Iranian films at the BFI.
2002 US President George Bush describes Iraq, Iran and North Korea as an 'axis of evil'.	Crisis in film production and distribution in Iran – few cinemas left, equipment crumbling.
	Situation made worse by competition from satellite TV and pirate DVD market.
2003 Thousands attend student-led protests in Tehran against clerical establishment.	
2004 February – Conservatives regain control of Parliament in elections. Thousands of reformist candidates were disqualified by the hard-line Council of Guardians before the polls.	Internet access available (to middle-class Iranians), proxy servers are used to bypass the blocking of sites by the government.
2005 Mahmoud Ahmadinejad, an ultra-conservative politician, becomes president; many of the previous liberal reforms are overturned.	
2008 UN accuses Iran of withholding information on its nuclear capabilities – sanctions threatened.	*Shirin* (2008), an Abbas Kiarostami film about Iranian passion plays, is shown at the Edinburgh Film Festival. For the first time in ten years the Iranian government wants to show his latest film but the director has refused permission.

Iranian cinema and the state

The history of Iranian cinema is inextricably linked to state influence – whether secular or religious. Iranian cinema has been seen as an important tool for:

- reinforcing the regime's point of view through 'teaching' the population
- representing Iranian culture to the world.

The great majority of Iranian film production is funded by the state which also enforces strict regulation and censorship in the context of Islamic beliefs. These include strict limitations on the way in which women can be represented; these conform to the strict dress and behavioural codes for women in Islamic society:

- hair must always be covered
- loose-fitting garments must be worn to disguise the curves of the female body
- women may only touch men who are their husband or family members.

This makes the realistic representation of relationships on film almost impossible, as the actors would have to be married or related in real life.

Figure 6.1 Young Iranians out shopping in Tehran.

INFORMATION BOX

i

Role of the censor

Film censorship is carried out in several stages:

- **Pre-production**: the script and names of cast and crew are submitted for approval and to receive a permit for production. (In preparing *Offside*, the director used aliases for several members of his crew in order to receive permission to film.)
- **Post-production**: once the film is completed it is then submitted to the censorship board who may pass it, require cuts or ban it completely. The final stage is to apply for a screening permit so that the film can be exhibited.
- **Rating and classification**: if a film receives a screening permit it is rated A, B or C. This is a very different form of rating to the British idea of classification of content; it is based on the perceived quality of the film and therefore what kind of distribution it will receive. For example, an A-rated film will be advertised on government television channels and play in the best cinemas at the most popular times, while a C-rated film will have very limited access to distribution and exhibition.

The result of this system is that the government is able to control all stages of film production in a fairly sophisticated way – films don't need to be banned; they can be given a C rating so that very few people will see them. This system also makes it virtually impossible for any US or European films to be imported as they would not pass the different stages of regulation.

Repressive regime vs. artistic expression

There is an apparent contradiction in the fact that Iranian cinema emerged as one of the most innovative and experimental national cinemas within the context of a repressive, fundamentalist regime. The reasons for this reflect the complex relationship between artists, the state and the nature of the Islamic Republic in Iran:

- There is not necessarily a clear opposition between filmmakers and the Islamic Republic (although there may well be) – Moshen Makhmalbaf was committed to Islam and a supporter of the revolution.
- Filmmakers have been supported by liberal segments within the government (particularly in the 1990s and before the election of President Ahmadinejad),

and have constantly stretched the limits imposed on subject matter by the religious conservatives.

■ Film has a unique position as an art form in Iran – too powerful to be ignored, it is not easy to 'Islamise' it, particularly as the religious laws make no ruling on cinema.

■ The high regard in which Iranian cinema is held in the West may be seen as a propaganda victory for the Islamic Republic, challenging some of the stereotypes about Iran. This could be even more important since Iran's identification as part of the 'axis of evil' and suggests one of the reasons for the paradox of the state funding films which are then banned.

Activity

This system of regulation means that many of the films defined as Iranian cinema have never been released in Iran – although they are often made there. This context makes the situation very hard for filmmakers who are faced with difficult choices – the kind that Western filmmakers rarely have to consider. Think about the following points and discuss your ideas with a partner:

■ Do you make a film which will pass the censorship rules but which may compromise your own vision?

■ If your film isn't released in Iran who are you making the film for?

■ Western audiences may appreciate Iranian art cinema but is this just preaching to the converted?

■ What about the safety of yourself and your family if you make a film which is critical of the Islamic regime? In 2001 the female director Tahmeni Milani was arrested for allegedly supporting 'counter-revolutionary' groups in her film *The Hidden Half*.

INFORMATION BOX

Cinema of exile

National cinema is usually analysed at two levels:

1   **Textual features**: the similarities in style and subject matter which can be identified as linking films from one country. (i.e. realism in British cinema).

2   **Industrial context**: the way in which national cinema is funded and distributed (i.e. the use of Lottery money to fund British films).

The concept of a national cinema is problematic because the idea of nationhood emphasises notions of coherence and unity, an agreement about the meanings linked to a particular nation – meanings which apparently make it unique.

The assumption that there is a definition of a nation which everyone can agree on is always problematic and particularly so in Iranian cinema; many Iranian film-makers are in exile due to their disagreement with the Iranian revolution. This aspect of Iranian filmmaking has been described in different ways, terms which can have varying connotations:

- **Festival films** (also known as Iranian art cinema): films made by Iranians which are not shown in their home country, but which receive distribution – and great acclaim – at Western film festivals such as Cannes and Edinburgh.
- **Cinema of exile**: films made by Iranians who have left Iran due to their opposition to the Islamic revolution.
- **Accented cinema**: films made in the West which have some link to Iran – often through the subject matter or the filmmakers who may be second-generation immigrants.

Festival films: Iranian cinema for Westerners?

An interesting complication in the reception of Iranian cinema is the different critical reactions to it outside Iran. The films of Kiarostami have received near universal praise among US and European critics, academics and the audience for art house cinema. An opposing reaction to the films however has accused Kiarostami (and other festival filmmakers) of a lack of political analysis of the situation in Iran. These films, the argument goes, pander to middle-class, Western audiences' taste for art house cinema and – in their concentration on the repression of women – choose easy subjects which reinforce stereotypes of Iranian and Islamic culture.

Case study
PERSEPOLIS: CINEMA OF EXILE

Persepolis was a critical and commercial (within the context of art house cinema) hit in the US and France (and to a lesser extent the UK). It won the Jury Prize at the Cannes Film Festival and was nominated for the Oscar for best animated feature.

The film is based on Satrapi's early life in Tehran and shows the repression under the Shah's regime. It also portrays the social restrictions, arrests and

continued

Figure 6.2 *Persepolis*.

Note: *Persepolis* is a French/US co-production co-directed and based on the graphic novel by Marjane Satrapi, a French-Iranian. It can be categorised as a film from the Iranian Diaspora and as such could only be studied as a supporting film in this topic area rather than as a key text.

executions that followed the Islamic revolution. The film has been condemned by President Ahmadinejad's government as 'Islamophobic' and 'anti-Iranian,' and has not been shown at mainstream cinemas in Iran. There have however been some screenings of the film in cultural centres in Tehran as reported by the Agence France-Presse (an international news agency):

> Around 70 people crammed into a small hall in a Tehran cultural centre on Thursday to watch the animated film in a rare chance for Iranians to see the film legally and in public. A similar screening of the film, which graphically shows its young heroine's brushes with the authorities in the early days of the Islamic revolution in the 1980s, also took place at the Rasaneh Cultural Centre in Tehran on Tuesday.
>
> 'The aim of this screening is to end the delusions surrounding the film which have been created by the media,' said the centre's public relations chief, Mahmoud Babareza.
>
> 'When a film is not shown people make all sorts of misconceptions. Cinema is cinema, after all, and it should not be put into a limited political context,' he told AFP.
>
> The film shown, a DVD copy with Farsi subtitles, was censored of half a dozen scenes mainly of a sexual nature before being deemed acceptable, but the screening took place with the full permission of the cultural authorities.

Some Iranians have already seen the film at home on bootlegged DVDs, which are discreetly but readily available in the capital for around two dollars despite being strictly forbidden.

For the full article go to: *Rare Iran screening for controversial film Persepolis* at: http://news.sawf.org/Entertainment/48162.aspx

It is also interesting to read the forums on the *Persepolis* site on imdb.com which has a discussion about the content and availability of the film with contributions from Iranians living in and outside of Iran.

Case study

FOCUS FILM: *10* (ABBAS KIAROSTAMI, 2002)

The film focuses on the life of a middle-class, divorced Iranian mother. It is structured around her conversations with her various passengers, creating ten chapters.

Figure 6.3 Mania Akbari in *10* (Abbas Kiarostami, 2002).

continued

10 has been chosen as a focus film for a variety of reasons:

- It is directed by Kiarostami, one of the most important figures in Iranian cinema, often described as the godfather of Iranian film.
- *10* was made in Iran – but it was refused distribution there.
- It is an example of the type of Iranian cinema described as 'festival films'.
- As a film made under conditions of strict censorship it demonstrates the way in which filmmakers can 'smuggle' through their ideas and views.
- The use of film form and narrative structure is characteristic of Iranian cinema's interest in experimentation.
- In the use of digital technology and documentary style filmmaking, Kiarostami explicitly questions the role of the director and puts the emphasis on audience interpretation.
- *10* provides insights into aspects of life in Tehran – from a woman's point of view – which are rarely seen in the West.

ACTIVITY

Before watching *10* read the following comments about the form of the film:

> [It is] the rejection of all elements vital to ordinary cinema (Kiarostami on *10*)

> [Kiarostami has always explored] the narrow line between illusion and reality that is the defining characteristic of cinema (Mulvey, 1995)

> The overwhelming impression left by *10* . . . is of an artist trying to create a new kind of cinema (Andrew, 2002)

> Anyone could make a movie like 'Ten.' Two digital cameras, a car and your actors, and off you go (Ebert, 2003)

These quotes suggest that Kiarostami is considered a great auteur by many, but that his films are controversial, not particularly due to their subject matter but because of their experimentation with film conventions.

We could summarise the key points from the previous quotes to provide a context for viewing the film:

- *10* subverts audience expectations about character, narrative, structure, visual style and so on ('the elements of ordinary cinema')
- it is difficult to define *10* as either fiction or non-fiction – it blurs the boundaries between the two ('narrow line between illusion and reality')
- Kiarostami is an artist rather than a moviemaker; he makes films for an educated elite (film studies students?) rather than for a mass audience ('trying to create a new kind of cinema')
- *10* seems like an amateur production; Kiarostami has fooled the critics again ('Anyone can make a film like *10*').

Having read these responses, how does it affect your expectations of the film?

- How might a filmmaker create a 'new kind of cinema?' Is it possible?
- What are some of the differences between documentary and fiction films?
- Does it matter if 'anyone can make a film like *10*'? What would a film look like that only a few people could make?

The first time you watch *10* make a note of the following:

- A brief outline of each chapter content – noting who is in the car, what they discuss.
- The predominant film style – type of shots (length, angle, distance), *mise-en-scène*, use of sound.

Making *10*: film realism

Some information about Kiarostami's working methods on *10* helps to inform the discussion of the film's style:

- The driver and the passengers in the car are 'acting', but are not professional actors.
- The actors were cast after auditions with Kiarostami in which they discussed their lives and experiences.
- Kiarostami prepared the script after long discussions with the cast, choosing what he wanted them to talk about in the film; this was often based on their real life experiences.

- Some of the chapters were more tightly controlled and scripted than others – we have no way of knowing for certain which these are.
- The 'actors' are actually in the moving car together, with the camera in a fixed position on the dashboard. Kiarostami was not usually present during the filming, leaving the actors to work without interruption or direction.
- Twenty-three hours of footage were completed – edited down to 90 minutes.

Kiarostami himself has said, 'I personally can't define the difference between a documentary and a narrative film.' (Saeed-Vafa and Rosenbaum, 2003).

This method of preparation – using ordinary people, developing a script from discussion with the cast – may be seen as similar to the work of British realist directors such as Ken Loach, Mike Leigh and Shane Meadows.

INFORMATION BOX – DOCUMENTARY AND FICTION TECHNIQUES

i

There are some conventions which we can identify as categorising films as either fiction or documentary.

Fiction film

Script, stars/actors, Blockbuster, Studio, SFX/CGI, non-diegetic sound, film created in post-production (through addition of effects, soundtrack and so on).

Documentary

Real world, interviews (with real people), voice-over, location shooting, natural lighting, diegetic sound, film created in production (little work in post-production beyond editing).

We expect a documentary to:

- Convey information about topics, issues, events or life in the present or past, based on fact not fiction.
- That events will be authentic and unstaged; they exist beyond the activity of filming them.
- Be real and not imaginary.

It is also assumed that a documentary-maker observes and records real events rather than intervening in them.

In film however the boundaries between documentary and fiction forms are becoming increasingly blurred.

ACTIVITY

10 and the documentary form

- Using the defining characteristics above, how would you define *10*?
- Why do you think Kiarostami uses documentary techniques? What is the intended effect on the audience?
- What does this method of working suggest about the role of the director in making a film? How does this differ from the concept of the auteur theory?

10: sample analysis

The following analysis suggests an approach to writing about *10*. It is structured by chapter and focuses on the key areas of representation, subject matter, film style and audience.

Opening and Chapter 10

10 begins with the film 'leader'; the film stock which provides a countdown to the beginning of the film proper. This is the first indication that Kiarostami is interested in **film form** as much as content, here revealing the **mechanics of film production**, reminding the audience that they are watching a film. The first shot of Chapter 10 is **shocking** because of the **visual style** – it really does look as if a home movie camera has been left on accidently. The image is grainy, the light is natural and the interior of the car familiar. This **amateur aesthetic** ('anyone can make a film like *10*') is different even from other fiction films which use **documentary techniques**, because of the use of a fixed, static – rather than handheld moving – camera.

Two characters are introduced in the first chapter: Amin, a young boy, and his mother, Akbira. Throughout the sequence the camera is fixed on Amin; the audience never sees his mother, only hears her voice and witnesses Amin's reaction to her. The effect of this is to make the audience focus intently on what is being said. The **fixed camera, lack of non-diegetic sound, use of mid-shots and close-ups** on a single character means there are no distractions for the viewer. It also allows the audience to do something we rarely get to do in the cinema because the **director** is in control of the visuals; namely create our own image of a character. The absence of Akbira on screen also creates a certain

suspense, a buildup to her entrance. Her appearance, when we do finally see her – beautiful, young, with bright lipstick and wearing jewellery – may **confound our expectations** of what an Iranian mother would look like. (This is likely to depend on the **audience's own background** and experiences.)

A further effect of the **film style** is to make the audience question the concept of an **auteur** as someone in control of his vision who transmits it to the audience. Here Karastami sems to be more interested in letting the action unfold naturally in **real time** – as if he wasn't there.

In Chapter 10 the conversation/dialogue serves a variety of functions. The dialogue provides context for the characters; Akbira is divorced from Amin's father; Amin is angry with his mother about the divorce and has been staying with his father for the weekend. It also introduces some of the key themes of the film: the position of **women in Iranian society** which encompasses gender relations and religious restrictions. Perhaps surprisingly there is explicit reference in the dialogue to the position of women, with Akbira making **feminist** statements about the role of a wife in Iranian society. Akbira is introduced as a woman frustrated by her situation who is battling against the restrictions imposed on her. Her strength of personality is evident in our first sight of Akbira as she rows over a parking space.

10 and narrative structure

The countdown

If the ten chapters are the leader what does it countdown to? Where does the film *10* start?

10 is structured around ten sections or chapters which all take place in Akbira's car and feature her conversations with five passengers. Initially it may seem that these are random sequences, but it soon becomes apparent that there are links between them. As viewers we begin to predict when certain characters will appear and how particular topics and themes will be developed.

Plot

10 has been described as a minimalist film in which very little happens, but there are storylines and plot developments which include:

- Will Akbari be able to mend her relationship with her son?
- Will Akbari's friend marry her boyfriend?

What other plot lines are there? Which ones are resolved at the end of the film? Which remain open?

ℹ

INFORMATION BOX – AUDIENCE THEORY: ACTIVE AND PASSIVE

One of the central debates in film (and media) studies is whether the audience is active or passive; both terms have particular connotations.

Active audience

In this conception the audience continually questions and challenges what it sees on screen, entering into a dialogue with the filmmaker. For political filmmakers this active position is important because it means the audience can be provoked by a film to continue this attitude outside the cinema – questioning the political and social world rather than just accepting the status quo.

In film studies this idea is demonstrated most explicitly in the work of various 'New Wave' filmmakers, but it is also apparent in genre theory.

Passive audience

The connotations of the passive audience are clear from the analogies used to describe it which often refer to the audience being drugged and duped. The theory of the passive audience is also specific to the mass media audience rather than for high culture. In film theory, authorship assumes a passive audience which is fed the ideas of a great director. In the 1930s the Marxist theorists of the Frankfurt School saw Hollywood (part of the culture industry) as one of the reasons for the continued oppression of the people – the passive experience of watching films taught people to be docile and reactionary.

ACTIVITY

Kiarostami has stated that his aim is to make films for an active audience who will interpret the material, rather than to provide the audience with a message. How does he attempt this? Consider narrative structure, plot, character, visual style. Do you think Kiarostami is successful in his attempt?

continued

For example, you may argue that by *not* using a conventional plot or characterisation, by *not* including cliffhangers and suspense, by *not* using continuity editing or non-diegetic sound to guide the audience, Kiarostami expects the audience to 'fill in' a lot of the areas which are usually done for us.

The concept of the active audience who are part of creating the meaning of the film may also explain the use of the 'countdown' to strucure the film. Kiarostami's film *10* is merely the countdown to the film the audience will create in their minds after watching it.

Themes

The themes of *10* include:

- Different types of relationships between men and women (husband and wife, mother and son, lovers, prostitute and clients).
- Power relationships between genders (women's lack of power, men's selfishness).
- The role of religion in Iran – and how it is the context for the other themes.

Looking at your summary of the different chapters, note where these themes are introduced and how they are developed. How does the film represent the relationship between men and women in Iran?

For example, in Chapter 10 Akbira talks about how her 'brain stagnated' during her marriage and she argues that women are not possessions to be owned by a husband. It is also clear that her son – who in many ways seems to be a symbol of her husband – blames her for the divorce and points out that she lied to get it, by attacking his father's character. This exchange is typical of the tone of the film – the situation for men and women is difficult and the film doesn't make judgements on one side over the other.

- The West: The influence of Western culture is also a clear theme in the film. What references are made to the West? (This might be through *mise-en-scène* or dialogue). How would you describe the representation?

Regulation and censorship

In analysing *10* it is important to remember the context of restrictions (in the wider society and the film industry) and censorship which may suggest some of the reasons for the choice of form and style:

- there is a ban on men and women who are not related being in a car together
- romantic or sexual relationships cannot be depicted
- women should not appear with their hair showing
- blasphemy – or criticism of the Iranian regime – is not allowed.

These restrictions on the film suggest another way in which *10* can be interpreted; it is a film about what can and cannot be shown on screen and therefore does two things. It:

- represents Iranian society with its rules and restrictions
- explores film form, making the audience aware of the constraints a director has to work within.

Some of the ways in which Kiarostami is able to work around the rules include:

- relationships between men and women are depicted in dialogue
- Akbira can only have female or child passengers; Amin is a child but is used to represent (a particularly macho type of) Iranian man
- the character of the prostitute remains off-screen
- Akbira's friend removes her veil – something forbidden in Iranian cinema – but her head is shaved.

Jafar Panahi, the director of *Offside*, refers to working within such a controlled society:

> **Many things in Iran always have certain problems. For each film that we make we have to think of creative ways of doing it. In Farsi we have a saying: 'if you can't get through the door then climb up through the window.' So this is what we have to do to find a way of achieving our aims. For each film this method can only be used once, and for the next one obviously we have to find an alternative way of doing it. (For the full interview with Panahi, go to:** *http://www.opendemocracy.net/arts-Film/offside_3620.jsp***)**

Offside (*Dir:* Jafar Panahi, 2005)

The second principal film for this area of study is *Offside*. It has been chosen because it shares some of the themes and style of *10*, which include:

- representations of the position of women in Iranian society
- use of a hybrid style of drama and documentary techniques
- 'smuggling' ideas past censorship restrictions.

In addition, *Offside* is an accessible film, providing clear identification with an appealing central character.

Figure 6.4 *Offside* (d. Jafar Panahi, 2005).

Context

The plot of *Offside* is about a young female football fan who wants to attend Iran's World Cup qualifying match against Bahrain, although Islamic law bans women from entering sports stadiums. It represnts the work of a director (Panahi, b. 1960) associated with the 'second' New Wave in Iranian cinema while Kiarostami (b. 1940) was one of the founders of the first wave. Panahi has continued to live and work in Tehran, although most of his films have never been shown there – including *Offside*. In a discussion of the inspiration for *Offside* Panahi explained that it was partly a result of the experience of trying to take his own daughter to a football match, coupled with the way in which sports and entertainment events are places where people can 'let themselves go' within the context of a heavily policed society.

Offside raises questions about the validity of many of the laws in modern Iran which restrict behaviour – particularly those regarding the position of women.

Women and football

In pre-revolutionary Iran women were free to attend football matches; the restrictions were part of the new Islamic laws governing behaviour. In 1998 when Iran previously qualified for the World Cup, women were given special dispensation to attend the matches. Five thousand women attended – sparking a debate about why women were not allowed in the first place. For many Iranians (men and women) the restriction was based on ideology rather than religious belief. In *Offside* this view is explored as the young women challenge the reasons for the ban, revealing the illogicality of it.

For more context on this area see: *Iran's female fans yet to win equality*

(Frances Harrison) at http://news.bbc.co.uk/1/hi/world/middle_east/5052000.stm.

Iranian law

For non-Iranian, Western audiences it is difficult to know how realistic the representation of people challenging authority under a repressive regime is. Would not the repercussions of such actions be too great? One of the most important characteristics of Iranian cinema is the way in which it shows that Iranian society is not a homogenous, repressed, terrified society but instead is composed of diverse individuals. It is also the case that many of the laws of the Islamic Republic are ambiguous and change frequently. Panahi makes the point that it is not always clear what is banned and what is permitted, that people have their own interpretation of the law in practice and that it is a natural reaction of people to do something they have been told not to do.

ACTIVITY

Rebellion against the regime forms the central plotline of *Offside* but how many other examples of individual mutiny can you identify in the film?

Themes

■ Representation of gender

The central character (as in *10* we rarely know the names of the characters) is represented as intelligent, brave and determined in her ambition to attend the football match. She is an easy character to identify with – transcending divisions of place, politics and religion – which is one of the reasons for the cross-over success of the film in the Europe. Closely linked to the representation of the gender of the central character is that of her age; as a teenager she symbolises the younger generation of Iran who are shown to be more radical than the older generation; this constitutes one of the other themes of the film.

■ The generation clash

The conflict between generations is a universal theme (and one which it shares with *Bend it Like Beckham*), and *Offside* conforms to the conventional expectation of this opposition, with the older generation represented as more religious and respectful of authority. The representation of youth could suggest future changes in Iran; they are shown to be more uncomfortable with the restrictions placed on them, more prepared to question their situation. This is evident in the character of the soldier who, as a young man conscripted into military service, is conflicted in his role, enforcing rules he doesn't believe in. This type of characterisation also shows the complexities of life in Iran – is it possible to retain your individual identity but also conform to the rules of society?

■ Nationalism and patriotism

As in other sports films, football in *Offside* is used as a backdrop to discuss the themes of patriotism and nationalism (another similarity with *Bend it Like Beckham*), to ask what it means to be an Iranian. The characters in the film, despite their many differences, are all united by their desire to see Iran win the game and qualify for the World Cup. The young women paint their faces in Iran's national colours and are fiercely patriotic. This nationalism is another example of the film's complexity – why would the women who are so restricted by the regime still be patriotic?

INFORMATION BOX: THE NATIONAL ANTHEM *i*

In *Offside* the National Anthem which is sung in celebration of Iran's victory is not the official anthem of the Islamic Republic but *Ey Iran*. *Ey Iran* was briefly the National Anthem in the 1940s and has a place in Iranian culture similar to *Men of Harlech* in Wales – a celebration of national identity which has been repressed. However, the singing of *Ey Iran* may be interpreted as a political act and therefore a dangerous one. (In this context it could be compared to *Nkosi Sikelel' iAfrika* in apartheid South Africa.)

Offside refers to the deaths of supporters at an Iran–Japan match in 2005; the official version stated that the fans had died in a stampede but other sources claimed that they had been shot by police for making anti-Islamic statements and for singing *Ey Iran*.

From the personal to the political

The festival films of Iranian cinema have been criticised for not being political; focusing too much on character and emotion rather than analysing the political and social structures of Iranian society. *Offside* takes as its starting point an individual action – wanting to get in to see the football match – and opens it up to deal with the wider contexts of Iranian society. In doing so the film suggests that many of the issues facing the central character are also universal ones which are as relevant to a Western audience.

Discussion

Which themes in *Offside* do you think are relevant to both a national and international audience?

The title

Offside obviously refers to a rule (often controversial) in football but what other reasons do you think there are for choosing this title? What other connotations or meanings does it have?

The ending

In keeping with the documentary style, much of the film was shot on the day of the actual Iran–Bahrain match at Tehran's Azadi stadium and therefore the ending of the film depended on the outcome of the game. Panahi has said that if Iran had lost he would have stopped filming, as he would not be able to have the ending he wanted. In fact the film ends with the 'prisoners' able to escape into the confusion of the celebrating crowds on the streets. Such a hopeful ending has been controversial, with the director accused of compromising his realist vision for a feel-good conclusion – one which is likely to be more popular with audiences.

ACTIVITY

What do you think of the ending? Is it unrealistic? How else might the film have ended? In exploring this point you should consider how the following affects your interpretation:

- the central character buys sparklers from a boy who has been arrested for selling fireworks
- she explains that she has attended the match in memory of her dead friend, 'one of the seven who died after the Japan game'
- the crowds are singing *Ey Iran*, not the official National Anthem.

ACTIVITY

Comparative analysis: similarities with *10*

To construct a comparison of the two films, make notes on the following:

What similarities are there in:

- characters (e.g. characteristics of central characters)
- narrative structure (e.g. loose, seemingly unstructured storyline, based in reality)
- film style (e.g. documentary hybrid, the importance of what isn't shown)
- the role of the audience (Is the message of the film clear or had the filmmaker left room for the audience's interpretation?)?

Conventions of Iranian national cinema

Although it is problematic to list characteristics of any national cinema there do seem to be some shared conventions of recent Iranian cinema:

- an interest in experimenting with film form and style
- women are often central characters; their role in Iranian society is the focus of many films
- there is a focus on contemporary society rather than on historical events
- ambiguity of style – documentary or fiction?
- films are 'open', leaving it to the audience to interpret the meaning.

EXAM QUESTIONS

- To what extent can Iranian national cinema be defined through a shared cinematic style?

- Would you define Iranian cinema as political?

Bibliography and Further Reading

Andrew, G. (2002) Drive He Said. *Sight and Sound*, October, BFI (also available online: http://www.bfi.org.uk/sightandsound/feature/34)

Ebert, R. (2003) *Ten. Chicago Sun Times*, 11 April (also available online: http://rogerebert.suntimes.com/)

Graffy, G. (2006) A nation of two halves. Film of the Month: Offside. *Sight and Sound*, June (also available online: http://www.bfi.org.uk/sightandsound/review/3260)

Issa, R. and Whitaker, S. (1999) *Life and Art: the New Iranian Cinema*. BFI

Mulvey, M. (1995) Moving Bodies. *Sight and Sound*, March, BFI

Saeed-Vafa, M. and Rosenbaum, J. (2003) *Abbas Kiarostami*. University of Illinois Press, p. 116

7 JAPANESE CINEMA 1950 TO 1970

This chapter will look at:

- the content and contexts of the focus films
- the characteristic features of Japanese film during this period
- the significance of this movement in terms of world cinema
- the influence of European and Western cinema on Japanese film
- the pleasures and challenges this period of national filmmaking offers as an 'alternative' to Hollywood

Suggested films from this period:

Rashomon (Daiei, Japan, 1950, Dir: Akira Kurosawa)

Tokyo Nagaremono (*Tokyo Drifter*) (Nikkatsu, Japan, 1966, Dir: Seijun Suzuki)

Saikaku Ichidai Onna (*The Life of Oharu*) (Shin Toto, Japan, 1952, Dir: Kenji Mizogochi)

Tokyo Monogatari (*Tokyo Story*) (Shochiku, Japan, 1953, Dir: Yasujiro Ozu)

Nihon no yuru to kiri (*Night and Fog in Japan*) (Shochiku, Japan, 1960, Dir: Nagisa Oshima)

Shinju ten no Amijima (*Double Suicide*) (Tokyo/Hyogensha/ATG, Japan, 1969, Dir: Masahiro Shinoda)

This topic area looks at the exciting period in Japanese cinema history when this previously isolated film industry (second only to Hollywood in size and number of productions) broke into world markets, and achieved both critical and commercial success. Covering a period from postwar economic boom to the decline of studio power and the rise of the independents, this topic engages with the principal genres and styles of filmmaking of the time, the jidaigeki (including the chambara), the gendaigeki, the shomingeki, the yakuza and the keiko-eiga.

CHAMBARA: effectively a subgenre of the jidaigeki films, in which sword fighting is the principal element. Most Samurai films fall into this sub-genre. The term is also used to describe the sword play in any film and has been used to describe the gunfights in the yakuza movies.

GENDAIGEKI: films that are set in the contemporary period and deal with present issues and debates. These films often tackle themes around family life and the changing nature of gender roles in postwar Japan.

JIDAIGEKI: a genre which was originally based on kabuki theatre, but which evolved to include any period drama film based prior to Japan opening itself up to Western influence (pre-1868). Most of the jidaigeki films come from the filmmaking traditions of the studios based in Kyoto.

KEIKO-EIGA: a style of filmmaking which has a distinctive (often overt) left-wing political message, or political aim, and is usually framed in a contemporary setting. Dismissively termed 'tendency films' by the Right, these films often reflected growing dissatisfaction with the nature of studio production, and the desire by many of a new breed of filmmaker to convey their own views on society.

SHOMINGEKI: a genre of (principally) comic drama films that deal with the lives of the middle class, and the difficulties presented by corporate life. Such films offer clear criticism of the nature of postwar Japanese culture through the gentle mocking of characters who have been industrialised.

YAKUZA: the Japanese gangster film. This genre deals directly with the young, organised criminal gangs that became established in urban Japan in the 1960s, and, through highly stylised ultra-violence, reflect key sociological divides in the postwar image of Japan.

Filmmaking in Japanese cinema from 1950 to 1960 is designed not only to examine the traditional and the new, but to encourage a wide engagement with the diversity of films within this period: traditional and New Wave, studio productions and independent productions, collective work and auteurist approaches, fiction and documentary. It is useful to consider the lineage of this period in Western film (both Italian neo-realism (see Chapter 11) and the French New Wave (see Chapter 12), and the effects of this period on subsequent generations of filmmakers both in Japan and internationally.

This significant moment in World Cinema can be usefully investigated (within a context of a range of skills which have been developed at AS level) to consider issues of textual study (see *AS Film Studies: The Essential Introduction –* Exploring Film Form – FM1), contextual study, and interpretation (see *AS Film Studies: The Essential Introduction –* British and American Film – FM2) including:

- The production contexts of Japanese cinema 1950 to 1970 in terms of the historical (industrial) production context, in relation to a broader context of World Cinema, and within the context of key filmmakers.
- Film form – changes in styles and approaches adopted in this period, and their relationship to subject matter.
- The social and political context of Japanese cinema 1950 to 1970 in terms of broader social and political changes that were shaping Japanese society during that period, and which are reflected in its films.

INFORMATION BOX – A BRIEF PREHISTORY i

Japanese cinema began in 1897 when Shiro Asano imported the first film camera, and quickly developed as a medium favoured by the cultural elite and the upper class (in contrast to cinema's development in America). This led to the adoption of literary and theatrical adaptations that were largely either period costume dramas or contemporary pieces (jidaigeki or gendaigeki) – a trend which still permeates Japanese cinema.

Western film impacted on Japanese film after 1917, both in terms of form and content, with the slapstick of early American comedy, the silent Hollywood westerns, and German Expressionism all having an influence. The full adoption of Western methods however was prevented by the unique feature of the benshi – a lecturer who commented on the action from the side of the screen (Akiro Kurosawa's brother was a benshi). This popular interpretive feature continued until the mid-1930s.

During the Second World War the film industry was nationalised and put to work for the Nationalist cause. After Japan's defeat it came under the control of the American occupying powers who ran it against a strict set of rules governing what could and could not be depicted (the jidaigeki was banned, and a number of films destroyed). As the threat of communism grew and the Cold War developed, Japan was seen as an important outpost of democracy, and (with the start of the Korean War in 1950), the controls over Japanese film were relaxed, and ceased with the end of the occupation in 1952.

Rashomon: summary

This is a film that deals not only with the story (of a rape and murder) but also directly with the nature of storytelling itself through presenting the differing accounts of four 'witnesses': the murdering bandit Tajomaru, the murdered Samurai Takehiro (through a medium), his wife Masako, and a nameless woodcutter. Central to an understanding of *Rashomon* is the issue of spectatorship, and the fact that the spectator is presented with contradictory information from which to determine the 'truth' of the event (even though director Akira Kurosawa does not provide them with any tangible way of reaching a conclusion). While the three 'suspects' present versions of the story from their perspective, the woodcutter's version, which is technically the impartial, objective one, is the one that seems least truthful (his version is coloured by his need to hide the fact that he stole the dagger from the dead man's chest).

Figure 7.1 *Rashomon* (1950, Dir: Akira Kurosawa).

Case study

AKIRA KUROSAWA (1910–1998)

Kurosawa's father was film obsessed, taking his children to see imported European films and home-produced jidaigeki films. This influence led Akira's brother Heigo to become a famous benshi, and the young Akira to enter the film industry as an assistant director to Kajiro Yamamoto who allowed him to direct his first film *Sanshiro Sugata* (Toho, Japan, 1943), at the height of the Second World War (this was attacked by censors at the time for being too Westernised). As the war ended he was in the middle of directing *Toro no O o Fumo Otokatachi* (*They Who Step on the Tiger's Tail*) (Toho, Japan, 1945), a period drama whose release was delayed by occupation censorship until 1952.

Influenced by the neo-realism of DeSica, it was ironically his jidaigeki *Rashomon* that brought the 40-year-old director on to the world stage, not the realism of his *Yoidore Tenshi* (*Drunken Angel*) (Toho, Japan, 1948). His subsequent jidaigeki films were matched by increasingly dark gendaigeki films, with both adding to his international acclaim.

A humanist with a clear sense of the dynamism of cinema as a storytelling medium, his films are dense, multi-layered fictions that comment on the human condition. They have had particular influence on American film with a number of them being remade as westerns – for example, the classic *Shichi-nin no Samurai* (*Seven Samurai*) (Toho, Japan, 1954) being remade as Hollywood's *The Magnificent Seven* (UA/Mirisch-Alpha, US, 1960, Dir: John Sturges).

His dismissal as co-director of the American film about the events surrounding the attack on Pearl Harbor – *Tora! Tora! Tora!* (TCF, US, 1970, Dir: Richard Fleisher, Ray Kellog, Toshio Masuda, Kinji Fukasaku) – on the grounds of incompetence, led to a dent in his international reputation and his attempted suicide.

Fêted by Coppola, Lucas, Scorcese and subsequent generations of filmmakers as one of cinema's masters, Kurosawa was able to raise the funds internationally to produce the personal projects and Samurai epics *Kagemusha* (TCF/Toho, Japan, 1980) and *Ran* (Herald-Ace/Nippon-Herald/Greenwich, Japan, 1985).

Akira Kurosawa died in 1998.

Unusually in a jidaigeki, Kurosawa presents the Samurai in a questionable light, as his claim of honourable suicide contrasts with the other witnesses' claims of a duel. Equally unusual is the fact that the spectator is presented with three individuals claiming to be the murderer (Tajomaru, Masako – both in inferring she may have been the murderess and by implication when the bandit suggests she asked him to kill the Samurai – and Takehiro who claims an honourable suicide), with no clarity of morality. Perhaps Kurosawa is suggesting that if there can be no knowable truth, if perspective (both physical and intellectual) shapes and distorts reality, then there can be no knowable morality, no right and wrong, just shades of grey (perhaps a fitting concern for a country rebuilding after defeat in a war of unimaginable horror and deprivation).

The story is told entirely in flashback through a framing device of the witnesses meeting in the rain at Kyoto's ruined Rashomon gate, and while in each of the four tellings of the story the characters are the same, the events and the characterisations are altered. The woodcutter claims he found the Samurai's body while collecting wood in the forest, while the bandit offers a tale of his own cunning, sexual prowess, honour and duelling ability. The Samurai's wife claims rape and the cold response from her captive husband, asking for an honourable death at his hand, then conveniently fainting when he continues to stare at her coldly. She also claims to have tried to drown herself. This is contradicted when a medium gives voice to the Samurai to reveal a tale of dishonour, of his wife asking the bandit to kill him, and of an honourable suicide. All versions are then confounded by the woodcutter revising his story to include elements of each telling, contradicting his initial story. This revision has rape, a duel, and the death of the Samurai by sword (this latter fact being added to conceal the theft of the valuable dagger which may – or may not – have been the weapon that killed him).

Rashomon won the Golden Lion Award at the 1951 Venice Film Festival and was influential and pioneering, both in terms of narrative structuring and of cinematic technique (such as using mirrors to reflect light on to the actors when shooting into the sun). Indeed, considerable attention was paid to the visual aspects of the film (the sound and dialogue seem to have lesser roles, secondary to the visuals), and its black-and-white images have an almost poetic quality about them. Not least in its successes is that of sharing the acting talents of Toshiro Mifune with the world.

Case study
TOSHIRO MIFUNE (1920–1997)

Born 1 April 1920 in Tsingtao, China, Mifune worked in the photography shop of his Japanese parents until 1939 when he was conscripted into the Imperial Japanese Air Force (aerial photography) for the duration of the

continued

Second World War. After the war he took a position with Toho Studios as a cameraman, and (after being put forward to new actor auditions without his knowledge), soon became a film actor.

Most associated with Akira Kurosawa (appearing in sixteen of his films), he is also closely associated with Senkichi Taniguchi (who was his first director), Kajiro Yamamoto, Hiroshi Inagaki, and Kihachi Okamoto. Internationally he worked with (among others) John Boorman, John Frankenheimer and Steven Spielberg.

Mifune developed the persona of the roving Ronin – the wandering Samurai – a simple, earthy warrior with wisdom and unmatched fighting skills, and this, coupled with his acting talent and range, made him the most famous Japanese film star of his time, making over 140 feature film appearances (both Japanese and internationally). A long-running dispute with Kurosawa meant that the two men did not speak for nearly thirty years, with a reconciliation coming in 1993, shortly before the deaths of both of them.

After retreating from public life in 1992, Toshiro Mifune died of organ failure in Mitaka, Japan on 24 December 1997.

ACTIVITY

Watch *Rashomon* and note down the basics of the parallel versions of events. Highlight the similarities in the versions, and consider where they diverge. Which story do you believe? Do you believe it in its entirety? If not, which parts are problematic to you?

In a group take the side of each of the four principal characters, and argue the case for their story. Is it possible to arrive at a final 'judgement'? What does this say about truth and perspective?

What do you feel the film has to say about women? Is Masako a typical representation of Japanese women of the fictional period, or is Kurosawa using her to pass comment on the contemporary position of women in Japanese society?

How does divorcing the Samurai from his 'telling' of the story through the use of a medium affect his version of events? Could the medium be representative of another medium of 'telling'?

Summary

TOKYO DRIFTER

Figure 7.2 *Tokyo Nagaremono* (*Tokyo Drifter*) (1966, Dir: Seijun Suzuki).

This yakuza film from 'pop-art' director Seijun Suzuki came towards the end of his studio career for Nikkatsu, and presages his emergence as an independent filmmaker. Ultra-violent and highly stylised, it is a film full of cinematic excess, and one which reflects a growing excess in broader Japanese culture at the time (perhaps reflecting in turn the identity crisis of the postwar generation).

After the crime syndicate, Kurata, is disbanded by its boss, its principal hit man Tetsu is offered a job by rival gang leader Otsuka. Honour (in true Samurai tradition) prevents Tetsu from taking the easy path and he turns down the offer, leaving Tokyo to avoid being killed by the spurned Otsuka. Otsuka places Viper – his chief hit man – on Tetsu's trail, and several confrontations ensue. Arriving at Umitani's, his boss's ally, Tetsu finds he has been betrayed by his boss, but manages to defeat his enemies and escape the clutches of the treacherous Umitani.

Case study

SEIJUN SUZUKI (1923–)

Born in Tokyo on 24 May 1923 (given name Seitaro Suzuki), Suzuki was deemed academically weak. Conscripted into the Imperial Navy for the duration of the Second World War, on his demobilisation and repatriation to Japan, he studied film at the Kamakura Academy. Passing the entrance exam for Shochiku Studios, he worked as an assistant director until 1954, when he moved to Nikkatsu Studios, where he began making his trademark ultra-violent yakuza films and pinku eiga films (sadomasochistic pornography).

Dismissed from the most sensationalist of Japan's studios for producing *Koroshi no rakuin* (*Branded to Kill*) (Nikkatsu, Japan, 1967), a film seen as too bizarre to make money, Suzuki was blacklisted (he sued the studio for wrongful dismissal and won) and did not make another film for nearly ten years.

He remade *Branded to Kill* as *Pisutoro Opera* (*Pistol Opera*) (Dentsu/ Shochiku, Japan, 2001), and recently completed a musical love story, *Operetta tanuki goten* (*Princess Racoon*) (Nippon Herald, Japan, 2005).

Suzuki's film modernises the chambara film, placing it in the highly stylised hip world of 1960s Tokyo, bright, colourful and violent, and in doing so presents a yakuza film that is full of both modern existential crisis, and Samurai ethics and codes of honour. Clearly influenced by the French *nouvelle vague* directors, Tetsuya Watari's performance as Tetsu offers more than a nod to Jean-Paul Belmondo and Alain Delon.

Mixing black-and-white, desaturated opening scenes with the symbolism of selected colours highlighted throughout for emphasis, Suzuki shows an obsession for geometric shapes (zig-zags, circles, triangles) that is reminiscent of Italian filmmaker Bernardo Bertolucci's work, and suggests a further indication of the conscious or subconscious influence of European cinema. He designed the snow sequence both for the dramatic effect of placing gun and sword play (and the resulting blood splatter) against it, and for its reflection of Tetsu's purity and nobility as a yakuza, of his single-minded determination and his honour.

Suzuki transforms the yakuza film into a combination of jidaigeki, film noir and western, with a Samurai code extending through it, an examination of the under-belly of urban Japan, and the use of the icons of the western (the bar-room brawls, the gunfights, and the landscapes that contrast with the suffocating intensity of the interiors). American film and American pop culture have found themselves infused with Japanese culture in *Tokyo Drifter* to the extent that it could be easily picked up thirty years later as an influence for a new American director, Quentin Tarantino.

ACTIVITY

Look at the colour scheme (including monochrome) in *Tokyo Drifter*. Does it amplify the story? What colours are particularly symbolic? Does colour tell you anything about Tetsu?

What particular scenes or sequences confirm the nature of this film as a jidaigeki or chambara film? Can you list the film noir elements in this film? What scenes or sequences remind you of any American westerns you may have seen?

What do you think accounts for the American influences in the film? Is there a reason that European influences were incorporated at this time?

In a group, discuss the possible audiences for this film, and try to assess which parts of the film would have been particularly effective in reaching them. Discuss how it makes you feel as a modern, Western audience.

The Japanese film industry 1950–1970

It is no simple coincidence that the immediate postwar period ended for Japan in 1950, just as the Korean War began. This development brought about a change of attitude in the occupying American powers, since they realised they needed Japan as a bulwark against communism, and it brought in an economic boom as the Americans bolstered both the economy and reconstruction efforts to ensure that the Japanese people recognised where their future lay.

This growing economy and the relaxation of film censorship (Japan was now considered 'friendly') meant that there was not only a financial impetus to increase film production, but there was also the impetus of a return to creative freedom. By 1952 (the end of the American occupation of Japan) the jidaigeki was firmly re-established and renewed as a popular genre, and the modernism of the gendaigeki films (promoted under the censorship codes of the occupation) was already an accepted part of Japanese film culture.

During the Second World War the film industry had been forced by the government to consolidate its operations around a tripartite studio system consisting of Shochiku, Toho and Shinko (absorbing the Nikkatsu Studio), which renamed itself Daiei. These companies were vertically integrated along the lines of the American model with production, distribution and exhibition all centrally controlled and fully exploited (Daiei allowed Nikkatsu's cinemas to remain outside the take-over, and this initially caused it some difficulty in finding exhibition for its product).

These studios worked with the occupying powers at the end of the war to ensure that 'preferred' styles of filmmaking were adopted by filmmakers, and to regulate (and police) exhibition. In return they were allowed to continue making films (an approach modelled on the occupation of Italy as opposed to the occupation of Germany where production centres were closed, distribution was taken over by the Americans, and exhibition was vigorously policed by the occupying armies).

Soon after the occupation a group of Toho Studio workers founded Shintoho ('New Toho') Studios, and in 1951 Toei ('Eastern Film Company') Studios were formed. In 1954 Nikkatsu Studios were reborn, separating once again from Daiei. All of these studios maintained their vertically integrated structures and, in the rebuilding of the war-devastated cities of Japan, took the opportunities presented to build extensive cinema chains in prime urban locations, where a population with growing disposable income could engage in movie-going once again. By 1954 these six principal studios were making one film each per week, and by 1960 this figure was nearing an average of two films a week. This was clearly a boom time.

Case study
KYOTO – JAPAN'S HOLLYWOOD

In 1925, in Uzumasa, a small suburb of Japan's second city Kyoto, the film star Brando Tsumasaburo founded a studio, and others soon rushed to join him in this new location. The studios continued to grow up until the outbreak of the Second World War.

After the war it became the centre of production for Toei, Shochiku and Daiei studios, and throughout the 1950s and 1960s it produced over three-quarters of all Japanese film. In 1971 Daiei's production ceased with its bankruptcy, Toei downsized to an alternative location, and by 1975 Japan's Hollywood was little more than a back-lot and movie theme park.

The American occupiers also initially encouraged independent production as a means of promoting democracy and ensuring that the studios (who had once supported the defeated Nationalists) would have some competition and something to anchor them to the commercial world. This sector grew throughout the 1950s and became significant with the sudden arrival of Japan's own New Wave in 1960.

Young filmmaker Nagisa Oshima was working for Shochiku when he made *Seishun zankoku monogatari* (*Cruel Story of Youth*) (Shochiku, Japan, 1960), a story of tainted individuals operating in a tainted world, which signalled a new direction alongside *Rokudenashi* (*The Good For Nothing*) (Shochiku, Japan, 1960, Dir: Yoshishige Yoshida), and *Koi no katamichi kippu* (*One-way Ticket of Love*) (Shochiku, Japan, 1960, Dir: Masahiro Shinoda). These films were hard-edged and supercharged, with tension both in the stories they presented and in the cinematic styles they adopted. Youthful, colourful, uncertain and intense, they introduced a world of casual sex and violence, of a new morality, that was far removed from the jidaigeki and gendaigeki films of the 1950s. The keiko-eiga film crashed on to the scene.

This was a new generation of filmmakers (and largely left-wing activists) who had been children during the war and who burned with the desire to redefine what it was to be Japanese. The movement however was not born out of the filmmakers' passion, but instead was a deliberate invention of the studio which was seeing its competitors stealing ahead by targeting the youth market, and a popular response to (and ticket sales for) imported films of the French *nouvelle vague*.

Angry at the continuation of the Japan–US Security Pact (which permitted the US a permanent military presence in Japan) which was renewed in 1960, Oshima made *Night and Fog* in Japan – with its clear reference to the French *nouvelle vague* film *Nuit et Brouillard* (*Night and Fog*) (Argos/Como, France, 1955, Dir: Alain Resnais). The criticism of both current and past policies (and of the

Figure 7.3 *Nihon no yuro to Kiri* (*Night and Fog in Japan*) (Oshima, 1960).

Communist Party and the student Left) for 'betraying' Japan was too much for Shochiku and they withdrew the film from release after only four days' exhibition. Oshima immediately resigned his position at the Shochiku and set up his own independent film company, heralding a new era of vibrant independent production and of individual authorial voices rather than studio-styled features.

At the same time, television began to impact on cinema audiences, and a significant decline in the studios' fortunes began. This was amplified when their stranglehold on exhibition was challenged by the Art Theatre Guild (ATG) which began offering collaborative production deals to New Wave directors, and then exhibiting their work in an expanding chain of independent cinemas. The ATG was to quickly become the main exponent and supporter of the Japanese New Wave throughout the 1960s.

The difficulties the studios experienced continued, and by 1971 Daiei had gone bankrupt, Nikkatsu had taken to working exclusively in the soft pornography market (making a type of sex film that became known as roman poruno) and the other remaining studios had fixed into genre production to survive with Toei promoting the yakuza, Shochiku comedy, and Toho the monster films (such as the very profitable and special effects-driven Godzilla franchise). This malaise heralds the end of the 'golden age' of Japanese cinema, yet at the same time marked out the foundations for its revival through independent production a decade later.

ACTIVITY

What is noticeable in the contexts of production of the different Japanese films you have studied? How does this manifest itself on screen? Is there a clear difference between films from the early 1950s and those of the late 1960s?

If you were a Japanese studio owner in the late 1960s experiencing the difficulties outlined above, what options would you consider in order to stay in business? Discuss your approaches with your peers.

As a group, select other New Wave cinemas from around the world and investigate their production contexts. How does the Japanese model compare with others? What are the principal similarities and differences? Are the results stylistically similar? What does this tell you?

How do you think audiences responded to the changes in cinematic production? What alternatives do you think they had? What power do you think they had?

Film form

In the early part of this period, the films produced were contextualised by a rigid system of censorship that prevented any image of sword play or Samurai activity, any glorification of the military, any image of the subjugation of another race, any implication of women in a subservient role and so on. Effectively the American occupiers outlawed much of Japanese cinema's heritage, and in doing so also outlawed much of its stock narratives and stock characters.

Many of the filmmakers working at this time had either been prominent before the Second World War or had developed their craft under the defeated Nationalists, and as such had much to prove to their American occupiers to enable their rehabilitation. One way of doing this was to distance current filmmaking practice from what went before,

Whereas Kurosawa adopted the challenging narrative structure of *Rashomon*, Kenji Mizoguchi returned to his pre-war themes of social problems, and the sufferings of women in Japanese society, in his *Saikaku Ichidai Onna* (*The Life of Oharu*).

Figure 7.4 *Saikaku Ichidai Onna* (*The Life of Oharu*) (1952, dir: Nagisa Oshima).

This is the story of a woman who falls from a respected position as a member of the Imperial Japanese Court to a beggar and disease-ravaged prostitute, and Mizoguchi depicted this through the use of a much more 'American' style of shooting than he used pre-war (shot-reverse shots, closer compositions, use of close-ups). He also introduced a 'Japanese-style' presentation of landscape that became the established marker of a Japanese film for Western audiences. Interestingly, this new filmic approach did not meet with a favourable response from audiences in Japan, but like Kurosawa the year before, Mizoguchi was fêted on the world stage, winning the Best Director Award at the Venice Film Festival.

Similarly, Yasujiro Ozu adopted a similar 'Japanese-style' presentation in his shomingeki film *Tokyo Monogatari* (*Tokyo Story*). Here he maintained his pre-war style of low camera angles and 360° shooting space, but avoided fades, dissolves, camera movement (the camera moves only once in *Tokyo Story*) and graphic matching in favour of *mise-en-scène* and the patterning presented in the place-ment of simple objects and colour design. Instead of relying on the power of editing, Ozu punctuated his sequences with brief, intensely symbolic moments from everyday life – empty streets, banners billowing in the wind, a small archi-tectural detail – and in doing so created an illusionary sense of timelessness.

Figure 7.5 *Tokyo Monogatari* (*Tokyo Story*) (1953, dir: Ozu).

While Mizoguchi was adopting an American style, Ozu was reflecting a new-found interest in a minimalist European style, stripped down and reinvented for Japanese cinema. This may be seen further refined in his later film *Ohayô* (*Good Morning*) (Shochiku, Japan, 1959) where his muted, neutral camerawork and ebb and flow of characters in and out of his frame was beginning to seem dated before the frenetic style of the New Wave.

Amidst the Japanese New Wave's replication of the naturalism of the French *nouvelle vague* came Nagisa Oshima's *Night and Fog* in Japan which offered a counterpoint both to the stylistic directions that mainstream Japanese cinema was taking and to those adopted by Oshima's peers. Assuming an almost theatrical artificiality, Oshima shot most of the film on sound stages, with dramatic lighting changes choreographed to carefully considered camera movement. With its use of vibrant colour, cinemascope, and an almost oppressive score, the film bears little resemblance to either Japanese or French tradition (indeed, it has more in common with the Hollywood musical which it could be seen to be a pastiche of).

Connecting both the style of established filmmakers and the exuberance of the New Wave filmmakers is the work of Masahiro Shinoda (who began his career as Ozu's assistant at Shochiku), specifically his *Shinju ten no Amijima* (*Double*

Figure 7.6 *Shinju ten no Amijima* (*Double Suicide*) (1969, dir: Shinoda).

Suicide). While starting his career working on 'youth subjects', his direction changed to explore style in period costume drama (a reinterpretation of the jidaigeki). In *Double Suicide*, Shinoda uses the aesthetic of the Bunraku puppet theatre as a contextualising device for his story of a rule-dominated society wherein any freedom or rule-breaking is but another part of a puppet master's manipulation. Beginning the film with the black clothed and masked puppet-hands manipulating the puppets, Shinoda switches to live action performance, yet does not remove the puppet-hands from the scene, lending the film a silent commentary that adds another dimension to his storytelling technique. Again concerned (like his master Ozu) with composition, framing, and the movement of actors within the frame, Shinoda shares with the New Wave directors an interest in fore-grounding the story and the cinematic style.

ACTIVITY

What for you is the most interesting feature of Japanese film style in this period? What makes you identify this above other features? Compare your choice with your peers. Discuss the similarities and differences of choice.

A number of the Japanese films in this period have been remade in the West (primarily in Hollywood). Compare the stylistic treatment of the original Japanese film and the Western remake. Which do you prefer? Why? Are there any stylistic carry-overs from one to the other? If so, why do you think this is?

Select a film from early in the period and one from late in the period. Compare them stylistically. In two columns headed with each film title, list the similarities, then list the differences between them. Do the similarities outweigh the differences or vice versa? What do you notice about the development of film style across the period?

Social and political contexts

At the beginning of the topic period Japan was still a beaten and occupied nation, reeling from eight million war dead, 600,000 civilian casualties, the devastation of the fire-bombing of its cities, and the horror of two atomic bombs being exploded on it. Its industries (including the film industry) were recovering slowly as Japan was rebuilt, and its people were beginning to reflect on the past and to consider who they were.

By the end of the topic period Japan had become a mighty global industrial and economic powerhouse, having rebuilt its infrastructure and its sense of nation.

However, change had come both in social and political understandings, and 1970 brought one era to a close with the ritual suicide of writer Yokio Mishima who represented the old guard of Japan, and gave birth to a new era with the terrorism of the Japanese Red Army.

The role of women had dramatically altered, and in response so had the role of men, with the new-found independence of the former impacting on the traditional values of the latter. Both masculinity and the nature of woman were questioned in Japanese film from *Rashomon* to *Double Suicide*, and both filmically and within the wider society an accommodation was reached.

Politically Japan polarised in the 1960s, as the march to the Left of the 1950s was tempered by the need to maintain good relations with the recently departed Americans, and to ensure a stable capitalist democracy close to mainland communist China, and close to the now divided Korea. In political terms Japan mirrored both Europe and America in activity and response to world events, and this is captured by the development of a radical documentary film movement in the 1960s.

Perhaps the biggest change in Japanese culture during this period is in the relationships between young and old, where issues of respect and responsibility became battlegrounds (as played out in Ozu's *Tokyo Story*). This battleground is one that perhaps shaped film most with an adherence to the traditional jidaigeki and gendaigeki on one side and the fast developing and new yakuza and keiko-eiga on the other.

ACTIVITY

Consider the gender roles presented in one of the films you have studied. How does the director portray these roles? What statement is the director trying to make? Compare these roles with those in another film from a different end of the period. What do you notice?

Consider how 'everyday' relationships are presented in Japanese film from this period. Are these relationships familiar to you (and hence modern) or are they removed from your experience? What would you have to do to make these relationships relevant to you?

What can you tell about the politics of a filmmaker from the films they make? Take one of the films you have studied for this topic and list any and all political representations in it. Does this indicate a political bias to you?

1 What elements of visual style are significant in defining a national cinema in the films you have studied for this topic?

2 In what ways do the films you have studied reflect wider issues within Japanese society?

3 How far do you think the films you have studied for this topic reflect the contexts in which they were produced?

4 How significant are the genre styles and conventions in the films you have studied to making a distinctive national cinema?

Further Reading

Anderson, J. and Richie, D. (1993) *The Japanese Film*. Princeton University Press

Bordwell, D. (1994) *Ozu and the Politics of Cinema*. Princeton University Press

McDonald, K. (2006) *Reading a Japanese Film: Cinema in Context*. University of Hawai'i Press

Phillips, A. and Stringer, J. (eds) (2006) *Japanese Cinema: Texts and Contexts*. Routledge

Richie, D. (1990) *Japanese Cinema: An Introduction*. Oxford University Press

Ritchie, D. (1999) *The Films of Akira Kurosawa*. University of California Press

Standish, I. (2006) *A New History of Japanese Cinema: A Century of Narrative Film*. Continuum International Publishing Group

Weisser, Y. and Weisser, T. (1998) *Japanese Cinema – The Essential Handbook* (4th edn.). Vital Books

Yoshimoto, M. (2000) *Kurosawa*. Duke University Press

Documentary

The Century of Cinema: 100 Years of Japanese Cinema (BFI, 1994)

Kurosawa (Wellspring, 2001)

Internet

http://www.brightlightsfilm.com/japan.html Bright Lights Film Journal – lots of articles about Japanese film and filmmakers

http://www.jmdb.ne.jp/ Japanese Movie Database

http://www2.tky.3web.ne.jp/~adk/kurosawa/J-AKpage.html Akira Kurosawa
  Database
http://pears.lib.ohio-state.edu/Markus/Welcome.html Kinema Club site –
  good academic papers and reference material
http://www.sensesofcinema.com/contents/00/7/japanese.html – article by
  Bill Mousoulis *Throw Away Your Books: Japanese Cinema*

8 MEXICAN CINEMA 1990 TO THE PRESENT

This chapter will look at:

- the content and contexts of key films
- the characteristic features of Mexican cinema during this period
- the significance of this movement in terms of World Cinema
- the influence of European cinema on Mexican film
- the internationalising of Mexican cinema
- the pleasures and challenges this period of national filmmaking offers as an 'alternative' to Hollywood

Suggested films from this period:

Sólo con tu pareja (*Love in a Time of Hysteria*) (Fondo de Fomento a la Calidad Cinematográfica, Mexico, 1991, Dir: Alfonso Cuarón)

Danzón (Fondo de Fomento a la Calidad Cinematográfica, Mexico/Spain, 1991, Dir: María Novaro)

Como agua para chocolate (*Like Water for Chocolate*) (Arau Films Internacional, Mexico, 1992, Dir: Alfonso Arau)

El Mariachi (Columbia Pictures Corporation, Mexico/USA, 1992, Dir: Robert Rodriguez)

La Otra Conquista (*The Other Conquest*) (ADO Entertainment, Mexico, 1999, Dir: Salvador Carrasco),

Sexo, pudor y lágrimas (*Sex, Shame, and Tears*) (Argos Producciones, Mexico, 1999, Dir: Antonio Serrano)

Amores Perros (Altavista Films Mexico, 2000, Dir: Alejandros González Iñárritu)

Sin dejar huella (*Leaving No Trace*) (Altavista Films, Mexico, 2000, Dir: María Novaro)

Y tu mamá también (*And Your Mother Too*) (Akkiaza Films International, Mexico, 2001, Dir: Alfonso Cuarón)

Japón (*Japan*) (No Dream Cinema, Mexico/Germany/Netherlands/Spain, 2002, Dir: Carlos Reygadas)

Mil nubes de paz cercan el cielo, amor, jamás acabrás de ser amor (*A Thousand Clouds of Peace Fence the Sky, Love, Your Being Love Will Never End*) (Nubes Cine, Mexico, 2003, Dir: Julián Hernández)

Batalla en el Cielo (*Battle in Heaven*) (Mantarraya, Mexico/Belgium/France/Germany, 2005, Dir: Carlos Reygadas)

Babel (Paramount Pictures, France/USA/Mexico, 2006, Dir: Alejandros González Iñárritu)

El laberinto del fauno (*Pan's Labyrinth*) (Tequilla Gang, Mexico/Spain/USA, 2006, Dir: Guillermo del Toro)

El Orfanato (*The Orphanage*) (Esta Vivo! Laboratorio de Nuevos Talentos, Mexico/Spain, 2007, Dir: Juan Antonio Bayona)

Arráncame la vida (*Tear this Heart Out*) (Altavista Films, Mexico, 2008, Dir: Roberto Sneider)

Mexican cinema has produced some significant films across its century of production, though after its 'golden age' ended in the 1950s these became fewer and fewer, as production turned towards the low end (but profitable) market of low-budget westerns and horror movies. However, at the start of the 1990s a new direction and dynamism in Mexican film began to impact on the world scene, and Novo Cine Mexicano (New Mexican cinema) was born.

INFORMATION BOX – NOVO CINE MEXICANO

New Mexican cinema is a film movement that began in the early 1990s and is remarkable in the fact that it has been populated almost completely by unknowns, from directors and writers, through to cinematographers

continued

and actors, catapulting them into fame. The movement has developed
from a purely Mexican base, through collaborations with Hollywood and
the influence of European cinema, to a truly international cinema. Many
of the filmmakers are from a documentary background, and accordingly
the neo-realist influence is evident in much of its output.

The characteristics of New Mexican cinema may be divided into micro and macro concepts. With a cutting-edge attitude towards editing, it used flash-cuts, enhancement through grading, colour distortion, and a host of other radical post-production techniques. While this is similar to what was happening in France during the 1980s (in the Cinema du Look), particularly in a shared use of contemporary music that stretches the medium, it is the narrative elements that make it significantly different. Largely built on a tradition of realism, with a significant neo-realist influence, the stories tend towards the superficially simple, while revealing deep commentaries on human nature and the human condition with all its violence, sexual tension and rich language.

In its emergence it brought a wave of new talent on the production side and this was matched by a similar wave of new talent on the acting side. Both groups began to function as an ensemble, which in turn meant that there was constant work and therefore constant opportunity for development. This was supported by the fact that Mexico lacked the division (or the snobbery of rivals) between the film and television industries and so there was a significant cross-fertilisation between the two media that enabled New Mexican cinema's rapid development.

INFORMATION BOX – A BRIEF PREHISTORY   *i*

Mexico was one of the first South American countries to engage with the new medium of the Lumière brothers within only a couple of years of its development. However, poverty and political instability meant that film in Mexico remained a sporadic 'here today, gone tomorrow' industry. By 1930 the industry was beginning to become more established and was important enough for the Soviet filmmaker Sergei Eisenstein to visit and teach. He had already spent time in Hollywood with Disney, yet had to be ordered back from Mexico because his fascination for their industry held him captivated.

Hollywood's early (unsuccessful) attempts at dominating the South American market were refocused with the outbreak of the Second World

War, and Mexico took advantage of this, building a successful industry that had influence across the entire South American continent. This was the beginning of the 'golden age' of Mexican cinema that saw output rise to seventy films in 1943, still a record for a Spanish-speaking country. This brought Mexican cinema to the attention of Hollywood, and soon not only were American filmmakers such as Orson Welles travelling south of the border to make films, but Mexican stars such as Delores Del Rio were being courted by Hollywood and brought over to appear in major star vehicles.

The 'golden age' of Mexican cinema began to fade in the 1950s, as television took a hold on the market, audiences declined, and South American politics brought a long period of instability. With a few notable exceptions Mexican cinema fell into producing low-budget horror, action, western and sex comedies, appealing to a large though undiscerning home market.

The role of the government

The end of the 1980s saw a sea change in Mexican politics and the Centre-right Partido Revolucionario Institucional (PRI) that had held on to power for seven decades was swept from power. In 1989, the incoming National Democratic Front Party appointed Ignacio Durán Loera as director of the Instituto Mexicano de Cinematografía (Mexican Film Institute, IMCINE). His approach and policies are directly responsible for creating the conditions for the New Mexican cinema movement to seed and flourish.

Loera campaigned for the repeal of the government's right to decide what films would be made, and in securing its agreement saw the majority of government funding withdrawn. This forced him into a position of seeking co-producers and international co-production. This injection of capital was matched by an injection of fresh ideas and new ways of working that Loera fostered by championing the support of new talent into the industry.

Summary
SÓLO CON TU PAREJA

Figure 8.1 Poster for *Sólo con tu pareja* (*Love in the Time of Hysteria*) (1991, Dir: Alfonso Cuarón).

Alfonso Cuarón's 1991 film *Sólo con tu pareja* (*Love in the Time of Hysteria*) (which literally translates as 'only with your partner') was the first feature film for this television émigré, and can be nominated as the film that launched the movement. Funding was secured from the Mexican government's Instituto Mexicano de Cinematografia (IMCINE), but the government refused to distribute it upon completion, though it was allowed into foreign markets, winning awards at the Mexican Academy of Film (the Ariel Awards) and at the Toronto Film Festival. Two years later the Mexican government allowed the film to be shown to the home market where it was received rapturously and became an instant success at the box-office.

It was the sexual content of this farce, along with its references to AIDS, that provoked the initial reaction from the Mexican government. The story itself is relatively simple, revolving around Tomás' multiple seductions and the complications arising from them. Tomás persuades a nurse into an encounter in his flat while simultaneously getting his boss to wait for a similar liaison in his friend's flat in the same apartment block. As he flits along the ledge outside the apartments in an attempt to keep both women satisfied, and more importantly to prevent each from knowing about the other, he discovers and falls in love with his new neighbour who has taken the flat between Tomás' and his friend's. Life, of course, cannot be that simple in a comedy, and so it is revealed that the new neighbour has a fiancé.

To compound Tomás' problems, the nurse he was with, who he then neglects after meeting his neighbour, decides to take some revenge on him for his behaviour. When he goes for a routine blood test she seizes her opportunity and alters the results to suggest that Tomás is HIV positive. This, of course, shakes him to the core and leads to a period of deep reflection on his lifestyle, attitude and behaviour. It also leads to a chase sequence finale that ends on the observation deck of the Latin American Tower in a filmmaker's homage to *An Affair to Remember* (Jerry Wald Productions, US, 1957, Dir: Leo McCarey).

ACTIVITY

Watch *Sólo con tu pareja* with a particular focus on the cinematography and editing. What do you think the director is trying to achieve with the style of the film?

In groups discuss the role of individual principal characters and what their function is in the narrative. Come back together and compare conclusions. Discuss how each character interacts with the others. What do you feel about the morality of your allocated character? What do you feel about the morality of the other principal characters?

How do you feel the film positions women? What do you think Cuarón is saying about gender roles?

Do you sympathise with Tomás' situation, or do you feel that the director is using his situation to talk about wider issues in Mexican society?

The Mexican film industry, 1990 to the present

The birth of New Mexican cinema opened the floodgates to a new generation of filmmakers who wanted to tell new stories that had little to do with monsters, action heroes or cowboys. Their stories revolved around the everyday activities and problems that were familiar to their audiences, and so films about abject poverty, violence, petty crime, failing relationships and a malfunctioning society all began to make an appearance. They seemed to embrace the neo-realist concept of a 'cinema of the humble' where lives float on a sea of politics, corruption, and the emptiness of a society at odds with itself. The filmic gloss that had carried over from the 'golden age' was swept away and a new style reflected a new content and an obsession with reflecting a modern Mexico.

Case study

KEY DIRECTORS OF NEW MEXICAN CINEMA

Alfonso Arau (1932–)

Arau was born in Mexico City to a middle-class family with a doctor for a father. He is seen as the 'father' of New Mexican cinema and forms a bridge to past cinematic movements, having directed his first film in 1973. His films during this period were unusual for dealing with social and political issues (particularly at a time when offering criticism of the ruling Partido Revolucionario Institucional (PRI) was a dangerous activity to undertake), and it is this determination to make films which reflect his society that places him firmly (intellectually and stylistically) at the heart of the New Mexican cinema movement. His *Como agua para chocolate* (*Like Water for Chocolate*) was made a year after Cuarón's *Sólo con tu pareja*, though it ended up being released in the home market the year before, and is often referenced as the first example of New Mexican cinema.

Like many of his compatriots in the New Mexican cinema movement he was courted by Hollywood, and has made several successful Hollywood studio movies. In 2004 the Santa Fe Film Festival granted Arau its lifetime achievement award, the Luminaria Award.

Alfonso Cuarón (1961 –)

Alfonso Cuarón was born in México City, and studied filmmaking at the Centro Universitario de Estudios. He was expelled from the University for making a short film in the English language and, with his career facing ruin before it began, he turned to television where he worked as a technician and then a director.

His first feature *Sólo con tu pareja* was controversially banned in Mexico for two years after its international release, and his second (equally controversial) feature *Y tu mamá también* was nominated for an Academy Award for Best Original Screenplay.

He has had a significant international career and has directed major Hollywood studio films including *Harry Potter and the Prisoner of Azkaban* (Warner Brothers, US, 2004), which was criticised for its darkness and adult address, and *Children of Men* (Universal Pictures, US, 2006).

Alejandro González Iñárritu (1963 –)

Alejandro González Iñárritu was born in Mexico City, and by 1984 he was a DJ on WFM, Mexico's top radio station. He studied filmmaking in the United States (Maine and Los Angeles) learning cinematography from Polish director Ludwik Margules, and directing from Judith Weston. By 1988 he was composing film scores, and by 1990 he was heading up production at one of Mexico's television companies, Televisa.

In 2000 he directed his first full-length feature film *Amores Perros* which presented three stories linked directly by a car crash and thematically by reflections on animal cruelty and the cruel attitudes of people towards other people.

The success of *Amores Perros* (nominated for an Academy Award for Best Foreign Language Film, winning a BAFTA for Best Film not in the English Language, and many others) propelled Iñárritu on to the international scene where he was again courted by Hollywood. *21 Grams* (That is That Productions, US, 2003) attracted American stars Sean Penn and Naomi Watts, and his next feature *Babel* attracted Brad Pitt and Cate Blanchett. This went on to achieve seven Academy Award nominations including Best Picture and Best Director.

Film director Alejandro González Iñárritu was first recognised for his debut in *Amores Perros*, written by his former colleague Guillermo Arriaga; the three intersecting stories presented in the film depicted life in Mexico City. Following the same hyperlink cinema attributes and with Guillermo Arriaga again, he directed *21 Grams* (2003), starring Sean Penn, Naomi Watts and Benicio del Toro. His last project, *Babel*, also interwove stories, but on an international scale, setting the four stories in Japan, Morocco, Mexico and the United States. It starred Brad Pitt, Cate Blanchett and Gael García Bernal; this film had seven nominations to the seventy-ninth Academy

continued

Awards, including Best Picture and Best Director. It was awarded Best Director prize at the Cannes Film Festival (2006), and Best Motion Picture in the drama category at the 2007 Golden Globes.

María Novaro (1951–)

María Novaro was born in Mexico City and studied filmmaking at the University Centre of Film Studies. She worked in the film industry as a sound mixer, a cinematographer and a director until making her first feature film *Lola* (Conacite Dos, Mexico, 1989). Her second feature *Danzón* cemented her position as the foremost female director in Mexico, and she is celebrated for her almost European expressionist style that uses a vibrant colour palette to convey and emphasise the emotion of the scene. Her 2000 road movie *Sin dejar huella* won a Mexican Academy Award (Ariel) for Best Cinematography, and won the Best Latin Cinema Award at the Sundance Film Festival.

Guillermo del Toro (1964–)

Guillermo del Toro was born in Guadalajara in Mexico and became interested in filmmaking at an early age. He executive produced his first feature at the age of 21, and directed his debut horror feature *Cronos* (CNCAIMC, Mexico, 1993) at age 29. The film won eight Ariel Awards (Mexican Film Academy Awards) and went on to win the International Critics Week Prize at the 1993 Cannes Film Festival.

Immediately courted by Hollywood, del Toro did not have a great experience there and returned to Mexico after shooting *Mimic* (Dimension Films, US, 1997). Here he set up his own production company and shortly after this released *El espinanzo del Diablo* (*The Devil's Backbone*) (Anhelo Producciones, Mexico, 2001). His dark fantasies were attracting bigger audiences and greater industry attention, leading him back to Hollywood where he made a name directing comic book adaptations.

His recent *El laberinto del fauno* (*Pan's Labyrinth*) achieved critical acclaim and reached audiences beyond the usual demographic for world cinema, and won three Academy Awards, with three other nominations.

In 2008 del Toro was named as director of *The Hobbit*, the latest in Peter Jackson's *Lord of the Rings*, and has moved to New Zealand for the four-year shoot.

As New Mexican cinema entered a new millennium it became reinvigorated rather than suffering the *fin de siècle* that many other national cinemas experienced at this time. Continuing economic success in Mexico was producing both prosperity and a modernising wave of construction that was serving to heighten the differences in circumstance between the rich and poor, and simultaneously placed a spotlight on the situation of the dispossessed, and those lost in a world of youth, skyscrapers and designer labels.

Summary

BATALLA EN EL CIELO

Figure 8.2 *Batalla en el Cielo / (Battle in Heaven)* (2005, dir: Reygadas)

In *Batalla en el Cielo*, Carlos Reygadas makes a clear distinction between the desperation of those who have nothing, and the boredom of those who have everything. The central character Marcos (Marco Hernández) and his wife are driven by extreme poverty to kidnap a baby for ransom. Meanwhile,

continued

his boss's daughter Ana (Anapola Mushkadiz) grapples with the emptiness of her life by prostituting herself for fun. Both pay the ultimate price for their actions, though the audience is again positioned to feel emptiness when Ana is murdered, and to suffer with Marcos as he processes through the pilgrims to his own death.

There is a restless longing for order and perhaps the simplicity of the past in Marcos' character, and he is made only too aware of his deficiencies through chauffeuring his boss's daughter around and being exposed to her empty lifestyle of beautiful, rich, bored friends, casual sexual encounters, and a complete disconnection with the lower echelons of society. He longs to taste this life, and he longs for her.

However, when she (rather surprisingly) takes him to her bed, there is an unsettling emptiness from both sides that makes the explicit sex scenes (and they are controversially explicit) unerotic, dissolute and devoid of passion. At the end of their intercourse she takes Marcos' hand, yet even here it is not with feeling, but more that she realises it is the thing to be done at this point. This single gesture captures the heart of the film – people are disconnected and simply go through the motions without feeling. When Ana is murdered there is a similar emptiness to the sudden event, and it is testament to the filmmaker that spectators recognise the same emptiness in themselves at the event that they see in the participants.

Perhaps to emphasise the meaninglessness presented in the film, the final scenes are filmed against the background of a pilgrimage, with an often handheld camera following chauffeur Marcos as he mingles with the crowd. The many bizarre images of the pilgrims are both captured from the 'real' and are supplemented by directed action, and the director has made conscious decisions to use and structure sequences with this footage. Here he seeks atonement and simultaneously meaning from a religion that dresses unfathomables as certainties and gives concrete meaning to things that are polysemic.

ACTIVITY

Look at the representations of rich and poor in *Batalla en al Cielo*. What does Reygadas do to differentiate between them?

Much has been made of the neo-realist elements in *Batalla en al Cielo*. What strikes you as particularly neo-realist, and where does the film diverge from a traditional definition?

The sequence in the fog is almost surreal in its editing and cinematography. How do these micro elements contribute to the 'feel'
of this sequence? What do you think Reygadas is trying to suggest
here?

The European influence

Both the Italian neo-realist influence and the style of the French New Wave can
be perceived in many of the films of New Mexican cinema, and there has in the
last decade been a move towards a more personal style of filmmaking that emulates many European products.

Carlos Reygadas' work is clearly neo-realist through its stark, constantly moving
camera, and its use of amateurs and non-actors, while María Novaro's films exhibit
the humanism of Renoir and the expressionist sense of mid-European cinemas.
The 'shock' collisions of editing that dominate much of the work of the directors
of New Mexican cinema have a lineage back to Eisenstein, though equally have
a reference point in Godard's work.

There has been a 'slickness' in cinematography, and a quirkiness of story in the
films of the latter part of the period that seem to reflect the work of the directors
of the French film movement, the Cinema du Look, and particularly the work of
Jean Jeunet. An obvious commonality of language and culture with Spain has
made the influence somewhat obscured, but nevertheless it is a strong one, not
least for the amount of co-productions Mexico and Spain enter into.

Case study
THE FILM SCHOOLS

The development of film schools in Mexico has been of major significance
not only in producing filmmakers for the Mexican film industry, but also in
producing filmmakers who are aware of film history, film language and a
range of international film styles, and who, through synthesising these
characteristics, produce films of a singular quality that appeal on the world
stage.

continued

The Centro Universitario de Estudios Cinematográficos (University Center of Film Studies, CUEC) was founded in 1963 within the National Autonomous University of Mexico, and has long acknowledged its debt of influence to the French New Wave.

The Centro de Capacitación Cinematográfica (Center for Film Realization, CCC) was founded in 1975 and is an independent film school run by the Mexican Academy of the Cinematic Arts. As such, its focus has always been on developing the authentic Mexican 'voice'.

The significance of these two film schools is in the fact that over 90 per cent of the filmmakers involved in making films within New Mexican cinema are graduates of these institutions.

The internationalising of Mexican cinema

The impact that New Mexican cinema has had on the world stage is undeniable, with more Mexican films reaching an international audience than at any other point in film history. Mexican films are being nominated for Academy Awards (and winning them), and are appearing in groups rather than singly in major film festivals such as Cannes and Sundance, where their constructional beauty, their stories, and the themes they address have a resonance that the big-budget US-produced event movies cannot compete with. This once filmic backwater has now become a powerhouse of film production on the world stage, and is using this position to attract US co-production that serves to further its impact on the market.

By Americanising its product (certainly in terms of its marketing) New Mexican cinema has been able to get over spectator reluctance to engage with foreign language films. The trailer for *El Orfanato* (*The Orphanage*) gave little clue that this was a foreign language film, and no clue other than the director's name that it was Mexican.

In part it is also due to the fact that many of the films of New Mexican cinema are dealing with real social issues, and as such are solidly connected to the visceral, making them unblinking in the face of controversial subject matter.

Summary

Figure 8.3 *Babel* (2006, Alejandro González Iñárritu).

Alejandro González Iñárritu's 2006 feature *Babel* is a multi-narrative drama that has an international cast including Brad Pitt and Cate Blanchett, and links events in Morocco, Japan, Mexico and the United States of America. It was also international in its production with companies from France, Mexico and the USA working together to co-produce it. Iñárritu was able to get the film made due to the international success of his earlier films, particularly *21 Grams*.

A disjointed narrative takes the spectator through a number of disparate but evidently connected events that include a tourist being accidentally shot in Morocco; a nanny crossing the border into Mexico for a family wedding; the self-destructive behaviour of a young deaf-and-dumb Japanese girl; and the life of poor Moroccan farmers. As the film progresses the connections become clearer. The confusions of language melt away, and the babble slowly begins to make sense.

continued

This is a vibrant film that achieved considerable critical acclaim and good box-office figures, helped in large part by the decision to use Brad Pitt as the principal marketing tool. As with *El Orfanato* (*The Orphanage*) there was little in the trailer to suggest that it was a foreign language film, and so it attracted an audience that it may not have done otherwise.

ACTIVITY

Watch the trailer for *Babel*. What clues are in there that large parts of this film are not in the English language? How are these clues de-emphasised?

Watch the film *Babel*. What marks it out as a non-American film? What characteristics does this international co-production share with other films in New Mexican cinema?

Compare this film with any of the Mexican films in the movement. Does the larger budget have an obvious effect on the film? How is this manifested?

Research the budget and box-office for *Babel*, and then do the same for any of the Mexican films in the movement. What correlations do you notice? What differences are apparent? What can you assume from what you have learned?

Key themes

A variety of themes have emerged from New Mexican cinema, some of which resonate further back through Mexican film history, and some of which are new evolutions from those that were there historically. Prominent themes include:

- Issues of gender and women's roles, including women's relationship between work and family life, empowered women, women with non-traditional lifestyles, sexuality, and the place of women in history.
- Regional themes that consider the relationship of the rural and the urban Mexico, and possibly the most significant of Mexican themes – the Mexican/ US border.
- Ritual and modernism are centred around religion and the economy, with neither being portrayed as a particularly positive force. Linked to this is

spiritual and material desperation, where little offers salvation or relief from the emptiness of life.

- Political issues both national and international, but also regional, and even the politics of small-town living. This is a theme that sits beneath much of what happens in New Mexican cinema, and is implicit in many of the stories.
- Disintegration – of society, of values, of morals, of institutions, of norms. This again is a key theme that is at the heart of most of the work in the latter half of the period. Social meltdown and the inability to react effectively to it runs through a number of the films and has crossed into the internationalised Mexican cinema.
- Sci-fi and new horror/thriller has become an emerging theme of the latter half of the period, possibly sparked off by the success of del Toro's *Cronos*, and its link to an historical staple of Mexican cinema.
- Sexual unfulfilment, and AIDS awareness. Both are 'difficult' subjects for a country mired in religious doctrine and superstitions.

As the movement heads towards the end of its second decade, an expectation would be for it to begin to founder or fade away. However, current trends would suggest that not only is it as strong as ever, but that it is once more evolving, with comedy becoming a prominent feature and costume drama emerging (a similar thing happened with the Cinema Déraciné movement in France towards the latter half of the 1990s).

Summary

ARRÁNCAME LA VIDA

Roberto Sneider's *Arráncame la Vida* (*Tear This Heart Out*) is a costume drama set in 1930s Mexico that offers an outstanding production design, and captures a spirit of the unchanging Mexico. A very different film from the documentary realism of many of the films of New Mexican cinema, it nevertheless shares many of the themes and certainly the production values and stylistic intent that mark out this movement as something interesting.

The film begins with the marriage of a young Catalina Guzmán (Ana Claudia Talancón) to Andrés Ascencio (Daniel Giménez Cacho), a charismatic general and city governor, who is significantly older than her. Immediately the spectator is placed in a position of having to deal with an enigma. She is consumed by the superficiality of his political world as he campaigns in the presidential race, a race he arrogantly assumes he will win, promising to make her the First Lady of his new Mexico.

continued

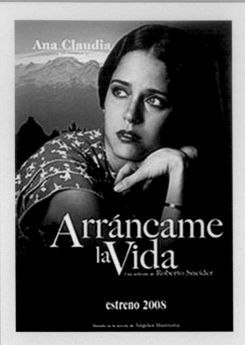

Figure 8.4 *Arráncame la Vida (Tear This Heart Out)* (Sneider, 2008).

Catalina discovers that Andrés has been having affairs with other women while married to her and has produced a number of illegitimate children from these illicit relationships. In revenge she too takes a lover, and then another, and it is at this point that the New Mexican cinema director becomes apparent, following a direction that is diametrically opposed to what would have happened in a traditional film where the wife would have remained long-suffering and faithful to her unfaithful husband.

Catalina finally falls in love with one of her lovers, an orchestra leader, the younger Carlos (Jose María de Tavira). He represents everything her husband is not: youth, vitality, rebellion, the new Mexico. Catalina has become empowered and self-determined, growing in strength from the relationship with someone whom she considers an equal. Indeed this could be seen as a political parable reflecting the fall of the Partido Revolucionario Institucional (PRI) and celebrating the rise of a new Mexico, one with something to say and something to be proud of.

Conclusion

There still remains a hunger for the quality of films that New Mexican cinema produces, and there is still a hunger on the part of the filmmakers to address the issues that are constantly emerging and evolving in their country. Unlike in many national cinemas, this movement has not become dominated by an 'old guard', the first of the New Mexican cinema directors clinging on desperately to their positions. Rather, through government incentive, through the Instituto Mexicano de Cinematografía (Mexican Film Institute, IMCINE), and through the film schools, Mexico has developed a culture that encourages the development of new talent to refresh the pool, and where established filmmakers work with aspiring ones to pass on skills and mentor them towards the same international success they have experienced.

It is this very sense of community and of Mexican nationhood that drives this movement forward and sees it continue to produce world-class films. New Mexican cinema proves that indigenous cinema can not only survive in the face of globalisation and Hollywood dominance, but that it can walk on to the world stage and stand shoulder to shoulder with the giants.

EXAM QUESTIONS ?

- To what extent do the stories depicted in the films you have studied offer comment on the society in which they were made?

- Explore how the themes highlighted in the films you have studied contribute to the creation of a distinctive national cinema.

Further Reading

De la Morte, S. (2006) *Cinemachismo: Masculinities and Sexualities in Mexican Film*. University of Texas
Haddu, M. (2007) *Contemporary Mexican Cinema 1989–1999*. Edwin Mellen Press
Hagerman, M (ed.) (2007) *Babel*. Taschen
Maciel, D. R. (1999) *Mexico's Cinema: A Century of Film and Filmmakers*. SR Books
Mora, C. J. (2005) *Mexican Cinema: Reflections of a Society, 1896–2004* (3rd edn). University of California Press
Noble, A. (2005) *Mexican National Cinema*. Taylor & Francis
Wood, J. (2006) *The Faber Book of Mexican Cinema*. Faber and Faber

Internet

http://terpconnect.umd.edu/~dwilt/mfb.html
The Mexican Film Resource Page with lots of links to other sites

http://www.imdb.com/video/screenplay/vi205879257/
Link to *Babel* trailer

9 GERMAN AND SOVIET CINEMAS OF THE 1920s

This chapter:

- considers general issues raised by studying films made in particular countries at specific historical moments
- offers a general indicative approach to films from Germany and the Soviet Union during the 1920s
- suggests ideas for approaching two case study films, one from each country

INFORMATION BOX

i

This chapter will be relevant to the section 'FM4 – World Cinema' in the WJEC's A level in Film Studies. It will be directly applicable to questions relating to 'German and Soviet cinemas of the 1920s' but you should note the particular requirements of this section of the syllabus. Notice in particular that you should be able to deal with two main films and have some idea of how the styles being considered might have been used in one further film.

Films mentioned:

As you work your way through this chapter you will need to watch at least some of the following films in full and at least short sequences from the others:

- *The Cabinet of Dr Caligari* (Wiene, 1919)
- *Nosferatu* (Murnau, 1922)
- *Metropolis* (Lang, 1926)
- *Strike* (Eisenstein, 1924)
- *Battleship Potemkin* (Eisenstein, 1925)

The historical moment

A simple consideration of the title of this chapter will give you a clear sense of the relevant time period. We are dealing with films made in the decade immediately after the First World War in two countries traumatically affected by that event. In Russia the war turned out to be the catalyst for a political revolution that transformed a country essentially organised along feudal lines into a communist state. In Germany the war meant that literally the whole population experienced the death of at least one relative, whether father, son, brother or uncle. In both countries the hardships experienced by men fighting on the front lines were by the end

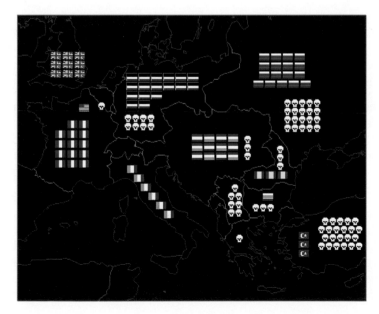

Figure 9.1 First World War losses. Reproduced by kind permission of Matthew White.

of the war to some extent mirrored by those endured at home where food supplies were at minimal levels, causing widespread starvation, disease and further deaths.

Films under consideration from this period need to be seen in relation to this context and are likely in some sense or other to reflect the historical moment. However, it is important not to make generalisations that are too sweeping or simplistically all-inclusive. Suggestions that a film 'has a theme of death' and this 'reflects Germany's experience of the First World War', first, tell us very little, second, neglect the complexity of responses that might be possible, and most importantly do not begin to deal with the details of the specific film in question that should be at the heart of any response.

ACTIVITY

- What do you know about this period in European history? Working with others if possible, try to build up a timeline of events in each country starting from any date you consider appropriate from 1900 to 1920 and concluding at any date you choose between 1930 and 1940. (It is likely that you will choose different dates to start and conclude your timelines for each country.)
- Research the historical detail behind the events within your chosen period for both Germany and Russia in a little more depth and then compare your timelines to those arrived at by another group that has been working on the same task. Explain why you have chosen to include particular events and outline your reasons for starting and ending your timelines at certain dates.

The categorisation of films

You will often see films made in Germany during this period referred to as 'German Expressionism', and a similar catch-all phrase, 'Soviet Montage', being used for Soviet films of the 1920s, but you should avoid categorising the films in too simplistic a way. You *should* work to identify general differences between German and Soviet films of the period and this will centre upon the particularly intense use of editing to be found in Soviet cinema, but make every effort to avoid simple categorisations.

Be aware that it may also be possible to find similarities as well as differences between films from the two countries made during this period. Thematically, for instance, you will find that in *Metropolis* (1926) Fritz Lang, the German director, and his fellow filmmakers are as intensely aware of the tensions between classes as are the Russian, Sergei Eisenstein, and those working with him on the films of the period. However, you should equally be concerned with the ways in which each director approaches this theme of class in their own distinctive ways and maybe how this reflects the different historical experiences of Germany and the Soviet Union.

At the same time you should also be looking to identify differences between films made within the same country and even between films attributed to the same director. For example, if you look at Eisenstein's *Strike* (1924) and *Battleship Potemkin* (1925) you will find similarities in terms of both style and thematic concern, but it will also be useful to remain alert to differences between these films; for instance, you could identify the range of uses that are made of comedy within *Strike* and then compare this to the extent that comedy is used in the later film. After making *Strike*, Eisenstein came to believe that this film was too theatrical and used too many comedy moments.

If you were to consider *Nosferatu* (1922) and *The Cabinet of Dr Caligari* (1919) you might notice, and give further consideration to, the way in which the director of *Nosferatu*, Friedrich Murnau, seems to have tried to escape the studio by filming on location, while Robert Wiene, who directed *The Cabinet of Dr Caligari*, was highly dependent upon set design within the staged space of the studio. The key question would be why each has chosen to use setting in the way they have and what each choice brings to the two films.

EXPRESSIONISM: this refers to the expression of the inner thoughts or emotions of the filmmaker or a character through the use of stylistic elements of film form. So, distorted shapes within the set design might be used to suggest, in some sense, a warped or perverted perspective on the world, and heavy shadows might be used to suggest the presence of darker aspects of human nature. The performance of actors (along with their make-up and clothing) can also become heavily stylised in order to further suggest psychological states. Clearly such heavy stylisation that moves towards symbolism is in direct opposition to the use of film to give a sense of photographic realism.

(It may well be that of the German films you consider you will come to see only *The Cabinet of Dr Caligari* as being fully expressionistic.)

MONTAGE: essentially this simply means to assemble a series of shots and so refers to the process of editing any film. Within the context of post-1917 Soviet cinema where the process of editing came to be so intensely linked to the creation of meaning, the term took on a slightly more specific use with the sequencing of shots being explored in especially intense ways (the common example given is the Odessa Steps sequence in *Battleship Potemkin*).

What you will see when you compare Soviet and German films from the 1920s is the way in which editing is quite simply a much more pronounced feature of film construction within the Russian films. Soviet filmmakers began to explore the ways in which each shot gained intensified meaning from its relationship to the shots deliberately placed before and after it. Eisenstein famously commented on the way in which it was in the clash (or tension) between shots that meaning was created. He suggested that placing two shots, A and B, together did not simply result in the creation of some amalgam AB but the emergence of X or Y, something new and larger than AB.

(Eisenstein was also, incidentally, interested in the way in which tensions could be created between areas of the frame within the composition of single shots. So, for instance, you could consider the ways in which different parts within the composition of single shots in the tenement attack sequence in *Strike* work in relation to each other. Clearly in this particular instance one of the reasons he has chosen to have such 'busy' shots is to give a sense of the chaos of the moment.)

ACTIVITY

- Working with others if possible, analyse the sequences of shots used in the scene on the Odessa Steps in *Battleship Potemkin* and the tenement attack in *Strike*. Decide where you are going to consider each scene to start and finish, time each scene, and then try to work out how many shots are used in each.
- Focus on trying to put into words the effect of each shot in relation to the shot that precedes it and also in relation to the shot that follows. Discuss this with others if possible, and see if you agree on potential meanings being created. (Be prepared to recognise that if someone sees something differently to you it may not be a question of one of you being right and the other wrong but that there may be a series of potential meanings contained in the clash between these shots.)
- You may like to find similar length scenes in German films from the period and play these alongside or after the Soviet film extracts to compare the use that is made of editing in each.

Case study

STRIKE (1924)

[Director/screenwriter: Sergei Eisenstein. Cinematography: Edouard Tisse and Vassili Khvato.]

Figure 9.2 *Strike* (Eisenstein, 1924).

Political background

This film, set in Tsarist Russia in 1912, was made in support of the Bolshevik government that had come to power in Russia after the 1917 Revolution. It is clearly made as propaganda for the new regime and puts forward a strongly Marxist message.

continued

ACTIVITY

- What is Marxism? Working in small groups if possible, research this political belief and agree on a short definition of no more than 100 words.
- What is communism and how does this relate to Marxism? Make sure you discuss, and if necessary debate, the relationship between these two terms.
- What is capitalism? Working in small groups if possible, research this political ideology/economic term and agree on a short definition of no more than 100 words.

Strike looks back to what it portrays very obviously as the brutality of pre-Revolution days when any attempt by workers to defend the simplest of rights for themselves was violently put down by the police, secret services and army on behalf of the wealthy industrialists and aristocratic upper classes. It is then a strongly political film with a very definite ideological standpoint. See, for example, how the wealth, space and grandeur that surround the industrialists or capitalists (as well as their clothing) compare with the poverty, confined space and basic furnishing to be found in the workers' homes.

ACTIVITY

- In small groups choose a recent mainstream Hollywood film that you have all seen and decide if there are any ways in which this could be seen to be making political points. List the political ideas contained in your chosen film and see if as a result you can identify a general political stance for the film.
- Could every film be seen as being political? List any films you have seen that you believe not to be political. Discuss your ideas on this within the group if possible.

Strike within the context of 1920s Europe

The title of this film in itself announces a particularly worrying form of worker action for those people with financial stakes in industrial concerns across Europe during the period; the concept of 'striking' is put forward as an imperative (almost a command). So, simply in itself the title creates a powerful impact that would be bound to antagonise capitalist governments in 1920s Europe faced with the fear that the recent Russian Revolution could lead to further revolts by workers in other countries. Hence, for example, in Britain this film and others from the Soviet Union were not shown for years other than in film societies with private (middle-class) memberships.

ACTIVITY

Find out when these Soviet films were finally approved for general release in Britain. Having seen *Strike*, were you surprised that it was banned in Britain? What does this tell you about life in Britain during this period?

The use of children

In the film the scheming of the factory bosses, the underhand tactics of the secret police and the brutality of the army defeat the strike, but we are never in any doubt where Eisenstein's sympathies are to be found. As evidence of his position, you could consider, for example, the use he makes of children within the film. There is, most shockingly, the child being dropped from the tenement walkway (see how this child and the idea of people falling are introduced through carefully organised intercutting in this scene); but immediately prior to this there is also the child playing around the hooves of the Cossack horses and then (in a carefully composed shot) sitting in the foreground as the struggle ensues in the background. Earlier, there is another child playing happily with a father who feels the strike to be a holiday before the same child is kicked away only a few scenes later as the hardship of having no income makes itself felt. This thematic concern with children and the use of their innocence in order to emphasise the brutality of the Tsarist regime is something that is also taken up in *Battleship Potemkin* in the famous Odessa Steps sequence. One possible study of the Odessa Steps sequence would simply involve analysing the way in which children and the idea of their innocence and vulnerability are employed.

continued

GERMAN AND SOVIET CINEMAS OF THE 1920S

169

INFORMATION BOX

This is a good opportunity to begin to consider in more depth the issue of the relationship between politics and film. Does all film fulfil a political role of some sort? Does this question centre on issues of representation: is the way in which the world is presented to us always inevitably giving a political perspective on that world?

ACTIVITY

■ Identify ways in which you feel Eisenstein makes clear his own perspective on the events he portrays. Make a list of these aspects of the film which may include elements of style as well as content.

(In fact, of course, it is always vital to recognise the way in which it is the combination of style and content that creates meaning; so, for instance, the decision to portray the factory boss as fat, smoking a cigar and laughing and then film him in close-up to emphasise these facts creates the idea of self-interested, uncaring bosses.)

■ If you have had time to watch *Battleship Potemkin* (in full or through the use of extracts) identify ways in which Eisenstein makes his 'take' on events clear here. In particular, look out for similarities and differences between the two films.

Strike and 'the Hollywood standard'

Eisenstein uses a series of approaches to film construction, each of which challenges the expectations of any reader brought up on mainstream American film. He thereby challenges what has, even as early as this in film history, become the Hollywood standard dominating filmmaking around the world; and in doing this he also challenges the capitalist system that this approach to filmmaking is seen to embody. Implicitly, he recognises film-making as being a political act that involves representing the world and one's understanding of the world in an inevitably political way.

Hollywood movies have traditionally tended to use a narrative structure that focuses attention on the individual, creating heroes who resolve problematic situations in such a way as to restore order out of chaos. The audience is encouraged to identify with these individual heroes, most obviously as a result of the amount of screen-time spent following their trials and tribulations.

ACTIVITY

- Think of several recent Hollywood films that you have seen and ask yourself whether this pattern could be applied to each of them. Who was the hero? What problems did he or she have to resolve? Did he or she succeed in restoring order? How could this basic narrative structure be seen to reinforce capitalism?

INFORMATION BOX

Understanding how such a structure could be seen to work towards reinforcing a particular ideology is one thing; deciding whether you agree that this is actually what happens is another. Do mainstream Hollywood films work to reinforce an understanding of the world that supports capitalism, or 'the American way of life' (whatever that might be)? Or, do the mainstream Hollywood films that you know actually challenge key capitalist ideas? Or, are these sorts of questions simply inappropriate because watching Hollywood films is actually about simple escapist pleasures? Decide for yourself how you feel about this and, as always, try to discuss your views with others.

Eisenstein by direct contrast and in opposition to Hollywood-style films emphasises the movement of social forces rather than the psychological make-up of individual characters; his film is built around the struggle between the workers and the industrial forces of capitalism. Individual personalities are not placed in the foreground by Eisenstein, but instead the whole social group (or class)

continued

of the workers is presented as a collective 'hero' while the capitalists *en masse* are seen as the 'villain' within the narrative structure. Characters are for the most part neither named nor focused upon in such a way as to enable the audience to identify with an individual and his or her struggle. Instead, actors work to portray character types, or what are suggested to be typical representatives of particular social classes; for example, the rich factory owners who sit around being waited upon in palatial surroundings while enjoying bizarrely indulgent (if not debauched) tastes, or the defiant worker who, despite recognising what the consequences will be for himself, refuses to betray his comrades.

Documentary style

Strike can in places take on the appearance of a documentary record of a historical event rather than a fictional narrative (this is in strong contrast to both the Hollywood norm *and* the expressionism of *The Cabinet of Dr Caligari*). When we glimpse the domestic intimacy in the homes of the striking factory workers, for example, as they are able to experience for the first time the joys of having time to play with their children, we are given that feeling of detached 'fly-on-the-wall' observation that we associate with the documentary. One of the reasons this happens is perhaps that we do not have a single central protagonist with whom we strongly identify.

But notice as well how the political is never far away. If we are to fully appreciate sequences like these in workers' homes we have to understand not only the extent of the pleasures of these moments of parenthood but also the oppressive nature of a system that never allows what would now be called 'quality time' as a possibility for workers.

ACTIVITY

- Can you think of any mainstream (or independent) fictional films you know that use documentary, or documentary-like footage?

(*Bloody Sunday* (Greengrass, 2002) might provide an interesting parallel text. In this film we do have two characters we are asked to identify with in a relatively strong way but, as with *Strike*, the main emphasis is on the roles played by large social groups.)

Use of intrusive images

At other points Eisenstein uses visual metaphors that immediately work to destroy the 'illusion of reality' that is so central to the Hollywood approach but which also form a marked contrast to his own documentary-style moments. For example, shots of police spies are intercut with images of animals such as an owl and a fox that it is visually suggested they resemble. And, most famously, the final massacre of the surrounded workers by armed troops is paralleled by shots of the bloodletting slaughter of a cow in an abattoir. The first set of animal images is used for comic effect in direct contrast to the seriousness of the abattoir footage, but in both cases what we are being shown is clearly anti-naturalistic in that these animals are not to be found within the imagined scene itself but are inserted by the film-makers as a form of commentary on the action. They break us out of the apparently 'real' scene and force us to think about what they might imply.

These sorts of shots used by Eisenstein have no place within any realistic representation of either the police spies or the violent onslaught on the strikers but work to create meaning above and beyond realism. At the same time, as suggested above, the effect of these two examples is very different: the first (showing the spies as various animals) works at the level of humour and ridicule; the second functions at the pitch of Shakespearean tragedy.

Analysing a scene

The most shocking scene for many viewers is the one mentioned earlier in which a small child is held aloft by a soldier on horseback and then dropped from a high walkway between the tenement buildings. This is made all the more effective by the fact that we have been alerted to the idea of the innocence of children just a few shots before as they are shown happily playing while the chaos of the struggle with the soldiers goes on around them.

continued

■ Working in pairs if possible, return to this sequence involving the invasion of the workers' tenement blocks and analyse it once more.

■ How does Eisenstein make us feel the power and dominance of the soldiers? Which images does he use to lead us towards the climactic moment of the dropping of the child? What is the effect of having such a complex of walkways; in other words, why do you think he might have chosen this location? Which shots does he hold longer than others, and why?

Use of editing

Filmmaking techniques that are carefully manipulative of audience response are clearly being used all the time here, but always it seems in the service not simply of generating response but of creating meaning for the spectator: conveying the unfair, unjust, brutal nature of the Tsarist regime is the overriding, ever-present aim. Editing is clearly seen as a major means of organising the form of the film in order to create meaning and not simply as a technique to be used to serve the narrative or plot progression.

Eisenstein as we have suggested is not interested in maintaining the illusion of reality, that concern which dominates the thinking of filmmakers attempting to create the standard Hollywood product. Instead, he wants to actively seek out ways of creating the maximum collision from shot to shot and sequence to sequence: the whole film is constructed around the juxtaposition of shots that comment upon each other. His interest to a large extent is given its clearest expression through his concept of montage: the arrangement of shots in such a way that the clash between them creates a new, enhanced meaning. Following the idea of this film as propaganda, the chosen style could be seen as an attempt to dogmatically force certain perspectives on to the spectator. More positively it could also be viewed as an effort to make the spectator active rather than passive in terms of intellectual engagement with the visual images flashing before her.

ACTIVITY

- From what you have read about this film and seen of it, why do you think you have been asked to watch it? What aspects of filmmaking has it required you to think about more carefully? List as many reasons as possible.

INFORMATION BOX

Here again it is worth flagging up the importance of returning to reread case studies like the one above and to rethink your understanding of the ideas involved as your work on film progresses. By now you may already have begun to question in a little more depth the whole notion of documentary, for example. In *Strike* Eisenstein uses a documentary-like style in places and in a sense the substance of what he is dealing with is non-fictional, since it is based on historical events. To what extent would Eisenstein argue he was documenting what had happened under the Tsars and to what extent would he agree he was creating a fiction?

Case study

THE CABINET OF DR CALIGARI (1919)

[Director: Robert Wiene. Screenwriters: Hans Janowitz and Carl Mayer. Art designers: Hermann Warm, Walter Rohrig and Walter Reimann. Cast: Werner Krauss (Caligari), Conrad Veidt (Cesare), Lil Dagover (Jane), Friedrich Feher (Francis).]

continued

Figure 9.3 *The Cabinet of Dr Caligari* (Wiene, 1919).

ACTIVITY

■ Watch this film and, as you do so, make quick notes about anything that with your knowledge of film studies strikes you as interesting. Areas to focus upon might include setting, costume and props, cinematography, editing, narrative, and characters. Ideally, try to work with a few other people so that you can each take one or two areas to concentrate upon and then pool your thoughts after having watched the film.

■ What was it all about? Individually, summarise the storyline in 200 to 250 words. Compare your summary with those arrived at by other people. Have some people emphasised different aspects, or has everyone agreed on the essential points?

■ What was it all about? Individually, list what you would see as being the key themes and ideas in the film. Compare your list with those arrived at by other people. Has everyone included essentially the same ideas? Debate and discuss any differences.

■ How might this film be seen within the context of the time and place in which it was made? Returning to the history of Germany in the period might give some clues, but hopefully you will also have ideas of your own. Discuss your ideas with other people.

Is this an examination of a psychological world?

One way of understanding this film is to suggest that as the audience we are confined in the central character's world of insanity and as a result see just what he sees: distorted perspectives, eerie lights and ominous shadows, a sharp, angular, thrusting world of fears. From this perspective the sets are used to convey the thoughts of Francis and to lay bare this character's emotions. The town of Holstenwall is a strange, nightmare-like place where the buildings have pointed roofs, the windows and doors are out of kilter, and curtains seem to hang over characters as a barely perceived threat. We open with Francis about to tell his story to an inmate in an asylum and close with him still confined in a space within the asylum surrounded by characters resembling figures from his dark imaginings.

Is this an examination of the nature of the world or of human nature?

Another way of looking at the film might be to see those who are murdered, along with Cesare and Francis himself, as victims of Caligari. He manipulates the helpless Cesare to carry out his wishes and, as the director of the asylum, has Francis totally within his power at the end. Frustratingly for Francis, if we take his perspective he alone knows who is responsible for the murders taking place in the world but is powerless to expose the villain; and worryingly for us as audience the character with the role of hero is unable to defeat evil and restore order. In this reading, Caligari becomes an embodiment of evil and the film takes on added symbolic power in its ability to talk about the nature of evil within the wider world. The film critic Siegfried Kracauer, who wrote a book on German cinema of the period entitled *From Caligari to Hitler*, suggested that films from this period had been able to project forward from the contemporary state of Germany in the 1920s to foretell the monstrous evil that was to come. Certainly, it would seem to be important to remember that when *The Cabinet of Dr Caligari* was made,

continued

the First World War and the horror of the trenches had only just ended (and in a powerfully real sense was still present in the shape of the physically and psychologically maimed casualties to be found on the streets of Germany). Asylums (and indeed the streets of the cities) would have been full of people who continued to 'live' the horrors of what human beings were able to inflict on others.

Undeniably, ideas of death and the bringing of death are at the heart of this film, as they are, for example, at the centre of *Nosferatu*. Once we have seen the film we can no longer avoid seeing the simple 'cabinet' of the title as in fact a threatening, if not frightening, image of a coffin. And, if we have seen *Nosferatu* we will be aware of how this very same image occurs time and again in this film. (There is, for example, one startling image of Orlok entering Harker's room in the middle of the night in which the door opens like the lid of a coffin.)

Logic and reading film

Logically, with an entranced Jane wandering through the opening scene in *Caligari* and Cesare standing in the asylum at the end, the main story has to be seen as arising from within Francis' insane imagination. This is clearly a difficulty for any reading that tends towards seeing the insanity as part and parcel of the character of Caligari, and yet it is not always the most reasoned account of events that we take away with us from a film. The power of some of the central images involving Caligari and Cesare (along with the final image of Caligari looking up in close-up in his role as director of the asylum) live on in our minds in such a way as to imaginatively carry forward the original concept of the writers Janowitz and Mayer, which was to present an examination of all-powerful authority as essentially evil.

ACTIVITY

■ How should we read, or understand, *The Cabinet of Dr Caligari*? Discuss your ideas on this once more with other people before writing an essay-style response (1200 words maximum).

■ Exchange essays with the people with whom you have previously discussed this issue and read each others' responses. Make sure to look for both similarities and differences to your own piece of work.

What should be the nature of film?

This was an early film that attempted to release mainstream cinema from any need to be involved in the straightforward re-creation of reality. The set design and the movement of the actors deliberately attempted to look alien and unreal. The aim it seems was to create an impression of a psychological state or the psychological world rather than any sense of the physical reality of a particular place, and perhaps in doing so to suggest the 'real' underlying nature of the world as a place of fear and dark forces. Film, it is being suggested by the filmmakers, can do things other than simply offer the photographic re-creation of life.

ACTIVITY

- What should film be used for? Is it best seen as a medium ideally suited to the photographic re-creation of reality or can it legitimately be used in other ways? Discuss this with others if possible.

- Consider actual examples of films you have seen recently or films you have studied, and discuss the ways in which they have used the medium.

- Have your views on this changed in any way since you began studying film?

Interestingly, the stylistic use of visual distortions continues into the final scenes within the asylum, and this raises further questions about how we should interpret the whole film, since even as we realise we have been hearing the story of a (supposed) madman we are still seeing the world as a nightmarish reality. Notice, too, the way in which if we identify ourselves with the listener in the opening scene, by the end we find we have been identifying ourselves with a person who is insane or, even worse, sane but trapped within the insanity of the asylum.

continued

ACTIVITY

Compare the techniques relating to *mise-en-scène* (and cinematography and editing, if you wish) that are employed here with those used in *Nosferatu*. What are the similarities and differences between the two films with regard to these areas of film construction?

Producers and audiences

Since the First World War, Germany had found difficulty distributing films abroad, since British and French exhibitors were refusing to show their products. However, French film enthusiasts acquired prints of this film and held screenings, so that eventually demand for the film was such that the French government lifted its ban and *Caligari* opened in France in 1922. What this reminds us of is that even this early in film history, filmmaking is a business that is being operated as an industry and is in some respects at least driven by audience demand. It may even be that one of the reasons Erich Pommer, the chief executive at the studio responsible for the film, Decla-Bioscop, accepted *Caligari* as a project was that he recognised that its novelty would be one means of generating interest abroad and perhaps as a result opening restricted markets to German products.

ACTIVITY

■ Try to find out a little more about German expressionist film from this period. Were there many other expressionist films? Was *Caligari* the first such film?

Genre and narrative structure

This film could also be viewed as an early horror film; it employs certain plot conventions that would be used and reused in later films in the genre. There is, for example:

■ the evil doctor/scientist who commits murder by manipulating a 'monster' who he controls;

- the mysterious fair peopled by freakish characters that comes to a town bringing terror;
- the 'monster' who, fairy-story-like, falls in love with a beautiful and innocent young girl;
- angry townspeople who, mob-like, chase the monster from their community.

It may indeed be worth considering the extent to which this film is actually doing no more than committing to celluloid horror stories that have always been part of folklore. (This may be worth further consideration in relation to *Nosferatu*.)

From the point of view of narrative structure the most interesting aspect of the film is that which has already been touched upon above. If we see Francis as being insane, then the framing of the central story by the episodes in the asylum could be seen as reassuring; order has been restored in the sense that the murders and the accompanying evil were all simply figments of the imagination of a madman. However, if Francis is seen as the hero and the close-up of the director's face towards the end of the film is the triumph of evil, then the film as a story has not performed its ritualistic taming of the horrors of the world, and the restoration of the world as a place of safety has not been achieved.

ACTIVITY

- Compare the genre and narrative structure employed here with that used in *Nosferatu*. What are the similarities and differences between the two films with regard to these two areas of film construction?

- List your ideas and compare them with those that other people have arrived at.

Expressionism

Janowitz and Mayer wrote a script containing a bleak, pessimistic view of postwar German society and showing authority as at least untrustworthy and potentially murderous. They also apparently put forward the idea that the sets for the film should be created from painted canvases. The designers Warm, Rohrig and Reimann then created both interior and exterior sets that used twisted shapes and sharp angles in order to suggest distorted perspectives.

continued

The performances of the actors were integrated into this overall approach, with both Krauss (Caligari) and Veidt (Cesare, the sleepwalker) moving in distinctive ways that suggest they are part of this strange world. Veidt with his tall, thin, angular appearance moves slowly, almost gliding along walls, while Krauss is hunched and moves in short, sharp steps. The use of the eyes by both actors is also interesting, and you may like to consider what each is suggesting at various moments through this most expressive aspect of acting.

ACTIVITY

Working with one other person if possible, see what you can find out about Expressionism as a movement in art and the theatre in Germany during this period. What were the features of the style? How was it employed? Why was it used? (Perhaps you will be able to come up with your own theories as to why it might have been a favoured style of the period.)

ACTIVITY

- Watch the whole of this film once more; and then, with a group of others if possible, choose one sequence of about six minutes to analyse in detail.

- Spend time discussing how your chosen sequence works in terms of its use of *mise-en-scène*, cinematography and editing.

- Individually write a commentary (1000–1200 words) discussing the ways in which one or two of these areas of film construction work to create meaning and generate audience response in your chosen sequence.

- Exchange your finished pieces with each other and read as many responses from other people as possible, noting similarities and differences to your own work.

- Compare ways in which German and Soviet films of the period use visual means to create tension and suspense.

- Is German and/or Soviet cinema of the 1920s better seen as a cinema fascinated by victims or a cinema engaging with ideas of oppression?

- In the films you have studied from this period, which features of film construction create the most powerful impression: cinematography, editing or *mise-en-scène*?

- In what ways do you believe it has been worth studying films from this period? Make sure you refer to details from the films themselves to support your ideas.

- What are some of the similarities and/or differences in the ways in which conflict is represented in the films you have studied?

- Consider some of the ways in which performance and movement are used in the films you have studied to convey themes and ideas.

- Is it necessary to put these films into the context of the social and political upheavals of the 1920s in Germany and the Soviet Union in order to properly understand them?

Further Reading

Abrams, N., Bell, I. and Udris, J. (2001) *Studying Film*. Arnold (Chapter 14)

Gillespie, D. (2000) *Early Soviet Cinema*. Wallflower (Chapter 2)

Hayward, S. (2005) *Cinema Studies: The Key Concepts*. Routledge

Kracauer, S. (1992) 'From Caligari to Hitler' in Mast, G., Cohen, M. and Braudy, L. (eds) *Film Theory and Criticism: Introductory Readings*. Oxford University Press

Lacey, N. (2005) *Introduction to Film*. Palgrave Macmillan (Chapter 5)

Marriott, J. (2004) *Horror Films*. Virgin Books

Thompson, K. and Bordwell, D. (2003) *Film History: An Introduction*. McGraw-Hill (Chapters 5 and 6)

10 SURREALISM

In this chapter you will study:

- Surrealism as an art movement
- what are Surrealist films?
- the relationship between fantasy and Surrealist films
- cinematic techniques in Surrealism and fantasy film
- narrative experimentation
- Gothic horror

The principal films discussed in this section are *The Phantom of Liberty* (Luis Buñuel, 1974) and *Alice* (Jan Svankmajer, 1988). There is also discussion of other relevant films that you could use in this topic.

Along with the principal films, you will also need to study one or two further films but in less depth.

Some suggestions for supplemental films:

Within this topic area you can study a maximum of two Buñuel films including the principal film. These could include:

L'Age d'Or (Buñuel/Dali, 1928)

Un Chien Andalou (Buñuel/Dali, 1930)

That Obscure Object of Desire (Buñuel, 1977)

Meshes of the Afternoon (Maya Deren, 1947) (for a discussion of this film see Chapter 17)

Orphée (Cocteau, 1929), a mix of fantasy and Surrealist filmmaking

Last Year at Marienbad (Alain Resnais, 1962). Often described as Surrealist influenced due to its experimental narrative structure, this would provide a good opportunity to debate what is and what is not a Surrealist film.

What is Surrealism?

The term *Surrealism* is now often used to refer to something which is unusual or odd. The original use of the term – and the one which makes sense in understanding the focus films – has a very specific meaning and objective which goes back to the beginning of the twentieth century. Central to Surrealism is the belief that reality is not orderly and logical but is in fact a collection of coincidences and chance occurrences. The only way to experience this 'true' reality is by allowing the unconscious mind free expression, rather than being stifled by the rational, conscious mind. Surrealist artists – in writing, painting, film – attempt to force the spectator to acknowledge the superior reality of the unconscious through shocking them with their art. Surrealist art must not be planned but must grow and develop unconsciously, rather than being designed to adhere to the artistic 'rules' and norms of society (a form of self-censorship). The resulting art work may initially look like a mess but the Surrealists believed that once viewers had overcome their prejudices – their belief in convention – then they could share the Surrealists' world. Central to the idea of the unplanned art was automatic writing and improvisation in poetry and painting.

The main problem in defining Surrealism is that – not surprisingly – it involves continual contradictions. Surrealists wanted to rediscover a childlike, uninhibited or 'primitive' response to the world through their art but they were also attracted to the scientific, rationalist research into the unconscious undertaken by Sigmund Freud. Freud asserted that unconscious thoughts – often revealed in dreams – can explain human behaviour, and he used dream analysis to reveal these thoughts. These ideas were very influential on Surrealism, driving the Surrealists' desire to connect with primitive impulses and to express themselves freely. Freud's work on the analysis of dreams linked to their belief in 'dream logic'. Rather than being a world of illogical events, the unconscious mind – as revealed in dreams – had a logic all of its own, different from the seemingly rational, conscious world. For the Surrealists, art can never be produced by 'wide-awake reason'; there must be a connection to the unconscious.

Surrealists were not only interested in the individual unconscious but also had political beliefs and aims. In an example of another contradictory aspect of the movement, they wanted to both liberate the creative unconscious and develop a plan of collective political action to overthrow what they saw as the corrupt authorities represented by church and state. In the late 1920s the Surrealist group entered collaboration with the Communist Party which led to disputes within both groups about the aims and nature of their political engagement. The Surrealist manifesto has a greater affinity with anarchism as a political movement, and this influence is evident in the work of Surrealist filmmakers.

INFORMATION BOX – SURREALISM 1924–1935 *i*

Although Surrealism, due to its subsequent cultural influence, cannot be limited to just one particular time and place, the movement was founded in France by a group of artists who had previously been associated with the Dada movement. (Dada was an artistic and cultural movement whose members emphasised the randomness of everyday life and developed a nihilistic point of view about the world – and art.) Surrealism was not just an artistic and literary movement but also a philosophy and a way of life. Despite being such a wide-ranging phenomenon, it was also a carefully organised and tightly controlled movement. Unlike other artistic movements of the early twentieth century the Surrealists were organised like a political party with hierarchies and a leader – André Breton – who was nicknamed the Pope of Surrealism.

The term *Surrealism* was defined by Breton in his first Surrealist Manifesto in 1924: 'Surrealism rests in the belief of the superior reality of certain forms of association neglected before; in the omnipotence of the dream and in the disinterested play of thought'.

Despite the careful organisation of the movement, there is no one dominant Surrealist style. Those art forms that are recognised as Surrealist include automatic writing through free association – 'the disinterested play of thought' (it is debatable how 'automatic' this work was; Breton later admitted to careful editing in his writing), and visual representations of the unconscious through the use of blots, blobs and fluid-like forms as in the work of Miro. The most famous form of Surrealist art is that developed by Salvador Dali and René Magritte which used the unexpected and shocking juxtaposition of unrelated images. The aim was again to represent the true reality of the unconscious which has its own logic; in recognising it the viewer would be able to share in this freedom of expression.

To look at works by Dali, Magritte and other Surrealist painters go to: www.tate.org.uk and click on Tate Collection.

Surrealist film

Surrealist film developed out of the experiments in Surrealist painting, sculpture and literature. It was specifically designed as an 'art cinema', reliant on private patronage and screened at artists' gatherings. This was an isolated movement which, due to its radical ideas, was designed to shock audiences. Two of the first – and most famous – of the Surrealist films are *Un Chien Andalou* (Buñuel and Dali, 1928) and *L'Age d'Or* (Buñuel, 1930) (for further discussion of *Un Chien Andalou* see Chapter 17).

The Surrealists' interest in cinema was shared by other avant-garde (see key term below) art movements of the period. Film was seen as the perfect form with which to capture the new post-First World War society as it was modern and technological. Cinema was seen as an art form which could explore desire and fantasy; it did not have to be limited by the restrictions of capturing everyday reality. The Surrealists found these expressions of uncontrolled desire in slapstick comedies (Chaplin, Keaton, Keystone Cops in the silent era; a contemporary equivalent would be Jim Carrey in the *Pet Detective* films and *The Mask*), where impossible events happened as normal, and also in horror films such as *Nosferatu* and the crime genre. The majority of these films were Hollywood genre films rather than examples of European art cinema which might have been more expected. This is

Figure 10.1 *L'Age d'Or* (Buñuel/Dali, 1928) – a famous Surrealist film.

another example of the way European, experimental cinema and Hollywood are inextricably linked (See New Wave, German and Soviet cinema).

The use of film as a Surrealist form again reveals contradictions in their ideas. In some ways film is ideally suited to a Surrealist aesthetic; the editing process is a form of juxtaposition which is central to the Surrealist approach of contrasting unrelated images. In the 1920s film was not yet established as a realist form, so there was room for experimentation and non-narrative films. The main obstacle was that film takes a great deal of preparation and planning – it can never be 'automatic' or unconscious.

AVANT-GARDE: taken from military terminology, *avant-garde* became an accepted term for describing art which was experimental, innovative and which challenged the artistic norms of the day. Although the term may be used to describe artists at any period since the beginning of the twentieth century, it specifically refers to a group of movements which developed during and after the First World War (1914–1918) in Europe. These included Futurism, Abstraction, Cubism and Dada.

Although routinely referred to as an avant-garde movement, the Surrealists were at odds with the aims of the more purely artistic movements – wanting to pursue social and political action as well.

Characteristics of Surrealist film

Surrealist films can be identified as:

- anti-narrative
- anti-cause and effect
- anti-rationality.

For example, in *L'Age d'Or* a cow stands on a woman's bed, advertising images come to life, and a man throws a series of objects out of a window including a giraffe and a priest. These inexplicable images – particularly the last – are clearly references to the ridiculous nature of slapstick comedy which the Surrealists admired. As with other movements studied in this section, the most striking characteristic is the experimentation with conventional – classic – narrative and the film language which developed along with it such as continuity editing. Rather than a seamless, logical movement from shot to shot and scene to scene, Surrealist films deliberately break these connections.

The Surrealist relationship to Hollywood cinema – like that of other European film movements – was characterised by a mixture of admiration and subversion. At the time of the early Surrealist films, Hollywood was just beginning its domination of European cinema in terms of film style and distribution. The conventions of Hollywood filmmaking – genre, classic narrative, continuity editing – were not yet fixed, allowing an experimentation in form in Hollywood as well as in Europe. In the 1920s France, Germany, Italy and Britain all had strong film industries producing popular genre films and art cinema (e.g. expressionism and montage). In the period of silent cinema (sound was introduced in Hollywood in 1927, quickly followed by Europe) directors were freer to move between film industries to work, without the obstacles of different spoken languages (e.g. Hitchcock worked in Germany, F. W. Murnau in Hollywood). Therefore while Surrealist cinema is certainly experimental in narrative form it is helpful to remember that the rules of filmmaking were not yet as firmly established as they were by the 1960s and the period of New Wave cinema. The classic Hollywood style was fixed with the introduction of sound which limited the possibilities for experimentation and led to the perception of an opposition between Hollywood and European cinema.

The techniques of Surrealist filmmaking were a way of expressing the logic of dreams and the unconscious – they are not a random sequence of events. As with other forms of Surrealist art the aim of the films was to provoke a response in the audience. This was done in the following ways:

■ Teasing the audience by encouraging them to make connections in the film which aren't there – a frustrating process. For example, *Un Chien Andalou* begins with the familiar inter-title 'Once upon a time' followed by 'Eight years later'. These become increasingly confusing as the film develops because the filmmaker disrupts our expectations about time in film: 'Around 3 o'clock in the morning', 'Sixteen years ago', 'In spring', and so on.
■ Juxtaposing unexpected images to disturbing effect – probably the most famous is the sequence at the beginning of *Un Chien Andalou* where a man is shown sharpening his razor – presumably in preparation for shaving – and then uses it to slit the eyeball of a woman who remains still and uncomplaining. (If you haven't seen this sequence you can watch it on the website *Chaotic Cinema: Surreal and Cult Films* at http://wayney.pwp.blueyonder.co.uk which also contains information on a wide range of other Surrealist films.)

- The use of a variety of filmic techniques – such as linking devices – rather than letting one form dominate. These include dissolves, superimposition of images, and also the use of continuity editing and motivated cutting. For example, in the eyeball scene mentioned above, the shock relies partly on the use of continuity editing which sets up the space of the scene very clearly and tricks us into believing that an eyeball is being slit open. There is also the use of discontinuities in editing; again in *Un Chien Andalou* a woman locks a man out of her room only to turn around and find him standing behind her.
- The lack of explanation for the actions of the characters. In conventional film such bizarre events could be explained through dreams and hallucinations – Surrealists rejected this emphasis on character motivation as it would only reinforce conventional expectations about human behaviour. The emphasis on character motivation and psychological explanation is dominant in Hollywood – and much other – cinema, making this refusal to explain an individual's behaviour one of the most disturbing aspects of Surrealist film for contemporary audiences. In popular genre it is probably only the horror film which – sometimes – has a killer without a motive who is seen as the most frightening kind.
- Emphasising the collision of scenes of sexual desire, violence, strange humour, blasphemy and social satire rather than a linear narrative with plot and character development.

The overall aim of this 'free-form' style (the closest approximation to automatic writing) was to reflect the workings of the unconscious and to provoke the spectator into an instinctive response rather than a learnt, conventional one.

INFORMATION BOX – EXPERIMENTAL FILM AND THE AUDIENCE *i*

As with other forms of experimental film discussed, the aim of Surrealist film was to create a direct response in the audience – one which would continue outside of the cinema and affect the audience's view of society. In this aspect Surrealism was originally a radical, even revolutionary, art movement, attacking what the members of the group saw as the hypocrisy of contemporary society. This attack was aimed at the powerful groups – the government, the church, the education system – and the way they controlled and regulated human behaviour. For Surrealists, throwing off these conventional ways of thinking and behaving and instead responding to primitive impulses could lead to revolution. As with other experimental film movements such as Soviet montage, German Expressionism and the French New Wave, the Surrealists believed that film was an extremely powerful medium which could provoke a direct response in the audience – a belief shared with propagandists.

Buñuel and Surrealist film

Surrealists used a variety of film techniques in a complex way. Rather than reject all forms of mainstream film they used elements of conventional narrative construction, such as character and continuity editing, to create a familiar world for the audience so that its disruption would be even more disorientating. This technique may be seen as another way of representing dreams which are often a mix of the familiar and the strange. This use of some forms of realism was central to resolving the contradictions of Surrealists' aims – the emphasis on primitive response and organised, political action – and is characteristic of Luis Buñuel's work. For Buñuel, Surrealism was an explicitly political movement:

> **All of us were supporters of a certain concept of revolution, and although the surrealists didn't consider themselves terrorists, they were constantly fighting a society they despised. The real purpose of surrealism was not to create a new literary, artistic or even philosophical movement, but to explode the social order, to transform life itself.**

(Luis Buñuel, My Last Breath)

Case study
THE PHANTOM OF LIBERTY (LUIS BUÑUEL, 1974)

The Phantom of Liberty was Buñuel's penultimate film and forms the centre-piece of a loose trilogy which includes *The Discreet Charm of the Bourgeoisie* (1972) and *That Obscure Object of Desire* (1977). By the 1970s Buñuel was recognised as a great auteur with an international reputation but he retained the social and political attacks which had always been central to his work. Fame and recognition did mean bigger budgets, a more polished look to the films and the involvement of European and international stars – Catherine Deneuve in *Belle de Jour* (1967), Fernando Rey and Carole Boquet, a former model and the 'face' of Chanel perfume, in *That Obscure Object of Desire*, and Monica Vitti in *The Phantom of Liberty*.

continued

Figure 10.2 *The Phantom of Liberty* (Luis Buñuel, 1974).

ACTIVITY

Many of the experimental and/or political films we have looked at in the World Cinema (and in examples of National Cinema) section are low budget and do not use stars. Buñuel's final films were produced and distributed within the mainstream French film industry with well-known, often glamorous stars and relatively high budgets.

■ Do you think it is possible to continue to make experimental films from within the mainstream?

■ What do you think are some of the pressures on a director working for a major studio who wants to use film to make a political attack on society?

■ It could be argued that the polished look and use of stars which are part of Buñuel's later work are in fact entirely appropriate to a Surrealist style. From what you know about Buñuel's aims and the objectives of Surrealism, make an argument supporting this view.

INFORMATION BOX – BUÑUEL AND CENSORSHIP

Due to Buñuel's consistent attack on the Catholic Church he made most of his films outside of his native Spain where he was unable to work. However, In 1961 he was invited by the Spanish government to return to Spain to make *Viridiana* – which was subsequently banned. The film climaxed with a parody of The Last Supper which turns into an orgy – a typical image from Buñuel's work. *L'Age d'Or* and *Un Chien Andalou* were also banned in many European countries (including Britain and France). The latter wasn't shown officially in France after its opening until 1979.

ACTIVITY

Analysis of Surrealist style

Before watching *The Phantom of Liberty* all the way through, watch the opening sequence carefully. The sequence is set in Spain, 1808, during the Napoleonic wars, when the Spanish people resisted Napoleon's troops to defend the cities of Madrid and Toledo. These events have become famous and the people who resisted the French soldiers are revered as heroes; the Spanish artist Goya celebrated the events in *The Third of May, 1808* (painted in 1814–1815).

■ Find a reproduction of Goya's painting or go to www. spanisharts.com/prado and click on the section on Goya. What similarities in composition, lighting and actions can you see between this painting and the opening of the film?

■ As you watch the rest of the film, make a note of any other references to this painting and the events depicted in it.

■ Why are the soldiers executing the people? How does this differ from the events depicted by Goya?

■ Why does one of the people about to be killed shout 'Down with freedom'?

continued

■ What different examples of reversals in terms of expected behaviour are represented in this sequence?

■ How is humour used in the sequence?

Sample analysis

The opening sequence is characteristic of Buñuel's Surrealist style through its reference to real historical events and the use of satire to attack bourgeois (middle-class, conventional) morality. The satire depends on a series of unexpected and inexplicable actions in which the soldiers are executing the people who refuse to be liberated and the 'heroic' resistance attacks the concept of freedom. By reversing the audience's expectations and usual understanding of the order of the world, Buñuel hopes to make us uncertain about a range of accepted institutions. This sequence is also a daring one because in Spain – and for revolutionary groups around the world – the civilians who stood up to the French were heroes, and here Buñuel parodies their actions, making them ridiculous. However, Buñuel is one of the civilians facing execution, perhaps commenting on his own inability to be free. Given this background here are some suggestions of what the sequence might mean:

■ The French revolution – with Napoleon as its figurehead – was actually terrifying for a population used to a clear hierarchy in which to live, which was why the Spanish attempted to resist it.
■ People have become so comfortable being told what to do and think by the authorities (the church, the state) that freedom is actually a frightening prospect – it makes great demands on the individual.
■ We should look again at those groups and individuals which the dominant institutions tell us are heroes and ask why they have been chosen.

There are still further questions provoked by this sequence though:

■ How would a Surrealist define liberty?
■ Can we be forced to be free?
■ How does this sequence relate to the title of the film?

This sequence also remains relevant to contemporary political culture – think about the use of the term 'freedom' by different politicians in the 'war on terror'.

After the opening sequence the action of the film moves to contemporary France where we are introduced to Veronique and a friend in a park who are shown a series of photographs by a man who tells them, 'Don't show them to adults'.

The audience is not shown the pictures:

■ Why not? What effect does this have on the spectator?
■ What do you think the images are of? Why?

Later on, the images are revealed to be pictures of architectural landmarks including the Eiffel Tower and the Taj Mahal – but the girl's parents are scandalised that their daughter has been looking at them.

■ In what ways are these events similar to the techniques of reversals in the opening sequence?

As with the opening sequence there are different ways of interpreting the photographs. Here are some suggestions:

■ The horror which the past (old buildings) provokes in people suggests that contemporary society has no understanding of the past and tries to live continually in the present – this would apparently be a bad thing.
■ The audience assumes that the pictures are of naked women and it seems ridiculous that people are scandalised by looking at pictures of old buildings. Buñuel is asking why this reaction should be ridiculous but it is considered normal when the pictures are of naked women. This could be another attack on the hypocrisy of conventional morality; the naked body is natural and nothing to be ashamed of and the scandalised reaction is hypocritical as the (male) viewer enjoys the images.

You may not find either of these interpretations satisfactory and probably have your own ideas. Or you may think that analysing the symbols of Surrealism in this way goes against the aim of the movement – to provoke an instinctive and primitive response.

ACTIVITY

Narrative structure

Surrealist films are often described as random but of course this is impossible and, from watching the opening and first sequences of *The Phantom of Liberty*, a pattern is already evident – in terms of technique if not narrative.

■ Once you have watched the whole film put together a flow chart listing the film's different sequences. You should find about twelve distinct episodes.

continued

- How is the experience of watching this type of structure different from a Hollywood film? What expectations to do with time and place are subverted?

What connections can you find between the different episodes? These might include:

- themes (religion, sex, violence, the family)
- characters
- place.

In addition to the links between subject matter there can also be links in the use of:

- satire
- Surrealist imagery.

One of the main ways in which the different sequences are linked is through the satirical technique of reversal; apart from those already mentioned, which other examples are there in the film? Do they have similar meanings?

INFORMATION BOX – BUÑUEL AND AUTHORSHIP

Buñuel may be defined as an auteur due to the consistency of themes and visual style which construct the personal vision of the world evident throughout his work. These include:

- Attacks on social and political institutions, particularly the state and the Catholic Church, which are developed through the themes of male paranoia, sexual repression and impotence, middle-class hypocrisy.
- The use of broken narratives and Surreal images which often resemble dreams.
- A visual style which has been described as 'detached' using static camera and long takes.

The influence of Buñuel's filmmaking may be seen in the work of Bertrand Blier (France), Bernardo Bertolucci (Italy) and Jan Svankmajer, whose film *Alice* is one of the focus films for this topic. The influence of the narrative structure of *The Phantom of Liberty* may be seen in Richard Linklater's film *Slackers* where it is used for a more obviously realist effect.

Fantasy films

There is obviously an overlap between Surrealist and fantasy filmmaking, but while Surrealism refers to a specific preoccupation with human psychology and the unconscious, fantasy films can be defined in much broader terms. Hayward (2000) defines fantasy films as including four basic categories – horror, sci-fi, fairy-tales and a particular type of adventure film which involves journeys to improbable places. The events in fantasy films break the normal rules of what is possible in the real world through the use of the supernatural, myths and legends. In this definition films such as *Planet of the Apes* (1967 and 2001), *Lord of the Rings* (Jackson, 2000), *Big Fish* (Burton, 2003), *Edward Scissorhands* (Burton, 1992), *Spirited Away* (Hayao Miyazaki, 2003), *City of Lost Children* (Caro/Jeunet, 1995) could be defined as fantasy films. However, the broadness of the category does mean that it can become rather meaningless – including *Shrek, Pirates of the Caribbean* and *The Truman Show*.

In this topic area it is useful to define fantasy films in the context of their link to Surrealism. This is evident in the way that fantasy is used in cinema as an expression of our unconscious – of creativity and imagination which is not repressed as it is in the real world. Fantasy is an exploration of desires and dreams which can be uplifting and exciting but which are just as likely to be dark and disturbing. Many of the ideas relating to the subconscious mind and dream states as places of creativity may be found in earlier artistic movements such as Gothic. Forerunners of contemporary horror fiction, Gothic novels have many of the characteristics and aims that we associate with Surrealism and fantasy – particularly the idea that the subconscious is a powerful, creative force.

Gothic horror

Some key novels are:

The Castle of Otranto (Walpole, 1764)
Frankenstein (Mary Shelley, 1818)
Dracula (Bram Stoker, 1897)

The novels that constitute the genre of Gothic horror – and the films which developed from them – share the following aims:

- to involve the audience emotionally rather than intellectually or morally – a reaction against reason
- to stir up fears, anxieties and desires which are normally repressed.

This concept of repressed identity is represented through the image of:

- Dual worlds (usually symbolic) which represent dark and light. Rather than merely representing good and evil these refer to the diurnal world – light and familiar – and the nocturnal world – dark and unknown.

In Gothic horror the diurnal world is the world of convention while the nocturnal world is the place where the artificial layers of social convention can be stripped away. This is a similar concept to the Surrealist idea of the subconscious and they also share the desire to provoke a reaction in the audience.

Case study
ALICE (JAN SVANKMAJER, 1988)

> **Whatever comes out of my subconscious I use it because I consider it to be the purest form, everything else in your conscious being has been influenced by reality, by art, by education and by your upbringing but the original experiences that exist within you are the least corrupted of all experiences.**
>
> (Jan Svankmajer)

Alice, an adaptation of *Alice in Wonderland* (1865) by Lewis Carroll, is a mix of Surrealism, fantasy and Gothic elements. The novel tells the story of a girl called Alice who falls down a rabbit hole into a fantasy world filled with illogical people, places and events. The world that Alice enters, which is full of distortions, where it is difficult to distinguish fantasy from reality, has an obvious appeal to Surrealist and fantasy filmmakers. The central conceit of two worlds – the 'real' world and that of Wonderland – has obvious links to Gothic horror.

Figure 10.3 *Alice* (Jan Svankmajer, 1988).

Alice and Surrealist style

The juxtaposition of impossible images and ideas seen in Buñuel's films is also evident in *Alice*. This includes the type of film it is: a mix of live action and object animation, which logically should not co-exist in the same world. Two further examples are found in the opening narration: 'Now you will see a film for children. Perhaps.' And 'Close your eyes otherwise you won't see anything.' The latter phrase is a good example of the dream logic of the Surrealists – the only way you will truly 'see' is to look at the world differently.

■ List the other examples of impossible images and ideas you see in the film.

ACTIVITY

Social and political messages

The narrative of *Alice* follows Alice as she goes on a journey. In a mainstream film the aim of this journey would be clear, and Alice – and the audience – would probably learn lessons and change along

continued

the way. In *Alice* the meaning of the journey isn't always clear but seems to have something to do with education.

- What symbols of the world of education are there in the film? Make a note of how these are used.

- Look at the trial sequence at the end of the film. How does this develop the comment on education? On institutions?

- What do you think is being said about the world of education in *Alice*? Does the film have a message about the role of education in society?

- How does the film's representation of education and the establishment (as represented in the trial) conform to what you would expect of a Surrealist film?

EXAM QUESTIONS

- 'The extraordinary is presented as ordinary and the ordinary as extraordinary.' How far does this statement capture your experience of watching the films you have studied for this topic?

- 'Surrealist and fantasy filmmakers use cinematic devices particularly creatively.' How true is this statement in relation to the films you have studied for this topic?

References and Further Reading

Bordwell, D. and Thompson, K. (1997) 'Surrealism', in *Film Art: An Introduction*. McGraw Hill

Bunnell, C. (2004) 'The Gothic: A Literary Genre's Transition to Film', in Grant, B.K. (ed.) *Planks of Reason*. Scarecrow Press

Cherry, B. 'Dark Wonders and the Gothic Sensibility: Jan Svankmajer's *Alice*', at www.kinoeye.org

Cook, P. and Bernink, M. (eds) (1999) 'Avant-Garde and Counter Cinema', in *The Cinema Book*. BFI

Hayward, S. (2000) *Cinema Studies: The Key Concepts*. Routledge

Kolker, R. (1983) *The Altering Eye*. Oxford University Press (pp. 93–99, 381–392)

11 NEO-REALISM

This chapter will look at:

- the content and contexts of key films of the movement
- why this originally Italian movement was such a significant development in world cinema
- the distinctive styles and themes of Neo-realism
- the institutional context behind the development of this movement
- the pleasures this different form of cinema offers to the spectator

Suggested Italian Neo-realist films:

Ladri di Biciclette (*The Bicycle Thieves*) (PDS-ENIC, Italy, 1948, *Dir*: Vittorio De Sica)

Ossessione (*Obsession*) (Industrie Cinematografiche Italiane, Italy, 1942, *Dir*: Luchino Visconti)

Roma, Città Aperta (*Rome, Open City*) (Minerva, Italy, 1945, *Dir*: Roberto Rossellini)

Riso Amaro (*Bitter Rice*) (Lux, Italy, 1949, *Dir*: Giuseppe de Santis)

Miraculo a Milano (*Miracle in Milan*) (PDS/ENIC, Italy, 1951, *Dir*: Vittorio de Sica)

Rocco e i Suoi Fratelli (*Rocco and His Brothers*) (Titanus/Les Films Marceau, Italy/France, 1960, *Dir*: Luchino Visconti)

L'albero degli zoccoli (*The Tree of the Wooden Clogs*) (Curzon/RAI/GPC, Italy, 1978, *Dir*: Ermanno Olmi)

Suggested non-Italian, Neo-realist films:

Pather Panchali (Govt. West Bengal, India, 1955, *Dir*: Satyajit Ray)

Shadows (Lion Internatiional, US, 1959, *Dir*: John Cassavetes)

La Battaglia di Algeri (*The Battle for Algiers*) (Casbah/Igor, Algeria/Italy, 1965, *Dir*: Gillo Pontecorvo)

The Northern Lights (Cine Manifest, US, 1978, *Dir*: John Hanson/Rob Nilsson)

Central do Brasil (*Central Station*) (MACT/Video Films/Riofilme/Canal+, Brazil/France, 1998, *Dir*: Walter Salles)

Bad ma ra khahad bord (*The Wind Will Carry Us*) (MK2 Productions, Iran/France, 1999, *Dir*: Abbas Kiarostami)

Chop Shop (Muscat Filmed Properties LLC/Noruz Films/Big Beach Films, US, 2007, *Dir*: Ramin Bahrani)

The initial period of Italian Neo-realism is one that grew out of Italian Fascist documentary production during the Second World War, and ran from 1942 through to 1952 (though Neo-realist films were sporadically produced until the movement effectively died out in 1960). It is, however, not the dates that are significant, but the effect this new style of filmmaking had in the aftermath of the war, and on subsequent Italian and other national cinemas (notably South American) to the present day.

The filmmaking covered in Neo-realism in Italy and beyond allows not only for the study of the two Italian focus films, but also the work of a wide range of filmmakers who were influenced by both the style and the underpinning philosophy of Neo-realism, and the contexts within which they worked. The broader issue of defining this movement as 'other' to Hollywood is a useful starting point to this study, as well as the consideration of these films within a wider context of their own national cinemas.

REALISM: a cinematic style that attempts both to use filmmaking techniques to create the 'illusion' of reality (and thereby allow an audience to engage with the on-screen subject as 'real'), and to select and shoot narratives that are representative of 'the real', without attempting to 'fix' a meaning on them (allowing the audience to 'read' a film's reality in a variety of ways according to their own view on the subject, and to what they see on the screen).

FRENCH POETIC REALISM: : a forerunner of and influence on Italian Neo-realism, and itself influenced by the German Expressionist movement (see Chapter 9 on German and Soviet cinemas of the 1920s). Poetic Realism offered a 're-created realism' that was highly stylised and studio focused, concentrating on replicating the 'real' world through the *mise-en-scène* in the studio. Despite the re-created realism, this form of cinema was highly symbolic, implanting the narrative with objects and actions that were symbolic of the main (usually male) character's situation. Some of the principal filmmakers of this movement include Marcel Carné, Julien Duvivier and Jean Renoir.

This key movement in World Cinema may be used as a platform to build on a range of skills developed at AS level, and a range of issues in terms of textual study (see *AS Film Studies: The Essential Introduction*, Exploring Film Form – FM1), contextual study and interpretation (see *AS Film Studies: The Essential Introduction, British and American Film* – FM2), including:

- The context of Italian Neo-realism – both historical production context and the broader social and political contexts that formed the movement.
- A new film form – the Neo-realist style and its relationship to subject.
- National cinemas – the adoption of Neo-realism as a focus of national film-making (and as a means of exploring national identity).
- Social and political institutions – how these films criticise not only the broader political institutions that govern society, but also the social institutions (family, peers, societies, religion) that operate on a micro (individual or small groupings) level.
- Production context – the films of this movement in relation to a broader context of World Cinema, and within the context of key filmmakers.

NEO-REALISM: a term first employed by Italian screenwriter Antonio Pietrangeli in 1943 when describing Visconti's *Ossessione* (a film he wrote the screenplay for).

Growing out of Italian Fascist documentary production, and influenced by the French filmmaker Jean Renoir's *Poetic Realism*, this movement

continued

set out to use a documentary style; to use location shooting rather than studio re-creation; to show the reality of everyday life (dropping in and out of the narrative with little by way of explanation of histories or prediction of futures); to focus on social reality (poverty, unemployment, political/social unrest/change); to use 'natural' dialogue and non-professional actors to deliver it; and to avoid literary adaptation, instead using 'real' stories developed for the cinematic medium.

Using long takes, deep focus cinematography, largely natural light, hand-held camerawork, and (in the original Italian movement) dubbed sound, the style was sparse, stark and documentary-like.

Case study

VITTORIO DE SICA (1901–1974)

Born in Sora in Italy, de Sica became an established actor ('Vittorio nazionale' – Italy's top film/theatre actor of the 1930s and 1940s), built his career under Mussolini's Fascist dictatorship, and was wealthy and popular by the time he started directing. Across a career of more than fifty years he appeared in over a hundred Italian and international films.

Between 1940 and 1944 he directed six films, sentimental comedies in which he showed some initial interest in the social subject matter that would later dominate his Neo-realist work. It was in 1942 that he met his principal Neo-realist collaborator, screenwriter Cesare Zavattini, and began developing his style through films such as *I Bambini Ci Guardano* (*The Children are Watching Us*) (Invicta/Scalera Film, Italy, 1943) and *La Porta del Cielo* (*Gate to Heaven*) (Catholic Film Centre, Italy, 1945). It was only through accepting the commission to shoot *Gate to Heaven* that he avoided being transported to the newly opened Fascist studios in Venice to work for the Nazi occupiers.

Renowned for his Neo-realist work, he received three Oscars for films after this period – *La Ciociara* (*Two Women*) (Champion/Marceau/Cocinor/SGC, Italy/France, 1960), *Ieri, Oggi, Domani* (*Yesterday, Today, Tomorrow*) (CCC/Concordia/Joseph E Levine, Italy/France, 1963) and *Il Giardino del Finzi-Continis* (*The Garden of the Finzi-Continis*) (Documento/CCC, Italy/West Germany, 1970). He continued his acting career, though this declined to small roles and cameos towards the end of his life.

Summary
THE BICYCLE THIEVES

Figure 11.1
The Bicycle Thieves (1948, de Sica).

Director Vittorio de Sica was an established actor and then filmmaker under the Italian Fascist dictatorship of Mussolini, and had already begun experimenting with Neo-realist themes before the Second World War was over. Taking the simple story of working-class dreams turned sour that he established in his successful feature *Sciuscia* (*Shoeshine*) (Alfa, Italy, 1946) – which won an honorary Oscar, as the Best Foreign Film category did not exist at this time – de Sica and writer Cesare Zavattini developed *The Bicycle Thieves* (which again won an honorary Oscar), a simple story of an unemployed man who finds a job, only to lose it, and his dignity, when his bicycle is stolen.

continued

In *The Bicycle Thieves*, de Sica develops an additional theme in his examination of the father/son relationship as pressure is added to pressure, disappointment to disappointment, and impotence to impotence as the pair trudge the streets of the city in search of the missing bicycle. Encountering government agencies, local political 'bigwigs', the Catholic Church, ex-fascists, black-marketeers, thieves and the police, de Sica's central characters interact with all that is Italy in the immediate postwar period.

INFORMATION BOX – ITALY AT THE END OF THE SECOND WORLD WAR

On 8 September 1943 Italy surrendered to the advancing Allied forces, and immediately the Nazis took over the unoccupied areas of the country (from Rome north). The Fascist dictator Benito Mussolini was rescued from captivity by the Nazis and flown safety to the Nazi-occupied northern Italian state. A fierce, inch-by-inch, battle then ensued for Italy, in which the Nazis carried out many atrocities against the Italian people, and in which many towns and cities were terribly damaged by bombing and artillery barrages. On 25 April 1945, a general insurrection against the occupying Nazis began in the northern rump of Italy, which led to the surrender of the German forces.

The postwar position was difficult, with high unemployment, returning prisoners of war, a dysfunctional civil service, a severely damaged infrastructure (bombed-out buildings, factories and shops destroyed, damaged water and sewerage provision), an occupying Allied Army (largely British and American), and a drive to reject all things Fascist (including the filmmaking system). People sold or pawned (a temporary sale where the property could be bought back at a higher price within a certain time limit) their belongings, and the black-market (the trade in illegal or stolen goods) was at its strongest.

Unemployment, crime and the breakdown of social structures were the burning issues of the day, with Italians (who had grown used to the ruthless efficiency of Mussolini's Italian state) recognising the inefficiency and ineffectuality of the new, emerging Italian state.

The Bicycle Thieves begins with unemployed Antonio Ricci (Lamberto Maggiorani) standing in the bombed-out ruins of a city along with a crowd of other unemployed men waiting for the day's announcements of job vacancies. Volunteering himself for a job as a bill-poster (someone who pastes up posters) he meets his first hurdle; the job is conditional on having a bicycle. Antonio falsely assures the government official that he has a bicycle, then rushes home to tell his wife his good news. Together they go to see Santona, a fortune teller, for advice, and at her (dubious, vague, and implied as fraudulent) instruction take their bed linen to the pawn shop in order to redeem Antonio's previously pawned bicycle.

Disaster strikes on Antonio's first day, when as he pastes a poster up his bicycle is stolen and, despite his efforts in chasing after the thief, he is met with the harsh fact that now, without the precious bicycle, he is destined to return to unemployment. De Sica here is clearly making a comment on the precious nature of the 'tools' of a job, and the importance of ensuring they stay in the hands of the Italian workers – whether this is a plea for a communist state, a criticism of the Allied occupation (in which many of Italy's assets 'disappeared'), or a metaphor for the Italian film industry is debatable.

Antonio then begins a relentless search for the stolen bicycle, taking with him his young son Bruno (Enzo Staiola). Antonio is constantly seen through the admiring eyes of his son, who expects his father to solve the problem and retrieve the stolen bicycle, and in this the spectator is continually confronted by Antonio's developing discomfort and shame in the realisation that he is not the man his son thinks him to be.

The search for the bicycle takes them to a communist union official, who leads them to a market of dismantled bicycle parts (Piazza Vittorio and Porta Portese) in the hope of finding it, but they are overwhelmed by the volume of bicycles and parts. Hearing that the thief may get a free lunch at a local church-run 'soup kitchen', Antonio and Bruno are mistaken for the homeless and destitute before being herded into church for Mass. Here they see the man they think is the thief and chase after him, Antonio again proving unable to resolve the situation.

In despair Antonio returns to the fortune teller (of whom he was critical when his wife sought her advice over the prospect of the job) and is offered clearly charlatan nonsense in response to his questioning as to whether he will find his bicycle again. A subsequent chase of the thief leads Antonio and Bruno through a brothel to a rough, downmarket area of the city, Via Panico, where there is an almost comic scene of the thief's (equally deceitful) mother coming to his defence when confronted by Antonio. The police here are seen as powerless, and as the criminal community unites, it is Antonio who is in danger.

continued

Retreating in defeat, de Sica presents Antonio with the temptation of row after row of bicycles outside a sports stadium. Despairing, Antonio succumbs to temptation and attempts to steal one of the bicycles, but is seen as inept even at this. The community again comes together in a way it did not when Antonio's bicycle was stolen, and stops Antonio, reuniting the stolen bicycle with its angry owner. Coming close to being arrested for the attempted theft, Antonio is met with the dismay of his son Bruno at seeing his father brought so low.

This ending to a story that would struggle to make a few lines as a news item in a local newspaper reveals de Sica's intent in this film – to find the drama of the everyday occurrence, the passion of the minute action, the emotion in the detail.

ACTIVITY

Look at the Pawn Shop sequence in *The Bicycle Thieves*, where Antonio and his wife are retrieving the pawned bicycle. What do you notice about the *mise-en-scène* here – what messages do you think de Sica is trying to convey? Compare this scene with the sequences at the open markets of Piazza Vittorio and Porta Portese. Do these scenes serve to show Antonio's plight as unique, or as simply one of many daily misfortunes?

Why do you think de Sica makes Antonio such a victim? What, in your opinion, is he a victim of?

Consider Antonio's relationship with his son. Is this a traditional father–son relationship? What is Bruno's role in his father's search for the stolen bicycle? Map Bruno's changing view of his father across the film. What do you notice?

Write down ten words to describe your opinion of Antonio (these may contradict each other if you consider your developing opinion across the film). With a peer, compare your lists of words. Are there any that are common to both of you? If so, why do you think you both arrive at the same conclusions about Antonio? If not, why do you think you have divergent opinions about Antonio?

How do you feel when Antonio finally gets to confront the thief? What did you expect would happen? How do you feel about the end of this confrontation? Does this affect your view of Antonio's actions in stealing the bicycle from outside the stadium?

What do you think de Sica is saying about class in the different results of the two bicycle thefts? Is he making a wider comment about Italian postwar society in this?

The bicycle is a central symbol of this film. If you were to remake this film today, what would you choose as the central symbol that is stolen? Write down a brief synopsis of your remake. How different is it to the original? Why have you chosen to make the story changes you have made? What does your story say about the society you have set it in?

Case study

ERMANNO OLMI (1931–)

The son of peasant factory workers, Ermanno Olmi's career began with company-sponsored filmmaking for the Edison-Volta electric company where he worked as a clerk. Rising to head of the film department there, Olmi became an accomplished documentary-maker, making industrial short films. His last, *Il Tempo Si e Fermato* (*Time Stood Still*, 1959) was successful enough for him to abandon the company and set up an independent film cooperative in Milan, 'Twenty-four Horses'. Here he made his first landmark feature in a Neo-realist style in 1961. *Il Posto* (*The Job*) (Twenty-four Horses, Italy, 1961) was a critical success, but his career was cut short by the commercial and critical disaster that was *And There Came a Man* (Italy, 1965), a biopic of Pope John XXIII, which caused him to abandon cinema and work in television. He did not return to film until 1978 when he made *The Tree of Wooden Clogs*.

Summary
THE TREE OF WOODEN CLOGS

Figure 11.2
*L'albero degli
zoccoli/The Tree of
Wooden Clogs*
(Olmi, 1978).

Winner of the Grand Prize at the Cannes Film Festival in 1978, *The Tree of Wooden Clogs* follows in an Italian tradition of 'peasant' films, but, rather than adopting the sentimental historicism of a 'pastoral' style (that wraps the poverty and hardship of peasant life in a rosy glow of rustic simplicity), Ermanno Olmi (who is of peasant descent himself) adopts a Neo-realist style, using non-professional 'peasant' actors, real locations, natural lighting, and direct sound using the local Bergamo dialect. The story is based loosely on his grandmother's stories of her peasant life, and this makes for a strong connection between director and subject.

The film has at its centre a warm view of traditional Catholicism as being at the heart of the rural, peasant life, and its morality and faith as essential to the nature of daily life. Olmi himself is a practising Catholic, and it is clear that his belief guides the construction of the film as a whole and that of the individual family narratives. The families of peasants attend Mass at the local Catholic church, say the rosary as they work, and see the Catholic priest as a central character in their lives. In a comic moment later in the film, Olmi has a newly-wed couple spending their honeymoon night in a convent where they have an aunt who is a nun, and has the nuns pushing single beds together for them and covering the headboards in flowers in tribute to the sacrament of marriage.

Other Italian directors (and indeed those of other national cinemas) of the time were choosing to make films that presented angry, revolutionary, workers' films, which often reflected the political struggles between extreme left- and extreme right-wing politics which shaped the political landscape of the 1970s. Indeed, where Olmi does introduce revolutionary politics, he does so as a backdrop to explore individual actions or attitudes that are often a counterpoint to the political arguments being expressed (such as the sequence of a socialist speaker's address during a local fair where Olmi concentrates attention on a spectator's attempt to discreetly pick up a gold coin he has spotted on the ground).

The film focuses on the members of three peasant families across a period of approximately a year at the end of the nineteenth century in Lombardy (northern Italy). They live on a large estate that is owned by an effectively absentee landlord (although he is in fact resident) and share a communal existence under his feudal authority, paid by him for their productivity, while he takes three-quarters of whatever they produce. The story is told in a series of 'vignettes' (sectionalised stories within stories, which while self-contained have a relationship to the film as a whole) which illustrate both peasant life and the central themes that Olmi is trying to present.

Crops are harvested; a hog is killed (presented directly with all the harshness and brutality that is entailed in such an action); a grandfather has a secret technique of growing tomatoes that allows him to be first to the market with them and he reveals this secret to his granddaughter; a village idiot wanders from home to home and is met with charity and given food, despite the peasants' poverty. Insulated from the outside world, the peasants pray, sing, and spend the evenings in front of the fire telling stories.

Three stories are central to the film, however: the struggle of one family to send their son to school on the advice of the Catholic priest (despite the loss of his labour to the family's income potential) and his subsequent sharing of his school lessons with them on his return home; the struggle of

continued

a widow to support her six children (despite the priest's advice to send the two youngest to the orphanage); and a honeymooning couple's trip to Milan where they witness a violent political protest, spend their wedding night in a convent, and rise the following morning to find a child available for adoption with a regular payment offered for his support.

The final sequence of the film is the one that gives it its name. The daily trudging to and from school results in one of the boy's wooden clogs wearing out. With no money to buy new ones, his father Batisi (Luigi Ornaghi) reluctantly chops down a poplar tree to make him a replacement. Sitting at the kitchen table working the wood into the clog, the action is given added importance and gravity by the addition of a soundtrack of organ music (Bach). The tree belongs to the landlord (as do all things on his land, even the peasants), and when he finds out what has happened he ruthlessly throws the family off the land and into an uncertain future. The unjust punishment is met with an acceptance that is in opposition to the protests of the city workers, but which is in line with Olmi's Catholic faith.

ACTIVITY

Most Neo-realist films deal with the present rather than with the past. Is Olmi's work really Neo-realist? If so, what tells you this?

Batisti's act of chopping down the tree is a central theme of the film, and indeed leads to the film's title. What do you think the tree symbolises? Is Olmi trying to convey a political message here? How successful is the use of the tree in conveying Olmi's message(s)?

Pick out five points in the film where religion has significance or where it directly impacts on the peasants' lives. Does religion have a largely positive or a largely negative impact on the peasants' lives? What do you think Olmi is trying to say about religion here? What kind of man does Olmi paint the priest as?

Compare this film with any from the period of Italian Neo-realism (1942–1952). What are the key differences between them both in terms of story and style?

In a group, explore either the male or female characters represented in the film. Do they differ significantly from modern men and women in both attitude and action? List their strengths and

weaknesses. Compare lists. Is there significant difference in the
strengths and weaknesses between genders? What impact does
Catholicism have on your chosen characters? Is its impact different
across genders?

Why do you think Olmi chose the 'peasant' backdrop when his
peers were making angry films about contemporary life?

The context of Italian Neo-realism

The Fascist dictator Benito Mussolini saw film as the most important medium
of the modern age, and was determined to bend it to the Fascist cause. Ignoring
his own concerns over the influence of left-wing intellectuals he allowed the
Marxist Umberto Barbaro not only to teach at the 'Centro Experimentale di
Cinematographia' (his newly commissioned film school) but demanded that the
work of the Soviet cinema (see Chapter 9) be taught extensively to ensure that
Italian filmmakers were aware of the latest developments in filmmaking technique.

Under the Fascists the Italian film industry saw a renaissance, with a return to the
prominence it once enjoyed in the Silent Era. Hundreds of features were made,
alongside thousands of newsreels and documentaries. Filmmakers were dispatched to Ethiopia, Spain, Albania, Germany, Greece, and anywhere else where
the Italian state had an interest.

FASCISM: Fascism was a nationalistic political movement that first
came into organised existence in 1919 as the 'Fasci di Combattimento'
Party under Benito Mussolini, who, in 1924, became the Fascist dictator
of Italy ('Il Duce'). Opposed to a rising tide of post-First World War
socialist and communist political approaches, Fascism promoted the
Italian state above the individual, the Italian race above all others, and
the ordinary Italian above the intellectual. Mussolini waged war in the
1930s in Ethiopia, in Spain (supporting the Fascist General Franco), and
in Albania, and joined forces with Germany's Adolf Hitler in 1936, declaring war on Great Britain in 1940. Overthrown by his own government in
1943, Mussolini formed a new government under the Nazi occupiers in
the north of Italy. He was executed by Italian partisans in 1945, and the
Fascist Party was banned.

Filmmakers such as Roberto Rossellini, Luchino Visconti and Vittorio de Sica enjoyed privileged lives at the Cinecittà studios in Rome, where they were well trained, well financed and well resourced. They made documentaries for the state-operated propaganda arm 'Luce', and 'White Telephone' features that met with state approval for showing Italy and Italian culture in a positive light (it is interesting to note that Visconti's *Ossessione* was actually destroyed by the state because it was deemed immoral and a corruption of Italian culture – any copies available today are from a single print rather than the negative, which Visconti was able to hide).

Figure 11.3 *Ossessione* (*Obsession*) (Visconti, 1943) was destroyed for being immoral.

PROPAGANDA: the purposeful manipulation of an audience's thoughts, behaviour, beliefs and attitudes, usually towards a common ideology. Filmmakers often use symbols, specifically charged dialogue or carefully constructed visual sequences to 'position' an audience. The Fascists believed film to be a powerful tool of propaganda, and ensured that all of their filmmakers were schooled in the techniques of propaganda.

WHITE TELEPHONE FILMS: : under the Fascist dictator Benito Mussolini, filmmaking was brought under state control. Mussolini dictated that Italian film must show Italy in a positive light, and should compete directly with film being produced in Hollywood. This led to the production of films set in the decadence of grand hotels, swish nightclubs and the first-class lounges of ocean liners, reflecting the similar decadence prevailing in 1930s Hollywood musicals and screwball comedies. The height of extravagance at the time was to have a white telephone (telephones were usually black), and this became the symbol of these films and their Art Deco *mise-en-scène*. The films were largely lightweight comedies, musicals and easily resolved dramas (most often set in the glow of Roman history, in the greatness of a Fascist future, or in the sophistication of an urban reflection of America), offering an idealised view of Italy far removed from its peasant economy.

By 1942 many of the Italian filmmakers were finding that their style, developed in newsreel and documentary production, was transferring itself into their work on features, with an accent on the stories of 'ordinary' Italians and the use of non-actors – such as in Roberto Rossellini's so-called 'Fascist Trilogy' of films which include *La Nave Bianca* (*Hospital Ship*) (ICI, Italy, 1942).

As the Fascist state crumbled and then surrendered to the advancing Allied Army in 1943 the Italian filmmakers found themselves in a precarious position. Rome was immediately occupied by the Nazis, and they began asset-stripping Cinecittà, taking much of the equipment back to Germany but using some to establish a new Fascist studio, Cinevillagio (The Film Village) in the Giardini della Biennale in Venice. In Rome during the Nazi occupation film continued to be made (indeed, Vittorio de Sica made one for the Nazis), but conditions were now unfavourable. Rossellini took the opportunity of secretly filming the occupiers on the streets of Rome, material that would later prove a foundation for *Rome, Open City*.

When the Nazi troops withdrew from Rome they took with them a number of Cinecittà's technicians, artistes and directors, and the filmmakers who would later found Neo-realism narrowly escaped being taken with them. With Rome left as an 'open city' (no power in control) the Italian partisan fighters took to the streets, killing those whom they deemed to have collaborated with the Nazi occupiers. Even if Cinecittà had been in a suitable condition for filming in, it would not have been wise for filmmakers who had been schooled by the Fascists and (some of whom) had made films for the Nazis to lock themselves behind the studio gates to continue their filmmaking. They needed to take to the streets, they needed to be seen making non-Fascist films, they needed to involve the communities that surrounded them, not only to show they were not collaborators, but also to show the advancing Allied troops that they were not the enemy.

Out on the streets they found the stories that would drive the Neo-realist move-ment — stories of individual heroism, of survival, of death, of love, and of the ordinary people. Using lightweight (documentary) cameras these filmmakers went on to the streets of Rome (initially), and then followed the Allied forces north as they advanced towards Germany (indeed, one of the most visually powerful films of this period is Rossellini's *Germania Anno Zero* (*Germany Year Zero*) (UGC/ DEFA, France/Italy, 1947) shot amid the ruins of Berlin). The Neo-realist devices of natural lighting, non-studio locations and non-professional actors were both a stylistic decision and a necessity in the war-torn ruins of the Italian cities and the ravaged countryside.

The poverty and desolation is evident in all the films of the early Neo-realist period, and especially so in de Sica's *The Bicycle Thieves*, which presents scenes set against bombsites and the ruined monuments of Fascism, and offers images of Italians drawing their water from 'stand-pipes' in the streets, and selling any possessions they may have retained through the occupation. This poverty is further expressed in de Sica's *Miracle in Milan* where the central character Toto organises the homeless, the tramps and the dispossessed into a community, and in his later *Umberto D* (Dear Films, Italy, 1952) where society is seen to have rebuilt itself, but the old are impoverished and have to resort to selling their property and begging in order to survive.

ACTIVITY

What choices do you think were open to the Italian filmmakers at the point of the Italian surrender in 1943? How do you think the decisions they made affected their filmmaking?

In a group, discuss how the Neo-realist style differs between films (or sequences) set in urban areas (and dealing with urban issues) and those set in rural areas (and dealing with rural issues). Do you feel there are any ingredients that unify these areas?

Take one of the films you have studied and transpose its locations (from ruin to polished, from bleak to comfortable). How does this affect the meaning of the film? Do you now need to adopt a different film style to Neo-realism to make it work? Is there anything in the narrative you now need to change to ensure that the story still works?

What differences in the contexts of production can you see reflected in the different Neo-realist films you have studied? Are the differences more marked between early and late Neo-realist films?

A new film form

The essence of the Neo-realist form can be traced further back into Italian film history than the earliest work of the acknowledged Neo-realist directors, though such film usually only offered some of the ingredients, or a presage of what was to come. One of the key proponents of a primitive Neo-realist style was the Fascist filmmaker Alessandro Blasseti whose 1930s films such as *1860* (Cines/Steffano Pittaluga Films, Italy, 1934) – the story of Garibaldi's invasion of Sicily in the unification of Italy – used location shooting, regional dialects and non-professional actors. What was missing however was the realism in the story – the simple realism of the humble.

A dark realism was brought to Italian cinema by Luchino Visconti's *Ossessione*, which was an adaptation of the American James M. Cain's novel *The Postman Always Rings Twice*. The harsh depiction of human nature, sexuality, desire and obsession is enhanced by a 'dirty' reality made possible by leaving behind the studio with its false sets, props and painted backdrops, and by seeking out the 'real' that could be offered by location shooting (the film was suppressed by the Fascist state, and then by MGM – which released its own version of the novel in 1946 – and it did not reach an international audience until 1959!).

Roberto Rossellini's *Rome Open City* took this new realism and refined it further. In the opening sequences of the film when Nazi troops are raiding an apartment building in an attempt to catch the partisan leader Manfredi, there are sequences that are so dark that it is hard to see what is going on. This is deliberate, since in reality these would have been the lighting conditions, and so it would have broken the reality of the scene to brighten it with artificial lighting. Similarly, later in the film when the partisan fighters attack a Nazi convoy a dog runs into the shot and is rapidly scared off-screen by the shooting. Most directors would have cut, re-set and retaken the scene, but Rossellini kept the dog's appearance in, rationalising that that is what could have happened in reality.

As well as using natural light, the filmmakers used (as much as possible) 'natural' settings, meaning that they could simply turn up and shoot in a location without over-concerning themselves with the *mise-en-scène*. A study of the background of these films often reveals interesting detail that is there largely by accident rather than by design (as it would have been in a studio-based film). This can lead to a greater number of interpretations, but it should be recognised that even though a filmmaker did not place the detail, they did choose not to re-shoot without it, and so any meanings read from this can be legitimately argued.

It was, of course the use of non-professional actors (or a mix of professional and non-professional) that most marks out the Neo-realist style. The tension created in their performances is due in part to their lack of being 'trained' into a style of acting, and in part to their natural affinity for the roles they are playing (a director may have chosen an actor for a particular look, or for any experience they may have had of the role they are playing). The Americans (in the form of Hollywood producer David O. Selznick) offered to back *The Bicycle Thieves* on condition that the lead role of Antonio be played by the Hollywood star Cary Grant, but de Sica refused, preferring to work with the non-professional Lamberto Maggiorani whose despairing look uniquely captured the spirit of the down-at-heel Antonio. This continued beyond the original Italian Neo-realist movement and examples may be found in later films such as Gillo Pontecorvo's *The Battle of Algiers*, in which the lead character Ali La Pointe is played by Brahim Haggiag – an illiterate farmer whom the director discovered in a marketplace – and Jacef Saadi, one of the surviving FLN guerrilla leaders, plays himself.

The stories themselves are a key feature of this new realism, featuring not the high drama of tragic events, but a 'cinema of the humble', where the real everyday dramas (that are often overlooked by dramatists) of unemployment, destitution, faith, hopes, morality and survival are played out. No grand symbols are offered for an audience to attach themselves to, but rather recognisable characters with recognisable narratives are developed, with time to focus on the small actions and agonies of decisions that are a part of everyone's lives yet receive scant attention in mainstream cinema.

ACTIVITY

Map out the turning points of the stories in the films you have studied. What kinds of events motivate these changes of direction? Compare these to the turning points in a mainstream Hollywood film that you have studied. Are the motivating events different? If so, in what way?

Look at the principal characters from the films you have studied. What is recognisably different about their performance? Do you think replacing them with 'stars' (such as Cary Grant or Leonardo Di Caprio) would make a difference to the films? If so, what differences would they bring to the films?

For you, what is the most recognisably different feature of Neo-realism's style? Once you have identified it, imagine the film with this element either taken away or replaced with a more mainstream element. What effect does this have on the film? Does it affect other elements of the Neo-realist style?

Does the documentary 'look' of these films add to the reality effect? If so, from the films you have studied, select a key sequence that illustrates this. What elements combine in this sequence to produce the documentary look?

National cinemas

The Neo-realist movement was essential in redefining Italian cinema at the end of the Second World War. For the preceding twenty years Italian cinema had been defined by its Fascist state sponsors, and it would have been hard to achieve distance from this association without such a radical departure, both in terms of form and of subject matter. While there were other forms of escapist cinema still being made postwar, and while the Hollywood studios lost little time in pouring money into a multitude of fast turn-around 'sword and sandal' Italian films, the new democratic Italian state recognised the need for a national cinema that helped define the new Italy both to the domestic audience and (possibly more importantly) to an international audience. For a brief period there were even considerable financial incentives offered to filmmakers to produce Neo-realist film, but the failings of this movement as a vehicle for redefining national identity soon became apparent.

First, the stark realism often presented an uncomfortable image of Italy, 'problematic' representations of aspects of Italian society, and messages about the Italian state that presented difficulties to the government. American pressure (Italy being occupied by Allied forces) coupled with a changing political landscape (the emerging East/West tensions and the development of the 'Cold War') meant that Neo-realist filmmakers would soon face the demand to tone down the realism of their films.

Second, this realism did not sit comfortably with the domestic audience, who at the end of the terrible period of Nazi occupation, and the battles on Italian soil between Nazis and the Allied forces, were ready for escapist entertainment, not a reminder of how low their country had fallen. Films showing unemployment, theft, poverty, despair, deceit and the callous disregard of the rich were sending messages that the domestic audience simply did not want to hear, and portraying values that (however accurate of the time) the audience did not want to recognise or associate with. This became amplified as Italy moved into the 1950s and prosperity began to return – the stark reality of Neo-realism simply did not match with the aspired-to reality of an Italy that was beginning to heal its war wounds.

Add to this the availability of American products which were being offloaded on to a hungry Italian market (there was an entire back catalogue of Hollywood film that had not been available to Italy due to the war), and the inevitability of the decline of Italian Neo-realism becomes clear.

As the movement declined in Italy it began to have an effect on other national cinemas, including British Social Realism, the French New Wave, the Realist movement in Indian film of the 1950s and 1960s (indeed, Rossellini went to make a film in India, and met an Indian actress who bore him a son who went on to become a filmmaker in his own right in India), the Cinema Novo movement of Brazil and the Los Angeles School of Black Independent Filmmakers. It was not simply their use of a realist style of shooting, but their sense of the importance of the stories of the poor and dispossessed (the 'cinema of the humble') and of a social realism, a spiritual realism, and indeed the realism that comes of hardship.

Case study

CINEMA NOVO

Brazil's Neo-realist-influenced Cinema Novo movement began in the early 1960s and rejected the slick, artificial and disconnected mainstream productions of the time, preferring to focus attention on the urban slums and the drought-ridden northeastern 'sertão' region, highlighting the poverty and deprivation suffered by the ordinary Brazilians. Generating politicised films, often set against a back-story of revolution, this movement was well received by the intellectual home audience, and critically applauded by the international film community, though it was not supported by the Brazilian government, nor by the masses who preferred American melodrama. The movement gained momentum with the liberal regime of President Goulart after the fall of the dictator Getulio Vargas.

Low-budget filmmaking techniques prevailed among directors such as Glauber Rocha, Nelson Pereira dos Santos and Joaquim Pedro de Andrade, and their unofficial motto became 'Uma câmera na mão e uma idéia na cabeça' ('A movie-camera in the hand and an idea in the head'). The movement evolved through the 1960s, adopting an almost anti-cinematic confrontational style. The military coup in 1974 and the resulting repression, the opposition of the Catholic Church, and the eventual loss of the Western art-house audiences who grew tired of the Marxist excess, led to the demise of the movement.

The Neo-realist influence is felt in the Cuban (state-sponsored) national cinema, and in much of contemporary South American and African production (particularly Mexican, Brazilian and sub-Saharan film). What is notable is that most of the countries whose filmmakers have adopted the Neo-realist style are those which have encountered the same kinds of social difficulties that Italy was experiencing at the time when Neo-realism developed (dictatorships, corruption, social inequality, extremes of poverty and desolation), and the link between Neo-realism and the social and political background from which it emerges is one that has been established time and again.

What do you think the subject matter's significance was in redefining a postwar national identity for Italy?

Look at a Neo-realist film from outside Italy. Compare it with one of the original Italian Neo-realist films. What similarities do you note? What differences? Can you identify the features that connect the films within the same movement?

Take one of the original Italian Neo-realist films such as *The Bicycle Thieves* and bring its story forward to a more contemporary Neo-realist national cinema. What would you need to do to it to make it fit this Neo-realist form? What would you be able to leave untouched? What does this tell you about the way the movement has evolved?

Discuss the representations of class and gender in the original Italian Neo-realist films, and compare these with similar representations in more contemporary Neo-realist film. What do you note about these representations? How significant an issue are these representations in the depiction of realism? Do these representations affect the way in which you perceive these films?

Social and political institutions

In *Rome Open City*, Rossellini offers a very clear view of the social and political institutions of the time. The police are seen as corrupt, the middle classes as self-serving, and the Church as righteous but ineffective with only the priest Don Pietro offering any sense of active opposition to the Nazi occupiers. The communist partisans, and the ordinary people in the form of the apartment dwellers and the children, are seen as the heroes of the film.

This theme continues in de Sica's *The Bicycle Thieves* where the opening scene of Antonio standing with other unemployed men waiting for job vacancy announcements serves as clear comment on the government systems. His criticisms go further in highlighting the ineffectual nature of most organisations (be they state in the form of the police, or community in the form of the union or the Church) in providing Antonio with active assistance in retrieving his stolen bicycle.

His next work, *Miracle in Milan*, sees a foundling (Toto) taken to an orphanage after his adopted mother dies, and later released into destitution. Toto organises the makeshift camp of homeless and displaced persons that he is invited to, and makes it into a productive and happy place – something the state could easily have achieved had it attempted it. These 'humble' people band together to face down the rich owner whose land they are squatting on (an owner who bears a

Figure 11.4 *Roma, Città Aperta/Rome, Open City* (Rousellini, 1945).

remarkable likeness to the dictator Mussolini, and who lives in a palatial building of the Fascist style), and to beat off repeated attacks by the police who have been bought by the landowner. De Sica is clearly championing the underdog against both the rich and the systems that support them, and in doing so suppress the poor.

The Neo-realist films are populated with such characters, and with such actions defining both the informal institutions of a society (families, collectives, societies) and the formal institutions that shape a society (government agencies, the Church, the military). In Gillo Pontecorvo's *The Battle of Algiers*, the formal agencies – the police and military – are seen as corrupt, using tactics that are worse than those claimed for their enemy the FLN guerrillas. The audience is positioned to have little sympathy for their deaths, whereas concern is generated for the 'family' of guerrillas who kill and bomb indiscriminately. The Neo-realist concern for the plight of the ordinary people is what allows this positioning to be acceptable to an audience, and it is this plight that makes the FLN guerrillas heroic.

Case study

GILLO PONTECORVO (1919–)

An Italian Jew, Gillo Pontecorvo's early experience in life was that of evading deportation by the Italian Fascists to the Nazi death camps, and acting as liaison between the Italian and French Resistance Movements during the latter part of the Second World War. An aspiring professional tennis player before the war, he was a key activist in Milan during the occupation, and was involved in several 'actions' against the Nazi occupiers in Turin. In 1945 he organised a general strike in the northern rump of Italy that led to the eventual uprising against the Nazis. Postwar he became a photo-journalist, and then a documentary-maker (a move that would lead to and inform feature film production).

Much of this wartime experience is expressed in his Oscar-winning feature *Kapo* (Vides/Zebra/Francinex, Italy/France, 1960), which details the story of a French Jewess deported to a Nazi concentration camp. Many of his wartime actions against the Nazis are transposed to Algiers for his later work *The Battle of Algiers* (including the scene where Omar steals a microphone from a French soldier, allowing him to broadcast encouragement to the striking Algerians).

In the 1990s he was Director of the Venice Film Festival, and continued to make films, though success eluded him.

Similarly, in Abbas Kiarostami's *The Wind Will Carry Us*, a car full of educated city dwellers are placed in contrast with superficially less sophisticated rural villagers, and the spectator is given a construction of the confusion they themselves face. The sophisticated 'engineers' are left impotent in the face of rural life, an impotence best symbolised by the group's leader Bezhad (played by Bezhad Dorani) continually climbing a hill above the village in order to get reception on his mobile phone.

This is a contrast that is also played upon in Rahmin Bahrani's *Chop Shop* where the unrelenting poverty of 12-year-old Ale (played by Alejandro Polanco) and his 16-year-old sister Isamar (played by Isamar Gonzales) in the heart of Queens, New York City is almost alien to the cinematic city so often presented to spectators. While the central story is reminiscent of Vittorio de Sica's *Shoeshine* or Satyajit Ray's *Pather Panchali*, it is the opening shots of day labourers that give it an immediate Neo-realist context (a contemporary re-creation of the opening of Vittorio de Sica's *The Bicycle Thief*), with a stark depiction of the 'humble', almost Third World poor waiting to be chosen for work, despondent in their desperation, and framed by the twin symbols of American wealth in the background: the Chrysler Building and the Empire State Building.

ACTIVITY

How are figures of authority characterised in the films you have studied? What do you think the filmmaker is trying to persuade you of in this characterisation?

What cinematic techniques do the filmmakers use to position the audience in relation to social and political institutions in the films you have studied? How effective do you feel these techniques are for a modern cine-literate audience?

How is community represented in the films you have studied? What is the attitude of these communities to outside authority? What values do you think the Neo-realist filmmakers were establishing with these representations?

Neo-realism may be described as reflecting society's need for social and political change. What social and political changes can you perceive as needed from the films you have studied?

Production context

Admiral Stone, the Commander in Chief of the Allied Forces in the Italian theatre of operations, decided that Italian cinema was too powerful a medium of propaganda to be left in the hands of the Italian state, especially since its filmmakers were all Fascist trained and, up until only a few weeks before the Italian surrender, had been working on Fascist films. His original decision was to close the cinemas, close the studios, and take over the distribution chain (as the Allies did later in Germany at the end of the Second World War). However, Roberto Rossellini and other filmmakers persuaded him to let them work, producing the anti-Fascist, Neo-realist films that have influenced generations of filmmakers around the world.

As Italy recovered and as the studios were rebuilt, the government introduced subsidies to promote this new form of Italian filmmaking, allowing it to flourish into the late 1940s. The Allied occupiers saw such films as a method of ensuring that Fascism did not resurface, and supported their criticisms of social division.

Case study
CINECITTÀ

Fascist dictator Benito Mussolini considered film to be an important tool in the Fascist state, both for control and propaganda, and decided that a film studio complex to rival Hollywood should be built to produce films which would show the world the glory of Fascist Italy. Located on the southeastern outskirts of Rome, Cinecittà (Cinema City) was constructed on the banks of the River Tiber in 1935 to 1936 from the ruins of a previous (and important) studio, Cines.

Opened by Benito Mussolini in April 1937, it was closely connected to the Instituto Luce – the state-run newsreel and documentary production facility. Mussolini's statement 'Il cinema è l'arma più forte' ('Cinema is the most powerful weapon') became the slogan for the new studios and, to show his commitment to this venture, Mussolini placed his son Vittorio in charge of production.

In order to ensure all filmmakers working in Cinecittà were working in the 'Italian style', a film school was established next to the studios. The Centro Experimentale di Cinematographia developed filmmakers, using the newsreels and documentaries of Luce through to the 'White Telephone' films of Cinecittà. This initial actuality and documentary experience of filmmakers such as Visconti, Rossellini and de Sica eventually fed through to the 'look' of Neo-realism.

In 1942 and 1943 Cinecittà suffered serious blast damage in Allied bombing raids, and when the Nazis took control of Rome in 1943 they stripped the studios of much of their equipment to install in Nazi-controlled studios in Venice. By the time the Allies liberated Rome the studios were being used as a refugee camp. Closed by Admiral Stone (the Allies' American Commander in Chief), they reopened in 1945 and a period of rebuilding and re-equipping ensued.

The studios are still in operation today, having been used for both Italian and international film productions including *Gangs of New York* (Entertainment/ Miramax/Alberto Grimaldi, US, 2002, *Dir*: Martin Scorcese, and *The Passion of the Christ* (Icon/Newmarket, US, 2004, *Dir*: Mel Gibson), and television productions including *Rome* (BBC/HBO, UK/US, 2005)

Changes in government and changes in the global political arena meant that as the decade ended the left-wing leanings of Neo-realism fell out of favour. Western filmmaking was positioned in the political confrontation with the communist East, and the Italian state wanted to show its Western allies that it was a modern, future-facing and prosperous democracy. Neo-realism did little to engage with any of these aims. Indeed, Christian Democrat future prime minister Giulio Andreotti wrote an open letter in the Party newspaper accusing the Neo-realists of slandering Italy before the world. He went further by enacting a law (*la legge Andreotti* – the Andreotti law) that served to promote Italian film (by ensuring minimum runs at all cinemas and taxing film imports) while introducing pre-censorship where scripts had to be approved by a government Ministry before funding could be granted. A film could also be denied an export licence, thereby effectively cutting off the funding opportunities offered by international co-production. Filmmaking had returned to being controlled by the state, just as it had been under the Fascists.

As the 1950s progressed, Italian life changed dramatically from a rural economy to the world's sixth largest industrial nation. The revived Italian film industry formed significant relationships with Hollywood, and American culture began to dominate Italian life. The government supported historical epics, horror films, the Commedia all'italiana and spaghetti westerns, and the number of films being made in Italy grew from a 1945 figure of only twenty to 201 in 1954. By 1952 however, Neo-realist filmmaking in Italy was virtually dead (though the success of Visconti's filmmaking allowed him to offer a finale to the movement as late as 1960 with *Rocco and His Brothers*).

Throughout the rest of the world the Neo-realist movement received a similar fortune at the hands of national governments, with it being supported by left-leaning governments to bolster their position against the right-wing opposition, then disowned, or, worse, repressed when the right-wing opposition assumed power. The exception to this has been the case of Cuba, where the communist government has consistently supported and championed the Neo-realist movement as a cinema of the people, and as such has funnelled significant funding to Neo-realist filmmakers through the ICAIC (the state-controlled film funding body).

ACTIVITY

Make a timeline of Italian Neo-realist film. Compare this against a timeline of postwar political events (you can create this from an encyclopaedia or an online resource). Are there any interesting points of connection between the two? If so, what can you conclude from this?

Were the Neo-realist filmmakers better off under the Fascist regime or under the postwar democracy?

Look at the political history of South America over the past half century, and compare it against the emergence of new Neo-realist movements.

Do you notice a pattern emerging? If so, what do you think this says about Neo-realist filmmaking?

Using the Internet, see what information you can gather together on Cinecittà (both historical and contemporary). What other Italian film studios can you find information on?

EXAM QUESTIONS

- Neo-realism has been described as the cinema of the humble. From the films you have studied, demonstrate how this focus is realised.

- How far does performance contribute to the Neo-realist nature of the films you have studied?

- There is a bleak, stark quality about the narratives of Neo-realist films. How do Neo-realist filmmakers employ cinematic techniques to achieve this?

- Although a realist cinema, many of the Neo-realist films rely on symbols to highlight the central themes of their subject. How effective at highlighting these themes are the symbols in the films you have studied?

Recommended reading

Bondanella, P. (2001) *Italian Cinema: From Neorealism to the Present* (3rd edn). Continuum International Publishing Group

Bondanella, P. (1993) *The Films of Roberto Rossellini*. Cambridge University Press

Liehm, M. (1984) *Passion and Defiance: Film in Italy from 1942 to the Present*. University of California Press

Marcus, M. (1986) *Italian Film in the Light of Neorealism*. Princeton University Press

Nowell-Smith, G. (2008) *Making Waves: New Wave, Neorealism, and the New Cinemas of the 1960s*. Continuum International Publishing Group

Rocchio, V. (1999) *Cinema of Anxiety: A Psychoanalysis of Italian Neorealism*. University of Texas Press

Rossellini, R. (1995) *My Method: Writings and Interviews*. Marsilio

Vermilye, J. (1994) *Great Italian Films*. Citadel Press

Williams, C. (ed.) (1990) *Realism and the Cinema*. BFI/Routledge

Internet sources

http://www.inblackandwhite.com
Useful overview of key Italian Neo-realist films and filmmakers

http://www.greencine.com
Megan Ratner's article on Neo-realism

http://www.articlemagazine.com/articlesp99/drothbarbody.html
The Cinema of Revolution by Daniel Rothbart – detailed exploration of Pontecorvo and *The Battle of Algiers*

www.gpc.peachnet.edu/~jriggs/film1301/notes10.htm
Study guide for Neo-realism

www.carleton.edu/curricular/MEDA/classes/media110/Voigt/paper5.html
Essay on Neo-realism

http://uk.youtube.com/watch?v=9805LvrMiw8 and http://uk.youtube.com/watch?v=0ecHvfiQi0I&feature=related
Martin Scorcese presents a two-part documentary about Italian Neo-realism

http://www.youtube.com/watch?v=MjL8NLanOeg
Trailer for *Chop Shop*

12 NEW WAVES

In studying this topic area you will consider the following:

- what is a new wave in film (and the other arts)?
- the influence of new technology on the development of New Wave cinema
- definitions of realism
- conventions of imitation in art
- the relationship between film and the audience

Principal films:

Breathless (*Dir*: Godard, 1959)

Chungking Express (*Dir*: Wong Kar Wai, 1994)

Along with the principal films you will also need to study one or two further films but in less depth.

Some suggestions for supplemental films:

Jules et Jim (Truffaut, 1962) to develop the study of the French New Wave

Festen (Vinternberg, 1998) which provides the opportunity to analyse the concept of New Wave cinema in more recent developments (there is more information on *Festen* on the companion website)

Schuzou River (Ye Lou, China, 2000) to develop the study of East Asian New Wave

This chapter introduces definitions of New Wave cinema which can be applied across different films and periods. The emphasis is on a comparative approach, developing an argument about what constitutes a new wave and the similarities and differences of films across movements.

New Wave includes the study of some of the most influential ideas and film styles in cinema; the experimentation with film language which at times is in opposition to Hollywood (or more generally mainstream) filmmaking. In the previous section we considered the complex relationship between Hollywood and indigenous cinema, and New Wave films can be considered in a similar context. While New Wave filmmakers may reject or attack Hollywood cinema they are also defined by it; they are 'not Hollywood'. It is also important to remember that many New Wave filmmakers are fans of Hollywood and are inspired by the genre form and visual style; this is particularly true of the French New Wave.

What is a new wave?

The following extract is taken from *The Oberhausen Manifesto* (Oberhausen is a city in Germany), a declaration – deliberately produced in the style of a political manifesto – by a group of German filmmakers in 1962, which was an attack on the West German film industry of the time:

> The new film needs new freedoms. Freedom from the usual conventions of the industry. Freedom from the influence of commercial partners.
>
> We have concrete ideas about the production of the new German film with its intellectual, formal and economic aspects.
>
> The old film is dead. We believe in the new.

ACTIVITY

- What do you think is meant by the phrase 'the usual conventions of the industry'? What aspects of film production, distribution and exhibition are being referred to?

- How can filmmakers challenge 'intellectual' and 'economic' aspects of cinema?

- What do you think a new German film would look like?

The *Oberhausen Manifesto* is typical of New Wave filmmakers' determination to overturn the conventions of the previous generation of cinema. It is unusual though in the writing of a manifesto. Most new waves comprise a group of individuals who may share the same aims about filmmaking, but have a different understanding of how these aims may be achieved. This is certainly evident in the films of the French New Wave where key directors Jean-Luc Godard, François Truffaut and Claude Chabrol make very different types of films.

The term 'New Wave' exists across a range of forms. There are new waves in painting, music, fashion, literature and theatre as well as film. New waves are cyclical; often becoming conventional and part of the mainstream. They are in turn challenged by a new style. New waves, which appear at different times and places and in different artistic contexts, are always about criticising what has gone before and trying to create a new form to replace it. Therefore these movements tend to be associated with youth, experimentation and the rejection of the values of a previous era which is often perceived as boring and conventional. It is for this reason that new waves are often controversial, as they are (or are perceived to be) an attack on traditional forms and values.

Case study
THE FRENCH NEW WAVE

Context

The filmmakers of the French New Wave have influenced cinema in two major ways:

- As critics on the film journal *Cahiers du Cinema* they developed the auteur theory.
- As film directors they challenged the established conventions of filmmaking in form, content and institutional practice.

Authorship theory

The key directors of the French New Wave – Jean-Luc Godard, François Truffaut, Claude Chabrol, Eric Rohmer – had been film critics writing for the French cinema magazine *Cahiers du Cinema*. This was the first film journal to treat cinema as an art form and to discuss it in an academic way. In the early 1950s this group of critics developed an argument through a long series of articles which became known as '*la politique des auteurs*' (auteur policy). Taken up by American critics in the 1960s these ideas became known as the **auteur theory** or **authorship theory**. This is problematic, as it suggests that the *Cahiers* critics were putting forward a theory which would explain the way existing cinema should be interpreted – and this is

continued

often how it is used now. Auteur theory was originally developed as a policy – a statement of intent – in this case an attack on the French cinema of the time, but more importantly a statement of intent about what film should be like.

> **POLEMIC:** a polemic is a subjective, passionate and strongly worded argument usually against an individual, a group or an idea. It is very often controversial and political, challenging established conventions. It is useful to think of '*la politique des auteurs*' as a polemical argument specifically about the present and future of French cinema which was translated into a theory about cinema in general.

In their writings the critics argued that film was primarily a visual medium rather than a literary one and that the director was the author of a film in the same way as a writer is the author of a novel. In one influential essay 'Le Camera Stylo' ('The Camera Writes') (1954), Alexander Astruc argued that the film director 'writes' a film with the camera as if he was an artist with a paintbrush. Rather than film language being used for the adaptation of a script, it should be the visual language which is most important. Therefore the director is the true auteur of a film because the visual language is the language of cinema; the script is literary, a different language entirely.

New waves and oppositions

An influential way of defining any New Wave cinema has been in terms of oppositions. This is a similar type of categorisation to that found in narrative theory. It is based on the assumption that new waves are in opposition to the mainstream form against which they are defined.

French New Wave as oppositional form

The French New Wave is defined as such because of its attack on the previous generation of filmmakers who dominated French cinema. One of the most influential directors of the New Wave, Godard, is quoted addressing a group of leading writers and directors of the French cinema in the 1950s; 'Your camera movements are bad . . . you no longer know what cinema is.'

As with the extract from the *Oberhausen Manifesto*, there is a declaration about what cinema *should* be in the future and how it will be different from the present and the past. In this case the 'old' cinema was referred to by the New Wave filmmakers as the 'tradition of quality' or the '*Cinema du Papa*'.

ACTIVITY

■ Quality is normally used as a term of praise; how might the New Wave use the term disparagingly? You could link your ideas to the other definition, the *Cinema du Papa*.

Characteristics of the French New Wave

Breathless may be seen as the quintessential film of the French New Wave, containing all the features that are characteristic of the movement:

Figure 12.1 *Au Bout de Souffle (Breathless)* (Godard, 1959).

continued

- **Shot on location in Paris and Marseilles in one month** (August to September 1959). (Some critics at the time referred to the films of the French New Wave as glorified travelogues for Paris.)
- **Natural lighting**
- **Handheld camera**
- **Experimentation with sound**: Unpredictable mixture of diegetic and non-diegetic sound, sometimes used as a counterpoint to the action on screen, sometimes to reinforce the action – but often in a melodramatic way.
- **Linking devices**: Godard uses techniques from early and silent cinema, such as irising, masking and the fade to black, to link scenes.
- **Uneven tone**: The tone of the film can change suddenly (e.g: from comic to tragic).
- **Elliptical editing**: Removing the continuity in time and space between shots. The most extreme form is the jump cut. The emphasis on elliptical editing is linked to a change in the narrative structure which could be characterised as:
- **Limited emphasis on cause and effect**: In conventional, plot-driven filmmaking each shot, each line of dialogue has a logical response; a reverse shot, an answer to a question. In *Breathless* there is an overall structure of cause and effect in the plot but often not within specific scenes and sequences.

Before looking in detail at the effects of discontinuities of narrative (limited cause and effect) and editing, it is useful to remind ourselves of what is meant by continuity in narrative and editing.

In studying any New Wave or mainstream cinema it is important to remember that narrative structure and editing are very closely linked.

Narrative may be defined as the *recounting of a series of fictional events which are linked in time and space*.

Features of classic narrative

- Events are organised in a cause-and-effect relationship and progress towards an inevitable conclusion.
- There is emphasis on identification with character.
- There is a high degree of closure (resolution).

In narrative films it is by linking together shots and scenes through **editing** that the moving forward of narrative takes place.

Continuity editing

■ Cutting breaks a scene into fragments; continuity editing creates a unity of time and space from those fragments.

■ Editing imitates the space of Renaissance painting, creating an illusion of depth on a flat screen.

■ Continuity editing aims to create coherence and orientate the viewer; it always positions the spectator on the same side of the action (known – from the theatre – as the fourth wall).

■ Continuity editing also creates dramatic focus, tempo and mood.

(Adapted from Buckland, 2000)

Textual analysis: opening of *Breathless*

The defining characteristics of the French New Wave may be seen in the opening sequence of *Breathless*.

Watch the first five minutes of the film and make notes on the following:

■ The film opens with a dedication to Monogram Pictures, one of the few independent film studios of the Classic Hollywood Studio system. How does this fit with what you know about Godard as a critic and as a filmmaker? Does it create expectations about what the film is going to be about?

■ What type of shot does the film open with? How does this subvert audience expectations? Consider the order of shots and subject matter.

■ There follows a sequence of shot reverse shots of Michel and a woman. Watch these carefully; how are they different from a conventional use of continuity editing? Consider the use of eyeline matches and the establishment of space between the two characters.

■ The most extreme form of discontinuity editing is the jump cut. How many jump cuts can you see while Michel is driving to Paris? What is the effect of these on the viewer? How do they affect the time and space set up in the film?

■ As with any film, the opening sequence of *Breathless* introduces the main character. What do we find out about Michel in this sequence? Consider his dialogue, actions, costume and mannerisms.

■ List the signifiers of genre in the sequence. Can you identify any differences between this and a Hollywood genre film?

■ Looking at the sequence again – and over your notes – make a list of the different ways that Godard reminds the audience that they are watching a film.

continued

Effect of discontinuity editing and the jump cut

> **ELLIPSIS:** an ellipsis is the omission of an implied word or a mark indicating where a text has been cut; for example, the use of dots (. . .). Elliptical editing is therefore the removal of implied action from a sequence. In some ways all editing is elliptical; a director won't show us every movement of a character but imply it. However, a jump cut is an extreme version of this type of editing, creating a disorientating effect for the audience.

The jump cut is used throughout the film, but can be clearly seen in Michel's actions of the first few minutes; he steals a car with the help of a woman, drives along abusing other drivers and some hitch-hikers, is pursued by police, pulls off the road, produces a gun and shoots one of the police. He then flees across the fields and arrives back in Paris.

This is all conveyed in a sequence of very brief shots, juxtaposing extreme close-ups with mid-shots (a jump cut between scenes) and jump cuts within a continuous shot (e.g. a sudden change in road as Michel drives). This creates a non-naturalistic ellipsis in the action. In a conventional film of the time this would have been conveyed in many separate shots, making sure that each event was fully explained. Jump cuts eliminate the smooth transitions which allow the audience to forget that they are watching a film and remind us that it is a constructed work, not reality.

ACTIVITY

- Does the use of discontinuities in editing confuse the audience?
- How does the audience make sense of what is happening on screen?
- How does it affect the construction of time and space on screen?

The French New Wave is *self-reflexive cinema* – films about the process of filmmaking more than about a particular story. For Godard, mainstream cinema's reliance on *unobtrusive techniques* led to the denial of film itself; the audience forgot that they were watching a film.

ACTIVITY

Today the techniques in *Breathless* are far more commonplace across film and television.

■ List examples of film and television programmes you've seen which use these techniques.
■ Do they have a similar effect on the audience to that intended by Godard?

New Wave cinema and new technology

Some of the aspects of film form derided by the French New Wave in the *Cinema du Papa* were a product of the limitations of existing technology. The sound cameras were heavy and difficult to move which in turn meant studio shooting that required artificial lighting, which was often unrealistic and lifeless. In the late 1950s the handheld camera was developed, which allowed filmmakers a greater freedom to film outside of the studio; to take cinema to the streets.

This development changed not only the look of films but also the institutional structure; films could be made independently, outside of the studios and for much less money, helping to make filmmaking a little more democratic.

ACTIVITY

■ Which new technological developments can you think of in filmmaking since the 1950s?
■ How have any of these changed the way films look or how they are made?
■ Which of these new technologies have you used?

Breathless is often cited by contemporary filmmakers (Tarantino, Scorsese) as one of the most influential films in cinema history; this would suggest that it was something new and different. Here is a synopsis of the plot of the film (warning: major plot developments revealed!):

Synopsis: *Breathless*

A small-time gangster, Michel, returns to Paris after shooting a policeman, to meet up with an ex-girlfriend, Patricia, an American studying journalism. Michel is on the run and the film follows his attempts to escape the police, get some money and make Patricia love him. The film ends with his death at the hands of the police after Patricia betrays him.

It is evident from this synopsis that the originality and difference which inspires people about this film is not to be found at the level of the plot, which is a mixture of the gangster and crime genres, both popular Hollywood forms of the 1930s onward. However, the narrative and use of genre in the film is not as conventional as it first seems and often subverts the audience's expectations. For example, the synopsis makes the film sound more action-packed than it actually is; despite being a fugitive Michel doesn't really do anything and spends most of his time walking the streets of Paris or in bed. Rather than the violence and suspense we would expect from this hybrid genre, there are long sequences where the main characters discuss topics – the meaning of art, abortion, William Faulkner, the relative attractiveness of women from different countries, Humphrey Bogart – which seem to have nothing to do with the plot. At times it seems that the people involved (director, actors, cinematographer) in the making of *Breathless* are playing at making a gangster film – they know that Jean Paul Belmond and Jean Seberg are pretending (or acting), and they know that the audience knows this too. In this film Godard no longer expects the audience to suspend disbelief; to believe that Michel exists and is on the run from the police.

If this is the case then it will mean that some of the usual pleasures offered by mainstream cinema – identification with character, excitement, suspense – will be lost. The whole emotional involvement we invest in a film relies on the suspension of disbelief – an unspoken bargain between the filmmaker and the audience. This deliberate attempt to change the type of pleasure an audience experiences when watching a film is one of the aspects which makes the movement and Godard in particular controversial, and can make the films difficult to watch.

ACTIVITY

To try to understand why Godard would want to make films in this way we need to look at the wider context of conventions of realism in film – and other art forms.

Read the following comments:

Art imitates life
Life imitates art
Art is a process of construction and selection

- In what ways is it true to say that art imitates life? Can you give examples from film and painting?
- Why do we expect art to imitate life?
- Does life imitate art? Have you ever imitated the actions in a film?
- How is art a process of construction and selection? Is this true of all art forms?

Realism and the imitation of life

Previously in Film Studies realism has referred to two types of visual style (or aesthetic). The first attempts to show the world as it is. It is associated with the representation of working-class experience and the discussion of social and political conflict. The second use of the term is rather different, as it refers to Hollywood cinema – the classic realist text – which is usually associated with glamour and escapism. In this context 'realist' refers to the idea of transparency, the illusion created by the film language that what we are watching is real and not just a film. The two uses of the term share the aim of convincing people of the truthfulness of what they are showing; creating the suspension of disbelief. In fact there is a central contradiction in the use of the term *realism* in any film; film is an imitation of reality – not reality.

This idea that art should imitate life is a very old one and it often affects the way we judge the worth of art; whether we think a painting resembles what it is supposed to represent (a landscape, a still life, a portrait) or not. It was only at the beginning of the twentieth century that artists began to question the accepted relationship between art and reality and instead pointed to the differences between the two. According to these artists representational art is in fact a selected, constructed and often more glamorous version of reality; not a mirror on the world at all. A similar comment could be made about film. The films which make us believe they are 'real' are also not a mirror but a construction. Therefore art does not imitate life (even when it tries to); film does not imitate life. This – if you agree with the statement as Godard obviously does – is a new wave of thinking about what art in general and film in particular is for. Art can be abstract, not representational, and films no longer have to adhere to the rules of filmmaking which had been in place for the previous fifty years.

INFORMATION BOX – IMITATION AND BREATHLESS

i

There are some interesting scenes in *Breathless* where Godard seems to be commenting on the idea of imitation in art, the assumption that film is a mirror on the world.

Humphrey Bogart

The central character, Michel, is a fan of Humphrey Bogart. Bogart was a Hollywood star in the 1940s; his persona was based on roles as a gangster but also as a romantic lead. Michel imitates Bogart in several ways – he dresses like him, smokes like him and is an anti-hero gangster. Why do you think Godard included this element in the film? Some suggestions:

Figure 12.2 Humphrey Bogart.

- it shows us that Michel is a fantasist who cannot tell the difference between reality and fiction
- it reminds us that Godard is a fan of Hollywood genre films and that *Breathless* is a homage to those films
- the reference to other film stars is a way of foregrounding film language, reminding us that this is a film.

It is clear that Godard wants us to think about the relationship between Michel, Bogart and us because he emphasises it through the film language. When Michel is being chased by the police he stops at a cinema and looks at the stills advertising the film *The Harder They Come*. The sequence cuts between close-ups of Michel and what he is looking at (a publicity photograph of Bogart) and lasts about a minute. This duration of shot, when nothing seems to be happening, is typical of Godard's films and is intended to make the audience question the images they are being shown. Some of the thoughts that might occur to the audience in this sequence include:

- Why do we admire particular film stars?
- Why do we copy certain aspects of a star's appearance (clothes, hair, body shape)?
- Is the still image of Bogart any less real in a film than the actor himself?
- Film isn't a mirror on the world but is in fact made up of layers of construction: Jean Paul Belmondo is playing Michel Poiccard who in turn is playing a character called Lazlo Kovacs, an imitation of Humphrey Bogart which in turn is a persona constructed by an American actor.

Renoir

Another reference to imitation comes in the bedroom sequence which makes up the central part of the film. Patricia is putting up a portrait of a girl by the Impressionist painter, Auguste Renoir. As with the Bogart sequence, Godard draws attention to the relationship between art and imitation. It is also typical of his films that high culture (Renoir) is treated in the same way as popular culture (Bogart). Rather than emphasising the difference between the two art forms, which had been the norm, Godard presents them both as images to be analysed and questioned.

- How may other references to popular and high culture can you note from the film?

In this context, Godard's reference to Hollywood films may be seen as a statement about definitions of art. At a time when Europe was seen as the only producer of film as art, Godard, first in the auteur theory and then in his films, challenged this, saying that art film was Hollywood film.

Realism in the context of New Wave cinemas means something new; it is the foregrounding of film language, the reality of the film itself. By making the audience aware of the technical aspects of filmmaking – the form – it is a constant reminder that you are watching a film, not life. This belief is based on questioning years of assumptions about the conventions of artistic practice.

Audience and new waves

> **I don't think you should feel about a movie. You should feel about a woman. You can't kiss a movie.**
>
> (Jean-Luc Godard)

Godard's stated desire to make an audience think – rather than feel – about film has been a contentious one, as it suggests the following:

- it isn't possible to think and feel simultaneously
- feeling is less useful than thinking
- the role of cinema as an escapist form leads to the audience becoming an unthinking mass.

These ideas about the audience have also been attacked as being elitist; i.e. New Wave films are made for a small intellectual audience who understand the theory behind the making of the film.

The most obvious way in which Godard attempts to stop the audience 'feeling' is through the different forms of disruptions and reminders that they are watching a film and not real life. This is an approach which is shared by most New Wave filmmakers, particularly in their use of film language, narrative and identification with character.

Chungking Express and narrative structure

So far, one of the defining characteristics of New Wave films has been the experimentation with narrative in contrast to mainstream conventions.

In *Breathless*, what aspects of the narrative structure could be defined as different to classic narrative? Consider:

- the characteristics of the opening and ending of the film
- does it conform to a three-act structure (beginning, middle and end)?
- how do the changes in mood and pace of the film affect the experience of watching it?

In the comparative study of *Chungking Express*, the disruption of conventional narrative structure is one of the key areas to consider. It is also useful to place these narrative techniques in a wider context of film styles.

Narrative experimentation – part of the mainstream?

While experimentation with storytelling forms is often seen as a challenge to mainstream conventions there are also examples of this experimentation in mainstream cinema. In *Love Actually* (Richard Curtis, 2003), *Crash* (Paul Haggis, 2004) and *Pulp Fiction* (Quentin Tarrantino, 1994), multiple story lines are used and in the latter the chronology is disrupted so that the film doesn't follow a linear pattern of beginning, middle and end. In *The Clearing* (Pieter Jan Brugger, 2004) (a thriller starring Helen Mirren and Robert Redford), two different time scales are used to tell one story. *Memento* (Christopher Nolan, 2000) continually comments on the audience's expectations of how a story should be told by the constant use of flashbacks due to the character's short-term memory loss. The portmanteau film – which told a series of separate stories – has also been popular with films from *Dead of Night* (1945), a British horror film, to American films such as *New York Stories* (1989) and *Four Rooms* (1995).

ACTIVITY

Narrative

- Which of the films mentioned above have you seen? Can you think of others which use narrative structure in an interesting way?
- Choose one film from your list – are there similarities with classic narrative? For example, is there a beginning, middle and end?
- Were you aware of the narrative form as you watched the film? Did it distance you from other aspects of the film such as characters, plot and so on?
- If experimental narratives are found in mainstream film then what effect does this have on definitions of new waves? What does it suggest about the relationship between Hollywood and other cinemas?

INFORMATION BOX – NARRATIVE STRUCTURE: THE FLASHBACK

The flashback is the most conventional way of disrupting time and space in a film. Because it is preceded by a transition (dissolve, fade) which is

continued

often accompanied by a voice-over (*I knew things would never be the same after that summer . . .*), the audience is not confused about the change in time and space which is still part of the continuity of the film. Some New Wave filmmakers have experimented with the flashback but removed the conventional signifiers so that the movement – whether in time or space – is unclear and disorientating. One of the most celebrated examples of this is *Last Year at Marienbad* (Alain Resnais, France, 1961), and *Pierrot le Fou* (Godard, France, 1962) would also provide a good analysis of this use of narrative.

Chungking Express tells two stories about two policemen, Cop 223 and Cop 663, and their love lives. The stories are independent from each other, but both are set in the bars, restaurants and hotels of Hong Kong. The *mise-en-scène* creates a vivid image of a modern, cosmopolitan city. It is a low-budget film and it uses many techniques associated with New Wave filmmaking – handheld camera, jump cuts – but adds new kinds of discontinuities such as the slowing down and speeding up of the film stock.

Figure 12.3 *Chungking Express* (Wong Kar Wai, 1994).

Chungking Express is a visually striking film which uses a variety of film language styles and has been compared to a music video. As with *Breathless*, at times it seems that Wong wants the audience to appreciate the form of the film more than the content.

Having watched *Chungking Express*, think about which of the two story segments you preferred. What do you think appealed to you about that one? Consider plot, character, genre.

The narrative form – two stories in one film – could be one of the ways in which Wong Kar Wai foregrounds the film language, reminding the audience that they are watching a film. In this respect, Wong may be compared to Godard – the form of the film, the film language is as important as the content. However, the subject matter in this film does seem to be important to the director – and very carefully thought through and structured. For example, the two stories are not completely separate but are linked through a variety of settings, characters and themes which may not be immediately apparent.

ACTIVITY

Watch *Chungking Express* and make notes on the following for each of the stories:

■ Write a brief synopsis for each story.
■ List the main characters. Who are they? What do they do? What are their names? What is their relationship with each other?
■ Describe the main settings which feature in each story.
■ How does each story end?
■ What other forms of narrative structure could be used to tell these stories? Why do you think this particular structure was chosen?

Looking at your notes, some connections should begin to emerge between the two stories. Here are a few.

Both stories feature policemen, known by their police numbers, who have been rejected by women but are unable to accept it. In both stories another woman appears – in story 1 a *femme fatale*; in story 2 a seemingly innocent young waitress – who offers romantic and sexual possibilities. The theme of obsession also structures both stories. Cop 223 buys tins of pineapple all with the same expiry date, 1 May, believing that by this date his girlfriend will return to him, while in story 2 Cop 663 follows the same routine every day.

■ What other examples of obsession are there in the film?
■ What else links the two stories? Consider character, setting and plot.

Hong Kong: East and West

Hong Kong is often seen as representing a crossroads between Eastern and Western culture due to its history as both a Chinese and a British colony. Britain invaded Hong Kong in 1842 during the war with China (known as the Opium Wars) over the free movement and trade of opium. It remained under British rule – which oversaw a liberal economy – until 1997 when Hong Kong was 'handed back' to China. This influence of different – often contrasting – cultures is evident throughout *Chungking Express* in the setting, costume, dialogue and musical soundtrack. The appearance of Brigitte Lin in her trench coat and blonde wig, the corporate logos and the use of American pop songs on the soundtrack are just a few examples of this. This representation of Hong Kong as a conflicted city – part British, part Chinese – also infects the characters. In *Chungking Express*, Hong Kong is a city which lacks an identity and is a place of anxiety in the buildup to the handover to a communist state. This is also evident in the characters. In both stories the policemen are filled with longing for something which has gone, they are unable to think or act rationally, they are in a state of complete self-absorption and isolation – perhaps Wong is using the characters as a metaphor for Hong Kong at the end of the twentieth century.

This theme of the conflicted state of Hong Kong as it faces an uncertain future is also found in other films of this period (these can be included in the East Asian New Wave topic); *Made in Hong Kong* (Fruit Chan, Hong Kong, 1997), *The River* (Ming Liang-Tsai, Taiwan, 1997) and *Schuzou River* (Ye Lou, China, 2000).

Defining a new wave: *Chungking Express* and Hong Kong cinema

As is evident in *Chungking Express*, Hong Kong Cinema is characterised by its mixture of references from Eastern and Western culture. These include the kung fu, gangster and thriller genres as well as influences from Chinese folklore and ghost stories.

Chungking Express has to be studied in the wider context of the Hong Kong film industry in the 1980s and 1990s which is unique in East Asian cinema. Hong Kong was one of the 'economic dragons' of the 1980s along with South Korea, Taiwan and Singapore. These countries experienced a rapid economic – and in some cases social – development throughout the period. However, of this group only Hong Kong developed a successful film industry (which has also been affected by the economic recession of the late 1990s; Wong Kar Wai has difficulties getting funding for his films now) and there are various possible reasons for this. In Hong Kong filmmakers have been free to express themselves with little interference from the state and censorship is very relaxed. This marks them out from other East Asian cinemas – particularly Singapore and China – where directors work within state-controlled, heavily censored industries. Another reason for the continued popularity of cinema-going in Hong Kong is that it is a small city with a high-density population where the social experience of the cinema has meant that it has remained dominant in the face of competition from TV and video.

Hong Kong cinema in the 1980s

As new waves are defined in part by their challenge to the dominant cinema which preceded them, it is important to consider Hong King filmmaking in the 1980s. The development of cinema during this period may be characterised by two international figures, Jackie Chan and John Woo. One of the most popular genres of this period was the kung fu comedies where Jackie Chan developed his star persona. Importantly for the development of Hong Kong cinema these were initially historical dramas, conventional of the time, but as the cycle progressed in films such as *Police Story* (1985) and *Armour of God* (1986) the settings, themes and characters were contemporary. A new hybrid genre – kung fu and ghost story – also emerged in the 1980s, combining the special effects of martial arts films with traditional Chinese ghost stories. The greatest critical and commercial success of these was *A Chinese Ghost Story* (Ching Siu-Tung, 1987), and the influence on contemporary cinema may be seen in *Crouching Tiger Hidden Dragon* (Ang Lee, 2000) and *Hero* (Zhang Yimou, 2003).

John Woo's films of this period also reflect the understanding of Eastern and Western styles and genres. Like Jackie Chan, John Woo now works in Hollywood (*Face Off*, 1997, *Paycheck*, 2003, *Mission Impossible 2*, 2000), but his Hong Kong action films introduced a new level of violence as well as a new type of Asian hero. In films such as *A Better Tomorrow* (1986) and *Bullet in the Head* (1990), the heroes are contemporary figures recognisable from Hollywood thrillers, but they also represent traditional values and a code of honour very similar to the heroes of the historical kung fu films. Woo's films have been controversial – partly to do with the representation of violence but also because of the misogynistic attitudes of the heroes.

This context of a thriving genre cinema based on contradictory influences which also emphasised action, violence and a macho code of behaviour is the context for the work of the Asian New Wave of the 1990s in Hong Kong, South Korea and China. Confusingly for our definitions of what a New Wave is, Hong Kong cinema of the 1980s (and also New Chinese cinema of the same period) was also referred to as New Wave.

ACTIVITY

The East Asian New Wave raises difficult questions about:

- What constitutes a New Wave in cinema?
- How many filmmakers does it take to make a New Wave?

continued

- Do New Wave filmmakers need to be linked by a particular place and time?
- Can a popular genre cinema (such as that of Hong Kong in the 1980s or Japanese horror films of the late 1990s) also be defined as a New Wave?

ACTIVITY

To construct a useful analysis of New Wave films, begin with the following questions:

1 What similarities are evident across the films in:

- film language (shots, editing, lighting)
- the use of new technology
- the context of production (studio, budget)
- subject matter?

2 In what different ways can the films be defined as realist? (Consider audience response as well as film language.) How are these films different from Hollywood realist cinema?

3 What type of filmmaking do these new waves reject? Are there similarities in the characteristics across the rejected film styles?

4 How would you define each of the films studied as belonging to a New Wave? Do you think each of the films has an equal claim on the term?

EXAM QUESTIONS

- In what different ways can the films be defined as realist? (Consider audience response as well as film language.) How are these films different from Hollywood realist cinema?

- How would you define each of the films studied as belonging to a New Wave? Do you think each of the films has an equal claim on the term?

Further Reading

The following all have chapters on the different New Wave movements covered in this topic.

Bordwell, D. and Thompson, K. (eds) (1997) *Film Art: An Introduction*. McGraw Hill

Buckland, W. (2000) *Teach Yourself Film Studies*. Hodder & Stoughton

Cousins, M. (2004) *The Story of Film*. Pavillion

Hill, J. and Church-Gibson, P. (eds) (1998) *Oxford Guide to Film Studies*. Oxford University Press

Vincendeau, G. (ed.) (1996) *The Companion to French Cinema*. BFI

13 SPECIALIST STUDY 1

URBAN STORIES – POWER, POVERTY AND CONFLICT

This chapter:

- offers a general indicative approach to studying and comparing films from different social and cultural contexts
- suggests ways of approaching two case study films

INFORMATION BOX

This chapter will be relevant to the section 'FM4 – World Cinema' in the WJEC's A level in Film Studies. It will be directly applicable to questions relating to 'Specialist Study 1: Urban Stories – Power, Poverty and Conflict'. (You should note that further films that could be used in relation to this part of the syllabus may be found in other parts of this book: *Chungking Express* is used as a focus film in Chapter 12 on 'New Waves' and there are sections on *The Bicycle Thieves* and *The Battle of Algiers* in Chapter 11 on 'Neo-realism'. You may also like to consider the material offered on *Strike* in Chapter 9 on 'German and Soviet Cinemas of the 1920s'.)

Films mentioned:

As you work your way through this chapter you will need to watch *La Haine* (Kassovitz, 1995) and *City of God* (Meirelles, 2002) in full and preferably several times. (Suggested alternative films to which you may like to try to apply a similar approach would be *Amores Perros* (Iñárritu, 2000) and/or *Tsotsi* (Hood, 2005).)

Approaching films from different cultures

In the process of watching films we each bring our own awareness of the world, or our own ideology, to bear on the texts before us. In this way we each create our own understanding of any given film. When we watch the films under discussion here, *La Haine* or *City of God*, we use our knowledge of the world and our way of seeing the world to help us to make sense of the array of images and sounds presented to us. Our individual ideologies may, for example, position us as pro-police or anti-police, or as somewhere in between these poles, and this will have a bearing on how we 'read' *La Haine*.

> **IDEOLOGY:** a person's or a society's set of beliefs and values, or overall way of looking at the world.

Any text (whether a film, a painting, a photograph, a book, a newspaper article, or any other work that demands that we should 'read' or interpret its words and/or images) has the potential to support our current ideological 'take' on the world, to slightly modify our perspective in some way, or to radically challenge (and even force us to totally alter) our perception of things. In any case, there will always be a complex interplay at work between us and the text before us.

When we approach a work such as *La Haine* or *City of God* there is perhaps (as the exam board suggests) an added complication in that these films are set within cultures and social contexts that may be very alien to us. However, it is as well to remember that this is really not that much different from the usual situation when we view a new film. In watching any film we will be attempting to bring our own knowledge and understanding of the world to bear on a set of circumstances that will to some extent be alien. As women or men, we may be attempting to understand a position more usually and easily identified with by the opposite gender. As black or white, we may be attempting to understand any number of potential configurations of ethnic backgrounds that are different to our own. As someone

living in the early twenty-first century, we may be asked to understand, empathise with, or even identify with someone living any number of years previously (or any number of years into the future).

To take two random examples: how can we understand the position of a woman involved in a domestic drama set in the United States immediately after the Second World War, or how can we understand the position of a man on a battlefield during that war? We are only able to do these things through the use of certain key strategies. First of all, we are able to identify similarities between our own direct experience of the world and any film character's experience; we know what it is like to live within a domestic environment, or we know fear and pain because we have experienced these things for ourselves. Second, we are able to use our observations of other people's experiences; we have, perhaps, watched our parents living out their relationship within the home, or we have seen fear and pain being experienced by friends. Third, we are able to draw on our mediated experience of the world to help us to understand events presented to us within films; we may have read books, or newspaper or magazine articles, or watched TV programmes, or listened to radio programmes, or viewed websites that have given us perspectives of one sort or another on women's lives in postwar America or on the experience of being a soldier on a battlefield.

When we come to view a film which is set within a culture that is distinctively different from our own we have at our disposal only these same basic approaches. We can use our own experiences, or our observations of the experiences of others, to help us relate to what we are being shown. Or, we can use our mediated experience to assist us. In this last area we can set out to improve our understanding of another social environment by deliberately researching the history, the politics and the culture of this initially alien society. However, in doing this we need to be aware that everything we read or watch in order to try to extend our knowledge and understanding will have been written or constructed from a particular ideological perspective and therefore needs to be watched or read in an active, questioning way. Equally we need to be aware that we ourselves will have been 'constructed', that our ideology is likely to have been largely passively absorbed from our social environment, and therefore our own immediate, instinctive reading of any situation needs to be questioned and 'unpacked'.

Culture and subcultures

In its widest sense, the term 'culture' refers to all human actions that are socially transmitted. However, it may also be used to refer more specifically to the way of life of a particular human group living at a particular historical moment and/or within a specific geographical location; in this sense we begin to talk of cultures rather than culture. The key identifying features of any culture are its customs, rituals and normal everyday practices. We could refer, for example, to 'the youth culture of the suburbs of Paris in the 1990s' in relation to *La Haine* or to 'gang culture in the slums of Rio de Janeiro in the 1980s' in relation to *City of God*.

CULTURE: (1) The way in which forms of human activity and interaction are socially transmitted. (2) The way of life of a particular human community living at a specific time and in a particular place.

Cultural theory also uses the terms 'subcultures' (cultures subordinate to a dominant culture) and 'counter-cultures' (cultures that are actively opposed to the dominant culture). Subcultures have tended to be working class and not to have articulated their politics, while counter-cultures have tended to have a middle-class base and have focused on explicit political and ideological resistance. You might like to debate whether either of these terms could be used in relation to any cultural groups found within *La Haine* or *City of God*.

Power and conflict

Relationships of power are found within any social structure in which there are differences between groups and/or struggles over material or cultural resources, in other words in every society. The key questions on which to focus are: Who has power, and who is in a position of subordination to that power? We should also consider the nature of the power in question: Is it economic power involving the accumulation of wealth and ownership of corporations, political power involving the ability to govern and make laws, or ideological power involving control over education and the mass media?

POWER: the various forms of control some individuals and groups within society have over other individuals and groups.

Marxists suggest that within the institutions of any society power is exerted on behalf of the ruling class. The institutions, perhaps schools or colleges, or the newspaper industry, are seen as being concerned to reproduce current relationships of political and economic power by promoting the dominant ideology. These institutions shape our cultural experience, set the social and political agenda, and present us with representations and ways of seeing that support the status quo. This construction of audience perception or reality is hidden in such a way that it seems normal or natural or 'mythical' (Barthes, 1972). Louis Althusser[1] suggested that in any society there were organisations such as the police, the courts and the army that were able to use physical force as power over others but there were also other institutions such as education and the media that were able to exert ideological control or power over citizens. Relationships of power can and do exist *within* all social organisations: within the family, within street gangs, within the police, between friends. But relationships of power also exist *between* social groups: between youth groups and the police, between different street gangs, between rich and poor.

> **REPRESENTATION:** the variety of ways in which individuals and groups are displayed to audiences within the media and other cultural texts.

Case study
LA HAINE (KASSOVITZ, 1995)

Figure 13.1 *La Haine* (Kassovitz, 1995).

Characters

Thinking about the characters involved can be a good way to begin to understand any film. In *La Haine* we have three main characters: the friends, Said, Vinz and Hubert. How would we differentiate these three young people? Their ethnic origins are made clear to us: Said is Arab African-French (Beur),

Vinz has a Jewish background and Hubert is black African-French. To them, drawn together by their shared youth culture, these differences seem unimportant; but each character is shown to be very aware of the ways in which others in France might look at his ethnicity. For example, because he is 'white', it is Vinz who is given the task of attempting to gain entry to the middle-class block of flats where they hope to meet 'Asterix'.

We could also consider the role each character is given within the narrative. We may notice, for example, that after the contextualisation of the documentary footage the film opens with Said contemplating the police in a very visually distinctive way and that we end the film in a somewhat similar manner. Vinz, of course, is strongly linked in plot terms to the key prop of the handgun: the object that is dangerous in that it is likely to 'go off' or explode with deadly consequences. The scenes in which we see Vinz link him to this object, not only physically in that he possesses it but also emotionally in that he displays himself as a 'loose cannon', as someone who could explode into violence. Hubert is the most carefully delineated character: we see him alone in his bedroom and at home with his mother, for instance, in scenes that do not move the plot forward but which increase our understanding of his character and intensify our sense of identification with him.

ACTIVITY

■ How would you differentiate the three central characters? Make sure you can refer to specific scenes in order to illustrate your case and compare your ideas with other people, if possible.

(In undertaking this task it is very important to remember that film is a visual medium and may 'show' us features of an individual character's make-up through performance and/or carefully constructed shots rather than simply 'telling' us in the use of dialogue.)

■ Which one (if any) is the central 'hero'? How would you justify your choice?
■ What role(s) does Samir, the Beur police officer, play in the film?
■ Are there any other minor characters who serve to tell us more about each of the key characters?
■ Why has the older character in the scene in the toilets been included in the film?

continued

Key scenes

In discussing the characters in the film you will notice how you need to be able to refer in detail to specific scenes in order to make your case for seeing Said, Vinz or Hubert in particular ways. This knowledge of the finer points of film construction is important when you come to write about this film or any other film. You need to be able to identify the ways in which elements of *mise en scène*, cinematography, editing and sound, and the structure of the narrative, create meaning and generate audience response.

It is always important to analyse the opening to a film since this is usually particularly helpful in identifying key themes and ideas for the whole film. Here, the first scenes are played out to the soundtrack of Bob Marley's '*Burnin* and *Lootin*', suggesting a particular way of seeing the documentary footage. Marley is strongly associated with radical politics and a willingness to confront state authorities that are seen both within the music and the associated youth culture as being repressive. As a result the actions of the rioters seem to receive a form of endorsement that might not have been achieved had a different choice of musical accompaniment been made. A full analysis of the start to the film would involve considering the sequence of shots found here in much greater detail and all the time in relation to both dialogue and music.

It is important to ground your understanding of the film in this sort of detailed exploration of individual scenes. You should therefore undertake careful critical analyses of each of the following scenes:

- The TV news crew attempting to interview Said, Vinz and Hubert about the previous night's riot when they literally 'look down on' the three friends in a space that resembles a bear pit or zoo enclosure.
- Hubert in his bedroom with iconic images of rebellious black Americans in the background (the boxer Muhammad Ali, and African-American sprinters Tommie Smith and John Carlos giving a black power salute at the 1968 Mexico Olympics).
- The police and local council authorities attempting to force young people, including Said, Vinz and Hubert, from the rooftop of one of the tower blocks.
- The three main characters sitting in a children's play area filmed and edited in such a way as to convey the sense of utter boredom being experienced.
- The DJ using his decks to blast out an anti-police message in a scene which is filmed and edited to convey an experience of momentary freedom, escape or release.
- The three central characters experiencing a surreal (but notice, heavily historically grounded) storytelling experience with an older man in a Parisian toilet.

- The two experienced plain-clothes policemen 'questioning' Said and Hubert while a younger trainee officer looks on.
- The scene at the late-night exhibition in a high-class art gallery at which the class divide becomes apparent.
- The friends being confronted by a skinhead gang (raising, as in the scene with the older man in the toilet, the issue of fascism).
- The final dramatic scene in which there is a critical change to the story that has been retold several times, so that it becomes a 'society' that is 'falling'.

Messages and values

La Haine was based on an actual event: the death of an 18-year-old black youth shot during interrogation by police in 1992. This context gives the central concern for the film, but the riots and the violent confrontation between the police and young people is placed within a much wider social context.

Multiculturalism and ethnicity within modern French society is clearly explored. For example:

- Hubert's posters are of Muhammad Ali and the 'black power' salute given at the 1968 Mexico Olympics;
- the Wailers' song *Burnin and Lootin'* links directly to ideas of black uprisings.

More positively, the three friends are of mixed ethnicity, and within youth culture the separate ethnicities are shown as evolving into a vibrant hybrid cultural fusion. There is a focus on the music, dance styles and street slang ('verlan') of this contemporary popular culture.

A strong sense of the nature of the working-class experience is given, for example, through location shooting among the bleak, stark walls and tower blocks of the estate and the deliberate choice of black-and-white film stock. In addition, by transporting the friends into central Paris strong contrasts are able to be given with the middle-class experience found here. (This also places the problem firmly within the heart of French society rather than leaving it as a peripheral issue out in the 'projects'.)

Racism is shown, most obviously in the scenes with the skinhead gang. Youth unemployment is a constant feature of the social 'backdrop': neither Said nor Vinz nor Hubert has a job. Police brutality is clearly an issue, though the role of Samir and the presence of black police officers within the *mise-en-scène* of several scenes suggests this is not a simple and clear-cut matter.

continued

Social exclusion, as shown by the scenes on the tower block rooftop, in the art gallery, and in the empty high-tech shopping mall, would seem to be creating an 'underclass'. An inevitable product of that, according to the film, would seem to be rebellion and social conflict.

ACTIVITY

- Compile a list of scenes that focus on issues of race.
- List your own points regarding ways in which working-class life (maybe in relation to or in comparison to the middle-class experience) is portrayed.
- List features of contemporary youth culture as shown in the film.

Social, historical and political contexts

The 'projects', or *les banlieues*:

- *Les banlieues* are satellite 'new towns' (for which read housing estates for the poor) up to twenty miles out of Paris that almost seem designed to keep the poor out of the middle-class centre of the city.
- The 'new town' in which *La Haine* was filmed had at the time an official population of 10,000 made up of sixty different nationalities or ethnicities.
- These areas are stereotyped in the media as places of urban deprivation, crime and drug use.

The French empire and imperialism:

- France was a major colonial power in the nineteenth and twentieth centuries with colonies in Africa, the Caribbean and South-East Asia.
- The struggle for independence was particularly bitter in some countries such as Algeria (which gained independence in 1962) and Vietnam (where the French were defeated at Dien Bien Phu in 1954).
- Some colonies, like Martinique, remain and are able to send representatives to the French Assembly. Other former colonies, like Senegal, remain closely linked to France and French culture.
- French policy towards non-white ethnic groups has always been one of 'assimilation' with people being expected to take on French cultural norms and values. Many Algerians, Moroccans and Tunisians,

in particular, who went to France to work during the 1960s, have to a greater or lesser extent resisted this policy.

- Maintaining the purity of the French language both at home and abroad was given a much higher priority than the British gave to upholding English usage in their colonies.
- Verlan, or 'backslang', began around Paris in the 1980s among second-generation ethnic minority young people who saw themselves as positioned between their parents' culture and French culture.

Racism:

- Immigration was limited by the French government during the economic crisis of the early 1970s.
- Fascist far-right groups (as in many other European countries during the period) have consistently blamed unemployment on immigrants.
- In the 1980s the National Front began to win some local elections and even parliamentary seats, especially in south and southwest France.
- Those who administered Vichy France during the Second World War collaborated in sending French Jews to the concentration camps.
- Kassovitz's father (who himself fled Hungary in 1956) was the son of a concentration camp survivor. (Kassovitz plays the skinhead captured by Vinz.)

The police and racism:

- There are two main police groups in the film: the neighbourhood plain-clothes police and the riot police.
- Racism (as in the UK) has been seen to be a particular problem in the police force.
- There were over 300 deaths in police custody or from police action from 1980 to 1995 when the film was made.

Case study

CITY OF GOD (MEIRELLES, 2002)

Characters

In *City of God* we have a narrator, Rocket, who is also our central character. This is his story, the narrative of one young man who is exceptional in that he manages to escape from the slums. However, as a narrator he is also an

continued

Figure 13.2 *City of God* (Meirelles, 2002).

observer of other people's stories, a character with a privileged position from which he is able to watch domestic, familial, communal, social and even national narratives unfold. Although this film may be Rocket's story, he is continually peripheral to, or on the edge of, a series of further narratives taking place around him. The status of being an observer fits well with his chosen profession of photographer. (Incidentally, the concept of 'shooting' with a camera contrasts interestingly with the more normal form of shooting (of necessity/unavoidably?) favoured by young men from the slums.) Before his eyes (and therefore before ours) human relationships involving short, energetic lives and brutal deaths are played out against an essentially unchanging social backdrop of extreme poverty. And yet, although the deprivation of the social environment remains constant, the nature of the slums is seen to change: the gang culture becomes increasingly violent as we move forward from the 1960s, the weaponry increasingly high-powered, the drugs more potent and the gang members younger.

ACTIVITY

■ How would you differentiate each of the key characters in *City of God*? List characters and refer to specific scenes in order to illustrate your understanding of their character. Compare your list with those arrived at by other people, if possible. Discuss any differences in the scenes chosen to illustrate specific characters and any related differences in the understanding of the characters.

(Remember that film is a visual medium and may 'show' us features of an individual character's make-up through performance and/or carefully constructed shots rather than simply 'telling' us something through dialogue.)

■ Would you agree that Rocket is the central character? Would you see him as the 'hero'? Or, would you see other characters as the main focus of the film? If so, which ones and why? How would you justify your choice? Would you see these characters as 'heroes' or 'anti-heroes'?

■ How would you characterise women in the film?

ACTIVITY

■ Consider the representation of gender in more depth. What roles do men and women play in the film? Could these be seen as stereotypical male and female roles in film terms and/or in social terms?

■ Would you agree that women are peripheral to the narrative and unimportant in plot terms? Do men or women 'drive' the narrative?

■ Would you consider this to be a 'male' text? If so, what features make it so? Given the nature of the social context is this inevitable?

Key scenes

The opening to this film focuses upon a chicken and its attempts to escape the violent death that almost inevitably awaits it. The images are of blood and instruments of death. The sounds are piercing, threatening and ominous. The sequences are of the chase, the pursuit and the desperate attempt to escape. We conclude this section of the film with the chicken being replaced

continued

by Rocket positioned between two equally threatening heavily armed groups: Ze's gang from the slums and the police. The themes of the film and the nature of our central character's experience of life would seem to be clear from the beginning. The importance of fate or chance in determining outcomes would seem to be demonstrated: a random series of events and coincidences have led to Rocket (as a 'normal' guy from the slums) being placed in a seemingly no-win situation.

And yet, if we watch the ensuing scenes we will find a key word recurring: 'study'. The emphasis placed on this concept would suggest that education at least is seen as offering a few individuals the opportunity to influence events and shape their own futures. Caught in the middle like the chicken, there seems no choice for most young boys from the favela (slums). For most, like Steak, who in a scene later in the film is handed his first gun by the gang leader, Ze, there is only the choice of who to kill in order to prove his manhood.

ACTIVITY

- Decide on a list of at least six scenes (or sequences of scenes) to analyse in more detail.
- If you are able to work with other people, debate the final list between yourselves and allocate one or two scenes to each person in the group.
- Prepare presentations on your chosen scenes, highlighting the messages and values you believe it is important to take from each and showing clearly how you feel elements of film construction are used to present these points.

(As in the paragraph above on the opening, don't be afraid to refer out from your scene to other parts of the film if it helps you to put forward, or further explain, an important idea. For example, if you were to examine the scene in which Steak kills for the first time you may wish to relate this to what Steak has to say when he is sent as a messenger to the rival gang leader Carrot, and/or to the scene in which Ze is killed at the end of the film.)

Messages and values

Early on in *City of God* when we are taken in flashback to the 1960s, there is an innocence attaching to the original gang, the 'Tender Trio', as they hold up a lorry and distribute gas canisters to the local community. But this sense of robbing from the rich (perhaps somewhat after the style of Robin Hood) comes to an abrupt end just fifteen minutes into the film with the murders in the brothel. By the end of the film, the young children who are becoming gang members are not yet into their teens but are already sure of one thing, the essential mantra is 'Kill: be respected.'

The cycle of one death (or set of deaths) leading to another is inescapable. Knockout Ned appears to start from the position that motivates the classic Hollywood western hero: revenge. He puts forward a moral outlook which centres on the naive notion that nobody who is innocent should be killed. Of course, he quickly becomes enmeshed in the unstoppable cycle of killings and ends up being killed by Otto, who ironically is motivated by the same sense of 'justice' that had originally driven Knockout Ned ('I want to get my father's murderer'). Shaggy and later Bene both want to leave the favela and their pasts behind, and escape to the idyll of a little farm in the country-side, but it is impossible. Even for the most cold-blooded of killers like Ze, there is no escaping an early violent death.

ACTIVITY

Examine the ways in which the killings in the brothel are presented to the viewer. Why is this material filmed and edited in the way it is? What effects are the filmmakers attempting to have on the audience and how have specific techniques been used in order to try to achieve these effects?

ACTIVITY

Choose two or three individual deaths (such as those of Shaggy, Bene, or Ze) and consider carefully the ways in which *mise-en-scène*, cinematography, editing and sound have been used to create meaning for the audience and to generate specific responses from the audience in these scenes.

continued

Perhaps the central relationship in the whole film comes to be that between Bene and Ze. It is important to ask ourselves how they are shown as being different and what reasons we are given for the differences between them. We seem to know little or nothing about their backgrounds, their families, their homes or their relationships with relatives. Bene has become the leader of a brutal, drug-dealing gang controlling territory within the favela while, it seems, remaining a chilled, 'good' guy, while by contrast Ze has since his youngest years been a psychotic killer. (The implication during Bene's death scene is, perhaps, that this is the only person Ze has ever loved.) Both characters, it seems, are what they are because of their individual psychological make-up; essentially they have been born this way. If we compare this with *La Haine* we find that characters in that film are given much more carefully delineated backgrounds that create them as distinctive and plausible individuals. In *City of God* the only explanation we have for Ze's nature is that he is too ugly to get a girlfriend, while there is no explanation at all as to how Bene has emerged from the cycle of violence as a freewheeling hippy.

ACTIVITY

Compile a list of scenes that focus in some way or another on issues of deprivation and poverty in the slums. This could include scenes showing the middle-class experience of life and therefore highlighting contrasts with life in the slums.

City of God shows the way in which it was only from the 1980s that cocaine came to replace marijuana as the dominant drug packaged and peddled by gangs in the slums (up until that point, cocaine had been seen as a rich person's drug of choice). It suggests that the drugs trade operates like any other business with the 'bosses' controlling certain franchises and employing managers, assembly-line workers and delivery boys. The film also exposes the involvement of arms dealers and the corruption of the police. But ultimately the film's political and social analysis of the situation is really quite thin. If the attempt is to show how each individual is a product of the social environment in which they have to live, it ultimately fails because Ze is simply an embodiment of evil. By contrast, *La Haine* succeeds so powerfully because Hubert is clearly not evil or easily dismissed as simply 'bad'.

Social, historical and political contexts

Social conditions:

- More than 6,000 people, most of them from the favelas, were murdered in Rio de Janeiro in 2007.
- Rio's wealthy middle class live in gated apartment blocks with private security in Copacabana, Ipanema or Leblon, in conditions that are in complete contrast to those of the hillside shanty towns.
- Police chiefs seem to be in no doubt that their job is to protect the status quo through control of the underprivileged (see *News from a Personal War* (Lund and Salles, *City of God* DVD extras)).
- Throughout the 1980s Brazil suffered chronic inflation and the country's foreign debt was higher than that of any other developing nation.
- There was a high birth rate and a migration of people into the city from rural areas during the 1980s and these trends continued into the 1990s.

History and politics:

- The struggle between left-wing socialist/communist groups and right-wing conservative forces stretches back into Brazil's past, to the 1960s and beyond.
- In 1961, the president, Janio da Silva Quadros, resigned, saying his attempts at reforms had been blocked by 'forces of reaction' (in other words, right-wing political forces).
- In 1964, the new president, Joao Bechoir Marques Goulart, attempted to nationalise the country's oil refineries and limit profits going abroad but was deposed by the army.
- Military rule lasted until 1985 with opposition political parties being suppressed, civil liberties being curbed, and strict media censorship being enforced.
- During the 1960s political prisoners politicised others who were in gaol with them so that the crime organisation, the Comando Vermelho, began to proclaim their enemy as the government, big business and the middle class.
- Also during the 1960s Roman Catholic priests began to criticise the government's failure to help the poor.

Meirelles seems to suggest in *City of God* that as one generation has replaced another since the 1960s the political dimension to crime in the favelas (if it ever really existed) has now most certainly been lost so that all that is left is a 'dog-eat-dog' world. This would be in line with the reading of the situation suggested by the more recent film *Elite Squad* (Padilha, 2008).

Figure 13.3 Police brutality feature heavily in *Tropa de Elite* (*Elite Squad*) (Padilha, 2008).

ACTIVITY

- Would you agree with this reading of the two films, *City of God* and *Elite Squad*?
  How important do you think it is to attempt to place such films within a social and historical context?
- *Elite Squad* has been described as a right-wing film that celebrates police violence. Would you agree with this assessment?
- Or, would you feel (as Jose Padilha, the director of this film, suggests) that what it really shows is that the actions of individuals are determined by the system in which they find themselves?

(Not only the author and the text but, just as importantly, the reading, must be seen as historically and culturally shaped.)

Crofts, S. (1988) 'Authorship and Hollywood', in Hill, J. and Church Gibson, P. *The Oxford Guide to Film Studies*. Oxford: Oxford University Press (p. 322).

Finally, remember that (as the quote above suggests) as we decide what we see as meanings being created in any film we may be constrained in what we can see by the historical moment and by the culture within which we are living our lives. To see *La Haine* as anti-police or *City of God* as ultimately failing to offer a firmly grounded socio-political analysis may say as much about someone's personal ideology as it does about the film itself.

EXAM QUESTIONS

- Compare the youth cultures to be found in two films of your choice.

- To what extent are the messages and values to be found in the two films you have studied similar or dissimilar? Make sure you refer to specific scenes to support your ideas.

- In order to understand the films you have studied, how important is it to be aware of relationships of power within the societies depicted?

- Through close attention to detail, compare and contrast two scenes, one from each of two films you have studied.

- How important is it to understand social, political and historical contexts in order to appreciate the films you have studied?

- What challenges do the films you have studied here present to the viewer?

Note

1 Louis Althusser (1918–1990): a French Marxist philosopher born in Algeria.

Further Reading

Barthes, R. (1972) *Mythologies*. Noonday Press
Hebdige, D. (1979) *Subculture: The Meaning of Style*. Methuen
Nagib, L. (2007) *Brazil on Screen: Cinema Novo, New Cinema, Utopia*. I.B. Tauris
Vincendeau, G. (2005) *La Haine*. I.B. Tauris

EMPOWERING WOMEN

In studying this topic area you will consider the following:

- representation of gender in films from different cultures
- developments in feminist film theory
- the link between representation and reality
- the role of film as an ideological form

The two principal films for this area are:

All About My Mother (Pedro Almodovar, Spain, 1997)

The Day I Became a Woman (Marziyeh Meshkini, Iran, 2000)

These two films were chosen for the following reasons:

- They conform to the specification's guidance that the choice of films can be 'eclectic in geographical range' and come from 'very different societies and cultural contexts'.
- By choosing to question the concept of gender identity, both films may be said to explore new ways of 'empowering women'.

Although the films have many differences it is interesting to note some of their similarities:

- Both films centre on female characters without conforming to a mainstream concept of positive representations of gender.
- The point of view in both films is female.
- The two films share a similar analysis of gender characteristics – that they are imposed rather than natural.
- Both directors may be viewed as 'outsiders' – Meshkini as a woman in a theocracy, Almodovar as a gay man growing up in the macho, religious culture of rural Spain.

Before watching the principal films it is useful to consider what the title of the specialist study, 'Empowering Women', actually means. To empower means to authorise, to allow, to make powerful; all of which are relevant to the feminist aim of achieving equality between men and women. The title is also ambiguous and suggests some relevant areas to consider:

- Can films empower people? How might we say that films 'authorise' or 'allow' people to do things that they have been prevented from doing?
- Is the 'empowering' taking place on screen or behind the camera? Can women (characters? spectators?) be empowered by a male director?
- Empowering has the connotation of being allowed or permitted to do something rather than having the right to do it. This could be problematic when considering notions of equality – who is being allowed and who is giving the permission?

To begin this area of study it is useful to have some background to the development of gender approaches in Film Studies, which grew out of feminist film theory.

Feminist film theory was influenced by the Second Wave feminist movement of the 1970s in the US and the UK. This 'wave' (the first wave was the Suffragette movement at the beginning of the twentieth century) was a civil rights movement which argued for equal opportunities – at work and at home – for women. Feminist film theory was an extension of this political movement and was initially interested in two main areas:

1   The role of women in the Hollywood film industry: was the emphasis on the 'great auteurs' in film theory ignoring women directors? This approach promoted the idea that equal representation of women on screen could only come from equal representation in the industry.
2   The way in which film used images of women: did this affect the way woman were treated in society? Is there a gap between the way women are represented on screen and in their real lives?

> **GENDER:** **gender** and **sex** are often used interchangeably but there are important differences:
>
> ■ **Sex** refers to the biological differences between men and women. Sex is fixed and does not change over time; it is the same across countries and across cultures, while gender is often different.
> ■ **Gender** refers to the social differences between men and women, girls and boys. These are the expectations that society has about men's and women's roles and responsibilities. These gender expectations will change over time, and will be different in different countries and among different cultures.

Gender identity

The study of representations of gender is important partly because gender is a political issue: Feminism is a social movement that questions gender inequalities and tries to change them, hoping to achieve gender equality, particularly in relation to work and pay. Part of the campaign for equal opportunities relied on pointing to the way in which gender expectations prevent equality – and affect men as well as women.

Gender as performance

One of the criticisms of the Second Wave feminist analysis of gender was that it often seemed to assume that gender was biologically determined rather than a result of society's expectations. This is seen most clearly in the formulation that the male is active and the female passive. In the 1980s and 1990s postmodern theorists argued that gender characteristics should be seen as a construction or performance – a form of clothing and props which are put on which mean both masculine and feminine. If this is the case then there is no longer the concept of naturally feminine and masculine – everything is an act.

In both the principal films studied in this section the characters – male and female – negotiate their gender identity, 'trying on' different forms. This is evident even in the tag line for *All About My Mother*: 'Part of every woman is a mother/actress/saint/sinner. And part of every man is a woman.'

The first published feminist works concentrated on the second area – the way in which film used images of women – which was termed 'image studies' but which we would now place in the context of the representation of women. In books such as Molly Haskell's *From Reverence to Rape* (1974), feminist theorists researched the following questions: What types of roles were played by women? How much screen time did they have (in comparison to men)? How close is the screen image to women's real experiences in the world? Do the films construct positive or negative images?

ACTIVITY

How useful do you think image studies is as an approach? You should consider the following: How can you judge whether a film role is an accurate reflection of real life? Whose reality is this judgement based on? Can everyone agree on what is a positive or negative image? Is it the purpose of film to provide realism? To provide positive images?

Image studies was extremely influential in terms of the development of feminist film theory but also feminist film practice. This was particularly evident in the rise of women moving into filmmaking, particularly documentary, a form that was perceived as being able to provide real representations of women's lives. However, these approaches were later heavily criticised as being naive – it is impossible to produce real images of women (or men), as film – even documentary – involves construction and representation. Another problem with image studies was one which is central to wider feminist debates. In talking about the *mis*representation of women it suggests that there is such a thing as an authentic feminine 'essence', something which all women share and which is different to men.

The theory of the male gaze

In countering these criticisms a new approach was developed which did not just rely on analysing images but also considered the spectator response and the way in which mainstream film constructed identification. Key questions in this theory were:

- What are the pleasures of watching mainstream (Hollywood) cinema?
- How does the 'apparatus' (the film language and film narrative) of cinema help the spectator to identify with a character?
- Do female spectators identify with female characters and male spectators with male characters?
- Do different genres appeal to the different genders?
- Do female film directors make different kinds of films to male directors? Is it possible to recognise a film directed by a woman?

The key theorists in this area were Laura Mulvey and Claire Johnstone, and their work continues to influence the current debate about film and gender. According to Mulvey, the pleasure of watching Hollywood film was a heterosexual, erotic pleasure; with images of women displayed – or objectified – for the gratification of the male spectator. This resulted from the particular conditions created by watching a film in the cinema and the film language and film style used by Hollywood:

Figure 14.1 Pleasure in cinema comes from a form of spying on others (on the screen) without being seen: a cinema audience watching Ginger Rogers.

1　**Pleasure in cinema comes from a form of spying on others (on the screen) without being seen**. This is an example of voyeurism which is particularly associated with *looking* to gain sexual pleasure. The cinema conditions are ideal for this: the dark auditorium where the audience is separated from each other; the screen which creates the illusion of looking into a private world which seems real (the suspension of disbelief).

In addition to this:

2　**Hollywood film also offers idealised characters**, heroes (usually male?) to identify with, whose world we share. We are encouraged to recognise ourselves in these ideal figures who are actually better looking, stronger, more intelligent and more successful than we are. This identification is therefore a form of narcissism (or vanity) because the hero is superior to us.

In this model there are two forms of 'looking' in the cinema:

■　voyeurism (spying)
■　identification (a form of narcissism).

Through identification it is the male hero who transmits the look of the male cinema spectator. It is a privileged position, as the male spectator sees the female character through the eyes of the hero – sharing the power of the hero.

It is this model which has been defined as the 'male gaze'; the male spectator simultaneously identifies with the hero and looks to the female for erotic pleasure.

VOYEURISM AND FILM: a voyeur is a person who gains sexual pleasure or satisfaction from watching others (although it can also refer to an extreme interest in scandal or tragic events), while remaining hidden. While film theorists have used the concept to explain our enjoyment of watching films, filmmakers have also used it as a theme in their work. The most celebrated example of this is Hitchcock, whose film *Rear Window* (1953) makes explicit the pleasures of spying on others.

The infamous scene in *Reservoir Dogs* (Tarantino, 1992), when Mr Blonde tortures his hostage, may also be read as an exploration of the voyeuristic impulse. Tarantino explicitly moves the camera away from the most horrific scene, asking spectators to examine their reactions. Disappointment? Wanting to see?

The male gaze is based on the idea that there is a gender imbalance in looking; the male is active and the woman is passive, or, 'men look, women are there to be looked at'.

This structure of looking and identification in the cinema affects the form of the narrative – women looked at as erotic objects slow down the story; women become static while the male is active, moving the story forward.

ACTIVITY

The theory of the male gaze in cinema raises interesting questions which should help to develop your ideas:

- Who do women identify with in films?
- If female characters are only used as objects to be looked at in Hollywood film, why do women enjoy watching them?
- Can you identify a 'female gaze' in film? Male stars such as Brad Pitt, George Clooney and Johnny Depp are often presented to be looked at and promoted as sexually attractive to the audience.
- Are the only pleasures in Hollywood cinema heterosexual ones? What happens when women are gazing at women?

continued

- Some film genres (war, westerns, buddy movies) practically exclude women – what happens to the male gaze then?
- How does new technology – particularly home viewing – affect the theory?

Popular feminism and the woman's film

In challenging the theory of the male gaze, feminist theory developed a more positive view of Hollywood cinema, suggesting that there was space for women in mainstream film. There were examples of films which did not merely use women as objects but as central to the narrative in roles more usually associated with men.

Central to this development is the work of Jackie Stacey (1987) who argues against the view that mainstream film is structured around the male gaze. To illustrate her argument she uses two films: *Desperately Seeking Susan* and *All About Eve* (a film which *All About My Mother* pays homage to) which are both about one woman identifying with and wanting to be like another. In *Desperately Seeking Susan* a shy, unconfident housewife (Rosanna Arquette) is fascinated by Susan (Madonna), a woman who lives outside the conventions of mainstream society and who is powerful and active. Similarly, in *All About Eve*, Bette Davis plays Margo Channing, the leading actress on Broadway, a successful and talented woman. In films like these there seems to be plenty of evidence that the male gaze is not always dominant.

Almodovar as auteur: deconstructing gender

One of the key characteristics of Almodovar's style as an auteur is his analysis of the way in which images are constructed. This is apparent at all levels of his films, in plot, character, theme, representations and *mise-en-scène*. *All About My Mother* is an example of reflexive cinema in that it draws the audience's attention to its status as a work of art, as a construction with a particular point of view – rather than as a form of realism (for more discussion of reflexive cinema see Chapter 12 on 'New Waves'). This reflexive nature includes:

- The stylised, created world of the *mise-en-scène* (e.g. Manuela's apartment in Barcelona), with its emphasis on the theatre with its inherent qualities of staging and acting.
- The foregrounding of works of art within the film – film, theatre and painting.
- The bizarre series of plot events – characteristic of the woman's film – are too exaggerated to appear realistic.

Figure 14.2 *Todo Sobre mi Madre* (*All About My Mother*) (Almodovar, 1999).

ACTIVITY

To analyse the way in which *All About My Mother* is a reflexive film, consider the following:

■ How many different examples of 'storytelling' are there in the film? What function do they serve?

For example, Esteban is writing a book called *All About My Mother*. Is it a biography of his mother? The screenplay of the film we are about to watch? The title is a play on the film he and Manuela have just watched – *All About Eve*, a film about the obsession of a fan for a famous actress. The plot line of that film is partially repeated in the plot of *All About My Mother* – a homage which serves to draw attention to film as a construction. Esteban's notebook is also presented in one of the most memorable shots of the film – where the camera seems to cross over to the 'wrong' side of the screen, perhaps foregrounding Almodovar's presence.

■ List the different ways in which characters are performers in the film – how does this affect the representation of gender?

It is soon apparent that all the characters in the film are performers in different ways – some more explicitly than others. Manuela appears at first to be a 'normal' character; she has a mainstream, professional career, a loving relationship with her son and is introduced in a traditional, domestic environment – preparing a family dinner. As the film progresses however, Manuela is also shown to be a performer of roles – she acts in the transplant training film (a role she then plays for 'real'), she talks about her days as a student actor when she played Stella in *A Streetcar Named Desire* ('the play marked my life', she says), she then understudies for Nina and once again plays Stella – a character who is pregnant. This emphasis on the different roles which Manuela plays leads us to question the role which society often claims is the most natural for a woman – that of mother. At the end of the film when Manuela is a mother again she is the non-biological mother of a child whose parents are a nun and a transsexual; as with many of the characters in the film the role she has chosen for herself is the most authentic one.

The clearest representation of the film's view of gender as a construction is found in the character of Agrado, a male female transsexual who is played by a female actor.

ACTIVITY

Watch again Agrado's monologue ('an alternative production') at the theatre.

■ How does the *mise-en-scène* emphasise the theme of performance?
■ What does Agrado's monologue suggest about gender characteristics?
■ During the monologue Agrado states: 'It costs a lot to be this authentic' and 'All I have that's real are my feelings – and the silicone'. What do these lines – which may seem contradictory – suggest about Agrado's (and by extension the director's) definition of authenticity?

All About My Mother and ideology

The analysis of the representation of gender in the film also suggests an ideological reading of the film. Through the character of Agrado we learn that to be authentic is to create your own identity – however that might be achieved. By contrast, to be fake is to take on the role that society has constructed for you. In this reading it may be argued that *All About My Mother* is a moral film, attaching value judgements to people's choices. The characters who conform (Nina and Rosa's mother) are judged most harshly.

Queer has traditionally meant odd or unusual and was used as a term of abuse for gay men, but it has now been 'reclaimed' by groups as a form of positive identification. (It should be noted though that it is still a controversial term.) Queer is not synonymous with gay but instead questions such narrow definitions of sexuality and gender. Queer refers to people who identify as gay, lesbian, bisexual, transgender, intersex, but also has a wider meaning in referring to anyone who doesn't feel part of the mainstream heterosexual (heteronormative) society.

New Queer Cinema is the term given to a group of films which emerged in the US in the early 1990s. The films were examples of independent cinema and were first shown at film festivals – particularly the Sundance Film Festival founded by Robert Redford – from where many gained cross-over distribution to a wider audience. These films had in common a central character that was on the margins of society – an outsider – usually due to their sexuality but issues such as race, gender, class and physical disability were also referred to. While there had been films which featured gay characters and story lines before, New Queer Cinema was different in that it *rejected the idea of positive representations* which would be acceptable to the heterosexual, mainstream audience and instead deliberately attempted to shock and anger that audience. In a similar approach, the term *queer* which had previously been used as a term of abuse was appropriated by some organisations and individuals and used as a positive form of identification.

Some examples of New Queer Cinema (US):

Poison (Todd Haynes, 1991)
My Own Private Idaho (Gus Van Sant, 1991)
Swoon (Tom Kalin, 1992)
Go Fish (Rose Troche, 1994)
The Living End (Gregg Araki, 1993)
Savage Grace (Tom Kalin, 2007)

UK:

Looking For Langston (Isaac Julien, 1988)
Young Soul Rebels (Isaac Julien, 1991)

All About My Mother as woman's film

One of the contexts and cultural reference points in *All About My Mother* is the Hollywood subgenre – the woman's film.

The woman's film is a form of melodrama which was at its peak of popularity in the 1940s with stars such as Bette Davis and Joan Crawford. Aimed at a female audience the woman's film was critically derided and only taken seriously with the rise of feminist film theory in the 1970s. For many feminist critics the woman's film provided a unique context in which to explore specifically female issues.

> **MELODRAMA:** the woman's film is a form of melodrama – a heightened and exaggerated form of drama. The term *melodrama* has traditionally been used pejoratively due to its reliance on coincidence, cliché, dramatic reversals of fortune and its appeal to the emotions. Other popular forms of melodramas are 'tear-jerkers', soap operas and chick flicks. Melodrama is particularly associated with camp (see below).

Generic elements of the woman's film:

- a central female character caught between the demands of home, work and romance
- a difficult relationship with a daughter/mother
- a female best friend as support, 'difficult' male lovers
- the heroine is punished for wanting too much (career and family and love).

The dramatic conflict of the woman's film can be represented as follows:

Home and/or work and/or Love/sexual desire

Central to the woman's film is a powerful female star who appeals to a female audience rather than one constructed for the male gaze.

ACTIVITY

Read the synopsis of *All About My Mother* below. What elements of the melodrama and the woman's film are apparent?

Manuela, a single mother in Madrid, sees her only son, Esteban, die on his seventeenth birthday as he runs to request an actress' autograph.

Manuela travels to Barcelona to find Esteban's father, a transvestite named Lola, who does not know he has a child. Ironically Esteban's last request of his mother was that she should tell him about his father. In Barcelona Manuela is reunited with her friend Agrado, meets a young nun Rosa, who is pregnant with Lola's child, and gets a job as an assistant to Huma, the actress with whom her son was obsessed. Rosa discovers she is HIV positive and Manuela gives up her job to nurse her and, on her death, adopts her son. At Rosa's funeral Manuela meets up with Lola and introduces him to his second son.

POSTMODERNISM AND GENRE: Almodovar has been defined as a postmodern director and one of the reasons for this is his use of genre; rather than making a melodrama or a woman's film he is commenting on the form. (This is similar – although in a very different context – to the way in which Tarantino has used the gangster genre and exploitation films.)

INFORMATION BOX – TYPES OF FEMALE STARS

i

In her book *A Woman's View* (a study of the history of the woman's film genre) Jeanine Bassinger (1993) has produced an 'abstract pattern' to explain the different roles played and personas developed by stars in Hollywood film.

1   Unreal women – fantasy figures, dream images, sex symbols, mostly appealing to men.
2   Real women – Women who are meant to be like the women in the audience ('the girl next door'), although they are as much of a construction as the other categories.
3   Exaggerated women – these are the kinds of stars who were most associated with the woman's film (Bette Davis, Joan Crawford). They are ferocious and strong in character, their characteristics

continued

– whether smile, hair, eyes, walk – are exaggerated. Importantly, a female star cannot start her career in this group but has to rise to it. The effect of their film history and star power combines to take them into something exaggerated, often dangerous and extra-ordinary. The exaggerated female stars mostly appeal to women.

ACTIVITY

- Do you think that there are still female stars who could be defined as exaggerated women? Why do you think they were so popular in the 1940s?
- Do the definitions apply to the characters in *All About My Mother*?

ACTIVITY

After watching *All About My Mother* and reading the definitions of the woman's film, melodrama and female star types, make notes on the following:

- How many points of similarity can you find between *All About My Mother* and the woman's film? Consider character, plot, casting and so on.
- How has Almodovar changed some conventions of the genre? What effect does this have?
- Why do you think Almodovar is interested in the woman's film – how does it fit into his ideas about gender?

All About My Mother and the camp aesthetic

Simply put, camp is a style – whether in film, fashion, comedy, behaviour – which relies on the exaggeration of gender characteristics. Camp representations may reverse gender expectations (the 'butch' woman or the 'effeminate' man) or take them to extremes: the diva and the macho man. This explains why action stars such as Arnold Schwarzenegger and Sylvester Stallone are camp.

The cultural critic Susan Sontag wrote a very influential definition of the camp aesthetic; the following is summarised from her 'Notes on Camp' (1964):

- Camp is a way of seeing the world as an aesthetic phenomenon, of being aware of the artifice and construction.
- Camp emphasises style over content.
- 'Camp taste has an affinity for certain arts rather than others. Clothes, furniture, all the elements of visual décor, for instance, make up a large part of Camp. For Camp art is often decorative art, emphasizing texture, sensuous surface, and style at the expense of content. Sometimes whole art forms become saturated with Camp. Classical ballet, opera, movies have seemed so for a long time. And movie criticism (like lists of "The 10 Best Bad Movies I Have Seen") is probably the greatest popularizer of Camp taste today.'
- Camp is often seen as 'bad' art, the phrase 'so bad it's good' is usually reserved for camp. It is not necessarily the case that camp art is always bad, though – it may be a matter of taste.
- 'The hallmark of Camp is the spirit of extravagance. Camp is a woman walking around in a dress made of three million feathers.'
- 'The peculiar relation between Camp taste and homosexuality has to be explained. While it's not true that Camp taste is homosexual taste, there is no doubt a peculiar affinity and overlap. So, not all homosexuals have Camp taste. But homosexuals, by and large, constitute the vanguard – and the most articulate audience – of Camp.'
- Camp does not reinforce societal values, but points out the inconsistencies – or hypocrisies – in society to show how any supposed norm (often to do with expectations about gender) is socially constructed.

ACTIVITY

Read the definitions of camp above and make notes on the following:

- What elements of camp aesthetic are evident in *All About My Mother*? Consider the *mise-en-scène* as well as the characters.
- How does the camp aesthetic link with the themes of the film?

The Day I Became a Woman

The second principal film for this study has a very different visual style and narrative structure to *All About My Mother*.

Figure 14.3 *Roozi ke zan shodam* (*The Day I Became a Woman*) (Marziyeh Meshkini, Iran, 2000).

Please note: For a detailed context of Iranian cinema and society please see Chapter 6 on Iranian Film.

ACTIVITY

Read the synopsis below. What are the main differences with *All About My Mother*? Consider structure, plot, characters.

The film is set on an island in Southern Iran and is structured around three different stories, each dealing with a different female character at three different stages of life. Each story is named after the central character: first tale: Hava, second tale: Ahoo, third tale: Hoova. The first story centres on a young girl on her ninth birthday who is told that she is now a woman; this involves a range of restrictions on her behaviour and dress. The second story is about a young woman who enters a bicycle race – something that is not acceptable for married women – and is threatened with divorce and exclusion from her village if she continues. In the third story an old woman who has come into some money attempts to buy all the consumer goods that she has never been able to afford before. The film concludes with the characters from the three stories appearing together.

Film style: realism?

One of the clearest contrasts between *All About My Mother* and *The Day I Became a Woman* is the visual style. While Almodovar uses a highly stylised *mise-en-scène* Meshkini's style seems much closer to realism; some of her techniques, such as long takes, emphasis on diegetic sound, use of non-actors, actually seem closer to documentary. However, the film has also been described as poetic, allegorical and even surrealist; terms which suggest an anti-realist style.

> **ALLEGORY:** the use of symbolism to represent deeper meanings which are often moral or political.
>
> **SURREALISM:** an art movement based on the unexpected and shocking juxtaposition of unrelated images.

Gender as performance

Although there are many differences between the two films they do share a similar approach to the concept of gender; both films explore the way gender is a construction, drawing the viewer's attention to this through the *mise-en-scène* and the dialogue.

ACTIVITY

After watching the film:

- Make a note of the different symbols of gender – this will include props and costume.
- Give examples of dialogue which explicitly refers to gender expectations.

Sample analysis

The first shot of the first story, 'Hava', is a long take of a rather tattered dark blue sail attached to the mast of a raft. Later in the film we discover that the sail is actually Hava's veil, one of the symbols of her new status as a woman. By giving the veil to the boys who have made the raft, she demonstrates her rejection of society's expectation that women should be covered. There is a poignancy in the way that the veil – a symbol of restriction – has become a sail, carried out to sea on the wind.

When Hava, her mother and grandmother are first introduced there is a clear contrast in their costume. The mother and grandmother wear the hijab as well as a covering on their nose and mouth; Hava, on her last morning as a girl, wears a flowery silk dress. The costumes draw a stark representation of Hava's circumscribed future life as a woman. In addition, Hava's young friend Hassan is dressed in a Western-style T-shirt (with an image of a footballer on the front) and shorts.

The dialogue in this sequence also emphasises Hava's move from a girl to a woman; her grandmother lays down rules that she must now adhere to: 'You're a woman now. . . . You mustn't play with Hassan or any boy'. . . . 'You must cover up your hair'.

When Hava questions the reasons for these, to her, seemingly arbitrary rules, she doesn't receive any answers. Through these references to the way in which Hava's position as a woman is governed by external forces, the director is arguing that gender characteristics are not natural but social.

Although the film emphasises the restrictions placed on women's lives in Iran there are also examples of the way in which the characters resist them; for example, Hava cleverly negotiates an extension to her freedom. What other examples of these acts of resistance are there in the film?

INFORMATION BOX – MAKHMALBAF FILM HOUSE

The director of *The Day I Became a Woman*, Marziyeh Meshkini, studied film at the Iranian film school known as the Makhmalbaf Film House, This was a school founded by Moshen Makhmalbaf, one of the most influential directors in Iran, who was part of the Iranian New Wave in the 1960s. The Film House has become inextricably linked with the Makhmalbaf family: Meshkini is married to Makhmalbaf, and his daughters – Samira and Hana – are also directors. The films of Samira Makhmalbaf would make a good case study for this topic as they also deal with the role of women in Iran, emphasising the possibilities of resistance. The success of the female members of the Makhmalbaf family is reflected across the Iranian film industry. It is interesting to note that there seem to be more prominent female directors in Iran than – for example – in the British film industry.

- How far do the films you have studied deal with political as well as personal issues?

- To what extent do the films you have studied make judgements about characters and society?

Further Reading and Resources

Arroyo, J. (2000) 'The Constructedness of Gender in the Cinema of Almodovar' in Fleming (ed.), *Formations*. Manchester University Press

Bassinger, J. (1993) *'A Woman's View: How Hollywood Spoke to Women 1930–1960*. Random House

Buckland, W. (2000) 'The Woman's Film' in *Teach Yourself Film Studies*. Hodder & Stoughton

Butler, A. (2002) *Women's Cinema: The Contested Screen*. Wallflower

Dyer, R. (1979) *Stars*. BFI

Haskell, M. (1974) *From Reverence to Rape: The Treatment of Women in the Movies*. University of Chicago Press

Mulvey, L. (1988) 'Visual Pleasure and Narrative Cinema' in *Feminism and Film Theory*, Penley, C. (ed.), Routledge

Nelmes, J. (1999) 'Women and Film' in *An Introduction to Film Studies*. Routledge

Phillips, P. (1999) 'Genre, Star and Auteur' in Nelmes, J. (ed.), *An Introduction to Film Studies*. Routledge

Sontag, S. (1964) 'Notes on Camp' in *Against Interpretation and Other Essays*. Picador.

Stacey, J. (1987) 'Desperately Seeking Difference', *Screen* 48

Stacey, J. (1994) *Star Gazing, Hollywood Cinema and Female Spectatorship*. Routledge

ILLUSTRATIONS

part 3

VARIETIES OF FILM EXPERIENCE (FM4): SPECTATORSHIP TOPICS

SPECTATORSHIP AND EARLY CINEMA BEFORE 1917

SPECTATORSHIP AND DOCUMENTARY

EXPERIMENTAL AND EXPANDED FILM/VIDEO

POPULAR FILM AND EMOTIONAL RESPONSE

15 SPECTATORSHIP AND EARLY CINEMA BEFORE 1917

This chapter will look at:

- the historical development of primitive and early cinema
- the pioneers of early cinema
- the development of film form from primitive to recognisable for the modern audience
- technological developments underpinning the period
- factors influencing the development of spectatorship
- developing national cinemas
- the industrialisation of film
- key elements that make this period distinctive and different

Pre-cinema developments

There are many points in history that could be identified as the key moment that led directly to the evolution of cinema, from the invention of the *camera obscura* during the Renaissance (though its origins go back to the Ancient Greeks), through to the invention of the *Fantasmagorie* by Belgian Étienne Gaspar Robert in 1798.

CAMERA OBSCURA: effectively a pin-hole camera on a grand scale. A room was made light-tight, except for a small hole opened to the outside world, which would suddenly reveal a mirror image of the outside world upside-down on the opposite wall. This was developed further as lenses and mirrors were invented, and now a corrected image can be seen. This is fundamental to the way a film camera works. There is an excellent *camera obscura* on the Royal Mile in Edinburgh, Scotland.

FANTASMAGORIE: (or in English, the Phantasmagoria): a 'magic lantern' show where still images were rear-projected from a movable projector on to a translucent screen, producing a 'suggestion' of a moving image. Later refined with a number of simultaneous projections, the 'magic lantern' show was in many ways responsible for building an audience for moving images.

Inevitably the developments in photography by Thomas Wedgewood, Nicéphore Niépce, Louis Daguerre and William Henry Fox Talbot at the beginning of the nineteenth century led to the necessary technical advances in image capture, and so could be highlighted as having special significance in the evolution towards cinema.

However, there were three men without whose experimentation the potential of cinema would have been delayed: English wilderness photographer Eadweard Muybridge, French scientist Étienne-Jules Marey and American manufacturer George Eastman. Muybridge and Marey experimented with photographic techniques of capturing the motion of objects and the movement of animals, though they were still using still photography to do this. Eastman worked on developing new kinds of material on which to record an image.

INFORMATION BOX – MUYBRIDGE'S HORSE *i*

Commissioned by the Governor of California in 1872 to find out if a trotting horse ever had all four of its legs off the ground at the same time, Muybridge placed twelve (still) cameras along a track, each connected by threads running across the track. As the horse trotted it broke the threads and caused each camera to take a photograph in sequence. By 1879 he had improved the system to incorporate twenty-four cameras, each with electronic timers leading to greater accuracy. He later took this idea and created the *Zoopraxioscope*, which projected a 'moving' image of a horse using sequential paintings of the original photographs to create the illusion.

Marey's *Photographic Gun, Chronophotographic Camera* and *pull-down mechanism*

As a scientist, Marey wanted to capture the motion of birds in flight, and to do this he developed his *Photographic Gun* in 1882. The device looked like a rifle (of sorts) and could record twelve sequential images on a rotating photographic plate using a disk-like shutter system. He developed this further into a larger, tripod-mounted system (the *Chronophotographic Camera*), which could capture more images that could then be superimposed on each other. His major contribution to cinema however came when he invented a 'pull-down' mechanism for celluloid film, which allowed it to be moved, momentarily held still and exposed, then moved on, frame by frame.

Eastman's *film*

Until 1888 all images were 'fixed' on to glass or gelatin 'plates' from which paper 'prints' were made. George Eastman changed all this with his celluloid roll film. Under the brand name 'Kodak', Eastman introduced this plastic material that could 'fix' an image, and then be wound on to 'fix' another image. A major hurdle for capturing motion had been overcome.

In America, Thomas Alva Edison (whose teams 'invented' the electric light bulb and the forerunner of the record player, the phonograph) had visited Étienne Marey to see his 'pull-down' mechanism, and from this he saw the potential of celluloid film in capturing moving images. The detail of developing a complete system of capturing, storing and replaying moving images was left to his young British assistant W. K. L. Dickson. Dickson developed two machines: the kinetograph to record images on, and the kinetoscope on which to view the images. More importantly for cinema, he perforated Eastman's celluloid roll with regularly spaced sprocket holes, and developed a sprocket mechanism (a 'toothed' wheel) powered by an electric motor, to drive the celluloid forward at a fixed and precise rate.

As commercial development offered financial reward, Edison built a studio (nick-named *the Black Maria* after the police vehicles of the day) in the grounds of his laboratory. Mounted on a turntable, to follow the sun (the thought of 'lighting' a scene had not occurred to the makers by this point), this studio was soon attracting many of the popular American vaudeville theatre performers who wanted to record their acts.

The design of the kinetograph (once they stopped running film horizontally and started running it through vertically) is the basis of all modern motion picture film cameras, but the kinetoscope was a fundamentally different experience. This primitive medium focused not on mass consumption of a film, but on an individual experience where a spectator peered into the kinetoscope through a small window-like aperture. Although a commercial kinetoscope parlour opened in New York in April 1894, this invention, with its short-lived run-times (originally only twenty

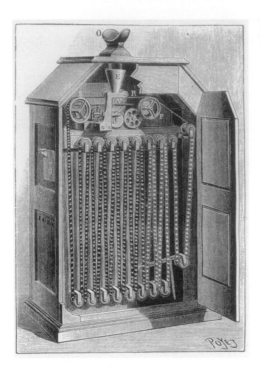

Figure 15.1 An interior view of the kinetoscope.

seconds, but which quickly extended to hold larger rolls of up to a minute of run-time) offered no real threat to the traditional and popular mass-market magic lantern shows, and vaudeville theatre itself.

Early cinema developments

Cinema, as it is recognised today, was born on 13 February 1895 when the French Lumière brothers patented *un appareil servant à l'obtention et à la vision des epreuves chronophotographiques*, a combined film camera and projector in one, portable, hand-cranked (rather than electric) lightweight unit. The keys to the success of this development were its portability – the camera could now go anywhere – and its ability to project an image to an audience (a key advantage over Edison's kinetoscope), which meant that the era of mass spectatorship (and all the associated industry of exhibition) could now develop.

In March of the same year they showed their first film *La Sortie des Ouvriers de l'Usine Lumière* (*Workers Leaving a Factory*) (19 March 1895, *ph.* Louis Lumière) shot on their new *cinématographe* to an audience of scientists and photographers in Paris. The response of this audience, and the growing demand for Edison's kinetoscope productions, led to the Lumière brothers opening the world's first cinema in the Salon Indien of the Grand Café, 14 Boulevard des Capucines, Paris on 28 December 1895. Cinema was born and quickly swept the world.

Case study
THE LUMIÈRE BROTHERS

Auguste and Louis Lumière were the sons of Antoine Lumière – a prominent Lyons-based portrait painter who abandoned art to establish a photographic manufacturing business in the mid-1800s. By 1894 Louis Lumière's invention of a photographic process three years earlier (at the age of 17) meant that the business had a large factory in Lyons, and was producing fifteen million photographic plates a year.

Returning from an exhibition of Edison's new kinetograph and kinetoscope, Antoine Lumière sensed the start of a new technological era and set his son Louis to work on a machine to compete with this American invention. Working with his brother Auguste, their experiments resulted in the *cinématographe* – a camera, printer and projector all built into one lightweight box. Hand-cranked to avoid the extra bulk and weight of an electrical motor, the *cinématographe* used a development of Étienne-Jules Marey's principle of intermittent motion and the pull-down mechanism, and Eastman's 35mm celluloid film stock. This was to set the standard for film stock to the present day, and set the standard for film speed (sixteen frames per second) until the advent of synchronised sound in the late 1920s.

The brothers launched commercial cinema in Paris on 28 December 1895 with a programme of ten films that lasted for approximately twenty minutes and included the following titles: *La Sortie des Ouvriers de l'Usine Lumière*, *La Voltige*, *La Pêche aux poissons rouges*, *Le Débarquement du Congrès de Photographie à Lyon*, *Les Forgerons*, *Le Jardinier*, *Le Repas de Bébé*, *Le Saut à la couverture*, *Place des Cordeliers à Lyon*, and *La Mer*.

The success of this projected film led to further factories, cinemas and international developments with the Lumière company becoming a name synonymous with French cinema. Closing their North American operations in 1897 (due to threats from the US government over 'improper' Customs documents), and having produced over 1,000 films within three years, they began to cut back on production, concentrating instead on manufacture of equipment and (in competition to Eastman) film stock. The Lumières sold their Cinematograph patent to Pathé in 1902 and abandoned production in 1905, though the company name still exists both in manufacturing and in distribution today.

By the middle of 1896 the Lumière's *cinématographe* was being used across Europe, the Russian Empire, and across India (its arrival in Britain was with a show in tents on the cliffs at Folkestone, Kent in 1896). Within another six months it was in common use in Egypt and Palestine, China, Japan and Australia. Within two years of its invention there was not a continent that had not embraced this new medium – comparatively it took the internet some ten years to have an even vaguely similar result, and twenty years before it was as commonly known and used. Driving this rapid expansion was the financial potential offered by exhibition. Film was relatively cheap to make (especially as at this time most films were *actualités* – simple documentary-like recordings of the world in front of the camera), and the audience was vast and hungry, with spectators often paying over and over again to watch the same short programme of films. The key players in the development of film already had successful manufacturing bases, and solid capital with which to develop this new medium. Profits were immense, and, since there were no language barriers to this silent cinema, a film could have a global audience.

The initial Lumière programme offers an indication of the type of film being made at this early stage, with actuality being the driving force. Thus spectators marvelled at the background movement of leaves in the wind in *Le Repas de Bébé*, scrambled for cover when the train comes towards them on screen for fear it would burst out in *Arrivée d'un Train en Gare de La Ciotat* (1895, ph. Louis Lumière), and tried to avoid splashes lapping over the screen edge from the sea in *La Mer*. Such actualities were primitive in form in that they used a solitary camera position and relied on the action in front of the camera to create excitement in the spectator.

ACTUALITIES: A primitive form of early cinema that captured simple events such as trains arriving or leaving, public events, and simple activities (such as a baby's breakfast). They differ from documentary in that they are simply recordings with no underpinning agenda or intention to position an audience.

PROSCENIUM ARCH: the primitive cinema relied on a fixed camera position with everything happening within the single positioned frame. The audience were in the same position in relation to the action as they were in the theatre, with the action 'framed' by the theatrical 'arch' that rises from the stage (though the Lumière films are somewhat unique in usually seeking a diagonal angle to emphasise the depth of the scene). This differs from later early cinema, which, once editing and a range of shot sizes were developed, 'moved' the audience around the action, creating a much more dynamic effect on spectators who themselves were developing a greater sophistication within the medium.

Figure 15.2 *Arrivée d'un Train en Gare de La Ciotat* (1895, ph. Louis Lumière).

Across the globe primitive filmmakers adopted the actuality form with films such as *Rough Sea at Dover* (UK, 1895, ph. Birt Acres), *The Derby* (UK, 1896, ph. R. W. Paul) and *The Corbett–Fitzsimmons Fight* (US, 1897, Edison). Soon primitive genres within these forms began to establish, with one of the most popular – 'the phantom ride' – being where a camera is mounted on the front of a moving train. The Lumières' *Leaving Jerusalem by Railway* (1896) is an early example of this, and also serves to illustrate another developing genre – 'the exotique' – which showed images of distant and exotic lands. It is important to note the sense of experimentation in what these filmmakers were doing, and the way their production was led by the demands of audience.

ACTIVITY

View a number of the early Lumière films (both the BFI *Early Cinema: Primitives and Pioneers*, Vol 1, and Kino on Video's *The Lumière Brothers' First Films* are useful sources). Can you trace developments in technique and experiment in these first films? Imagine you had never seen

continued

a moving image before – what effect do you think these films would have had on you?

Do you notice any developments in the background action of their films? Is there anything to suggest that they quickly learned to control elements of background action? Is there anything to suggest that they were beginning, even at this earliest stage, to direct action? If so, what do you think they were hoping to achieve, and what effect would it have had on the spectator?

INFORMATION BOX – BIRT ACRES

American Birt Acres initially settled in Ilfracombe in Devon in 1885, and quickly became a successful photographer while working on photographic inventions. Introduced to R. W. Paul in 1894, the pair worked together to develop a camera along the lines of the *cinematographe*. Shooting the first successful film in Britain, *Incident at Clovelly Cottage* (UK 1895) outside his Barnet (London) home, Acres patented his kinetic camera shortly after, and the following year his kinetic lantern – a projector which was also known as the cinemascope.

In 1896 he formed the Northern Photographic Works – a company manufacturing celluloid film – and in 1898 he unveiled his Birtac 17.5mm camera for the amateur market; the first home-movie camera. He continued in film production and manufacture until his death in 1918.

INFORMATION BOX – R. W. PAUL

Successful electrical engineer Robert Paul was approached in 1894 to make illegal copies of Edison's kinetoscope. Realising there was no British patent on the machine, Paul produced a number of copies and began selling them, developing a camera with Birt Acres in 1895 in order to produce films to show on them. He improved his camera in subsequent years, and developed and patented his own projector – the theatrograph – in 1896.

The success of his film business, a 1,200 per cent profit in his first year of operation (1896–1897), led him to build Britain's first film studios in Muswell Hill, London in 1898, producing over eighty short dramas in its first few months of operation.

He became disillusioned with film in the latter half of the first decade of the twentieth century, closing his studios in 1910, and destroying the majority of his negatives. Paul returned to electrical engineering and continued successfully until his death in 1943.

Drama and the development of the fantasy film

Edison realised the theatrical potential for his kinetoscope and quickly began recording popular vaudeville theatre acts. This potential became even clearer when the medium developed into a projected one, with a limitless audience. The Lumière brothers offered the first fiction film with *Le Jardinier et le petit espiegle* (aka *L'Arroseur arrosé*) (France, 1895, ph. Louis Lumière) in which a 'naughty boy' plays a comic trick on a gardener (later remade by James Bamforth as *The Biter Bit* (UK, 1900), and Thomas Edison as *Weary Willie and the Gardener* (US, 1901), and followed this with a 'directed actuality' in *Démolition d'un mur* (France, 1896, ph. Louis Lumière, Dir: Auguste Lumière). It was this later film that exposed a further potential for cinema, since audiences marvelled at it as it was rewound, as they could see a demolished wall reconstruct itself. Such was the simplicity of the birth of cinema special effects.

These early fictions rapidly took off with film companies establishing themselves worldwide to produce 'moving picture shows' in which the audience's desires for wonders and marvels were addressed with energy. Two British filmmakers, George Albert Smith and James A. Williamson, developed a range of cinematic techniques such as the use of close-ups, the pull focus, the point-of-view shot, shaped masks (such as keyholes), continuity of action and moving camera shots. Together they formed what was to become known as 'The Brighton School'.

INFORMATION BOX – THE BRIGHTON SCHOOL

A group of filmmakers based along the English south coast, centring on Brighton, the foremost of whom were George Albert Smith, a Fellow of the Royal Astronomical Society, and James A. Williamson, chemist and

continued

photographer based near to Smith's pleasure garden in Hove (near Brighton).

Smith is most likely to have been the first filmmaker to divide up continuous action into a number of shots in his *Grandma's Reading Glass* (UK, 1900), and he pioneered the use of insert editing and vertical wipes in the technically accomplished *Mary Jane's Mishap, or Don't Fool with Paraffin* (UK, 1903).

Williamson's 'Kinematograph Company Ltd' started by processing others' films, and projecting them (including Smith's) but from 1898 he began making actualities. His work developed into reconstructions of historical and current events in films such as *Attack on a China Mission* (UK, 1900), and into the fantastic (or trick cinematography) with films such as *The Big Swallow* (UK, 1901) in which the filmed subject approaches the camera and appears to eat it and its operator. Perhaps his key achievement is the development of a film genre – the chase film – through his *Stop Thief!* (UK, 1901), and through this the initial development of continuity editing.

No one was more effective at displaying fantasy than French filmmakers George Méliès, who pioneered 'artificially arranged scenes' (*mise-en-scène*) for his own productions, and Ferdinand Zecca who directed films for Pathé. Both made films based on history, operas, fairy-tales and the Bible, with Zecca's *La Vie et la Passion de Jesus Christ* (France, Pathé, 1902) being the second time Christ had appeared in this new medium (the first being in Alice Guy-Blanché's similarly titled earlier film for Lumière – Alice Guy becoming the first female director when she started work for Gaumount in 1896 with *La Fée aux choux*). Both men exploited the range offered by studio constructions, and trick photography (double exposures, time-lapse, over-cranking, under-cranking, hand-tinting and colourising), and their films set a new standard in production.

Case study

GEORGE MÉLIÈS

Magician, and owner of the Theatre Robert Houdin in Paris, George Méliès was in the audience at the Salon Indien when the Lumières unveiled their

Cinematographe, and immediately afterwards approached them to buy this new invention (they turned him down). Fascinated by the potential of this new medium he travelled to London where he viewed Robert Paul's camera-projector design, and subsequently developed his own in early 1896.

An accident in one of his early attempts at filmmaking set him on a course which made him universally recognised as one of the greatest filmmakers of his time: his camera jammed while filming a street scene and it took some moments to fix – when viewing back the film, this jam caused objects to transform into other objects, and people to appear/disappear in the frame. He had inadvertently discovered 'trick' photography, and, more importantly, saw its ability to manipulate filmic time and space.

In developing his elaborate and ever longer films, Méliès was the first to introduce split-screen cinematography in *Un Homme de têtes* (France, 1898), double exposure in *La Caverne Maudite* (France, 1898), and the first dissolve in *Cendrillon* (France, 1899). He was also the first to introduce nudity to the evolving medium with *Après le Bal* (France, 1897).

He built an elaborate glasshouse studio in Paris in which he was able to completely control the use of natural light in order to enhance his productions. Here he filmed his most extraordinary films such as *L'Homme-*

Figure 15.3 *Le Voyage à travers l'impossible* (Méliès, France, 1904).

continued

orchestre (France, 1900) (in which he used multiple-superimposition to have the same man playing all the instruments in an orchestra), *Le Voyage dans la Lune* (France, 1902) (in which he included animation and hand-tinting of every frame, and which led to international fame and his setting up a film exchange in North America) and *Le Voyage à travers l'impossible* (France, 1904) (which was his most costly film up to this point, confirming his position as the most prominent filmmaker of the day).

Unfortunately his filmmaking developed little beyond this point, and he was overtaken by other narrative filmmakers. He abandoned cinema in 1912, and in 1915 turned his studio into a variety theatre, resuming his pre-cinema career. The First World War years and the poverty of the postwar period impacted on him and in 1923 he was forced to sell the Theatre Robert Houdin when he went bankrupt.

Awarded the Legion of Honour for services to cinema, George Méliès died almost penniless in 1938 in a Paris tobacconist kiosk that he operated.

The transformation of primitive cinema

In the decade or so since its birth, this new medium of cinema had undergone a significant set of transformations. First, the nature of the medium had developed away from its early actualities to clearly signposted entertainments, and in doing so helped shape audience expectation of what the medium was to be. The serious was replaced with the frivolous, the intellectual with the entertaining, and 'reality' with drama. This is not to say that actualities and travelogues disappeared – they remained popular with audiences as part of a programme of entertainment – but they certainly soon took second place to works of fiction.

Second, a filmic *language* was beginning to evolve through the experimentation of the pioneers of film, which offered an ease of production, and a recognisable set of codes and conventions of the medium. This filmic language made film more understandable to a mass (and often uneducated) market, made it more formulaic (and hence repeatable – the vital key to industrial success), and offered new filmmakers a template to work to, thereby both speeding them into production of similar films, and allowing them to develop this language faster.

Third, the audience for film had begun to evolve. No longer shocked by the arrival of a train or fearful of waves splashing, and no longer content to simply watch unstructured actuality, they demanded ever greater spectacle and stronger stories to shape the lengthening films put before them. While George Méliès was perhaps the genius of spectacle, it was an English producer, Cecil Hepworth, and an American director, Edwin S. Porter, who did most for the development of narrative.

SPECTACLE: the 'camera-trickery' of early cinema that initially excited and has led to this period being termed a 'cinema of attractions'. Of course this developing use of spectacle developed the audiences' sense of cinema not merely as a visual medium but as one that provoked sensation (of being run over, of exploding, of going to the moon). As primitive cinema underwent its transformation, it was recognised that the audience needed more than spectacle alone – spectacle had to be carried by emotional involvement, by strong stories, and identifiable characters, for it to continue to be a key element of cinematic expression.

NARRATIVE: the *story* of the film, usually (at this time) told linearly and in chronological order. Film narrative involves not merely the story but the methods employed to make sense of that story, and a set of conventions (of shot, of screen direction, of editing) had to evolve in order for a 'standardised' way of telling cinematic stories to evolve.

INFORMATION BOX – CECIL HEPWORTH *i*

Hepworth was the son of a Magic Lantern showman, and quickly developed an interest in the new medium of film. Indeed, he wrote *The ABC of Cinematography* (the world's first manual on the subject) in 1897, and *Animated Photography* in 1898. He began making films in 1897 for Charles Urban who had founded the Warwick Trading Company the year before, and in 1899 he set up his own company, the Hepworth Manufacturing Company, at Walton-on-Thames. Within a year he was releasing over a hundred films a year (as producer, though he did undertake all the technical roles from writer to editor on occasion), and in 1903 he built a studio in the style of Méliès but used arc lights for additional lighting. His key collaborators were the directors Percy Slow and Lewin Fitzhamon, and with the latter he made the pivotal film *Rescued by Rover* (UK, 1905). This film was so successful with the paying public that over 1,200 prints were released, and it had to be reshot three times due to the negatives wearing out. *Rescued by Rover* marks a clear departure from primitive cinema with its continuity of screen direction, its sophisticated use of parallel editing, its strong central narrative and central characters, and its use of the language of film (including an

continued

awareness of the 180° Rule (see *AS Film Studies: The Essential Introduction*, Chapter 3, 'FM1 Creative Project')).

The Hepworth Manufacturing Company competed easily with films being imported from the world market. After the First World War, however, his film technique began to date, and in 1924 he went bankrupt, ending his career in film directing trailers and adverts.

INFORMATION BOX – EDWIN S. PORTER

Unusually for this period, Porter's work as director is recognised beyond that of the production company Edison. Working out of Edison's New York East 21st Street Skylight Studios he used his skill as an editor to combine actuality and fiction footage to great effect, and later used an actuality style of shooting to weave the actuality footage into his *Life of an American Fireman* (Edison, US, 1903). The success of this film led to what was considered the most significant film of the decade in an early western, *The Great Train Robbery* (Edison, US, 1903), a film that defined parallel editing, and was masterful in manipulating the spectator through the filmic space. The final shot (of a sheriff firing directly out of the screen) is reminiscent in effect of the Lumière train rushing towards the spectator.

Porter made hundreds of films for Edison and became head of production, a post he was fired from in 1909 as the company felt his methods were outdated. In 1915 he left production altogether to return to an earlier career in projection.

ACTIVITY

Look at a number of Hepworth and Porter films (and at least at *Rescued by Rover* and *The Great Train Robbery*). What significant differences can you see in these films from those at the beginning of film's first decade? Make a list of advances under the headings *Story* and *Technique*.

Keep this list safe, and repeat the exercise with films from later in the period (e.g. a Griffith, a DeMille or a Sennett), comparing them with early primitive cinema.

Compare the two lists. Is there anything that stands out about the Hepworth/Porter list? What further development in film language happened beyond these two filmmakers?

Do you think there were significant developments in spectatorship during this period?

The industrialisation of cinema

The first industrial filmmaker was of course Edison, whose production line was in operation before film had ever been screened, and Edison was determined to keep control of the American market (he would have loved to have also controlled the world market) in the face of growing competition from other countries' filmmakers. By 1908 Edison had been dramatically eclipsed by the French company Pathé, which was undisputedly the world's largest production company.

INFORMATION BOX – PATHÉ

i

Backed by France's leading industrialists, Charles Pathé bought the patents to the Lumière *cinematographe* in 1902 and set about making an improved camera (such was the success of this that it is estimated that over half of the films shot up until 1917 were shot on a Pathé camera). Manufacturing his own film stock, Pathé opened a studio at Vincennes, and introduced a production-line style of operation (one that Hollywood would later replicate). The company established a network of film sales agencies across the globe (which they quickly turned into film rental agencies, seeing that there was more money to be made in distribution rather than in outright sales), and opened a chain of per-manent cinemas, including the world's first luxury cinema, the 'Omnia-Pathé', in Paris. In 1909 Pathé introduced the world to the 'Pathé Journal' – the newsreel – a form that would last long into the television era. The success of Pathé continues to this day.

In America the industry boomed, with a gradual shift away from the fairground and vaudeville theatre sites to fixed, cheap exhibition venues that became known as 'nickelodeons' (the price of admission was a nickel). The industrialised cities of the northeastern states had a high proportion of unsophisticated immigrant workers from Central and Southern Europe for whom the theatres offered no real

Figure 15.4 The front of Comique movie theatre, a nickelodeon theatre in Toronto, Canada, c. 1910.

entertainment due to the inaccessibility of the language. Silent film, however, was clearly universal, and was an instant success in these new venues at the heart of industrial America. This was not a uniquely American phenomenon however, and across Europe storefront cinemas (the entrance was either between storefronts, or a storefront itself) began to spring up.

The nickelodeons were not the luxury palaces that cinemas became in the 1930s, but rather simple halls with bench seating, a screen and a projector (though they soon adopted gaudy trappings as the money rolled in). Since the projectors were often in the same room as the audience, and there was no need for silence in which to hear dialogue, the cinema experience was a very different (and noisy) one. It was not uncommon in America for a film producer to make a movie on the roof of an apartment block (easily accessible space with good light in overcrowded cities, full of tall buildings and long shadows), process and print it in an apartment below, and rent out the basement in order to show the finished film. Nickelodeons developed quickly because they were easy to establish, they were unregulated, and offered considerable profits. In 1905 the Kalem Picture Company was founded with an investment of $600 (a considerable amount in those days). By 1908 the company was making two films a week at a cost of $200 each, and returning a profit of $5,000 a week.

With this sort of profit available, and a completely unregulated industry (one effectively founded on the illegal replication of the Lumière and Edison machines), it is unsurprising that it attracted criminal elements and provoked violent disputes. Battles were fought between rival nickelodeon owners, thugs were hired, equipment destroyed, and in one dramatic case over 300 spectators were killed when a nickelodeon was firebombed by rivals. All this was to gain control of cinema and the lucrative exhibition and (to a lesser extent) distribution opportunities.

In 1909 Edison along with his two chief American rivals, Biograph (Edison's ex-assistant W.K.L. Dickson) and Vitagraph (legally the only ones in the United States with the patents to make motion pictures), combined with the more established of their European or 'immigrant' rivals Essanay, Kalem, Lubin, Pathé-Méliès and Selig to form the Motion Picture Patents Company. Arranging with Eastman Kodak to supply only them with film stock (using their combined power to present Eastman with a *fait accompli*), they demanded $2 per week from exhibitors to 'rent' Edison-based equipment (which they may have already owned without having ever paid anything for the rights under Edison's patent). The MPPC also established a national film exchange – the General Film Company – to distribute the films of this cartel. Within two years, through the use of legal and less than legal means, the General Film Company had taken over all fifty-seven of the leading film distributors in America with the exception of William Fox's Greater New York Rental Company. Fox was able to resist, as his company owned enough exhibition venues, and produced enough films, to remain self-sufficient.

By 1911 Edison had achieved an effective monopoly over the established American cinema industry, but at this point made the mistake of trying to take control of the other companies in the cartel. The MPPC began to crumble, and a number of filmmakers saw the opportunity to regain their independence.

Case study
BIOGRAPH

W.K.L. Dickson left Edison's employ in 1895 to found the American Mutoscope and Biograph Company with inventors Herman Casler and Henry Marvin (whose mutoscope was already designed to be an effective competitor for Edison's kinetoscope), and investor Elias Koopman, inventor of the pocket lighter. In 1896 Biograph became the first American company to screen a film made by an American company, to an American audience, and quickly overtook Edison as the principal company in the emerging film industry, opening European offices (Dickson went out to manage the London office) and quickly developing both an international reputation and international sales. Biograph soon focused its energies purely on production.

In 1901 Biograph made the first ever western, setting the format of a popular genre for years to come. It was the first company to shoot a drama in California (Hollywood was not born at this time), and gave the renowned

Figure 15.5 Florence Lawrence – the Biograph Girl circa 1918.

director David Wark Griffith his first opportunity to direct. Indeed, it was Griffith's overwintering of his actors in California that led to his discovery of a village near the small town of Los Angeles which was to become Hollywoodland, and eventually Hollywood.

Biograph launched the careers of countless directors and actors including Mack Sennett (who, later working for the Keystone Studio, not only gave the world the unique comedy of the Keystone Cops, but 'discovered' and launched Charlie Chaplin), Florence Lawrence (the 'Biograph Girl' who was later to become the first 'star'), Lillian Gish, Lionel Barrymore (founder of the Barrymore acting dynasty and grandfather to Drew Barrymore), and Mary Pickford. Moving to Hollywood, Biograph was among the first to establish permanent studios there (in 1911) where it began developing the first full-length feature films: D.W. Griffith's biblical epic *Judith of Bethulia* (Biograph, US, 1913) is seen as the first American feature, running at around ninety-four minutes when projected at 18fps. Griffith left Biograph shortly after this and the company never recovered from the loss of its star director. Biograph ceased production in 1918.

The birth of Hollywood

The difficulties with the MPPC and the General Film Company came to a head in a series of legal disputes over patents and monopolies, and as they played out in court over several years from 1910 to 1916, a number of filmmakers (both established and new independents) sought to escape the difficulties the MPPC presented. Slowly a migration west took place, to the furthest and remotest point the relentless railroad had reached, and furthest away from the disputes of New York, Chicago and Atlanta.

The suburb village of Los Angeles that was to become Hollywoodland had much to offer these filmmakers, not least being within a hundred miles of the Mexican border if trouble from the east coast came calling (the border shifted significantly south during the twentieth century when America bought what is now southern California from the Mexicans). All year round sunlight, constant good weather, space, a varied landscape (coastline, city, mountains and desert), cheap labour (largely American Indians, Mexicans, and Chinese railroad labourers who had been abandoned at the end of the line) and cheap raw materials (the forests of the area were destroyed to make the studios), combined to make the lure of this new-found filmic paradise irresistible. In 1911 studios were established by Biograph, Essenay, Kalem, Selig and Vitagraph in southern California, and Nestor opened the first Hollywood studio on Sunset Boulevard. Independents Thomas Ince, Carl Laemmle (founder of Universal Pictures), William Fox (founder of Fox Pictures which later became Twentieth Century Fox) and Adolph Zukor (founder of Paramount Pictures) quickly followed.

The opportunities offered by this new location led quickly to the development of early examples of the genre films which would span the next century of film: the western (with stars such as Tom Mix), the melodrama (with stars such as Lillian Gish and the 'vamp' Theda Bara), chase films (epitomised by the Keystone Cops and Harold Lloyd), comedy (Charlie Chaplin, Fatty Arbuckle), and the historical/biblical epic (such as those of Cecil B. DeMille). Film as spectacle had arrived on a grand scale, and there was nothing beyond the scope of these Hollywood filmmakers (archaeologists in the southern Californian desert recently uncovered full-sized pyramids and a sphinx, constructed by the studio craftsmen of Hollywood, and abandoned after Cecil B. DeMille had finished shooting against them).

By 1916 the full-length feature film was the dominant form in America (supported still by newsreels and comedy shorts in sometimes lengthy programmes), and the nickelodeons developed into grand palaces of fantasy, suited to the length of time a spectator would need to sit in order to consume the product. Spectators themselves had developed considerably within a short space of time and were now fully conversant with the (now established) film language, understood the underlying principles of narrative direction and character development, could follow spatial and temporal changes, and were beginning to develop allegiances towards particular film companies' product, particular directors or particular actors.

Case study
THE BIRTH OF THE STAR

Thomas Ince persuaded the 'Biograph Girl', Florence Lawrence, to switch to working for his company. Ince placed her opposite his most popular actor, King Baggot, in her first film for him, but before its release played a spectacular publicity stunt. Planting a story in the press that Florence Lawrence had been tragically killed in a collision with a streetcar, he watched as news spread across the industry. He then, in full fury, went to the newspapers to complain about the vicious lie being spread about the demise of his new actress, accusing Biograph of being at the root of it. His finale to this sting was to announce that 'proof' that she was alive would be revealed when she would appear at the première of his new film later that week.

The stunt was an absolute success, with a huge crowd appearing to see if Florence Lawrence was alive or dead. When she stepped out of the car with King Baggot the crowd went wild, and in scenes repeated around stars ever since there was a crush of fans trying to kiss, touch or take trophies from this first star.

One of Hollywood's most prolific directors at this time was D.W. Griffith, who left Biograph in 1913 to join Mutual/Reliance-Majestic where he went on to make *The Birth of a Nation* (Mutual, 1915), before seeking independent status and making *Intolerance* (D.W. Griffith, US, 1916). Griffith continued this path through to 1919 when he formed United Artists with actors Charlie Chaplin, Douglas Fairbanks and Mary Pickford.

Case study
INTOLERANCE

Figure 15.6 *Intolerance* (1916, Dir: D.W. Griffith).

While much has been written about D.W. Griffith's 1915 American Civil War/Klu Klux Klan epic *The Birth of a Nation*, it is his 1916 anti-war film *Intolerance* that is perhaps more indicative of the late stage of this period, with a scale and a degree of self-indulgence that one of the early pioneers such as George Méliès could never have imagined.

continued

Griffith was overawed by the mammoth nature of the Italian epics such as *Quo Vadis?* (Cines, Italy, 1912, *Dir*. Enrico Guazzoni), and *Cabria* (Itala, Italy, 1914, *Dir*. Giovanni Pastrone), both in terms of scale and in terms of *mise-en-scène*, and was determined that his filmmaking would equal if not surpass their efforts. The result was *Intolerance* – a film that audiences rejected, ironically because its structure was counter to that which had become the established norm largely through the work of Griffith himself.

The film is in four parts – the carnage of ancient Babylon, the massacre of the sixteenth-century Protestant Huguenots in France, the persecution of Jesus by the Pharisees in Judaea, and the 'Modern Story' of strikers gunned down, a boy falsely accused of murder, and a narrow escape from the gallows – with each part interwoven, separated by the highly symbolic image of a woman (Lillian Gish) bathed in a shaft of light, rocking a cradle with the three Fates sitting behind her.

The sheer scale of the production is worthy of a contemporary Hollywood blockbuster: full-scale replicas of the walls of Babylon were built, along with a garish attempt to outdo Pastrone with an enormous reconstruction of the Babylonian palace; immense battle scenes were enacted with thousands of extras employed; the French Court of the Reformation is stylishly replicated; and the Judaea of Christ's time is recreated in exacting detail.

It is, of course, Griffith's focus on the human condition that makes this film more than just an exercise in spectacle (but what an exercise in spectacle it is), with the social chaos of each period set against the intimate moments of key figures (usually women). Griffith also offers a rich vein of metaphor throughout the film and (often bluntly) uses this to highlight his key theme of intolerance.

The film was a financial disaster however, and lost Griffith all the money he had earned from *The Birth of a Nation*. Audiences wanted the traditional narrative structure that Griffith helped develop and enshrine, and by becoming a victim of this his filmmaking was never to return to its previous heights.

Filmmaking in the rest of the world

Until the dominance of Hollywood was recognised in the world market in 1918/1919, France had clearly been at the forefront of production (thanks largely to its industrialised process defined by its two key production companies Pathé and Gaumont), with Italy close on its heels. Italy developed studios in many of its principal cities, and was the first to produce the lengthy feature films and epics that became the mainstay of feature film production internationally to the present day. Germany and Russia both engaged in significant production (though much of their early work was lost in the upheavals of the First World War and of the Russian Revolution).

Second to Pathé's position as foremost producer of film was Denmark's Nordisk company, which introduced the renowned director Carl Dreyer to the international stage. In Latin America, Brazil was a dominant producer (developing its own genre of 'singing films' – 'fitas cantatas' – where singers behind the screen would try to synchronise with the filmed musical numbers), closely followed by Argentina and Mexico, offering stories of the gauchos (Argentinian cowboys), outlaws, and stories of real life – a primitive form of documentary reconstruction.

Filmmaking in both India and China was driven by the British through the colonial system, with India developing an indigenous cinema which focused on Indian histories and myths, while China tended towards filmmaking by colonists who told 'Chinese' stories for Western audiences (often based around Chinese immorality and drug dens), though an indigenous cinema evolved late in the period. Japan embraced film quickly, though it developed approaches that were radically different from those of Western cinema ('voicing' a film's dialogue from behind the screen, having a narrator complete with illustrating stick who would point out and explain the scene to the audience, and the 'chain' drama in which film sequences were interspersed with live performance to create an interdisciplinary work).

ACTIVITY

Consider the international developments in cinema listed above. How do you think they relate to their audiences? How does this compare with the developments in Western cinema? If possible, compare the structure of any of the films of these national cinemas of this period with an American film of roughly the same date (you may find some of these short films available on the internet), looking at shot composition, editing, narrative construction and so on. What similarities do you notice? Are there any fundamental differences? Account for the nature of each production and assess the sophistication of each production's audience. Do you think the spectator differentiated significantly between national cinemas in this period?

The First World War and the end of an era

The outbreak of the European war in August 1914 had an immediate and irreversible effect on European cinema, and by extension, world cinema. As soon as hostilities began, the French government ordered the stopping of all filmmaking activities, and many of the key personnel were dispatched to the Western Front to fight the Germans. As this bloody conflict wore on over the next four years, with a continuous and terrible slaughter, it was unlikely that many of these film specialists ever returned to take up their cameras again. Although filmmaking was resumed in France during the war, the French industry never really recovered.

As Pathé was at this point the world's leading film producer, this was a disaster both for the French industry and for the world market. A huge hole opened in production and distribution, and it was the Italians who initially filled it with their own product and by taking over the distribution networks established worldwide by the French.

In Germany production was reduced, though not stopped completely, but it lost most of its export markets by being at war with them. Danish film suffered in consequence of the war as Nordisk owned cinemas in Germany, which led to their films being boycotted by France and Russia (their biggest markets outside Germany). When the Germans took over these cinemas their last market was closed to them and the financial loss of losing their exhibition outlets nearly ruined them.

British filmmaking ceased temporarily, but the government soon saw the propaganda potential and encouraged certain forms of cinematic expression. The French experience of skilled film technicians enlisting to fight was replicated in Britain, and again many talented filmmakers were lost to the bitter trench warfare. The Americans (who did not enter the war until 1917) were quick to fill the production gaps with their product, which increased in popularity with the British audience throughout the First World War.

When the Italians joined the war in 1916 they did not follow the French and British examples of closing their film industry, though the financial impact of war curtailed activity. The American industry mopped up the distribution opportunities in Latin America, and began supplying films to replace those lost by reduced Italian production.

When America entered the war in 1917, the US War Industries Board declared film an 'essential industry', meaning that film personnel were exempt from the draft. While other national cinemas were destroyed, both financially and in the loss of their talented filmmakers, the American industry was positioned for global dominance. It achieved this dominance in 1919, months after the end of the First World War, when it was able to offload four years' worth of back catalogue on to a reconstructing European market, and was in a financial position to begin buying into European production, distribution and exhibition markets. Grateful postwar audiences were only too eager to watch these films and escape the horrors of the postwar period, while being drawn into an attachment to American film that would see out the century. In 1919 Hollywood had a boom year, as early cinema became a mature cinema, and as American film finally fulfilled Edison's vision of global dominance.

- Early cinema is described as 'a cinema of attractions'. Do you believe that early cinema is based on spectacle alone or are there other factors determining its development for spectators?

- Describe the key points for you in the development of spectatorship from primitive to mature, and assess their impact on the direction of cinema.

- Which for you was more important in developing cinema from its primitive stage: technical invention or the evolution of a film language?

- Film spectators evolved from a magic lantern and vaudeville theatre tradition. In what ways did this impact on early spectatorship and the development of this primitive medium?

- Assess which elements of film form had most impact on the development of spectatorship in early cinema.

Resources and further Reading

Books

Baliol, T. (1985) *The American Film Industry*. University of Wisconsin Press

Barnes, J. (1998) *The Beginnings of the Cinema in England, 1894–1901*. University of Exeter Press

Chanan, M. (1995) *The Dream That Kicks The Prehistory and Early Years of Cinema in Britain*. Routledge

Christie, I. and Gilliam, T. (1995) *The Last Machine*. British Film Institute

Elsaesser, T. and Barker, A. (eds) (1990) *Early Cinema: Space, Frame, Narrative*. British Film Institute

Popple, S. and Kember, J. (2004) *Early Cinema: From Factory Gate to Dream Factory*. Wallflower Press

Robinson, D. (1998) *From Peep Show to Palace. The Birth of American Film*. University Presses of California, Columbia and Princeton

Shipman, D. (1995) *Cinema: The First Hundred Years*. Weidenfeld & Nicolson

Thompson, K. and Bordwell, D. (1993) *Film History: An Introduction*. McGraw Hill

Withall, K. (2007) *Early and Silent Cinema: A Teacher's Guide*. Auteur

Film

Cinema Europe: The Other Hollywood – Don Taffner's DLT Entertainment – six part series on European Early Cinema, narrated by Kenneth Branagh
Early Cinema: Primitives and Pioneers Volume I – BFI DVD – includes Lumière, Méliès, Acres, Paul, Smith
Early Cinema: Primitives and Pioneers Volume II – BFI DVD – includes Pathé, Hepworth, Porter
Landmarks of Early Film Vol 1 – Image Entertainment – a collection of over forty fillms made during the opening decade of cinema
Landmarks of Early Film Vol 2: The Magic of Méliès – Image Entertainment – fifteen Méliès shorts and including a documentary 'George Melies: Cinema Magician'
The Lumière Brothers' First Films – Kino on Video, with eighty-five Lumière films from 1895 to 1897, and a narration by renowned French filmmaker Bertrand Tavernier
The Movies Begin – A Treasury of Early Cinema, 1894–1913 – Kino on Video – DVD box set – over 130 early films!

Internet

www.imdb.co.uk – Internet_Movie Database
A fantastic resource, includes filmographies of early cinema filmmakers

www.screenonline.org.uk – ScreenOnline
The BFI's excellent site with comprehensive information, and the opportunity to see some early British film online

http://website.lineone.net/~luke.mckernan/Links.htm
Early Cinema Gateway, listing links to various useful sites

http://easyweb.easynet.co.uk/~s-herbert/momiwelcome.htm
The unofficial MOMI (Museum of the Moving Image) site. Cannot be bettered for a detailed and informative look at Early Cinema

http://www.earlycinema.com
A host of great information, biographies, timelines and so on, focused on early cinema

http://inventors.about.com/library/inventors/blmotionpictures.htm
History of the motion picture – full of biographies, company case studies and information

http://www.institut-lumiere.org/english/frames.html
The official French site dedicated to the Lumière brothers

http://www.filmsite.org/pre20sintro.html
Superb set of resources on pre-1920 films

16 SPECTATORSHIP AND DOCUMENTARY

This chapter will look at:

- film form in relation to the 'real'
- the evolution of the documentary form
- issues of uses of documentary
- spectator response to the 'real'
- 'types' of documentary and their effects on the audience
- contemporary resurgence of documentary
- alternative delivery platforms and the new documentary user

What is documentary?

'Documentary' is a term that is popularly asserted to have been first used by John Grierson, to describe Robert Flaherty's film *Moana* (Famous Players – Lasky Corp, US, 1926), coming from the French *documentaire*, or travelogue, a form that grew out of the *actualities* of early cinema (see previous chapter). While accurately describing one aspect of *Moana* – a travelogue – the term took on new meaning in relation to the film's approach to depicting the 'real'. However, a more familiar use of the term occurred soon after the birth of cinema in the writings of a Polish filmmaker Boleshaw Matuszewski, who proposed a use for the new medium as a museum of contemporary life, capturing activities that would be of 'documentary' interest.

INFORMATION BOX – ROBERT FLAHERTY

Canadian explorer and prospector Robert Flaherty was fascinated by the Inuit (Eskimo) peoples of northern Canada, and began shooting short films of their lives (ethnographic films). In 1916 he lost all 30,000 feet of his feature documentary when a burning cigarette started a fire in his editing room. Deciding to reshoot and refocus the film, he produced a documentary feature revolving around one central character and his family, *Nanook of the North* (Revillon Frères, US, 1922). The success of this film defined not only the nature of the ethnographic documentary, but gave a resurgence and direction to documentary filmmaking, and got the major world film studios interested in financing them.

Documentary is an approach to the 'real' as opposed to the fictional, and in dealing with issues of fact, of real events, of actuality, the approach is both popular with audiences and highly significant in terms of study. John Grierson later further explained documentary as not just the approach to actuality, but as the 'creative treatment' of actuality, and it is this creative treatment that defines both subject and documentary form. It also clearly implicates the hand of the filmmaker as being behind the structured representation of the subject (and by association the expected audience response), and brings out the central question of documentary in relation to the 'real' – whose 'real' is shown on screen?

The very act of structuring images gives them meanings they do not possess on their own (see the 'Kulishov effect' and the concept of montage in Chapter 9: German and Soviet Cinemas of the 1920s), and so, to a major extent, a filmmaker cannot depict the 'real', but instead offers a partial or selective view of the 'real' which should be considered in relation to production context, ideology and intention. It could be argued that the only true documentaries are those made in the primitive period of early cinema, the *actualities*.

ACTIVITY

- Consider a documentary you have recently watched. How can you be certain it is documentary, and not a fiction film? What tools do you think the filmmaker uses to ensure you accept this as a depiction of the 'real'?
- Are there any points when you felt it seemed less 'real'? If so, why do you think this happened?

■ Read the rest of this chapter, and then rewatch the documentary you identified above. Does it appear different to you now? If so, in what way? Why do you think this is?

Actualities

The earliest films were (almost by definition) documentary films, as they recorded either the 'real' or a simulation of a real event. Thomas Edison's *Fred Ott's Sneeze* (US, 1984, ph. W.K.L. Dickson) was a simple film of a man who sits facing the camera and sneezes, and this could be described as a documentary of a sneeze. However it is unlikely that the cameraman waited patiently until a sneeze arrived, and so either the subject was made to sneeze or was asked to simulate a sneeze, either way affecting or replicating the 'real'. Similarly with the Lumière brothers' *Sortie des Ouvriers de l'Usine Lumière* (*Workers Leaving a Factory*) (France, 1895, ph. Louis Lumière), they depict a real event (workers leaving at the end of their shift) and yet on close examination the factory workers appear over-dressed, and a number of them seem to be acting exuberantly for the camera.

Figure 16.1 *La Sortie des Ouvriers de l'Usine Lumière* (*Workers Leaving a Factory*) (19 March 1895, ph. Louis Lumière).

Again, this is either a replication of reality, or a shaped and managed reality, where the manipulation of the 'real' is lost beneath the spectacle of the new.

The *actualities* were dominated by the novelty or spectacle of the event, and many films simply showed panoramas, shots from vehicles, or simple actions without any manipulation of the image. Indeed, the filmmakers themselves had no motive to manipulate the image since the audience of the time devoured anything put in front of them, and so simply recording the 'real' was a filmmaker's easiest option. From these images, however, drama could emerge and could refocus both the *actualities* and the spectator's view of the event on screen. Alternatively, where cameras were not present, filmmakers could reconstruct an event (a popular technique in contemporary television documentary), as the Williamsons' Kinematograph Company did with *Attack on a Chinese Mission* (UK, 1900, *Dir*: James Williamson) in replicating an incident from the Boxer Rebellion in China at the end of the nineteenth century.

Charles Urban, a significant British producer of the period, was determined to use film as an educational tool rather than as the extension of the music hall theatre that he feared it was becoming. As early as 1903 he had begun a series of films that depicted the more inaccessible parts of the world and their peoples through his Bioscope Expeditions, and from the same year was producing an 'Unseen World' series which included such titles as *Through the Microscope* (UK, 1907) and *Rodents and their Habits* (UK, 1908).

After the First World War the radical art movements that developed before and in the interwar period gravitated towards film both in European democracies and in the newly formed Soviet Russia. Denis Kaufman (who adopted the name Dziga Vertov – 'Spinning Top') developed a Kino Pravda (or Cinema Truth) style of documentary production that was based on combining multiple angles on an event to capture the essence of its 'truth' and to avoid merely offering a representation of the 'real'. If someone noticed they were being filmed, then the filming was instantly stopped, as it was assumed the subject's behaviour would be influenced by the knowledge that they were being captured on film. Using the principles of montage, Vertov collided images, used techniques of multiple exposure and superimposition, and reflected the subjects he captured through the rhythms he created.

In Germany the *actualities* developed painterly qualities in the abstract work of filmmakers such as Walther Ruttman, whose interest in rhythms and the patterns in life betrays the influence of Vertov. Focusing on a day in the life of Berlin, set to symphonic music (composed for the film by Edmund Meisel, though the film itself does not have synchronised sound), *Berlin: die Sinfonie der Großstadt* (*Berlin: Symphony of the City*) (Deutsche-Vereins Film/Les Productions Fox Europa, Germany, 1927, *Dir*: Walther Ruttman) fused the style of the *actualities* with the Kino Pravda editing techniques to create a film that interprets the 'real' and gives the city itself a sense of life independent of its inhabitants. This sparked a range of 'City Symphony' films in the late 1920s with Ruttman contributing several more.

CITY SYMPHONY: a short-lived style of documentary from the late 1920s/early 1930s in which 'themed' images were connected together with a concentration on rhythm and emotional impact, and were set to a separate composed soundtrack. The focus was often on abstract images (shadows, shapes, movement) to create comment or make meaning. Key proponents were Walther Ruttman, Eugene Deslaw, Wilfried Basse, and the artist Man Ray. The popularity of cine clubs across Europe at this time not only exposed the movement to willing spectators, but also inspired many to produce their own films of the same style.

In France, the young Brazilian artist Alberto Cavalcanti (who was later to become significant in British wartime documentary and feature production) presaged Ruttman's work by making *Rien Que Les Heures* (*Nothing But Time*) (Alberto Cavalcanti, France 1926) as a day in the life of Paris (this was begun after Ruttman's film but released earlier). Further south, Jean Vigo worked on another city symphony *À Propos de Nice* (*On the Subject of Nice*) (Jean Vigo, France, 1929, *Dir*: Jean Vigo), and engaged Boris Kaufman – Dziga Vertov's youngest brother – as cinematographer, with both firmly committed to the principles of Kino Pravda. Also in 1929 the influence of Ruttman's abstract documentaries reached the young Dutch filmmaker Joris Ivens, who used the theme of rain to paint a cinematic portrait of Amsterdam in *Regen* (*Rain*) (Capi-Holland, Netherlands, 1929, *Dir*: Joris Ivens). All of these films represent the 'real', yet do so by using a range of cinematic devices that perhaps allow the spectator to perceive deeper realities in the image than that of the superficial surface.

ACTIVITY

- Look at any of these early *actualities*. Can you see any intentional comment on the subject in them? Do you think the filmmaker is trying to position the spectator in any way?
- If you have access to a video camera, try to make a short film in the style of these *actualites*/early documentaries (a street symphony, for example). What difficulties do you face in representing what is there in reality? How do your decisions position the audience?

The British documentary movement

At the same time as these abstract documentaries were being made, John Grierson, influenced by the work of Robert Flaherty, produced and directed his first film on a grant from the HM Treasury Department of £2,500. *Drifters* (Empire Marketing Board, UK, 1929) was a film about the herring fishery industry, and in using a combination of Flaherty's ethnographic observation and the Soviet (futurist) style of placing the relationship between man and machine at the core, with ordinary working people as 'heroes', this led to a success both for Grierson and for documentary.

Figure 16.2 *Drifters* (Empire Marketing Board, UK, 1929).

By not concentrating on a historical view of his subject, Grierson was concerned in *Drifters* to show the fishing industry as something contemporary, using modern equipment and modern techniques, and he emphasised the professionalism and the social interaction of the fishermen at sea, and the importance of the herring fishing industry to the economy and to Britain. In doing so he emphasised the importance of the wider working-class community to industrial Britain, and offered the first glimpse of a theme that would run through much of the later work to which he was connected. This film, which was shot entirely on location (except for some innovative underwater cinematography which was constructed at the Marine Biological Research Station in Plymouth), at a time when British film was distinctly studio-bound, marked out the direction for a new movement in British film.

Case study

John Grierson was born on 26 April 1898 in Deanston, Scotland, graduating from Glasgow University after a period in the Royal Navy during the First World War. He spent four years in the USA at the University of Chicago, developing an interest in mass communications while on a Rockefeller fellowship grant. It is here that he met Robert Flaherty, whom he termed the 'father' of documentary. He spent some time in New York, and helped prepare Sergei Eisenstein's *Bronenosets Potyomkin* (*Battleship Potemkin*) (Goskino, USSR, 1925) for an American audience, re-editing it to comply with New York State censors. This period ignited not only an affinity for the Soviet promotion of ordinary people as heroes, but also for Eisenstein's editing techniques.

On his return to Britain, Grierson approached the Empire Marketing Board (a trade promotion body for the British Empire) with a plan to persuade them to use film as a medium of communication. Securing funds from the Treasury, he was commissioned to make *Drifters* (which premièred at the London Film Society as support to the first British screening of Grierson's edit of *Bronenosets Potyomkin*).

The success of this first film led him to a position as Head of the Empire Marketing Board Film Unit, which grew from Grierson and an assistant in 1930 to a staff of over thirty by 1933. Developing new filmmakers such as Paul Rotha and Harry Watt, he also hired in talents from abroad in the form of Alberto Cavalcanti and Robert Flaherty. In 1934 the Empire Marketing Board was dissolved and Grierson's team became the GPO Film Unit, producing such important works as *Night Mail* (GPO, UK, 1936 *Dir*: Harry Watt/Basil Wright), attracting new talent such as Basil Wright and Humphrey Jennings to the team of filmmakers, and using the talents of contemporary 'emerging stars' in both literary and music fields such as Louis McNeice, W.H. Auden and Benjamin Britten. Members from the GPO Film Unit took Grierson's influence into a range of other developments including the Strand Film Unit, the Realist Film Unit and the Shell Film Unit. Grierson himself left in 1937 to found the Film Centre as an advisory service to documentary filmmakers.

Two years later, as war appeared on the horizon, the Imperial Relations Trust sent Grierson to Canada to organise production there, resulting in the development of the National Film Board of Canada, and he went on similar trips during the war years to Australia and New Zealand. Returning to Britain in 1946, he worked from 1948 for the Central Office of Information

continued

(the government film production arm) but was prevented from significant documentary production by the economics of postwar Britain. He later moved into television where he spent several years before returning to Canada, where he ended his career as a university lecturer. He died in Bath, England, on 19 February 1972.

The most successful period for the British documentary movement (which may be seen as being left-wing or socialist in its viewpoint) was from the mid 1930s through to the end of the Second World War. Government agencies such as the GPO (General Post Office – also responsible for telephones, telegrams and mass communications generally) developed film units (the GPO Film Unit was to become the Crown Film Unit at the outbreak of war), companies such as Shell and ICI developed film units to promote their work, and a large number of independent film units were established as commercial enterprises, making commissioned documentaries for a variety of employers. At a time of polarised politics, organisations such as trade unions and the Left Book Club (an organisation dedicated to bringing left-wing literature to working people) also sponsored documentary production. One of the most significant films of the period is *Night Mail*.

Case study
NIGHT MAIL

Figure 16.3
Filming *Night Mail*
(Watt/Wright,
1936).

Perhaps the most celebrated film documentary in history, this film focuses on the GPO's 'Postal Special' – a post train that travelled up the country from London to Scotland. Celebrating the postal workers' skills, efficiency, unity and determination to deliver the post on time, directors Harry Watt and Basil Wright created heroes out of 'ordinary' working men doing 'ordinary' jobs.

The film is structured around the journey of a post train, which carries mail north from a central London sorting office, dispatching it at 'automated' points in mail bags (collecting outward-bound mail at the same time), and at key station junctions (again collecting more outward-bound post). The postal workers on the train sort the mail, package it into destination mail bags, and dispatch them.

A key moment in the film comes when a young postal worker is instructed in the 'automated' system, prepares a mail bag dispatch, and successfully operates the machinery for the dispatch. The influence of the Soviet filmmakers may be seen at its clearest in this sequence, with heroic compositions of the workers, an emphasis on the machinery and a rhythmic style of editing.

The film ends with a poem that was composed especially by the young popular poet W.H. Auden, and is read by Louis McNeice. The music for the film was composed by the esteemed Benjamin Britten, with all the elements of the final soundtrack directed and developed by Alberto Cavalcanti.

ACTIVITY

- Watch the film *Night Mail*. Now, watch it again, this time with the sound turned off. What do you notice about the visual structuring of the film? Can you see any direct influences? How important do you feel the soundtrack is to the overall success of the film?
- Watch the film again, but this time turn the brightness down so all you have left is the soundtrack. What do you think is significant in the soundtrack? What do you notice about the way it is structured? Do you notice the multi-layering of sound? What effect does the soundtrack have on you?

Documentary as propaganda

The Soviet leader Vladimir Lenin is credited as being the first to recognise the significance of film as propaganda, though its importance as a medium of persuasion had been put to use nearly two decades before. Albert E. Smith of the Vitagraph Company filmed scenes of the Spanish–American war in 1898, adding material shot back in the USA to ensure the right image and gravity was achieved. In 1899 The Biograph Company sent W.K.L. Dickson to Africa to cover the Boer War (at one point working with a young Winston Churchill), where he was well supported by the British military in promoting a 'correct' view of the conflict (British servicemen were even dressed in Boer uniforms to stage reconstructions of events for the camera). Needless to say, his films were informed by the British view on the conflict, and were somewhat less than impartial.

PROPAGANDA FILM: A film made with the express intention (either by the filmmaker or by those commissioning the film) of persuading an audience of the validity of a particular viewpoint, and positioning them to share that viewpoint. Documentary works particularly effectively as a medium of propaganda due its nature of representing the 'real' and in the audience's unquestioning belief in its depiction of 'truth'.

Governments (British, American, Soviet, Nazi German, Fascist Italian and Japanese, among many others) have used the power of documentary as a propaganda tool in order to shepherd their people into a particular belief or cause, and history shows that it has been an effective technique.

When the First World War broke out, both the British and German governments were quick to make documentary-like films that portrayed the enemy in a poor light, often using a 'newsreel' form to further convince the audience of the authenticity of their claims. Many British audiences were convinced of atrocities being carried out in 'plucky little Belgium' by the German occupiers, through the implications of dubious 'reconstruction' films – a belief firmly held by that war generation for decades, despite evidence to the contrary; clear testament to the power of film documentary as propaganda.

With the postwar Russian Revolution, documentary was put to work for the benefit of the Soviet state. Documentaries were produced by many of the Soviet filmmakers, with the intentions of promoting the Soviet cause, and 'educating' a population which may not have fully understood what the revolution had been about. Dziga Vertov, along with many other filmmakers, was sent out across the Russian states on 'Agit-prop' trains, where he shot and screened countless short documentary films for the Soviet cause.

Political ideology took Joris Ivens to Spain in 1936 to make a documentary about the Spanish Civil War, sponsored by a group of prominent American writers, artists and intellectuals who were all politically of the Left. The resulting film, which focuses solely on the Republican forces' struggle against the Fascist forces of General Franco, includes 'found sound footage' of earthquake sounds from the feature film *San Francisco*, which they ran backwards over images of bombing to 'create' the feeling of the 'real'. Blatantly biased to the Republican cause, *The Spanish Earth* (Contemporary Historians Inc, US, 1937, *Dir*: Joris Ivens) was clearly propagandistic, yet its artistry could not be criticised, and indeed, such was the critical reception that Ivens was wanted both for a US government project and another (on the Chinese–Japanese war) by his sponsors (he went to China and directed *The Four Hundred Million* (History Today Inc, US, 1939), a film constructed under the permanent censoring presence of the Chinese Chiang Kai-shek government).

Figure 16.4
A poster advertising *Triumph des Willens* (*Triumph of the Will*) (Leni Riefenstahl/Nazi Party, Germany, 1935).

The similar difficulty of propagandistic documentary that is constructed with considerable filmic talent is met when looking at the films of Nazi filmmaker Leni Riefenstahl. While her hastily constructed short film *Seig des Glaubens* (*Victory of Faith*) (Nazi Party, Germany, 1933) is little more than a homage to Hitler on his becoming dictator of Germany, it is her grand-scale epic documentaries – *Triumph des Willens* (*Triumph of the Will*) (Leni Riefenstahl/Nazi Party, Germany, 1935) and *Olympische Spiele* (*Olympia*) (Leni Riefenstahl, Germany, 1936) – that are most problematic. Central to the problem is Riefenstahl's continued assertion that she was not a Nazi and was not sympathetic to the Nazi ideology, which (since she had complete control over the production and editing of both films) is at odds with the powerful opening sequence of *Triumph des Willens* which begins with a dissolving title sequence announcing:

On September 5

1934

*20 years
after the outbreak
of the World War*

*16 Years
after the start
of German Suffering*

*19 months
after the beginning
of Germany's rebirth*

*Adolph Hitler flew
again to Nuremberg
to review the columns of his faithful followers*

This alone could be considered evidence of the propagandistic intent, but when it is coupled with the opening images of Hitler's plane descending from the clouds, a god returning to earth with salvation for the German people, then both the propaganda aim and Riefenstahl's allegiance are confirmed.

Similarly, in *Olympische Spiele*, her coverage of the Nazi Olympic Games in Berlin, 1936, Riefenstahl claimed (as she did with her earlier documentary) that she was simply recording the event, but again the opening sequence offers a clear sense of underlying ideology and intention. The film opens with an Olympic torch being handed through the generations from the 'cradle of civilisation' that was Greece, to the modern Nazi state overseen by Hitler himself, with the suggestion that Nazi Germany is the natural successor to the Ancient Greek empire and that it is the new cradle of civilisation. Couple to this the imagery that Riefenstahl uses which echoes the Nazi theme of strength and racial purity, and Riefenstahl's simple recording of the event becomes a masterpiece of Nazi propaganda.

When the Second World War broke out, the propaganda elements of documentary became more obvious (in retrospect), though to an audience sympathetic to the views being expressed they may not have seemed so blunt. In America, Hollywood feature film director Frank Capra was drafted in to make the *Why We Fight* Series between 1942 and 1945, and contracted both Robert Flaherty and Joris Ivens for some of the work. Boris Kaufman also found himself in America as a refugee, before moving north to Canada where he worked on Grierson's propaganda films at the National Film Board of Canada. In Britain documentary-making was centralised under the Ministry of Propaganda in the form of the Crown Film Unit, where many Grierson-trained filmmakers such as Basil Wright, Humphrey Jennings and Harry Watt produced numerous films alongside European refugees and émigré directors such as Alberto Cavalcanti. In Nazi Germany filmmakers were dispatched to film all the major military and 'security' tasks, and much of this footage (such as the liquidation of the Warsaw Ghetto, the operation of the concentration camps – e.g. Majdanek – including the details of the systematic mass murder of those sent there, and the atrocities of Operation Barbarossa – the brutal war against the Soviet forces) was used in the war crimes trials at Nuremberg.

In postwar Britain a milder form of documentary propaganda developed through the government communication agency the Central Office of Information (still existing and responsible for the commissioning of everything from the recent advice leaflet on how to deal with a terrorist attack, through to the annual drink-driving advertisements). This development, designed to build a common purpose in the population in the immediate and difficult postwar years, highlights an interesting point about propaganda: propaganda is always assumed to belong to a perceived 'enemy' view, whereas a nation's own material is viewed much more sympathetically. Thus, when considering the issue of documentary film propaganda it is more useful to detach any nationalistic preconceptions, and consider it in simpler terms of whether a film is made with *the expressed intention of persuading an audience of the validity of a particular viewpoint*, and whether it positions that audience *to share that viewpoint*.

ACTIVITY

Propaganda is usually a term used to describe the work of the vanquished in a conflict. Examine the films of the Crown Film Unit of the 1940s. Do you feel that they are trying to persuade an audience of the validity of a particular viewpoint? If so, what is the viewpoint being promoted? What propaganda techniques do the documentary-makers use to position their audience? Do you feel that these techniques work?

continued

> Now view one of Leni Riefenstahl's films (such as *Triumph des Willens*). Try to remove any thoughts of what the Nazis did in the run-up to war and in the war period, and watch the film as the audience of the time would have done (a film such as *Triumph des Willens* was effectively a party promo film designed to attract followers). Which sequences do you feel are most powerful, and why? What filmic techniques are being used by the filmmaker in these sequences? Which sequences affect you personally? How do they make you feel? What on-screen devices do you think are employed to provoke this reaction?

Notions of the 'real'

The early actualities were simply recordings of events that had little intention behind them other than to capture what was happening in front of the camera. This view, however, does something of an injustice to those behind the camera in much the same way as the term 'primitive' does in describing the period. Many of these camera operators had extensive photographic backgrounds, and were aware both of the importance of composition and of the significance of the selection of angle in conveying the scene.

As soon as a camera is set up, and a preferred angle chosen from which to capture the subject, everything outside that angle is excluded from this representation of the 'real'. This can either exclude inadvertently through assuming the importance of one aspect of the scene and prioritising it over other aspects of the scene, or deliberately through choosing to highlight one aspect of the scene in order to use it to reinforce a particular message or viewpoint (or even through filmic necessity – losing a part of the scene that does not work in terms of composition, or reframing to cut out an object or person that distracts from the focus on the main subject). What is not included in a scene (everything that is off-camera) is still part of the 'real', but it simply does not exist in terms of on-screen reality.

As the nature of filmmaking is largely based around hiding or disguising the constructional elements that go towards making a film in order to infer a sense of the 'real', any documentary, simply by virtue of setting up a camera, can only represent a particular sense of the 'real', a partial (partisan, if not biased) view. As this considers only the setting up of a camera and the selection of a shot, when it comes to what the filmmaker actually decides to shoot (and whether they shoot the same thing over a number of takes), the question of documentary's relationship with the 'real' becomes even more complex. The choice of what is shot makes the 'real' a subjective (personal view) reality as opposed to an objective (detached, impartial view) reality, though the latter should always be questioned as the filmmaker makes a number of choices to 'create' this objective style. Truly objective filmmaking has always been a practical impossibility, since decisions of angle and composition matched with choice of what is shot, and for how long, are joined with the fact that film cameras are usually loaded with a maximum of ten minutes of film before the magazine needs detaching, the 'gate' (the point of entry for light, where each frame is exposed) needs cleaning, and another magazine is loaded. At best, objective documentary can offer ten-minute portions of partial reality.

This subjective selection process is amplified when editing is introduced, as this is where choice between shots and between parts of shots is made, and where decisions to create meaning through the combination of shots are considered. When a filmmaker sets out to make a documentary there is usually an inherent angle that develops from their initial interest in the subject. With Flaherty's *Nanook of the North*, for example, it was the Inuit's 'natural' state, uninfluenced by modern civilisations, which interested him, and he structured his documentary to capture this (even famously getting Nanook to hunt in a traditional way with spears when this practice had long since been replaced in his community by hunting with a rifle). Flaherty offer the audience his 'real', a version of reality that either he saw himself, or that he wanted others to see.

ACTIVITY

If you have access to a video camera, choose an event to capture (something simple and repeatable, such as a Sunday League football team's activity, or the arrival and departure of boats in a port). Try to select camera positions and compositions that allow you to show the 'real'. Is there already a view of the event forming in your mind, which is influencing your practical decisions?

Shoot a few shots and then assemble them into a short sequence. What has influenced your decisions in constructing the sequence the way you have? Have you already developed a message you want to convey with this sequence?

Make another edit, this time varying the assembly. Did you find yourself instinctively returning to the original edit due to the point of view on the subject you have developed? What could you do to make this less subjective?

Types of documentary form

Whether an investigative documentary, an ethnological documentary, a documentary reconstruction, a drama-documentary, a docu-soap or a mockumentary, there are a number of variations on documentary form that are available to the filmmaker. Bill Nichols (1991, p.132) describes four dominant documentary forms (or as he calls them *modes of representation*) as *expository, observational, interactive and reflexive*.

INVESTIGATIVE DOCUMENTARY: the most common type of documentary that introduces a 'problem' or question, which it then goes on to solve. Dramatic filmic techniques are often used to heighten the tension and draw the audience into the documentary world. Much television documentary follows this format.

ETHNOLOGICAL DOCUMENTARY: a type of documentary that looks at the lives and culture of a particular group in a scientific or analytical fashion. This would include a wide range of films from many of the Nazi documentaries made about other races to 'prove' the entitlement of the Aryan race to be declared a 'master race', through to the television documentary series *A Child of Our Time* (BBC, UK, 2000–2006) which follows the developmental issues of a group of children born in the year 2000.

DOCUMENTARY RECONSTRUCTION: usually part of a documentary, where events are reconstructed for the camera, sometimes using the locations and people involved, and sometimes using sets and actors. In contemporary documentary such reconstruction is usually labelled as such, though early filmmakers were less concerned with the legitimacy of such approaches (Edison filmed some scenes for his documentaries on the Boer War at a New York golf-club, passing it off as the 'real').

DRAMA-DOCUMENTARY: a type of documentary that dramatises an event (or series of events) and uses the techniques of the fiction film to construct the 'real'. Such documentaries may include 'voice of God narration' to lessen the demand on the dramatisation to explain complex underpinning issues. A good example of the drama-documentary may be seen in *The Somme* (Darlow Smithson Productions, Channel 4, UK, 2005, *Dir*: Carl Hindmarch).

DOCU-SOAP: very much a television development, this type of documentary follows a set of characters through a series of events across a series of documentaries (usually a three-, six- or eight-part series). Their lives, opinions and emotional states are very much to the fore, with the surface subject of the documentary often reduced to the situation of backdrop. A long-running example of this (with worldwide spin-offs) is *Airline* (Granada/LWT, ITV, UK, 1999–2005)

MOCKUMENTARY: a fiction film that uses documentary form to suggest it is actually a documentary. Often comic in nature, the mockumentary can be so effective in using documentary form that audiences become convinced they are watching a true documentary (many people have fallen into this trap with *This is Spinal Tap* (Mainline/Embassy, US, 1984, *Dir*: Rob Reiner), which used a very familiar and convincing 'rockumentary' style to detail the life of fictional band 'Spinal Tap').

The expository mode

This is a most commonly used form that uses a 'voice of God' narration (or in the case of silent cinema, inter-titles) to shape the message of the documentary and to position the audience in relation to it. The disembodied narrator has a power granted by the very fact that they are not seen, and their words take on an authority that is usually amplified by a specific style and tone of delivery (so specific that it is recognisable when being mimicked in satirical television programmes).

This form will often use the techniques of the fiction film to reinforce its message, and a range of image techniques (e.g. use of filters, tracking, craning, dissolves, post-production effects) are usually matched with a musical score that unifies and enhances sequences. Often the images will be doing little more than supporting the voice-over.

As the views expressed are always mediated by the voice-over, this is a form that has strict control over meanings and over spectator response. Understandably it is one of the forms most often adopted for propaganda purposes.

The observational mode

This form of documentary often seems to be the most authentic in dealing with the 'real' as it presents itself as simply recording the things that happen in front of the camera. The principal techniques it uses to do this include long takes (which in themselves infer that the filmmaker has not interfered with the 'real' by editing things out of the shot), sync-sound (again adding to the illusion of reality, and, by not using the 'polished' soundtracks of the expository mode, placing the form closer to a 'raw' reality), the absence of a 'voice of God' narrator (the narrative is pieced together from 'overheard' conversations in small segments of the 'real' that are stitched together to provide a coherent information line), and continuity editing (which functions in the same way as in a fiction film to establish the construction of time and space). This form was popularised in Britain in the late 1950s by some of the filmmakers of free cinema, in France at the same time by the *cinéma vérité* movement, and in America in the early 1960s by direct cinema.

The interactive mode

This documentary form is often considered to be the 'purest', as it does not try to hide the medium (nor indeed the filmmakers and their processes). Filmmakers interact with their subjects, often conversing directly with them on camera, and can interact with what is being filmed, acknowledging their reactions to the 'real' and the effects of their being there with a camera. Often using the interview as a vehicle to structure the interactive documentary, the interaction between filmmaker and interviewee is often cited as one of the strengths of this form (though of course it must be remembered that the documentary-maker can shape the 'real' through the questions asked and, equally importantly, those not asked). The documentary *The Thin Blue Line* (BFI/Third Floor/American Playhouse, US, 1988) is often cited as a prime example of this form in its suggestion (through various contrary views presented by witnesses) that the audience is free to construct their own view of the truth – whereas Errol Morris has used all the traditional tools of the documentary-maker in his construction, selection and ordering of sequences, and in doing so simply positions the spectator.

Case study

ERROL MORRIS

Errol Morris was born in Hewlett, New York, on 5 February 1948. He graduated from the University of Wisconsin-Madison and was briefly a graduate student at both Princeton University and the University of California-Berkeley where he was studying for a Ph.D. before dropping out to make his first film *Gates of Heaven* (Gates of Heaven, US, 1980), which follows the fortunes of two pet cemetery owners.

His most controversial film is *The Thin Blue Line*, which is billed as the only film ever to have solved a murder. Here Morris investigates the murder of Robert Wood, a Dallas police officer, and proves the wrongful conviction of Randall Dale Adams, who was on Death Row awaiting execution for the murder.

It is his use of the interactive mode that has led to audiences responding to his 'authenticity', and to his becoming America's most respected contemporary documentary-maker. He has won several awards for his work, including the Oscar for Best Documentary Feature Film for his *Fog of War: Eleven Lessons From the Life of Robert S McNamara* (@radical.media/ Globe Department Store/SenArt Films, US, 2003).

A distinctly British adaptation of the interactive mode is in the work of Nick Broomfield who, while making documentaries since the mid-1970s, achieved widespread fame through a number of celebrity-based documentaries during the 1990s. Adopting a personalised, participatory approach, he encourages his subjects to interact with him and with his camera, and in these interactions they reveal much about themselves to the audience.

Case study
NICK BROOMFIELD

Documentary filmmaker Nick Broomfield was born in London on 30 January 1948. He studied politics and law at Essex University, where he made his first film *Who Cares?* (BFI, UK, 1971) about a threatened working-class community in Liverpool. Graduating from Essex, Broomfield gained a place at the National Film School where he received the Grierson Documentary Award for *Behind the Rent Strike* (NFT, UK, 1979).

Spending a number of years making documentary films in America with fellow NFT graduate and partner Joan Churchill, he returned to Britain in the mid-1980s to find it a very different and deeply divided place to the one he had left in the 1970s.

His work from this point onward is characterised by a false naivety, and the device of presenting himself to his subjects as bumbling and almost amateurish. This deliberate technique is one that yielded startling results in his most successful film *The Leader, His Driver and the Driver's Wife* (Lafayette Films, UK, 1991) about the South African neo-Nazi leader Eugene Terreblanche, where the normally cautious Terreblanche happily and openly explains his racist views.

His later work explores the nature of the mass media through a number of documentaries focusing on 'celebrities'. The 'truth' that emerges from his encounters in films such as *Kurt and Courtney* (Strength Ltd, UK, 1998) and *Biggie and Tupac* (FilmFour/Lafayette Films, UK, 2002) owes much to his documentary persona, his blunt, direct approach, and his willingness to ask the awkward questions that spectators themselves are wanting asked.

The reflexive mode

This is perhaps the most 'difficult' of the four modes, as it is the one that not only looks at its subject, but also draws attention to its own nature in constructing a filmic representation of the subject. This mode has a natural affinity with avant-garde filmmakers, and is often represented by films that draw attention to themselves as films through direct reference to the tools and devices of the medium. These films are less about the filmmaker's relationship with the subject, and more about the documentary's relationship with the spectator. Documentary filmmaker Chris Marker is a key proponent of this form of documentary. Audiences who have been developed through more traditional forms of documentary often find the challenges this form offers disconcerting.

For example, in the documentary about Japanese fashion designer Yohji Yamamoto, *Notebook on Cities and Clothes* (Road Movies, West Germany, 1989, *Dir*: Wim Wenders), the director is filmed filming the designer with a film camera as the designer cuts cloth. The footage shot by Wenders is later seen on a Steenbeck editor in a sequence where the director is commenting on the similarity between fashion design and the design of a film, and is seen cutting the footage. The edited material is later incorporated into the fabric of the film (though not without first being seen playing on an in-car screen as Wenders drives to meet Yamamoto). The parallels between the documentary task and the fashion design task are repeatedly illustrated, bringing the nature of film to the fore.

Figure 16.5 *Notebook on Cities and Clothes* (Road Movies, West Germany, 1989, *Dir*: Wim Wenders).

Case study

CHRIS MARKER

Chris Marker was born as Christian Bouche-Villeneuve in Paris, France on 29 July 1921, studied philosophy under Jean-Paul Sartre, and was a member of the French Resistance during the Second World War. A committed socialist, he developed his style of filmmaking through working with surrealist filmmakers such as Alain Resnais.

Renowned for stretching documentary form into the personal essay, his films have had considerable influence on more contemporary filmmakers dissatisfied with the constrictions placed upon them by dominant documentary form.

Best known for works such as *Sans Soleil* (*Sunless*) (Argos/BFI, France, 1982), and *Le Tombeau d'Alexandre* (*The Last Bolshevik*) (Argos/BFI, France/UK/Finland, 1993), Marker creates films that are awash with audio/visual information beneath the very personal commentary of a voice of God narrator, the very richness of which creates a freedom of interpretation.

Marker is seen as a poet-documentarist whose work seeks not to establish meaning, but rather to explore meaning through the very personal nature of constructing the documentary.

ACTIVITY

- Select a documentary with which you are familiar, and consider it in relation to the four documentary modes identified above. Does it fit comfortably into an individual mode, or does it use a range of techniques that makes it straddle modes?
- Taking two of the four modes identified, make a list of the techniques and features that define them. Are there any techniques or features that appear in both lists? If so, why do you think this is?
- Using the list of documentary types (see key terms above), in a group try to list as many documentaries as you can under each heading. Discuss why one or two of the types of documentary lists will be easier to fill than others.

Personal documentary

The immediate postwar period was a time of crisis for documentary-makers, who were wrestling with a film form that over the past decade had become closely associated internationally with propaganda, and had thus lost validity in the eyes of the audience. Similarly, merely documenting reality seemed somehow insubstantial when faced with the horrors of recent reality that were being slowly revealed to the public postwar. These conditions gave rise to a new style of documentary-making – the personal documentary.

The personal documentary sets out not to offer a universal view to which spectators can ascribe, but rather personal (and often less common) views on a subject, which are then used to illustrate or cast light on more universal themes and issues. Many of these personal documentary filmmakers were from left-wing backgrounds or from radical art movements, and had seen both oppression (both physical and intellectual) and conflict firsthand during the war.

Georges Franju's *Le Sang des Bêtes* (*Blood of the Beasts*) (Forces et voix de la France, France, 1949) offered an audience still too close to the slaughter of the Second World War a frank look at the daily life of slaughterhouses. While peppered with surrealist imagery and the casual brutality of the slaughterhouses set at the gates of Paris (a significant motif itself), the film is often reminiscent of newsreel imagery of the Nazi concentration camps. Franju's use of music (for instance, 'La Mer' ('The Sea') plays over the image of a slaughterman sweeping a sea of blood across the slaughterhouse floor towards a drain) adds a personal commentary to the images, and his casual juxtaposition of the suffering animals and the homes and churches overlooking the slaughterhouses implicates them (by their inaction) in the slaughter, and in doing so edges towards questions about the role of France in the Second World War that were certainly not being publicly raised at the time.

Similarly, in *Nuit et Brouillard* (*Night and Fog*) (Argos/Como, France, 1955, *Dir*: Alain Resnais) the juxtaposition of monochrome archive footage of the Nazi concentration camps in operation, and newsreel footage of the horrors found there on liberation, with full-colour images of the deserted camps as they were at the point when the film was made, offers a powerful and personal commentary on the nature of the subject through a commentary that explores the difficulty of capturing the past. Resnais' frank, direct approach, often setting the frenetic archive/newsreel footage against long, slow, tracking shots, placed reality and memory in tension, and stirred a wider debate around whether the underlying drive that led to the camps had been extinguished, or whether (like the colour images) it had merely adopted a different image. His inclusion of the image of a gendarme in a guard tower at one of the French transportation camps led to the film being censored and banned from the Cannes Film Festival – the confirmation of collaboration and complicity in such crimes was too much for many French to bear.

Free Cinema

The Free Cinema movement launched in London's National Film Theatre in 1956 built on the concept of the personal documentary, and called for a cinema that would allow directors to express through film their deep commitment to personally held views. Citing admiration for the work of Georges Franjou it included among its key proponents Lindsay Anderson, John Fletcher, Karel Reisz and Tony Richardson, most of whom became key directors of feature film production in the British Social Realism movement (kitchen sink dramas) of the late 1950s/early 1960s, and made some of the films that were at the heart of 'Swinging Britain' throughout the 1960s (see *AS Film Studies: the Essential Introduction*: FS3 – 'Swinging Britain 1963–1973').

While launched in 1956, the movement included earlier films by the filmmakers reaching back to *O Dreamland* (UK, 1953, *Dir*: Lindsay Anderson) about the popular culture of an amusement park. It also promoted screenings of films from across the globe including Franjou's *Le Sang des Bêtes*, Lionel Rogosin's *On the Bowery* (Film Representations/Rogosin, US, 1956), the story of an alcoholic in New York, and Wlodzimierz Borowik's examination of the lives of prostitutes, *Paragraf Zero* (*Paragraph Zero*) (Pol, 1956).

At the heart of this movement was the position of the filmmaker not as social commentator, but rather as observer. They did not promote a universal view (as the films of the British documentary movement did), but rather left meaning to the conclusions of the spectator, and in doing so freed themselves to look at (often) contentious subjects (or in some cases the obvious and everyday that is overlooked because of its familiarity). In Britain, Free Cinema was supported in part by the British Film Institute (through its Experimental Film Fund), and as the filmmakers were not having to work under the restrictions usually imposed by the commercial sector, they also had the freedom to work in ways and using techniques that were outside the conventions of the industry at that time. A number of films were also made as part of the Ford Motor Company's *Look at Britain* Series.

Two films of the time stand out above the others – *Every Day Except Christmas* (Graphic Films, UK, 1957, *Dir*: Lindsay Anderson), and *We are the Lambeth Boys* (Graphic Films, UK, 1959, *Dir*: Karel Reisz) – as key examples of what Free Cinema was about. Both offered the importance of ordinary people, with Anderson observing the workers of Covent Garden Market, and Reisz putting ordinary working-class young people on the screen, allowing them to speak for themselves in their own voices. Through their observation, in both cases a clear sense of community, unity and social identity emerges, and of course (from a contemporary perspective) they offer a view on a way of life that has either vanished or has evolved out of recognition. One of the strengths of the movement (best exemplified in Anderson's documentary) is the use of sound to structure and amplify the images, and the experimentation in sound design for the non-fiction film echoes back to the work of Alberto Cavalcanti in the 1930s.

ACTIVITY

Choose a topic that you feel should be addressed by a personal documentary style. Think about what could be observed and recorded to develop the topic. List some key components you would include, and how you would film them.

- What kinds of compositions would you choose to frame these components with?
- How would you complement the images with sound? Think about what sound effects you could use, what music, what actuality, and how it should be mixed together.
- Write out a treatment (a step-by-step description) of your idea and show it to your peers. What meanings do they see in it? What do they think you are trying to say? Are they right?

Direct Cinema

The observation technique of the Free Cinema movement was paralleled in America during the early 1960s by a similar movement that became known as Direct Cinema. The key technique of this movement was to use the lightweight cameras and portable synchronised sound-recording equipment to get close to their subjects and let them *talk*. Up to this point (due to the difficulties of recording synchronised sound on location) documentaries had largely concentrated on action – seeing subjects *doing* rather than *talking* – but films of this movement, such as *Primary* (Drew Associates/Time Magazine, US, 1960, *Dir*: Robert Drew) allowed the subjects of the films (both events and people) to speak for themselves without mediation by an imposed narrator.

In order to avoid the effect of the camera on the subject, the filmmakers in this movement gravitated towards subjects for whom the camera would not be an unusual object, such as the US Senators in *Primary* (one of whom was later to become President John F. Kennedy), Bob Dylan in *Don't Look Back* (Leacock-Pennebaker, US, 1966, *Dir*: D.A. Pennebaker) and Marlon Brando in *Meet Marlon Brando* (Maysles Films, US, 1965, *Dir*: Albert and David Maysles). A late arrival to the movement, Frederick Wiseman, was to take it in a different direction by adopting an approach where his crew would spend enough time with the documentary subjects for them to become comfortable with, and eventually largely ignore, the camera. The technique worked and he produced the outstanding *Titicut Folies* (Frederick Wiseman, US, 1967) about a Massachusetts institution for the criminally insane (which did not find a wide audience until 1991 when a legal ban on distribution obtained by the State of Massachusetts – for fear of how the documentary portrayed their system – was set aside).

These films differed from other film movements that had gone before, as they were intended for television, not cinematic release. The style they adopted (handheld camerawork, 'loose' movement, simple compositions) were all informed by the destination of the work, and so began an evolution in documentary form, away from the cinematic and towards the televisual. In the 1970s these filmmakers largely turned to portable video cameras to continue their work.

ACTIVITY

Consider the effect of the camera on the subject. What techniques would you use to ensure that the subject was not 'acting' for the camera? How would you judge what was worth recording and what was not? What decision processes would help in sifting through the hours of footage you would have assembled using a direct cinema approach?

The contemporary resurgence of documentary

On a cold mid-week October night in 1998 at Flicks Cinema in Deal, Kent, the Kent International Film Festival screened a new film documentary *The Buena Vista Social Club* (Road Movies, Germany, 1998, *Dir*: Wim Wenders). This small two-screen cinema in an equally small coastal town had an audience queuing around the block for this documentary, and people were turned away when the auditorium reached capacity. By contrast, on the other screen the Hollywood feature *There's Something About Mary* (TCF, US, 1998, *Dir*: Bobby and Peter Farrelly) was playing to an audience of three people. Documentary was back on the big screen and was at the start of a renaissance.

Rather than playing to the demands of the small screen of television, filmmakers approached documentary with the cinema screen in mind, as exemplified in the Oscar-winning *One Day in September* (Redbus/Passion Pictures, UK, 1999, *Dir*: Kevin MacDonald), and *Touching the Void* (Pathé/Film 4/UK Film Council/Darlow Smithsonian, UK/US, 2003, *Dir*: Kevin MacDonald). These are both grand-scale films which use all the cinematic devices of mainstream Hollywood cinema (from Michael Douglas offering the narration in the former, to helicopter action shots in the latter).

American Michael Moore's work has significantly raised the profile of documentary both as a cinematic and a televisual product through his controversial films *Bowling for Columbine* (Momentum/Alliance Atlantic/Salter Street/Dog Eat Dog, Canada/Germany/US, 2002) and *Fahrenheit 9/11* (Miramax/Dog Eat Dog/Fellowship Adventure Group, US, 2004), both overtly challenging to the mainstream, overtly political, and overtly critical of the role of big business in the life

Figure 16.6 Michael Moore's *Bowling for Columbine* is a provocative film that challenges American views on gun control.

of America. Using a mix of styles, Moore's documentaries have a modern pace, structure and energy that set them apart from their predecessors, and have spawned a revitalised American documentary movement.

One of the key figures in this movement is Morgan Spurlock, whose first documentary feature *Supersize Me* (The Con, US, 2004) was an immediate and worldwide success, as it addressed the impact of fast food on health through Spurlock himself choosing to eat nothing but items on the McDonald's menu for thirty days. Its effects were wide-reaching, being attributed to a worldwide fall in profits for the fast food giant McDonald's, and forcing the company to end its Super-size promotion. Spurlock has subsequently built a genre out of the thirty days' concept through a series of television documentaries where subjects volunteer to have the cameras follow them on their thirty-day missions (e.g. to live as a Muslim).

The authored documentary

With documentary's resurgence has come a development in documentary form, giving rise to the authored documentary, whose parentage lies in the interactive mode and the contemporary focus on personal documentary. In the authored documentary the documentary-maker is the 'star' of the documentary, leading the audience on an often idiosyncratic journey through a story of personal interest to them. A subgenre of this form will often involve the documentary-maker undergoing elements of whatever it is they are investigating (such as Louis Theroux auditioning for a job on a Norwegian cruise ship in *Louis Theroux's Weird Weekends: Off-off Broadway* (transmitted BBC2, 9 June 1999), or Lisa Rodgers undergoing a consultation for plastic surgery in *The Perfect Vagina* (Channel Four, 17 August 2008). This is a form that has proved popular with audiences, partly due to the reaction of the 'author' (usually over-emotional) to what they are 'discovering' as the camera rolls, offering an implicit heightened sense of 'the real', and a suggestion that there is lack of restriction editorially. Key exponents of this form are Michael Moore and Morgan Spurlock.

Both Moore's and Spurlock's successes have helped draw attention to an additional area of documentary exhibition, the internet, where there are countless sites now offering downloadable documentaries. Made using the technical advances offered by modern consumer or pro-sumer products, these documentaries are able to reach audiences that they would never have been able to reach through traditional distribution/exhibition methods, and spectators are opening themselves up to global markets rather than being limited to what is showing at the local cinema or broadcast on television.

Case study

INTERNET DISTRIBUTION

Michael Moore's *Slacker Uprising* (Dog Eat Dog Films, US, 2008) is one of the first major documentary features to be released as a completely and legally free online download (available to residents of the United States and Canada). Moore made it available for three weeks from 23 September 2008, and it broke all download records in its first twenty-four hours. It was also made available for a three-month run from September 2008 on Lycos Cinema.

This follows on from the significant online success in distributing documentaries such as *Loose Change* (Louder Than Words, US, 2005, 2nd edn, 2006, Final Cut, 2007) that achieved over forty million viewngs with the website getting over 100,000 hits a day.

At the start of the twenty-first century, documentary is once again fashionable, smart and accessible, with technology democratising the form by allowing even those of limited means access to documentaries and the opportunity to make them themselves.

EXAM QUESTIONS ?

■ Which styles of documentary offer the spectator the most opportunity to engage directly with the 'real'? Refer to at least *two* documentaries in your answer.

■ 'Documentary-makers shape spectators' views on their subjects and tell them what is real and what is not.' Consider this statement in relation to your experience of documentary film. Refer to at least *two* documentaries in your answer.

■ Which particular filmmaking techniques do you feel have been most effective in making you engage with representations of the 'real'? Refer to at least *two* documentaries in your answer.

■ Documentary is a constantly evolving medium. What do you consider to be the most important changes in documentary film spectatorship? Refer to at least *two* documentaries in your answer.

Resources and further Reading

Books

Aitken, I. (1998) *The Documentary Film Movement: An Anthology*. Edinburgh University Press

Barnouw, E. (1993) *Documentary: A History of the Non-fiction Film*. Oxford University Press

Bruzzi, S. (2000) *New Documentary: a Critical Introduction*. Routledge

Hardy, F. (ed.) (1966) *Grierson on Documentary*. Faber

Izod, J. and Kilborn, R. (eds) (2000) *From Grierson to Docusoap: Breaking the Boundaries*. University of Luton Press

Nichols, B. (1991) *Representing Reality*. Indiana University Press

Internet

http://www.bfi.org.uk/sightandsound/feature/425
Sight and Sound magazine listing of Free Cinema programmes

http://www.filmsite.org/docfilms.html
Useful general overview of documentary

http://www.nickbroomfield.com/home.html
Nick Broomfield official site

http://www.michaelmoore.com
Michael Moore official site

http://www.errolmorris.com
Errol Morris official site

http://www.screenonline.org.uk
BFI's ScreenOnline archive – excellent articles, biographies and resources on diverse documentary-related subjects

http://www.supersizeme.com/
Official website for the film *Supersize Me* with details on Morgan Spurlock

www.youtube.com/watch?v=7E3olbO0AWE
View the full-length *Loose Change* documentary

17 EXPERIMENTAL AND EXPANDED FILM/VIDEO

This chapter considers:

- the relationship between the film on the screen and the audience in terms of a communication process
- the exploration of radical alternatives to mainstream film language and representation as being a process that filmmakers have engaged in throughout film history
- the challenge to conventional expectations that such 'experimental' film involves

INFORMATION BOX

i

This chapter will be relevant to the section FM4 – Varieties of Film Experience: Issues and Debates in the WJEC's A level in Film Studies. It will be directly applicable to questions relating to Experimental and Expanded Film in Section B of that paper, but should also suggest general approaches to film that will be applicable to other areas being examined.

In addition, you will also find the case study on *Man with a Movie Camera* to be relevant if you are looking at German and Soviet Cinemas of the 1920s under Section A: World Cinema and investigations undertaken into *Un Chien Andalou* (Buñuel, 1928) and *Meshes of the*

Afternoon (Deren, 1943) to be relevant to Surrealism again under Section A: World Cinema.

It is important to note that WJEC A level work on Experimental Film is essentially concerned with the interaction of elements of film construction with the spectator. Its focus is, in other words, on what goes on at the interface between the viewer and the film.

films mentioned:

If you are working your way through this chapter you will find it useful to have watched some of the following films in full, and helpful to have access to scenes, clips and single shots from at least some of the others.

- *Metropolis* (Lang, 1926)
- *The Cabinet of Dr Caligari* (Wiene, 1919)
- *Un Chien Andalou* (Buñuel, 1928)
- *Meshes of the Afternoon* (Deren, 1943)
- *La Jetée* (Marker, 1962)
- *Man with a Movie Camera* (Vertov, 1929)
- *Tout va bien* (Godard, 1972)
- *Dreams That Money Can Buy* (Richter, 1946)

film as a communication process

Before we begin to look more directly at experimental film (and 'popular film and emotional response' in the following chapter) a few general observations regarding the nature of film may help to give a context for these investigations.

Film is fundamentally a form of communication, and as such it could be said to involve the transmission of messages with senders encoding and receivers decoding those messages. This is a process, in other words, under which there is an attempt by the sender of the message to influence in some way the state of mind of another person. From this perspective a certain meaning is seen as being placed in a text by the author, and it is the job of the reader to discover that meaning and thereby share something of the accompanying understanding of the world.

However, another way of looking at communication would be to see it as the production of meaning during an *interactive* process. From this perspective film could be said to involve created texts interacting with readers (in this case viewers or spectators) to produce a variety of possible readings. Under this interpretation of the communication process the reader becomes a factor, perhaps the key factor, in the production of meaning. Meaning is no longer singular and clearly defined by authorial intention, but is plural and created in the relationship between the individual reader and the text.

Much of what is dealt with in this chapter focuses on what happens at this interface between film and spectator as meaning is being made.

ACTIVITY

- Working with one other person, choose a film that you both know well and, without discussing your ideas, both write down what you would see as the central message that has been placed in this film by the filmmakers.
- Compare your written responses. Are they the same, similar or different? Discuss your ideas and see if you can arrive at an agreed definition of the main authorial message.
- Attempt the same process with a couple of other films, if you have time.
- Do you think other people would agree with either your individual readings or your agreed readings of these films? If possible, find other people who know the same films well and, without showing them your written outline of the main message of the film, ask them how they see the film. (They may, of course, say they have never thought of the film in question as having a 'message'. What would be your response to this?)

A common, or shared language

Whichever approach is taken you should notice that both of the perspectives on communication given above (the one deriving a single intended authorial meaning and the other a variety of possible meanings) are dependent upon the idea of there being some sort of shared knowledge of the medium, a language held in common between the sender and receiver (or the producer of the film and the audience). Without a shared language of some sort there can be no communication.

One way of considering film studies as a subject is to suggest that what we are essentially interested in is this language of film. To a large extent this is quite clearly a visual language.

We are all very familiar with at least one form of visual language since we use it every day when we smile, or scowl, or make any one of the 1,001 facial expressions open to us to express our feeling or communicate our understanding. This is directly used in film via the directed performance and movement of actors. But there are other visual areas, as you are well aware, such as the nature of the setting in which the action in a film takes place, the clothing being worn by characters, and the objects that are placed within the frame of each shot. Beyond this there is the variety of angles and distances of perspective that can be given to the viewer and the multiplicity of possible ways in which a number of shots can be sequenced. (All of this leaves unexplored the variety of ways in which film also uses sound to create a complex aural language.)

Film 'language'

So, film operates as a language; it communicates with the spectator through the use of images and sounds. In the opening to *Metropolis* (Lang, 1926) it is the combination of the ordered formation of the workers, the nature of their shared movements, the uniformity of their dark clothing, their movement into an enclosed cage-like space, and their transportation in a downward direction that gives us a

Figure 17.1 The downcast workers in *Metropolis* (Lang, 1926).

sense of the oppressed, ordered and confined existence of a whole group (or class) of people. We do not need to have the situation explained to us in words because it has been explained using the language of film. In addition, our understanding is confirmed when we immediately have these shots set in contrast to the free-and-easy movements within open spaces enjoyed by members of the elite upper class within this society.

It is the way in which visual indicators are combined both within a single shot and from shot to shot within a carefully arranged sequence that is critical to the creation of visual meaning. It is the combination of spoken word, sound effects and musical soundtrack that works to create meaning within the sphere of the aural. Over and above this, it is the choice of certain sounds from within the spectrum of such possibilities in combination with the choice of certain visual indicators from within a corresponding range of possibilities that ultimately constitutes the language of film. An amalgam of these visual and aural languages makes up this language of film.

Both our responses to a film and the meanings we take from a film can only be created from this one source. Therefore, if we are to be able to 'read' film with any confidence, we need to explore the nature of this language in some detail.

ACTIVITY

Watch the opening to *Metropolis*. Why do you think a film like this might be controversial? Why might some people be shocked by it? How would reception of this film vary from place to place and from time to time over the period since 1926?

(*Note*: this film is mentioned in Chapter 9 on 'German and Soviet cinemas of the 1920s' and will be relevant to any studies you are undertaking in this area for Section A of FM4.)

Films as 'constructs'

What all of this should remind us is that what we see on screen is not 'the real' itself but a re-presentation of 'the real', a construct. The basis of Film Studies really depends upon coming to terms with the idea of films as constructs; that is, that they are built by filmmakers from a series of component parts that we can identify, and that since they have been constructed we can take them apart and see how they have been put together. We can explore the choices that filmmakers have made in particular films and attempt to suggest reasons why those choices might have been made. In doing this we will be attempting to explore possible meanings that could be created as viewers interact with the film text before them.

In considering both 'experimental film' (and 'popular film and emotional responses' in the next chapter) we will be attempting to explore this communication process and the intense creation of meaning occurring at that moment of interaction as the audience experiences the film. The regulation and censorship of film essentially amounts to society's response to the intensity of that moment of experience: officials given authority by society attempt to regulate which members of the community should have access to the potential meanings available at that film–audience interface. If you are old enough, for example, you are permitted to attend a showing of an '18' certificate film and are allowed to experience the particular intensities of the engagement with the screen that are on offer.

Experimental film

ACTIVITY

- What is experimental film? Discuss your initial understanding of this term with others. Attempt a definition in no more than 200 words.
- Try to draw up a list of films you think might qualify as being 'experimental'; perhaps you do not know the names of individual films but you can think of types or styles of film that would come under the category of 'experimental'.

Return to basics

When attempting to come to terms with a new Film Studies concept it is often useful to go back to the key approaches to film with which we started, what we could refer to as the Film Studies 'toolbox'. Films are constructed through the use of *mise-en-scène*, cinematography, editing and sound, and the fictional films we have spent most of our time dealing with have also employed ideas relating to narrative and genre. In order to understand experimental film we could again revisit these basic concepts. Logically, experimental films are likely to be using the same fundamental areas of film construction but in experimental ways.

We might, for example, expect some experimental films to use setting in unexpected, non-realistic ways. In this sense the expressionistic sets used in *The Cabinet of Dr Caligari* (Wiene, 1919) (see 'German and Soviet cinemas of the 1920s') would be experimental. In *Tout va bien* (Godard, 1972), considered in more detail later in this chapter, the set is revealed to the audience as exactly that, an area constructed for staged performance. We might also expect actors to use performance and movement techniques that push at the boundaries of what is normally expected in mainstream film. Thus, in *Un Chien Andalou* (Buñuel, 1928) (see 'Surrealism'), two characters 'dance' a performance of male lust and female withdrawal in the face of that exhibition of desire. In *The Cabinet of Dr Caligari* the movements of both Caligari and Cesare are highly stylised.

We might expect at least some experimental cinema to use the camera in similarly challenging ways. Thus Andy Warhol's *Empire* (1964) comprises a single static long shot of the Empire State Building lasting eight hours, while *La Jetée* (Marker, 1962) uses still photography. We might also expect editing to be used in unexpected ways. Thus *Un Chien Andalou* cuts from a man being shot indoors to a man dying outdoors as he falls past the back of a naked statuesque woman – the gunplay is unexpected and the cut even more so; we are disorientated and confused, and in that sense a prime objective of experimental film has been achieved.

In terms of narrative, there is often no recognisable narrative to be found in experimental film. There may be characters and we may see them experience moments of love, boredom, uncertainty, joy and all the other emotions, but in story terms whatever happens to them fails to obey the normal cause-and-effect pattern employed by mainstream narrative. There may be no characters at all. There may not even be any recognisable objects from the real world. Ultimately, we may face a totally abstract experimental film employing colour, size, shape and light, all of the fundamental components of our everyday visual experience of the world, but offering nothing more than the experience of watching a kaleidoscopic pattern employing these basic elements. Consider, for example, the opening to *Dancer in the Dark* (von Trier, 2000). How do you react to these images employing colour, shape and light, and how would you react if this was the whole film, a three-and-a-half-minute abstract short film?

In short, we can be sure that in an experimental film either the style or the content or both will be radically different from the experience of film offered by mainstream cinemas. However, we can still use our normal approaches to film to help us to gain at least some understanding of experimental film. We can talk about the setting used and ask why it might have been employed. We can discuss the actors' performances and what meanings they may have conveyed. We can consider the cinematography and editing, and in both cases analyse why we think the film may have used these elements of construction in certain ways.

When we move into the area of totally abstract film (known as 'absolute film'), things may become slightly more difficult. Yet we will still be dealing with the basic elements of cinematography (and photography and painting) – light and colour, shape and perspective, composition and form.

ACTIVITY

- Working with one other person, undertake a study of television advertisements and promotional music films. Take one of these areas each, find examples that seem to you to be in some way 'experimental', and record them. (You may like to first of all discuss with a wider group of students what you already think might be similar between experimental film, advertisements and music promos in order to clarify your thoughts before beginning the task.)
- Show your examples to each other and discuss the aspects of each that seem to be alternative or experimental in some way. Are there any factors you would see as key differences between most, if not all, advertisements and promotional music videos, and films more normally defined as experimental?
- Would it be valid to study certain sorts of advertisements and/or music videos within this area of Film Studies? If you think it might, give reasons to justify your decision.

Three alternative/experimental films

In order to further explore the nature of experimental film you could consider three short films: *Un Chien Andalou* (Buñuel/Dali, 1928), *Meshes of the Afternoon* (Deren, 1943) (both of these films will also be relevant to 'Surrealism') and *La Jetée* (Marker, 1962). The first two of these films use a surrealist approach to disrupt our normal expectations of film structure, and the third is created almost entirely from photographic stills and therefore challenges our expectation of film form. Watch all three films, looking for ways in which each could be said to challenge our general/'normal' perceptions of what film 'should' be.

ACTIVITY

- *Un Chien Andalou* (1928) is a seventeen-minute surreal short made by Luis Buñuel and Salvador Dali (a painter whose work you may like to research). How easy did you find it to watch this? If you found it difficult, what made it a difficult viewing experience? If you found it easy, what was it about it that made it easy to watch? How could it be said to challenge our 'normal' perceptions of what film should be?

continued

- What was it about? How would you explain this film to a friend who has not seen it? (Write a quick 250-word account as if explaining it to a friend.)
- Try to analyse what you were doing as a spectator as you were watching this film. Take a few minutes to note down as many ideas as you can about the reception process that was going on. Were you consciously attempting to approach the film in certain ways, and if so, did these approaches help or hinder your appreciation of the film?
- What meaning(s) did you take away from the film as a whole, or from particular scenes? Were you always able to find meaning, and if not, did this upset or annoy you in any way?
- How did you respond to the film in general and to particular scenes: with amusement, laughter, bemusement, confusion, boredom, fear, uncertainty or in some other way? Were you curious or intrigued? List as many words as possible to describe your response to the whole film and to particular scenes.
- Identify any sections to which you responded in a particularly strong way. Why did these sections cause such a strong response and what was the nature of your response? Which individual shots do you recall most clearly and why?
- Discuss your ideas with other people if possible. Compare their points with yours, as always looking for similarities and differences.

(From this you will notice that when dealing with experimental film, in addition to falling back on the usual areas of film construction as a means of exploration, we can also bear in mind key phrases used in A level Film Studies, 'the creation of meaning' and 'the generation of audience response'. Even if meaning becomes more problematic, audience response (and as a first measure this means our own response) is still available as a valid means of exploring any film with which we are confronted.)

FURTHER ACTIVITY

Follow the same process as in the task above, and answer the same questions, for *Meshes of the Afternoon* (Deren, 1943).

Figure 17.2 *Meshes of the Afternoon* (Deren, 1943).

ACTIVITY

- Watch *La Jetée* (Marker, 1962). Did you find this to be effective or was it difficult to watch? If you found it difficult what was it that made it so? Was it easier or more difficult to watch than *Un Chien Andalou* or *Meshes of the Afternoon*? Why?
- Again, use 250 words to explain what this film was about to a friend who has not seen it.
- Was it easier to explain than *Un Chien Andalou* and *Meshes of the Afternoon*, and if so, why?
- In what ways was this different from your usual experience of film? List as many ideas as possible. Would you describe this film as 'experimental'? Give reasons to support your answer.
- List scenes and shots that you found particularly effective in some way, noting for each both in what way you felt they were effective

continued

and what it was about the content and/or style of the scene/shot that made it effective.
■ Discuss your ideas alongside those of other people if possible, looking in particular to see where you have responded in the same ways and where differently.

Other terms used for 'experimental' films

The films we are interested in here have been categorised under various other headings apart from 'experimental': 'avant-garde', 'alternative', 'underground' and 'independent', for instance. You may like to go through each of these terms and consider in more detail what they each imply about the films they are trying to delineate, but briefly:

■ 'Avant-garde' being French for 'advanced guard' suggests these are films that are in some way ahead of other films being made during the same period (something of an elitist assertion, perhaps).

■ 'Alternative' implies these are films that are in some challenging way different from mainstream movies and that they have been consciously shaped as such in order to offer some sort of alternative to the mainstream.

■ 'Underground' puts forward the notion that these may be films that defy social conventions and censorship, and that they therefore might tend to operate in a hidden, subversive way.

■ 'Independent' suggests these tend to be films made by individuals or small groups without the backing of mainstream film studios.

In general terms the tag of 'experimental' suggests some rejection of mainstream filmmaking conventions and a willingness to attempt innovative approaches to film construction.

Simply because they are mainstream and commercial, most of the films we are used to seeing in the cinema are immediately subject to certain restrictions that do not apply to experimental films. Most films must above all be designed to take money at the box-office if they are to have a chance of being made, and in order to do this they are put together in such a way as to fulfil rather than challenge the audience's expectations (they tell a story and follow certain 'rules' of continuity, for example). If you choose to make experimental films you immediately avoid the need to make money and please the audience, and you also immediately imply that some filmmaking at least should be founded upon other considerations. You also implicitly accept that few people are ever likely to see your work (although some commercial advertisements and some music videos might be seen to set up interesting contradictions in this respect).

ACTIVITY

- Research the history of experimental film. When were the first such films made? Have there been high points and low points in the history of these films? Are there any reasons for this? Has this form of expression been especially popular in any particular countries during any particular periods?
- Choose any experimental film of your choice that you have not previously seen but which has interested you from the research you have done and try to get hold of a copy. How easy is this? If you find it difficult, why is this? Is the subject matter difficult and therefore only of interest to a small target audience? Is the film not easily available because it lacks the marketing support of a big studio?
- Show your chosen film (or a short extract) to a small group of other film students and explain both your interest in the film and your understanding of it. Allow time for the group to discuss the film.

Case study
MAN WITH A MOVIE CAMERA (1929)

(Director: Dziga Vertov. Cinematographer: Mikhail Kaufman. Editor: Elizaveta Svilova.)

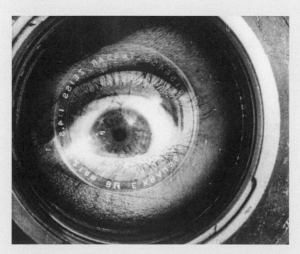

Figure 17.3 *Man with a Movie Camera* (Vertov, 1929).

continued

'Vertov'

Vertov was born Denis Arkadievitch Kaufman. 'Dziga Vertov' was a pseudonym he adopted meaning 'spinning top'. Fundamentally, in his filmmaking he rejected the use of narrative and professional actors, believing that film should use camera techniques and editing to create its effects on the audience.

ACTIVITY

- What would such a pseudonym suggest to you? List as many suggestive possibilities as you can that arise from such a name. Compare your ideas with those of at least one other person.
- Find out more about Vertov and his work, if you can, and also about the woman who is mentioned in the credits as the editor, and the cinematographer who is also called Kaufman.

Differences between this film and mainstream films

This is a complex film containing over 1,700 shots (more than twice what most Hollywood films of the same period used). It does not try to give the impression of being a straightforward, objective presentation of reality with a cause-and-effect narrative structure. Instead, it explores montage as a means of editing film without regard to continuity of location (space) or chronological sequence (time). Vertov takes the fundamental feature of the film medium, its ability to transport the viewer through time and space, and refuses to limit the resulting freedom by imposing any need for continuity. He equated the filmmaker with an eye ('kino-eye'), looking around and gathering shots from many places and linking them creatively for the spectator. As in *Strike*, Eisenstein's film from the same period (see 'German and Soviet cinemas of the 1920s') there is the juxtaposition of machines and human labour in this film but here, it seems (after the Revolution), the workers are participating cheerfully rather than being oppressed.

ACTIVITY

- Construct a table that shows differences between this film and mainstream films using the headings of *mise-en-scène*, cinematography, editing and narrative structure.
- Compare your table to those constructed by other people. Discuss differences and add to your table any extra ideas that might arise.

Genre: city documentary?

This film could be seen to belong to a genre known as city documentaries. It seems to begin to lay out a typical day in the life of a particular city. There is a woman asleep, the shops are closed, the streets are empty; a few people come out, the city wakes; and so on. In this sense much of it does in general follow a movement from waking, to work, to after-work leisure time. However:

- the order and time sequence is often broken and jumbled, with episodes from earlier in the day returning, many in fast motion;
- this is not one city, it is a mixture of Moscow, Kiev and Riga;
- the cameraman and the camera continually intrude, announcing their presence as part of the filmmaking process (and as part of 'modern' life).

ACTIVITY

See if you can find any more examples of the city documentary, also sometimes known as 'city symphonies'. Why do you think this second term was seen to be appropriate for these films?

Homage to the camera and filmmaking

The cameraman (is he what in conventional terms might be the hero?) can, it seems, move effortlessly through space and time, so that the filmmaker's power to control our perception of reality is revealed and the taken-for-

continued

granted nature of reality is itself brought into doubt. Film representation is revealed as a manipulative construction. From the outset this film flaunts the fact that the camera can alter everyday reality. See, for example:

- the opening image in which through a double-exposure effect the cameraman climbs on top of a giant camera;
- the use made of stop-motion to animate objects (e.g. crayfish on a plate);
- the construction of a street scene achieved by exposing each side of the image separately.

The camera is in fact personified, for example, through the way in which:

- the camera lens itself is seen to be moving a blurred shot of flowers sharply into focus;
- stop-motion is used to allow the camera out of its box, on to a tripod, and then to walk off;
- a deep-focus shot is composed looking over the city with the camera in the foreground panning in manic fashion.

In a manifesto of the Kinoks ('cinema-eyes') film group from 1923 Vertov stated his belief in the central importance of the camera: 'I am the cinema eye. I am the mechanical eye. I, a machine, can show you the world as only I can see it.' He is clearly putting forward a serious challenge to mainstream cinema with its emphasis on staged dramas, but at the same time we should not miss the humour in Vertov's work

ACTIVITY

- How did you react to this film? Did you enjoy it? Did it please you, and if not, why not? If it did, what sort of pleasure did you derive from it: was the pleasure to be found in the narrative, or in the characterisation, or in the play with film construction that was going on, or in the ideas as a whole that were being addressed, or in some other aspect(s) of the film?
- Through group discussions compare your thoughts on this with other people's reactions to the film.

Case study

TOUT VA BIEN (1972)

(Direction and screenplay: Jean-Luc Godard and Jean-Pierre Gorin. Cast: Jane Fonda (American journalist), Yves Montand (her French filmmaker husband).)

Figure 17.4 *Tout va bien* (Godard, 1972).

Brecht and alienation theory

ACTIVITY

■ Research Bertolt Brecht's alienation theory which he devised in an effort to change the relationship of the audience to plays they were watching in the theatre.
■ Write a short (maximum 300 words) summary of this theory.

continued

With Brecht's ideas in mind, see how Godard places you (forces you to place yourself) as a player in the game of construction of meanings that is going on in this film. His effort it seems is to expose the normally hidden techniques of the film production process that usually allow the viewer to escape into a fantasy world. In doing this he reveals film to be an imaginative fantasy and yet, it could be argued, he succeeds in making it all the more part of the real world. See:

■ how the audience is disorientated by being addressed directly;
■ how our expectations are further challenged by the fact that the set is exposed as being just that;
■ how the easy adoption of the point of view of, and therefore identification with, one or two characters is (to a large extent) refused.

The audience and its relationship to film

Tout va bien even in complying with the narrative love story structure exposes it as a myth and yet reveals, perhaps in an even more meaningful way, the importance of relationships with others and, paradoxically, the ultimate isolation of the individual. Classic realist, or classical Hollywood, narrative allows you to escape from the real world into a fantasy where you can in some sense be whatever character incarnation you have chosen (via identification) in your imagination. Godard attempts to refuse us this possibility as he also attempts to refuse to allow us to sit as voyeurs, or unseen observers; instead, his effort it seems is to force us to become active participants in the construction of meanings.

Despite refusing to allow the conventional participation of the audience, he still through his own adaptation of film construction urges the spectator to participate. This time, however, the involvement that is encouraged is that which demands the conscious adoption of a reasoned point of view (or if you like political stance) in relation to the material presented in the film, even if it is necessarily recognised that this perspective is inevitably going to shift and change in response to ongoing changing experiences of the world.

Differences between this and mainstream films

The use of subtitles and mixed English and French dialogue further disrupts the easy smoothness of classic film narrative, forcing an intensified concentration on what is being said. In addition, the dialogue itself refuses to conform to the simple (or simplistic) pattern of easily understood exchanges used in Hollywood; instead, the arguments or debates that are being presented are complicated and intellectually demanding.

The camera refuses to allow you to identify with one character. All the time as a spectator you are being challenged, especially as a viewer more used to Hollywood-style screen images. (At this point the use of Jane Fonda, a well-known and highly politicised Hollywood actor from the period, becomes additionally interesting.) Who is the woman who comes on to remove the coffee cups, for example, as the central couple is arguing? You might make up scenarios, wanting her to be the maid in order to maintain the fantasy narrative perhaps; but it is just as likely that she could be part of the catering staff on the set, and perhaps even more likely that she is an actor pretending to be a member of the catering corps.

ACTIVITY

- Construct a table that shows differences between this film and mainstream films using the headings of *mise-en-scène*, cinematography, editing, sound, genre and narrative structure.
- Compare your table to those constructed by other people. Discuss differences and add to your table any extra ideas that might arise.
- How did you react to this film? Did you enjoy it? Did it give you pleasure, and if not, why not? If it did, what sort of pleasure did you derive from it: was the pleasure to be found in the narrative, or in the characterisation, or in the play with film construction that was going on, or in the ideas as a whole that were being addressed, or in some other aspect(s) of the film?
- Through group discussions compare your thoughts on this with other people's reactions to the film.

Accessing experimental film

If the space available for showing 'ordinary' independent films (that is to say, those that follow the basic tenets of realism and present narratives grounded in cause-and-effect chains of events) is small, then the screening possibilities for experimental film are minimal. The films we have considered here have gained some currency within film circles but many lesser known filmmakers have worked away in the experimental field for much less recognition. The films we have looked at here, while not easily available are at least reasonably accessible; much other experimental work is far less easy to get hold of, only ever really being seen at film festivals, art galleries or special screenings at universities.

ACTIVITY

- Watch a few of the early works of Hans Richter, for example, *Rhythmus 21* and *Rhythmus 23* along with one or two others, followed by the film *Dreams That Money Can Buy* (Richter, 1946).
- Discuss your response to the early films with other people, if possible, before watching *Dreams That Money Can Buy*. In particular, how do you respond to Richter's use of abstract cinema and how do you find the language with which to discuss it?
- After watching *Dreams That Money Can Buy* decide if there are any similarities between this and other experimental films you have seen. How did it compare to the earlier Richter films?
- In groups, take one dream sequence each (created for the film by the artists Max Ernst, Fernand Leger, Man Ray, Marcel Duchamp, Alexander Calder and Richter) and after you have discussed it at some length prepare a short presentation on meanings and responses to this section of the film to be given to the rest of the class.

EXAM QUESTIONS ?

- Is the most challenging aspect of experimental film the lack of an immediately recognisable narrative structure?

- Apart from the lack of an immediately recognisable narrative, what other challenges do experimental films present to the viewer?

- In what ways have the films you have studied been designed to make spectators see the world differently?

- Experimental films are seen by only very small audiences. What arguments would you put forward to convince someone of their importance?

CONCLUSION

■ The range of films available to audiences is much broader than that found in mainstream cinema.

■ Experimental films can challenge audiences in many ways and may be seen as containing a whole range of potential meanings.

■ Audiences may be seen as active participants in the construction of meaning.

Resources and Further Reading

Books

Abrams, N., Bell, I. and Udris, J. (2001) *Studying Film*. Arnold. (Chapter 15)

Gillespie, D.C. (2000) *Early Soviet Cinema: Innovation, Ideology and Propaganda*. Wallflower

Hayward, S. (2005) *Cinema Studies: The Key Concepts*. Routledge

MacDonald, S. (1993) *Avant-garde Film: Motion Studies*. Cambridge University Press

O'Pray, M. (2003) *Avant-garde Film: Forms, Themes, Passions*. Wallflower

Phillips, W.H. (2005) *Film: An Introduction*. Bedford/St Martin's Press. (Chapter 8)

Rees, A.L. (1999) *A History of Experimental Film and Video*. BFI

Useful website

www.bfi.org.uk

18 POPULAR FILM AND EMOTIONAL RESPONSE

This chapter considers:

- the relationship between the film on the screen and the audience in terms of a communication process
- the idea that spectators will find that particular films and particular sequences within films draw out from them certain, often strong, emotional responses
- the possibility that film may 'shock' in a variety of ways and intensities, and that it may as a result be both disturbing and challenging to spectators

INFORMATION BOX *i*

This chapter will be relevant to the section FM4 – Varieties of Film Experience: Issues and Debates in the WJEC's A level in Film Studies. It will be directly applicable to questions relating to 'Popular Film and Emotional Response' in Section B of that paper, but should also suggest general approaches to film that will be applicable to other areas being examined.

It is important to note that WJEC A level work on 'Popular Film and Emotional Response' is essentially concerned with the interaction of elements of film construction with the spectator. Its focus is on what goes on at the interface between the viewer and the film.

Films mentioned:

If you are working your way through this chapter you will find it useful to have watched some of the following films in full and helpful to have access to scenes, clips and single shots from at least some of the others:

- *Reservoir Dogs* (Tarantino, 1991)
- *The Big Shave* (Scorsese, 1967)
- *Taxi Driver* (Scorsese, 1976)
- *Freaks* (Browning, 1932)
- *Psycho* (Hitchcock, 1960)
- *Morocco* (Sternberg, 1930)
- *Let Him Have It* (Medak, 1991)
- *Paths of Glory* (Kubrick, 1957)
- *Sweet Sweetback's Baadassssss Song* (van Peebles, 1971)
- *The Crying Game* (Jordan, 1992)
- *Once Were Warriors* (Tamahori, 1994)
- *Romper Stomper* (Wright, 1992)
- *American History X* (Kaye, 1998)
- *Birth of a Nation* (Griffith, 1915)
- *Sweet Sixteen* (Loach, 2002)
- *My Beautiful Laundrette* (Frears, 1985)

IMPORTANT NOTE

Before engaging with this chapter you should read the opening section to the previous chapter, 'Film as a communication process'.

The consumption of films by fans and audiences

Films (which are, crucially, commercial products as well as creative works) are made by the industry for specific target audiences. If the distribution company's marketing strategy works effectively, as members of the target audience we will be drawn to the cinema to consume (with others) the product on offer. We will be expecting (or at least, hoping) that this experience will give us sensual, emotional (and perhaps intellectual) pleasure. And, if we are fans of the movie series of which this film is a part, or of the genre, star or director, we will be anticipating the event in a particularly strong fashion.

Figure 18.1 Watching as part of an audience, we are in a crowd but engrossed in our own pleasure and unaware of the others around us.

As members of the audience we will at moments be so engrossed in our own pleasure that we will become oblivious to the presence of others. But, equally we will remain part of a crowd (or even of a community, we might say) so that we will often be aware not only of our own excitement, but also of the emotions of others who are present. We will be conscious of the fact that we are in some way sharing our emotions and experiences with others. Often we will go to the cinema with others, whether family or friends, in a deliberate attempt to share these moments of intensity. And often, our choice of who to accompany to particular films will be governed by our knowledge of their likes and dislikes; we go with them because we know they are already, or could become, a fan.

ACTIVITY

- List people with whom you have been to the cinema and the films you have seen with them. How did you make the choice to go to particular films with particular people? Was it on the basis of their known or presumed likes and dislikes?
- Are there particular types of films you watch on DVD with particular people? Do you have conversations with particular people about particular types of films? When you are doing these things do you see yourself operating as a fan?

Emotional response to film

ACTIVITY

- List your favourite genre, favourite film star and your favourite film of the year. Beneath each explain in as much detail as possible the emotional response each has drawn from you. (How do you respond emotionally to the typical situations and typical characters found in your favourite genre? Are there emotions you know you will be experiencing when you sit down to watch one of these genre films? How do you respond emotionally to the types of roles played by your favourite star? What are your emotional expectations when you see their name attached to a film? What was the range of emotions that your favourite film of the year made you feel? Are there particular scenes, or exchanges between characters, you can recall that made you feel certain emotions?
- To what extent do you think it is the emotional response you have had to this particular genre, to this star and to this film that has made each of them a favourite with you?
- Discuss your emotional responses to each with a group of people who have attempted the same exercise. Try to explain as fully and as clearly as possible your responses to your chosen genre, star and film.
- Listen very carefully to other people's explanations to see if they have responded to films in similar emotional ways to you or perhaps in very different ways. Make a note of any types of emotional response you had not considered along with the name of the genre, star or film which produced that response.

What exactly is an emotion, or an emotional response? We could describe an emotion as a feeling. This may help a little but it really only substitutes one rather vague word for another, equally vague one. To what extent should emotions be seen to be linked to thought? Can a spectator experience fear while watching a horror movie without that experience being linked in some way to a thought process? The emotion of fear created in the presence of a screen displaying a sequence of images in a horror film may manifest itself in a bodily, or physiological, way (there may be a start, a jump, a scream, a cold sweat) but there will also be a mental or psychological sensation, in this case, of terror. In a way that is noticeable to us and often to others, we will have been moved, stirred or even perturbed by what we have seen and heard; a physical change of some sort may have come over us but we will also have experienced some inner psychological change, a feeling that may be fleeting or may stay with us for a few minutes, a few hours, or (in some form) for even longer.

We can all too easily assume that simply because we have experienced a certain emotion at a certain point in a film others will respond in the same way, but if we reflect on discussions we have had with others about films and if we think about the experience of watching films with others, we will realise this is not always true. Sometimes, for example, people will laugh at points in films that we don't find funny, or even more disconcertingly at points that we find deadly serious. As we watch films we can each experience fear, and pleasure, and desire, and surprise, and shock and a whole array of possible emotions, but we will not all experience these emotions equally at the same moments in a film. If that is the case, what is it that determines our individual predisposition to respond in particular emotional ways at certain points in certain films?

You should think carefully about these sorts of things, but you shouldn't worry about finding right answers since questions like these continue to fuel debate among 'experts' working in the field of human emotions. Your job is to recognise that there is an intense interaction with the sounds and images occurring as we watch films, and that filmmakers are deliberately setting out to engender emotional responses. Through your observation of the use of *mise-en-scène*, cinematography, editing and sound you are able to explore the ways in which emotional response is created.

ACTIVITY

- Compile your own list of the various types of emotional response film might elicit from the spectator.
- Compare your list with those compiled by other people. Discuss any differences and similarities, and add to your list if possible.

Film and the creation of 'shock'

One emotional response that could be on your list of emotional responses to film would be 'shock'. Films, like books, plays, paintings and other forms of cultural production, have always been seen to have the ability to shock an audience. The nature of this shock can cover a wide range of possibilities. The early audiences for films in Paris in 1895 were apparently 'shocked' simply by the sense of realism created by the filmed image of a train moving towards them. It might 'shock' some people to be shown experimental, avant-garde or alternative film simply because they had never thought of the possibility of there being forms of film other than realist narratives. However, most people's initial response when considering this issue is to see 'shock' in terms of scenes of a graphic sexual or violent content in more popular mainstream films. These are certainly the areas that receive most media coverage in relation to 'shocking' film.

ACTIVITY

- List the range of ways in which you see film as being potentially 'shocking', and try to give an example for each. In order to comply with Film Studies good practice you should try to refer to specific scenes within particular films.
- Compare your list with the lists compiled by other people, if possible. Discuss differences and similarities among your ideas.

Content and form

In carrying out the activity above you should have become aware of the way in which 'shock' in film can be talked about in terms of either the content (or subject matter) and the form (or style) of the film under discussion. Clearly the opening eye-slitting subject matter of *Un Chien Andalou* is itself shocking, but so too is the film construction in terms of the way in which use is made of close-ups and an editing cut from the blank face of the woman with her eye being held open to the actual eyeball-cutting shot.

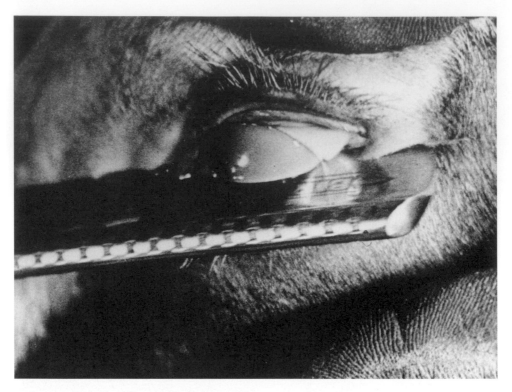

Figure 18.2 The famous eye-slitting scene in *Un Chien Andalou* (1928).

ACTIVITY

- You might like to compare the way in which the scene from *Un Chien Andalou* is constructed with the slicing off of the policeman's ear in *Reservoir Dogs* (Tarantino, 1991) which is handled in an altogether different way.
- Both scenes will draw a sense of shock from most spectators on a first viewing but perhaps the nature of the shock is different in both instances.
- Consider the use of *mise-en-scène*, performance, cinematography, editing and sound in both cases.
- For both scenes consider whether the nature of the shock changes on a second viewing, and if so in what ways.
- Are there other emotional responses that you or other spectators have had to either of these scenes? Could you imagine the possibility of further emotional responses that neither you nor anyone you have spoken to has had but which might be possible for other spectators?

As you discuss or think about films and scenes from films that create an emotional 'shock', always make sure you are considering both content and film form. Try to decide on the nature of the shock experienced and the intensity of that shock. Is it a physical shock that affects your bodily response in some way?

ACTIVITY

- If you have access to the film, watch the Scorsese short *The Big Shave* (1967) which is found in a collection of early Scorsese movies. In what ways might this be seen to be 'shocking' in terms of both content and style?
- Try to analyse the way the film has been put together in terms of its use of *mise-en-scène*, cinematography, editing, sound, genre (not forgetting the genre of TV advertisements) and narrative structure, in order to shock.
- Do you think there is any way in which the 'shock' in this film short may be said to be used to any social or political purpose? Consider what was happening during the period in both American foreign policy and home affairs.

ACTIVITY

- Watch *Taxi Driver* (Scorsese, 1976) and analyse the way in which the bloodbath scene has been constructed, with Robert de Niro as Travis Bickle acting as some sort of vigilante in a brothel. As always take careful note of *mise-en-scène*, cinematography, editing and sound. Could the exciting cinematography be said to express pleasure in violence?
- See what you can find out about the controversy that surrounded the film and this scene in particular, when it was first released.
- To what extent was this controversy the result of particular emotional responses that had been caused by the scene?

i

INFORMATION BOX

For the purposes of the A2 exam you must refer to popular film in answering this question. However, looking at more experimental film such as *Un Chien Andalou* and *The Big Shave* may help you to consider more carefully mainstream films such as *Reservoir Dogs* and *Taxi Driver*. These exercises might also help you to reconsider experimental film more fully if you are also studying the topic 'Experimental and expanded film/video' dealt with in the previous chapter.

Please remember to answer on the correct type of film for the exam but also be aware that a short, sharp reference to an experimental film while answering a question on popular film, or similarly a short, sharp reference to a popular film while dealing with experimental film, may help you to make a point particularly clearly. Any such reference must be made quickly and succinctly, and must help to further your argument in some way. Imagine a conclusion to an essay on popular film, for example, that points out how not only popular film but also experimental film relies upon the creation of emotional response sometimes in very similar ways and certainly using the same construction techniques of *mise-en-scène*, cinematography, editing and sound. Potentially, this may enable you to leave the reader on an interesting reflective point that really shows you to be somebody who is thinking carefully about the nature of film in the widest sense.

The historical perspective

It is useful to place the idea of the 'shocked' emotional response to film into some sort of historical context, recognising that certain forms of shock can continue to remain shocking over time (the previously mentioned eye-slitting scene in *Un Chien Andalou*, for instance, or the representation of disability in *Freaks* (Browning, 1932)), while others may over time lose much of their power to shock (the shower scene in *Psycho*, for instance). However, notice from these examples that it is a mistake to believe that the events, characters and character relationships that filmmakers have tried to show on film have simply become progressively more shocking over time.

- View *Freaks* (Browning, 1932), with others if possible, and make notes throughout on your emotional response at various points. If you watch it with others, try to also take note of any response you notice in other people along with some indication of what it was in the film that you thought caused the response.
- Afterwards, allocate plenty of time to discuss your response and the responses of others as fully as possible.
- Research the history of the film if you have time (it was, for instance, banned in the UK for thirty years). What connections can you see between the history of the film and the concept of emotional responses to film?

Alterations over time in what is seen as shocking may be brought about as a result of changing social values that lead to accompanying adjustments in what is deemed conventionally acceptable in film. For instance, rather bizarrely one might think, Hitchcock was apparently pleased to manage to get a shot of a toilet pan past the censors and into *Psycho* (1960). Similarly, the lunchtime rendezvous in the hotel room with which *Psycho* opens was at the time seen to be pushing the boundaries of acceptability.

Filmmakers have always attempted to gain some sort of emotional response from spectators, and for their part spectators have always responded emotionally to film. More than that, spectators have always attended the cinema in order to have their emotions aroused and with the expectation that this will take place. This is, after all, a basic function of storytelling. Stories gain emotional responses from listeners, readers or viewers. Effective storytelling encourages us to feel human emotions by allowing us to sympathise, empathise or even identify with characters and their narrative experiences. As spectators (and as readers) we presumably find this process to be pleasurable or we would not return time after time to films (and stories), but in what ways is it pleasurable? Entering the window of the hotel room at the opening to *Psycho* would seem to encourage the notion of film as voyeuristically pleasurable, but what is the connection between voyeurism and emotional response? What sorts of emotional response does voyeurism bring about? Are we being permitted to give rein to a type of human interest in others that might more normally be considered socially unacceptable? If so, what sorts of emotion do we experience at this point?

What emotions are engendered by the vigilante bloodbath scene in *Taxi Driver* or the ear-cutting scene in *Reservoir Dogs*? Do these emotions involve pleasure of some sort? If so, what is the nature of this pleasure? If it is not pleasurable, why do spectators watch these sorts of scenes, deliberately exposing themselves to a certain type of emotional response?

- If possible, watch the opening scene to *Morocco* (Sternberg, 1930) featuring Marlene Dietrich through to the end of her stage performance.
- Discuss with others what might have been deemed rather shocking about this film. If you are uncertain about this try acting it out. Find a performance space and get someone who enjoys and perhaps has some experience of acting to volunteer to play the Dietrich role.
- Is this scene still shocking today? Or does it depend for much of its shock on transgressing the particular norms and values of the society in which it was first made and shown? Are we now too sexually sophisticated and open to be concerned by this sort of behaviour?

INFORMATION BOX

If you do not manage to find a copy of *Morocco* (Sternberg, 1930), Dietrich appears on stage within the opening few minutes of the film as a cross-dressing female in a black dinner jacket and top hat (Figure 18.3).

Figure 18.3 Dietrich in *Morocco* (Sternberg, 1930).

How are we supposed to read this entrance? Is it a display of lesbianism, sexual ambiguity and/or strong female independence? In the face of catcalls and jeers from the largely male audience who clearly do not like her initial presentation of herself, she is defiant and coolly provocative. She moves with poise and confidence towards a party around a table to the left of the stage, gracefully takes a flower as a love token, kisses full on the lips an apparently straight (but clearly at this moment sexually challenged) female sitting with a male partner, and turns back towards the stage after giving the woman a final sexually meaningful look.

(Unfortunately, by the end of the film Dietrich is fulfilling the Hollywood stereotype of the love-struck woman faithfully following her man as she trudges off across the desert behind a rugged Gary Cooper playing the part of a soldier in the French Foreign Legion. The strong, independent female of the opening has been transformed in true Hollywood style into the woman who forsakes all to follow her man!)

'Shock' as sudden and unexpected, or long-drawn out

'Shock' in film usually occurs as something sudden and unexpected so that the viewer is as it were caught unawares. But it is worth bearing in mind that this is not always the case; sometimes the shock effect is achieved in a rather more long-drawn-out fashion. For example, the shock of the finally extremely quick moment of execution in *Let Him Have It* (Medak, 1991) is essentially achieved through the painfully slow movement towards this in the preceding scenes. (This is also an example of a different sort of shocking content as we are forced to witness what amounts to state violence against an adult with the mental age of a child.) On a similar theme, Kubrick makes the inescapability of the execution by firing squad in *Paths of Glory* (1957) unbearably painful as he gives us an experience of shock not as something sudden but as something of prolonged intensity.

ACTIVITY

- Watch either/both of the two scenes mentioned above and attempt to record your emotional response in as much detail as possible by noting how you are feeling throughout the viewing.
- Compare your responses with those of others who have watched the same scene(s).
- Watch the same scene(s) again and by making further notes attempt to see if your emotional response alters on a second viewing.

ACTIVITY

- Working with others, if possible, in order to pool your ideas, list the range of different sorts of violence that have been dealt with so far in this section and try to give your own examples of films in which similar events occur. Make sure you consider any films you have studied while preparing for other parts of this A level but also remember that it is just as valid to include films you know from your own experience.
- Prepare a short presentation, introducing two or three films you have mentioned during discussions but which other people don't appear to have seen.
- Show short clips from these films that you consider shocking, explaining how you believe the various elements of film construction have been used in order to create the emotional response of shock.

ACTIVITY

'Shock' suggests a state of being stunned by what you have seen. It is felt to be repulsive in its brutality, so that you (and probably all those watching with you) are startled, surprised by what you have witnessed, knocked off balance, and probably very silent. But consider another form of possible emotional response, the tearful response. Is this part of 'shock' or is it something different? For instance, did you have a tearful response to the executions in *Let Him Have It* and/or *Paths of Glory*, and if so, was this because of the shock you experienced or due to something else? Discuss this with others who have seen the same scenes.

Sexual content

As with violence so of course there are various types of sexual material that might be seen to be shocking and that might create certain sorts of emotional response. There are plenty of films you could consider under this heading, but as a few examples you might look at scenes from:

- *Sweet Sweetback's Baadassssss Song* (van Peebles, 1971) which opens almost immediately with underage sex;

- *The Crying Game* (Jordan, 1992) which involves an interesting and challenging sexual twist to the plot;
- *Once Were Warriors* (Tamahori, 1994) which has scenes of domestic violence,
  one of which involves teenage rape and the other which amounts to rape within
  marriage.

ACTIVITY

- Working with others, if possible, in order to pool your ideas, list the
  range of different sorts of sexually related material you have come
  across in any films you have seen that you believe could be seen as
  shocking. Make sure you know the titles, directors and dates of any
  films to which you refer. Make sure you consider any films you have
  studied while preparing for other parts of this A level.

Racism and extreme politics

If we move on from issues of sex and violence, it could be argued that the most
shocking elements in films are not the actual incidents that are portrayed but the
ideas that are expressed and that underpin the events. In *Romper Stomper*
(Wright, 1992) or *American History X* (Kaye, 1998), for example, it is the extreme
right-wing politics and accompanying racial hatred that audiences may find most
disturbing. Both films could be accused of giving a platform to fascist ideas: in
Romper Stomper Russell Crowe as Hando reads directly from Hitler's *Mein Kampf*
and in *American History X* Edward Norton as Derek gives a powerful 'race hate'
speech almost directly to the camera. Do we as viewers have an emotional
response to these sorts of scenes?

For *Halliwell's Film and Video Guide* the first of these films amounts to 'a violent
excursion into Australian low-life and one that refrains from any implied comment
on the anti-social action it presents'. For us as film students, the second half of
this sentence should form the focus of our attention as we examine movies such
as these: How should these films be read and how would different audiences
respond? Is it possible to find evidence from within the construction of these films
to suggest the way in which the filmmakers ultimately wished their film to be
understood? Is it likely that different audiences will respond in different ways?
Could Nazi skinhead gang members gain their own gratification from watching
these films? If they could, is that shocking in itself or simply inevitable and not
something that should concern the filmmakers? (*Birth of a Nation* (Griffith, 1915)
would provide an interesting parallel text for investigation. This early, much-
heralded 'classic' is about as racist as you can get, with the Ku Klux Klan being
portrayed as heroes!)

ACTIVITY

- Are there any films you have seen either as part of this A level course or independently that have contained ideas you have found disturbing? Discuss your ideas with others, if possible, making sure that you explain as clearly as you can what it was about the ideas that troubled you and identifying specific scenes in the films where you felt you could see these ideas being expressed.
- Is this sort of response simply an intellectual response? Or would you argue that disturbing ideas can in themselves create an emotional response?

Audiences

As we have said, in considering 'shock' and other emotional responses to film you will inevitably need to consider the variety of possible ways in which films could be read by different spectators. Not everyone will respond to a melodramatic 'weepie' in the same way, nor will everyone be emotionally shocked by the same events in the same scenes. It may well be that the filmmakers place a certain meaning within the texts they produce through the ways in which they construct that text; but it is also true to say that they have no ultimate control over the ways in which viewers will actually respond to the material they have put out into the world.

DECONSTRUCTION: this theory challenges the assumption that a text has an unchanging, unified meaning that is true for all readers, and also the idea that the author is the source of any text's meaning. The approach suggests instead that there is a multiplicity of legitimate interpretations of a text.

Theories such as this, developed particularly during the 1970s, tended to emphasise the viewer's control over the creation of the film being watched. However, other theories have attempted to demonstrate how the spectator is fixed in place by the text (or by the system of values within the text) so that audiences are manipulated by filmmakers into seeing things, and therefore thinking, in certain ways.

The tension between concepts of the reader/spectator as on the one hand active and in control, and on the other as passive and a victim, lies at the heart of ideas regarding the experience of spectatorship, or the process that is taking place as we view films.

ACTIVITY

Watch either *Romper Stomper* or *American History X* and answer the following questions:

- With which characters is the audience invited to identify?
- What types of audience would visit the cinema to see this film? What would be their reasons for going? What would be their emotional responses?
- Why might censors, or a government, consider cutting or banning this film? Would their concerns be to do with potential emotional responses to the film?
- Are there any sections you believe could, or should, have been cut?
- What certificate is your film given in Britain, and would you agree with this? Justify your response. Undertake some research to see if the film has been given different classifications in different countries.

Regulation and censorship

Does the implementation of censorship and/or classification mean that there is a fear that the material could create too strong an emotional response within certain groups in society? Does it imply that people outside of any group permitted to see the film are not deemed to be as able as others to deal with their emotional responses to film? Films have always been seen to have the power to bring about antisocial behaviour, especially among the working class and the young. To what extent is it a heightened emotional response that has been feared in these circumstances?

'Fans' and 'fandom'

Finally, you may like to briefly consider the issue of 'fans' who bring with them a particularly intense form of emotional response and emotional attachment to certain films. 'Fans' are people who enjoy films in a particularly intense and impassioned way. We could be talking here about fans of films in general, whether as a form of entertainment or as a means of creative expression, who attend the cinema and view films with a special passion; or we could be discussing the fans of particular genres, cult movies, film series, stars or directors.

The study of 'fandom' is the investigation of what it means to be a fan: how fans express their likes and dislikes, and in doing so how they carve out a role for themselves within the wider film industry. Fans do not just watch films, they talk (a lot!) about them, and they often write about them (whether via text messaging, e-mail, internet sites and forums, or more formal reviews). In doing these things could they be said to have, through the expression of their passionate responses, real power within the industry in determining the products that are made and offered for sale? (Or are fans actually quite weak, easily manipulated creatures who because of their impassioned responses are at the mercy of an industry that spends millions on publicity and advertising?)

The director, Bryan Singer, has spoken about the difficulty of making the film *X-Men* (2000) knowing that fans of the Marvel comic-book series were ready and waiting to judge every decision he made. This was a fantasy world over which he clearly felt the fans had some sort of 'ownership' that had existed prior to his appointment as director of the film and that would continue into the future after the film was made. Yet, at the same time, Twentieth Century Fox had clearly made a calculated commercial decision to make a film for which there was an easily recognisable, emotionally committed, pre-existing audience. For the studio, the attraction of this target audience was not only that its members would boost box-office figures but more importantly that it constituted a ready-made fan-base. As a group of fans they already had fanzines, websites and e-mail networks in place that would guarantee massive publicity for the film.

EXAM QUESTIONS ?

- Creating the opportunity for emotional responses in popular films is simply to do with manipulating the audience: mainstream films don't attempt to use emotional responses to make any more considered points. From your experience would you agree with this?

- Would you agree that strong emotional effects are achieved in some films by the careful use of film construction techniques and in others by the subject matter itself?

- After the shock of the initial viewing, do subsequent viewings lessen or intensify the impact of shocking images and/or subject matter?

- After you have watched a melodrama or a romantic comedy, does the emotional response change on subsequent viewings, or does it always seem just as intense and fresh as the first time?

CONCLUSION

■ Films can create a range of emotional responses, but they will always create some sort of emotional response.

■ Filmmakers can use constructed emotional responses in order to challenge audiences or to make them think about issues they may previously not have considered.

Resources and Further Reading

Books

Abrams, N., Bell, I. and Udris, J. (2001) *Studying Film*. Arnold (Chapter 15)

Hayward, S. (2005) *Cinema Studies: The Key Concepts*. Routledge

Hill, A. (1997) *Shocking Entertainment: Viewer Response to Violent Movies*. University of Luton Press

Medved, M. (1992) *Hollywood vs America: Culture and the War on Traditional Values*. HarperCollins

Phillips, W.H. (2005) *Film: An Introduction*. Bedford/St Martin's Press (Chapter 8)

Slocum, D. (2001) *Violence and American Cinema*. Routledge

Internet

www.bbfc.co.uk (The British Board of Film Classification)

www.bfi.org.uk

part 4

VARIETIES OF FILM EXPERIENCE (FM4): SINGLE FILM – CRITICAL STUDY

INTRODUCTION TO
SINGLE FILM – CRITICAL
STUDIES

19 INTRODUCTION TO SINGLE FILM – CRITICAL STUDIES

Single Film – Critical Study offers an opportunity to explore one of a number of set films through close analysis of both text and context, and by synoptically bringing to bear any previous learning developed through the study of film. The macro and micro aspects of film form from FM1 (see *AS Film Studies: the Essential Introduction*) will be a starting point to explore the film language and styles adopted in these films, and consideration of the approaches to making meaning employed by the filmmakers will prove a valuable vein to mine. The contextual study of these films will encourage the consolidation of the work carried out in FM2 and (most likely) in FM3.

Each of the following films has been selected in part for the critical reception it received on release (and in some instances since), and an intelligent engagement with the various critical voices would facilitate a deeper understanding of what these films meant to spectators. The debates engendered by these films are likely to position the spectator, and this is another element in understanding the significance of these works.

The films may also be approached through the use of critical frameworks, where some will suit particular films more than others. Thus one could explore the performance styles and use of stars in one of these films, while another could be usefully explored through adopting a gendered approach. This flexibility should allow you to engage with the chosen film in a way that best suits your interest, and part of the study around these films should include your own responses to them.

The films are examined as part of the FM4 paper, and have a choice of three questions focused on them. Two of the questions are general and apply to all of the films, and one is specific to each film. The general questions will revolve around the critical approaches that apply to the films and the critical debates engendered by them. The individual question tends to be focused more on the text as a specific starting point for the exploration of broader concepts, either within the film itself, or issues outside of the film.

Each of the films for this section is discussed below, and that discussion will highlight some, though not all, areas of interest that could be further explored. Accordingly the discussion should be seen not as a definitive route map through a chosen film, but rather as a starting point, or springboard, for further consideration and research.

Modern Times (Chaplin, US, 1936)

Figure 19.1 Charlie Chaplin in *Modern Times* (1936).

> **Because they could get movement into the actual shots, comedy directors depended less on cutting for pace. A great part of the early comedies was played in long shots, embracing the whole action on a screen at one time. Even now there is little constructive cutting in Chaplin's films . . . except for the purposes of emphasis.**

(Alberto Cavalcanti, 'Comedies and Cartoons' in Davy 1938, p. 77)

Cavalcanti was writing just two years after the release of *Modern Times* but this view of Chaplin's films has continued. His work is frequently seen as depending simply upon staged vaudeville-style performance taking place in front of a camera. The use of editing and cinematography to create meaning and generate specific responses from the audience is not, it is assumed, an important part of his approach. This has meant that a focus on performance has been expected of anyone wishing to critically analyse Chaplin's work.

To an extent this dominant understanding of Chaplin's work is not surprising, since the Tramp who plays a central role in almost all of his films became a powerfully iconic image during the early twentieth century and remains an immediately recognisable character. A range of 'Tramp' toys were made throughout the 1920s and 1930s, comics and cartoons featured the character, look-alike and walk-alike competitions were held for members of the public to mimic the character, and Chaplin himself often played to the role before the newsreel cameras.

We might like to reflect on why this character was so popular and perhaps try to consider why his antics are often no longer seen to be so funny. Older cinema-goers are on record testifying to the cliché of 'rolling in the aisle' while watching Chaplin's silent movies. Is it possible at the distance of almost a century from his first emergence to understand this phenomenon? The character was essentially an extension of the classic circus clown: he revelled in basic knock-about humour but at his heart there was a well of sadness. The Tramp (almost) never got the girl, he almost always left the film walking away in long shot down an empty, dusty road alone with a heavy, laboured gait until there was a kick of the heels, a change of posture and an increased stride as he threw off the past and determined to carry on whatever. This final aspect is where Chaplin takes his character beyond the circus clown. This is his moral: the importance of carrying on in the face of adversity. (It is also his acknowledgement of what he sees his audience as doing every day.) You will find the moral given in the inter-titles at the end of *Modern Times* but it is most successful perhaps when it is shown in performance as described above as at the end of *The Tramp* (1915) or *The Circus* (1928).

ACTIVITY

- Do you agree with this analysis of the Tramp? There is no reason why you should: Chaplin has often been criticised for being overly senti-mental, for example. Perhaps you agree with some of this analysis but would add to it or modify it in certain ways.
- Write a short essay analysing the role of 'The Tramp' and the role he plays in the Chaplin films you have seen. (You may want to leave this task until you have watched more of the films.)

ACTIVITY

Why would this type of character find a currency with the early film-going public not only in America but across Europe and around the world? Are there reasons that might account for such a phenomenon? Discuss this with others if possible and list as many potential reasons as you can.

ACTIVITY

- Research briefly the history of the United States during the period 1914 to 1936; that is, from the time Chaplin became involved in films to the making of *Modern Times*. Focus on social conditions in the country but major headings for consideration will be immigration, the First World War and the economic depression of the 1930s.
- As you are doing this you may like to watch films such as *The Tramp* (1915), *Easy Street* (1917), *The Immigrant* (1917), *Shoulder Arms* (1918), *The Kid* (1921) and *City Lights* (1931). What are Chaplin's key themes in these films and how would these concerns reflect the period in which these films are being made?

When Chaplin tried to remove himself and his main character from a film, as he did with *A Woman of Paris* (1923) in which he had only a small walk-on part, the movie was a box-office failure. But if we watch this film and consider some of the shots and the relationships between the characters, we find evidence that Chaplin was more than simply a performer. One of the central relationships is a love triangle between a woman and a man, and his mother. Speaking to the mother the man has just dismissed his relationship with the woman, not realising she has been nearby and able to overhear what has been said. There follows a shot of all three together but with strong lines breaking the composition and dividing the characters one from another. This is a director who knows how to use the camera and screen space in effective, creative ways.

This does not mean we should neglect to consider the costume, performance and make-up of our central character in *Modern Times*: the bowler hat, the clipped black moustache, the heavy eyebrows, the dark make-up around the eyes, the shoulders-back and stomach-out body posture, the battered outsized shoes, the outturned feet, the cane walking-stick, the over-large trousers and too-tight jacket. Nor that we should neglect to consider the specific values that might attach to these sorts of elements within the context of the period. But we should not confine our interests to these performance-related fields.

Consider the opening to *Modern Times*. A flock of sheep, tightly packed, move forward, with one black sheep in their midst. This shot dissolves into one of men jammed together emerging from a subway with railings and the strong line of the subway sign above them herding, enclosing and entrapping. This dissolves into men crossing a street to join others moving from left to right, all flowing in the same direction, following the strong lines of the road and a stone balustrade towards the factory that dominates the screen. A further dissolve takes us into a narrow corridor crowded with workers; there are windows like grilles to one side, pipes and girders above and a row of 'clocking-in' machines along the other wall. From here we cut to a shot inside the factory completely dominated by machinery and with the workers enclosed in a small space within the frame. A straight cut takes us to another huge machine with one man dwarfed to one side and others further in the distance within this vast space dwarfed still further. All of this displays a very careful use of editing, cinematography (notice the dominant camera angle looking down on the men) and *mise-en-scène* to create meaning.

ACTIVITY

Research the economic concept of 'Fordism' (named after Henry Ford, founder of the Ford Motor Company) and the management theory, 'Taylorism' (named after F.W. Taylor who published his *Principles of Scientific Management* in 1911).

ACTIVITY

Watch the opening to *Metropolis* (Lang, 1927) and list similarities and differences between this film and *Modern Times*.

ACTIVITY

■ Describe in detail the use of cinematography and *mise-en-scène* in the shot that introduces our 'hero' working within his section of the assembly-line.

■ Find a further single elaborate shot or a sequence of edited shots such as those outlined above that you find particularly interesting in its construction and explain to others how you see this shot or sequence as working to create meaning.

■ (Most obviously, perhaps, you may like to consider the significance of the edited sequence from the point where the Tramp leaves hospital after his nervous breakdown to his arrival outside the closed factory.)

Modern Times is a natural film for the character of the Tramp to graduate to making. The essence of the Tramp is that he embodies the concept of liberty; he understands that free time is real wealth and that work is wage slavery. He is from his inception entirely anti-capitalist and implacably opposed to the regimentation and order imposed by factory work. This is a comedy and we have sequence after sequence of contrived comedic set-pieces, but notice what this allows Chaplin to insert in the spaces between. The repetitive, mind-numbing nature of work drives the central character to a nervous breakdown, a father is shot dead by the police, two orphans are taken away by the uncaring authorities, a middle-class woman denounces a poor street urchin ('the gamin') for stealing a loaf of bread, the store burglars are nothing more than the hungry unemployed, the police are heavy-handed in their treatment of striking workers as a matter of routine, and the Tramp makes every effort to return to prison because you're better off 'inside' than outside in the middle of an economic depression. Finally, when almost at the end of the film the Tramp and the gamin have secured jobs, the authorities immediately destroy their happiness.

ACTIVITY

- Watch *Zero de Conduite* (Vigo, 1933) and list themes that are similar to those found in *Modern Times*.
- Consider the teacher who resembles Chaplin's Tramp: why has this character been given certain characteristics of the Tramp and in what ways might this be seen as important for the thematic concerns of the film?

ACTIVITY

- Watch *À nous la liberté* (Clair, 1931) and note any similarities with *Modern Times*.
- How does Chaplin use ideas from Clair and to what extent do you think he adapts those ideas to his own ends?

> **In recent years Chaplin's achievement has sometimes been under estimated by critics without historical perspective, or perhaps influenced by the public smears of the 1940s.**

(Robinson, 1996, pp. 84–85)

Bibliography

Davy, C. (1938) *Footnotes to the Film*. Lovat Dickson

Hayes, K. (2005) *Charlie Chaplin: Interviews*. Jackson: University Press of Mississippi

Mast, G. (1979) *The Comic Mind: Comedy and the Movies*. Chicago: University of Chicago Press

Mellen, J. (2006) *Modern Times*. London: BFI

Robinson, D. (1984) *Chaplin: The Mirror of Opinion*. Bloomington: Indiana University Press

Robinson, D. (1996) 'Charlie Chaplin' in Nowell-Smith, G. (ed.) *The Oxford History of World Cinema*. Oxford: Oxford University Press

Figure 19.2 *Les Enfants du Paradis* (Pathé Cinéma, France, 1945, *Dir*: Marcel Carné)

Les Enfants du Paradis (Children of Paradise) was made by Marcel Carné during the Nazi Occupation of France during the Second World War and its production was beset with problems from the film's inception, not least having to have members of the crew work in secret because they were Jewish, and the producer being removed from the film because of suspected distant Jewish ancestry. It began shooting in 1943, and, because of the Vichy government edict that feature films could be no longer than ninety minutes, actually began life as two separate films: *Le Boulevard du Crime (The Boulevard of Crime)* and *L'Homme Blanc (The White Man)*. Production was halted when the Allies landed in Normandy and, although it could have restarted, it did not do so until after the liberation of Paris in 1944, by which time one of its stars, Robert le Vigan, had fled after being condemned by the Resistance as a collaborator. The film was finally premièred in 1945 and stayed in the cinemas for a record fifty-four weeks.

The film's title refers to a particular section of a theatrical audience who inhabit the cheapest seats, known in British theatre as 'the gods'. The film itself is set in the 1830s in the theatrical district around the Funambules Theatre in Paris, and is the story of unrequited love where four men are all in love with the courtesan Garance (played by the actress Arletty).

The two originally planned films conjoin to become two 'epochs' spanning the film, with the first set in the mid-1820s and the second less than a decade later. The story is a convoluted tale of love, intrigue, betrayal, and ultimately suffering, and is pure melodrama from start to finish. As Bosley Crowther wrote on its release: 'Marcel Carné is Platonically observing the melancholy masquerade of life, the riddle of truth and illusion, the chimeras of *la comédie humaine*.'

The *masquerade of life* is one suited to the becostumed characters that act as ciphers for Carné's story which focuses on the comedy of the human condition (something more commonly referred to as the tragedy of the human condition). This in itself suggests a viewpoint that is in opposition to the norm.

Shot initially by Roger Hubert, who was replaced in 1944 by Philippe Agostini, the film is exquisite in its use of cinematography, with a complementary use of a vibrant and rich *mise-en-scène*. Deep focus cinematography is matched with a constantly moving camera that settles on scenes before moving on to others. The opening scene offers a view of a specially constructed set for the Boulevard du Temple that ran to over a quarter of a mile long, but that could house the many hundreds of extras used in so many of the scenes. Vibrant and complex in its construction, this is clearly filmmaking at its best.

Thematically, the essential drive is to explore issues of freedom in all its many forms (artistic, personal, national), and this is highlighted in the opening scene, and particularly through the modern, almost proto-feminist depiction of Garance. This connects and contextualises the other grand theme of the piece, that of love, and the freedom to love. However, the love that Carné offers the spectator is not the romantic love of many of his contemporaries, but rather a realist love in all its many forms, unique to the individuals who bear it.

Carné makes much play of the boundaries between the real world and the world of the theatre, and even takes this division inside the theatre where the occupants of the cheap seats are constantly present as both witness to (spectator) and informal commentator on (chorus) the events of the story. It is this boundary around a fictional world that will have been familiar and significant to the spectators who had suffered the surreal yet hyperreal Nazi occupation, with its casual violence matched with glories of excess. The transgressions of these boundaries have significant implications for those who perpetrate them, and drive the complex narrative forward, giving a relatively loose tale structure. Indeed, the theatrical coincidences that make the plotting so complex and convoluted are themselves a transgression of these same boundaries with the reality of coincidence in life being brought to its extreme end to the point where it appears as a simple theatrical device.

The film offers a set of stereotyped characters that thematically introduce issues of masculinity and femininity. Each of the male characters offers a differing version of masculinity, none of which are particularly successful or satisfying to those embodying them. There is indeed much contemporary criticism which suggests that the character Lacenaire has been created to represent homosexuality, and rather than being in love with Garance is actually jealous of the attention she receives from the male characters. The female characters are more assured in themselves and more assertive in their expectations, and as such the film is more closely connected to contemporary cinema than to the immediately postwar cinema of France.

Les Enfants du Paradis is a fine example of a key French film movement known as Poetic Realism, which is defined as having a heightened sense of aestheticism that promotes representational issues above all others. Often dealing with characters on the edges of society, they are marked by a sense of nostalgia and often regret.

In 1971 the French Film Academy awarded it a special Cesar, naming it the best French film in the history of talking pictures, and in 1995 it was voted Best French Film of the Century in a critics poll.

Note

1 Crowther, B. (1947) The Screen in Review: *Les Enfants du Paradis*. *New York Times*, 20 February.

Supporting Media

http://uk.youtube.com/watch?v=UU4PTm-abG0
Opening sequence

http://uk.youtube.com/watch?v=JpmADgSQaxM&feature=related
Trailer

Vertigo (Hitchcock, US, 1958)

Figure 19.3
Vertigo
(d. Hitchcock,
US, 1958).

Vertigo is one of the most admired films in cinema history made by an undisputed auteur; a director whose achievements as an artist have been compared to Shakespeare's.

Some evidence of the status of the film and director:

- In 1954 *Cahiers du Cinema* (the film journal where Truffaut, Godard *et al.* developed *la politique des auteurs*) was devoted to the career of Hitchcock
- For Andrew Sarris (1968), American translator of *la politique des auteurs*, Hitchcock belonged in the Pantheon: the highest category reserved for the very few great directors.
- In a poll conducted by *Sight and Sound* (2002) critics voted *Vertigo* the second greatest film of all time (*Citizen Kane* was first). In the same poll Hitchcock was voted the second greatest film director (beaten by Orson Welles).
- In his analysis of Hitchcock's films, Robin Wood (1965) claimed: '*Vertigo* seems to me Hitchcock's masterpiece to date, and one of the four or five most profound and beautiful films the cinema has yet given us.'

ACTIVITY

What effect does this weight of critical approval have on your expectations of the film?

It is also important to remember that:

- The initial reception of *Vertigo* was not so affirmative; even positive reviews saw the film as a prestigious, star-led thriller rather than as a work of art.
- The context of auteur theory has been widely attacked; this would question the validity of the concept of Hitchcock as a great director.

Robin Wood argues that Hitchcock should be taken seriously as an artist because of the 'thematic and formal unity' evident in his work – nowhere more so than in *Vertigo*.

Buckland (1998) summarises the key features of Hitchcock as an auteur:

- The narrative is based around an investigation. This is either by the hero investigating a suspected crime or the hero is himself being investigated.

The structure of the investigation leads to other themes:

- confession and guilt
- suspense

- the perfect murder
- the wrong man.

These themes are explored through a distinctive visual style which includes:

- emphasis on editing and montage
- high number of point-of-view shots
- shooting in a confined space.

INFORMATION BOX – IDENTIFICATION AND POINT OF VIEW

The success of Hitchcock's films is reliant on the careful manipulation of spectator response; one of the techniques used to effect this is identification with character. In film, identification with character is created in a number of ways:

- Sympathy with characters, an emotional identification which allows us to empathise with the character.
- An 'intellectual identification' where the audience has the same information as the characters.
- Point-of-view shots which although rarely used can place the spectator in the character's position.

ACTIVITY

- Watch the sequence where Scottie is following Madeleine through San Francisco at the beginning of his investigation.
- How are the different techniques of constructing identification evident in *Vertigo*?

Hitchcock's films represent a world in chaos with no structure or rational order. This is an unstable place with no God, a frightening unpredictable place where things happen by chance and without explanation – whether you are a good or a bad person. You might be killed in the shower, attacked by birds, mistaken for a spy or murderer, your favourite uncle turns out to be a murderer, the woman you're in love with doesn't exist. . . .

ACTIVITY

Read the definitions of Hitchcock as an auteur. How can *Vertigo* be defined as a Hitchcock film? Give evidence of specific themes and use of film language.

THEME AND FORM: The idea that there is a link between theme and form has traditionally been one of the definitions of great art. In film this concept suggests that the form – narrative structure, shots, editing – is not just there to deliver the themes but has meaning in itself. For example, one of the characteristics of Hitchcock's style is his use of camera almost as another character in the film. In the opening of *Psycho* (1960) the camera seems to consider other windows before going through the motel window where Marion Crane is lying on the bed, and in the first scene of *Rear Window* (1953) the camera looks around Jeff's room while he sleeps. In both cases this spying on characters who don't know we are there is part of the theme of the film – the pleasures of voyeurism.

ACTIVITY – NARRATIVE FORM AND THEMES

Vertigo was criticised on its release because of the implausible plot and the failure to conform to conventional narrative and genre expectations (Hitchcock was often referred to as the Master of Suspense in publicity material).

- Can you apply the narrative theories of Todorov, Propp and Lévi-Strauss to *Vertigo*? Which aspects of the theories are applicable?
- Does *Vertigo* conform to a classic narrative structure?

Vertigo is usually defined as a thriller, a genre structured around creating suspense for the audience.

- At what stage is information revealed to the audience? Do we gain information at the same time as Scottie? How does this affect the construction of suspense in the film?
- How does *Vertigo* conform to and subvert the conventions of genre?

Some points to consider in the analysis of narrative and genre:

- *Vertigo* opens in disruption – rather than equilibrium – with the race across the rooftops and the death of the policeman. At the end of the chase Scottie is left hanging from the roof by his fingertips and a reverse zoom shot visually represents his fear of falling: the vertigo of the title. It is not clear how Scottie is rescued from the roof top and this has become the focus of much analysis of the film. While for some critics it is an example of Hitchcock's playful attitude towards the details of plot (there is a very similar incident at the end of *North by Northwest* (1958)) others have read it as much more symbolic; Scottie remains hanging, unable to move throughout the film, never the one to take action, he is always propelled by more powerful characters.
- *Vertigo* 'breaks' the rules of the thriller genre by destroying the suspense and solving the puzzle two-thirds of the way into the film. This is a very disorientating experience for the audience as we no longer have our narrative and genre expectations to guide and reassure us. A similar effect is created in *Psycho* when the central character, the one with whom the audience identifies, is murdered in the shower.

ACTIVITY

If *Vertigo* doesn't conform to the conventions of genre, why do you think Hitchcock chose to work in that genre? What themes are associated with the thriller? How do these themes link with the themes of *Vertigo*?

ACTIVITY

- To continue the formal analysis of *Vertigo*, identify the different examples of double motifs and repetition (plot, character, *mise-en-scène*) in the film – the most explicit being that of Madeleine and Judy.
- Apply a feminist reading to the film; does *Vertigo* reinforce the male gaze?

Bibliography

Buckland, W. (1998) 'Film Authorship: The Director as Auteur' in *Teach Yourself Film Studies*. Hodder & Stoughton

Spoto, D. (1992) 'Vertigo' in *The Art of Alfred Hitchcock*. Fourth Estate

Wood, R. (1965/1989) 'Vertigo' in *Hitchcock's Films Revisited*. Faber and Faber

The Battle of Algiers (Pontecorvo, Algeria/Italy, 1966)

Figure 19.4 *La Battaglia di Algeri* (*The Battle of Algiers*) (Igor Film, Italy/Algeria, 1966, *Dir*: Gillo Pontecorvo).

Shot in a neo-realist style using amateur actors and location-based shooting, Gillo Pontecorvo's *La Battaglia di Algeri* covers a period in Algiers during the Algerian war of independence from 1954 to 1957, and is based on real events that happened during that time. It focuses on the string of battles between the FLN (the National Liberation Front), the French colonists, and eventually, as the situation escalates, the French Paratroops.

The film is episodic in nature and revolves around several central characters, including Ali la Pointe, an FLN cell commander, Saadi Yacef, the rebel FLN military commander. Petit Omar, a child messenger for the FLN, Djamila, Zohra and Hassiba, the three FLN activists who carry out bombings, and Colonel Mathieu, the commander of the French Paratroops. While the French eventually liquidate the cell structure of the FLN and effectively win the Battle of Algiers, Pontecorvo ends the film with newsreel-style footage of rioting Algerians which offers the view that the French have lost control of Algeria as a whole.

The narrative is built around a set of sequences that demonstrate the methods of the FLN and of the French local population and then, eventually, of the French Paratroops. Pontecorvo makes no attempt to flinch from the atrocities committed by all sides in the conflict, nor from the attacks against civilians that became a feature of the conflict. The French colonists are shown discriminating against native Algerians and then turning their prejudice into violent action through lynch mobs and vicious attacks.

The FLN takes over the Kasbah at the heart of Algiers and immediately begins a campaign of ruthless control by executing the criminals and 'traitors' of the Kasbah. With their grip on the Kasbah maintained through violence, they extend their campaign by taking the violence out of the Kasbah and into the French colonial suburbs. The violence escalates until there is a series of café bombings that are both shocking in terms of the narrative but also in terms of the buildup through the editing, and in terms of execution though the cinematography. The camera lingers on the aftermath in a documentary style, moving among the wreckage and survivors.

This set of atrocities brings the French Paratroopers to Algiers to crush the uprising, and Pontecorvo shows their strict military tactics, but also intimidation, torture and murder to destroy the network of cells that has organised the uprising. While the spectator is positioned relatively neutrally by the narrative, a degree of sympathy is engendered for the FLN, and this is strengthened by the fact that they are crushed by superior numbers (giving them almost the position of victim), but even more significantly in terms of positioning the audience, they are betrayed by traitors and those tortured into betraying them.

The film has incredible staging set against the backdrop of the real locations where the dramatised events occurred. Pontecorvo spent two years before commencing shooting in Algiers scouting locations, researching the script and the people the characters were based on, and being guided by the insurgence leader Saadi Yacef to get the political and historical perspectives on the conflict. Towards the end of these two years, Pontecorvo began casting from among the local Algerian Arabs or Kabyles, choosing them not for their acting ability but for the intensity of their 'look' and the emotional effect of their appearance. Indeed, by the end of the casting process, the only professional actor involved in the production was Jean Martin, who took the role of Colonel Mathieu.

Pontecorvo was determined to re-create the uprising visually, and chose to do this by re-creating the 'feel' of the Kasbah with its frenetic over-population and confusion. To do this he engaged the participation of thousands of local Algerian extras and shot sequences in the narrow streets of the Kasbah, emphasising the scale of the uprising and the power of the FLN in commanding the people. Pontecorvo got his camera in among them, resulting in a cinematagraphic honesty and an enhanced level of naturalism. There are moments when the scenes are reminiscent of Roberto Rossellini's *Roma, Città Aperta* (*Rome, Open City*) (Minerva, Italy, 1945), with a stark and oppressed quality heightened through the carefully positioned camera, wrapped in the swirling masses of the Kasbah. Equally his use of the long shot (particularly of the rioting scenes) and the innovative handheld camera give a heightened documentary, an almost newsreel feel that further contextualises the more formally staged sequences.

Marcello Gatti shot the film in black and white to re-create the newsreel style, and pioneered the handheld techniques that lend vibrancy to the riot scenes and the scenes of the suppression of the uprising by the French Paratroops. Although Pontecorvo stated that no newsreel footage was used in the film, had he included any it would be impossible to distinguish from the restaged events and stylised form.

The film was an instant hit with critics and audiences alike (though it was banned in France), which is all the more surprising when reflecting on the fact that experimental film was in vogue at this point – a neo-realist film about an almost forgotten conflict would not have been an obvious choice for critical plaudits. The film won the Golden Lion at the Venice Festival, was nominated for three Academy Awards, and won the International Critics Award at the 1966 Cannes Film Festival.

Supporting Media

http://www.youtube.com/watch?v=Ca3M2feqJk8
La Battaglia di Algeri trailer

http://www.youtube.com/watch?v=2N6wAm0nZrQ
Ennio Morricone documentary discussing his music for the film, and also including interviews with Gillo Pontecorvo

Sweet Sweetback's Baadasssss Song (van Peebles, US, 1971)

ACTIVITY

Without knowing much more than the title of the film, its rating and where it was made, discuss with others your expectations of this film. Try to consider the implications of each part of the title. If you or others know anything of the reputation of this film share those ideas as you would before going to watch any film with friends.

ACTIVITY

- Watch the film in one sitting in conditions as close to those found in a cinema as you can manage. Don't take notes at this stage but try to be as aware as possible of both your own responses and anything you can gauge of the responses of others at various points throughout the film.
- As soon as the film ends, discuss your responses with others in as unstructured a way as possible and certainly without a list of questions you feel you have to answer. This is your chance to see if other people have responded in the same way as you to the characters, to events in the narrative, and to the style of filmmaking.

Sweet Sweetback's Baadasssss Song was made on a budget of $200,000. Melvin van Peebles wrote the screenplay, composed the music, directed the film, edited it and played the lead role. It was initially released in 1971 in just two cinemas, one in Detroit and the other in Atlanta. However, within less than two months of its release it had made it to the top of the box-office ratings. The film took more than $15 million in its first year, a record for an independent film at that time. On the back of *Sweetback*'s success in drawing a young black audience, MGM rewrote a film they were making about a white police officer, and before the end of the year released *Shaft* (Parks, 1971). A series of films followed that came to be known as Blaxploitation movies. In these films the black heroes achieve their goals, or at least are not defeated by the white system.

ACTIVITY

Watch *Shaft* (or another Blaxploitation film of your choice). List any similarities or differences you can identify between it and *Sweetback*. You should consider all of the usual elements of film construction (*mise-en-scène*, performance, cinematography, editing and sound) along with narrative features such as overall structure, character types used, the sorts of events included and the handling of the various phases of the narrative, especially the ending or resolution.

During his most famous speech in Washington in 1963, the black civil rights leader, Martin Luther King, emphasised his belief in non-violence:

> **We must forever conduct our struggle on the high plane of dignity and discipline. We must not allow our creative protests to degenerate into physical violence.**

But he knew the debate was raging within the black community as to whether the fight-back should involve something more than pacifist marches, and he warned the white majority:

> **Those who hope that the Negro needed to blow off steam and will now be content will have a rude awakening if the nation returns to business as usual.**

(Worley and Perry, 1994, p. 314)

Just over a year later Malcolm X, speaking in Mississippi, was suggesting:

> **I don't think . . . you will find the upcoming generation of our people, especially those who have been doing some thinking, will go along with any form of non-violence unless non-violence is going to be practiced all the way round.**

(Worley and Perry, 1994, p. 142)

Both of these men were assassinated: Malcolm X in 1965 and Martin Luther King in 1968. In 1966 there were race riots in more than forty cities across the United States and in the same year the Black Panther Party for Self-defense which advocated the importance of violently confronting the racist white community was formed. The Black Panthers welcomed van Peebles' film as revolutionary. In it, the black hero hospitalises two white police officers, kills two more while evading capture, and (at the time, more outrageous than anything) escapes to Mexico.

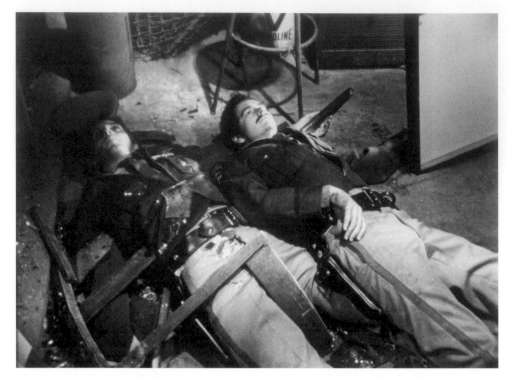

Figure 19.5 The dead policemen in *Sweet Sweetback's Baadasssss Song* (1971)

ACTIVITY

Working with others if possible, research the history of African-Americans in the United States. Decide how you are going to divide up the task within the group. You should aim to cover the period of slavery, the migration of the black population from the South into northern cities, the Civil Rights Movement of the 1960s, racial segregation in the South during the 1950s and 1960s, and social conditions for African-Americans in US cities in the 1960s. Bring your findings together and debate how to present the material in a handout of no more than two A4 sides.

Sweetback sets out its confrontational political agenda from the beginning: 'This film is dedicated to all the Brothers and Sisters who had enough of the Man.' This is a film that stars 'The Black Community'. The suggestion is that ordinary black people are going to see themselves represented on the screen in a way that they can recognise and in a way that has not been achieved until this point. Clearly an audience was attracted to the film but whether this was because of the film's highly charged political message or because of the X-rated sex has been heavily debated. Is the audience being exploited to make a profit? Are black actors (and perhaps the starring 'Black Community') being exploited to the same end? Or is it insulting to the audience that went to see the film in 1971 (and to the audience that has subsequently viewed the film) to suggest they have been nothing more than sexual voyeurs?

The film echoes the classic runaway-slave narrative: Sweetback is pursued throughout. Ironically, he uses the very image of slavery, the handcuffs, to severely beat the first two officers. The release of the pack of dogs to hunt him down towards the end of the film is again reminiscent of the pursuit of an escaped slave. Both the cuffs and the dog pack recall a film from 1958 directed by Stanley Kramer, *The Defiant Ones*, in which a black convict (Sidney Poitier) escapes, handcuffed to a white racist (Tony Curtis). In this earlier film, though, the men are eventually recaptured and learn to respect each other.

Poitier starred in rather comfortably middle-class films with a race angle such as *The Blackboard Jungle* (Brooks, 1955), *Lilies of the Field* (Nelson, 1963), *To Sir, With Love* (Clavell, 1966), *Guess Who's Coming to Dinner* (Kramer, 1967), *In the Heat of the Night* (Jewison, 1967) and *They Call Me MISTER Tibbs!* (Douglas, 1970). These films offered white liberal America's answer to the race issue – assimilation into white, middle-class society. They embodied the very antithesis of both the political position and the filmmaking style adopted by van Peebles.

ACTIVITY

Watch one or two films starring Poitier and identify as many ways as possible in which these films are different both thematically and stylistically from *Sweetback*.

How do we respond to the central character? Is it possible to identify with him? Isn't he too emotionally controlled, distant and cold? Is he without emotions, or incapable of emotions? Are we to assume this is as a result of his experience of life, or his experience at the hands of the Man? He is capable of sudden, extreme violence. He is perhaps ultimately nothing more than the stereotypical black male stud. Does he offer something to which black males should aspire? Or is this a (white) middle-class critical position that fails to appreciate the working-class African-American context?

How do we respond to the representation of sex and the representation of gender? The women take in the street urchin, Sweetback, but then rape him as a 10-year-old. Or, is this as Black Panther leader Huey P. Newton claimed, baptising him into manhood?[1] Women in the film express great natural pleasure in sex. Is this threatening to middle-class sensibilities and values? But aren't women also seen to be nothing less than happy with working as prostitutes? Is the representation of black women as whores and black men as gigolos and pimps politically positive or progressive? Or is this *concern* again a (white) middle-class perspective?

Note

1 Newton, H. P. (1971) 'He Won't Bleed Me: A Revolutionary Analysis of *Sweet Sweetback's Baadasssss Song*', *The Black Panther*, June 19.

Further Reading

Bogle, D. (2001) *Toms, Coons, Mulattoes, Mammies and Bucks: An Interpretative History of Blacks in American Films*. London: Continuum

Donalson, M. B. and Donalson, M. (2003) *Black Directors in Hollywood*. Austin: University of Texas Press

van Peebles, M. (1996) *The Making of Sweet Sweetback's Baadasssss Song*. Edinburgh: Payback Press

Worley, D. and Perry, J. (1994) *African American Literature: An Anthology of Nonfiction, Fiction, Poetry and Drama*. National Textbook Company: Chicago

Solaris (Tarkovsky, USSR, 1972)

Figure 19.6 *Solaris* (Creative Union of Writers and Cinema Workers, USSR, 1972, *Dir*: Andrei Tarkovsky).

Andrei Tarkovsky's *Solaris* can only be described as one of the most significant films of the science fiction genre, with its hallucinatory meditations on the nature of grief, and its lyrical pace and rhythm. Tarkovsky presents his narrative through slow and complex storytelling, and a visually stark *mise-en-scène* reflected in a similarly stark cinematography.

The plot of *Solaris* is relatively standard science fiction fare, and yet, unlike most contemporary science fiction films, reveals so much about the human condition, and the very nature of humankind.

Chris Kelvin (Donatas Banionis) is sent by The Academy of Science to a space station orbiting the planet Solaris, with the task of convincing the three scientists on board the station that their studies of the planet have achieved no tangible results and that they should abandon the space station. The planet is actually a great consciousness that has connected with those aboard the space station (and indeed, probably with the space station itself) and which allows their thoughts to become reality. The scientists are all suffering hallucinations and mental break-down, and their behaviour has become strange and strained. One of the scientists has killed himself and has left a videotaped oblique message for Chris that shows him as tormented by visions of a lost loved one.

He soon begins to see other people on the space station, and comes to realise that these are not hallucinations, but beings with a tangible sense of reality. Below the space station, the surface of the planet Solaris boils. Like the scientists, Chris barricades himself inside his room only to wake to find a woman who is the image of his dead wife Hari (Natalya Bondarchuk) in there with him. He lures her to his spacecraft and launches her into space. Later that day Hari appears to Chris again, and this time he approaches her more calmly. Introducing her to the scientists as his wife, they suggest that she may have been created by Solaris, shaped from Chris' memories and made from neutrinos.

One of the scientists comes up with a plan to bombard Solaris with Chris' brain-wave pattern in the hope that it will prevent the planet from creating any more of these apparitions, and as they carry out this plan islands begin to form on the surface of Solaris. Hari asks the scientists to destroy her and Chris is then left with the decision to return to Earth or stay on the space station above Solaris in the hope that he can once again encounter Hari.

The film ends with Chris at his father's house, with his dog and his father. However, something is wrong, and water is falling inside the house. His father seems to be ignorant of this, and as the camera pulls back it is revealed that everything is on one of the islands that have emerged on Solaris.

Central to Tarkovsky's film is the concept of 'truth', a concept that is portrayed as something shifting and intangible, and one that underpins the scientists' slow unravelling. Chris is presented as a practical scientist and evangelist for human advancement, yet he too crumbles in the face of truths about himself and his relationship with his wife. Humankind is seen as self-deceptive, and even when the truth of a situation is unveiled, it is ignored in favour of a more convenient theory that supports an aggression or a destructive response.

The destructive nature of humankind is another theme that Tarkovsky examines in *Solaris*. Each of the inhabitants of the space station is led to self-destruction through their unconscious guilt and self-loathing. This is externalised by the proposition that they blast Solaris with a massive dose of radiation in one last attempt to understand what the planet is. In this, Tarkovsky symbolises the human race's principal failing, its natural state of aggression and of destroying what it does not or cannot understand. To some extent he could be seen to be making an observation about his own Soviet society, or indeed about the West's attitude to the Soviet Union.

Solaris is at the edge of human endeavour, and the failure of the scientist at this furthest outpost introduces another theme, that of human reliance upon technology. The boundaries that contain humankind are pierced by technology with little regard for the consequences, and little appreciation that boundaries are sometimes not only for constraining endeavour, but also for protecting endeavour from what is outside the boundary. This is, of course, a symbolic representation of humankind's psychological self with the boundary representing the division between the conscious and the unconscious self. Inevitably, when these two identities are exposed to each other, the result is a breakdown of reality.

In this breakdown, Tarkovsky introduces his last major theme – that of love, a love bound to guilt, regret and longing. All who inhabit the space station suffer some form of longing springing from guilt and regret. It is this that causes Solaris to create the 'guests' for them, perhaps in an attempt to fill the void that eats away at them, or perhaps to torture them with what they can never have again. The inhabitants of the space station are all empty, drained of love and therefore drained of life. They appear soulless and unable to engage on human terms, and it is only through the apparitions that surround them that their passions and humanity are reignited, albeit briefly.

The ending sees Chris engage with the Solaris' created representation of his father and his father's house, even though he recognises that it is an illusion. He does this because underpinning the entire film is a desire for reconciliation and closure, and by accepting the superficial creation as real, Chris sets himself on a path towards achieving inner peace once more.

Supporting Media

http://uk.youtube.com/watch?v=5_0UPh5FELg
Final sequence of *Solaris*

http://uk.youtube.com/watch?v=1Tob56Mebl8&feature=related
Original trailer

http://uk.youtube.com/watch?v=IFtNG1wZ4zU
Interview with Andrei Tarkovsky (part 1)

http://uk.youtube.com/watch?v=6oRTH659KBA&feature=related
Interview with Andrei Tarkovsky (part 2)

Happy Together (Wong Kar Wai, Hong Kong, 1997)

Figure 19.7 *Happy Together* (Hong Kong 1997 *Dir*: Wong Kar Wai).

Wong Kar Wai is an art house auteur producing visually distinctive films which deal with difficult concepts about existence and belonging. He has also been described as fashionable, cool and hip which partly explains his cross-over appeal, as well as the description of his films as style over substance. Crucial to understanding the films of Wong Kar Wai is the influence of living and working in Hong Kong during the buildup to and handover from Britain to China.

INFORMATION BOX – HONG KONG i

Hong Kong has always been a colony. Initially it 'belonged' to China but became a British colony after the opium wars in the mid-nineteenth century. Hong Kong was administered by Britain (people in Hong Kong had British passports) until the agreement to 'hand back' Hong Kong to China in 1997. This process became known as the 'handover' and the people of Hong Kong were now Chinese citizens.

ACTIVITY

What are the connotations of the terms used to describe Hong Kong's situation such as 'belonging' and 'handover'? Can you imagine what it might feel like to live in a country going through this process?

Wong Kar Wai as auteur

The earlier films of Wong Kar Wai have a very distinctive visual style (this changed in later films such as *In The Mood For Love* (2000)). The characteristics include:

- harsh lighting and saturated colours
- shift between black and white and colour
- non-naturalistic colour filters
- wide-angle lenses
- in shot speed changes, moving from 'normal' (twenty-four) speed to twelve or eight frames per second (or the other way round); this creates a signature style of blurred scenes
- long takes, mobile camera
- jump cuts
- almost no conventional establishing shots
- characters filmed through glass, an emphasis on reflections
- overall, the style is anti-realist.

The cinematographer on nearly all of Wong Kar Wai's films is Christopher Doyle and his contribution to the overall look of the film is clearly vital. In his published journal (1997) of the shoot for *Happy Together*, Doyle refers to 'our signature style' and discussions with Wong Kar Wai about the structure and direction of the narrative, indicative of a collaborative artistic process.

ACTIVITY

- Choose two sequences which you feel illustrate the 'signature style', and identify the different characteristics. How does this style reflect the characters' relationship?
- In *Happy Together* there are very marked shifts between the use of black and white and colour. Make a note of which scenes are in colour; what links these different scenes?

Happy Together deals with many of the key themes associated with the work of Wong Kar Wai:

■ Desire and loss: relationships are usually transient or unrequited; the films often deal with the 'missed moment' when two people could have met.
■ Personal and national identity: can people be defined by belonging to a specific nation?

These major themes are then explored through particular motifs and ideas:

■ Journeys: *Happy Together* is a road movie, the characters have travelled from Hong Kong and Taiwan to Argentina.
■ Time: *Happy Together* has a very specific time span (1995–1997) but within that there is little indication of linear or chronological time. The visual style seems to be a way of representing time and memory as fragmented and uncertain.
■ The city: a harsh, crowded, alienating place. *Happy Together* is unusual in that it is set in Buenos Aries rather than in Hong Kong, but it is represented in a similar way.
■ Repetition and doubles: the narrative is full of repeated narrative events and the characters repeat their actions; Ho and Lai's relationship is always about 'starting over'.
■ Allegories: *Happy Together* is not a realist film; its themes are presented allegorically with the characters symbolising cultural and political concepts.

ACTIVITY

■ How many examples of repeated actions, settings and plot events can you list in the film?
■ How does *Happy Together* differ from a conventional narrative structure?

Representation of national identity

Happy Together is set in Buenos Aries, a port like Hong Kong, which underlines one of the main themes, that of transience and impermanence. Although the film was shot on location in Buenos Aries, the stylised nature of the visuals means that it is not a realist representation of place. The narrative of characters leaving home for a strange, exotic location is a frequent one in Hollywood cinema of all genres – interestingly, American characters often go to Asian cities, and in *Happy Together* Argentina has a similar function for Ho and Lai.

Themes of national identity are evident from the beginning of *Happy Together*. The film starts with a close-up of Lai and Ho's passports, symbols of one form of identity: nationality. The shot contrasts the passport photos of Asian faces with the line declaring them to be 'British nationals'. The immigration stamp is dated May 1995, two years before the handover. The stamp suggests a deadline: what will Lai and Ho be after this date? Immediately after this image, which raises the issue of the handover, comes the title: *Happy Together*.

ACTIVITY

■ How else is the passport used in the film? What does it symbolise about the characters' relationship with each other and with their country?
■ What different meanings does the title have? How does it relate to characters and places?

Happy Together as allegory

In Wong Kar Wai's films the characters are symbols of ideas and places as well as of particular personalities and relationships. In *Happy Together* the relationship between Ho and Lai could represent the situation of Hong Kong in the run-up to the handover:

■ The constant reference to the relationship 'starting over' suggests the end of one relationship (Britain and Hong Kong) and the beginning of another (with China).
■ The repeated breakups, aggression and anxiety in the relationship suggest the difficulties of living under the rule of another country and anxieties about the future.
■ The characters' feelings of being trapped (reflected in the claustrophobic settings) in a relationship which has no future is indicative of Hong Kong's impotence in defining its own identity.
■ Ho and Lai are caught up in an obsessive relationship – unable to live together or apart. The concept of living apart together is perhaps a hopeful representation of Hong Kong's future as a Chinese colony.

Asian cinema and sexuality

Happy Together was the subject of some controversy on its release in Hong Kong owing to its representation of gay relationships; homosexuality had only been decriminalised in Hong Kong in 1993. In fact *Happy Together* was one of several Chinese language films of the period which deal with homosexuality. These include:

Yang + Yin: Gender in Chinese Cinema (Stanley Kwan, 1996)
The Wedding Banquet (Ang Lee, 1993)
Farewell My Concubine (Chen Kaige, 1993)
Lan Yu (Stanley Kwan 2002)

ACTIVITY

- Genre: Compare the use of the iconography of the road movie in *Happy Together* with more conventional examples such as *Thelma and Louise* (Ridley Scott, 1991). *Happy Together* could also be compared to *Stranger Than Paradise* (Jim Jarmusch, 1984) in its use of genre and visual style.
- Authorship: Watch some of Wong Kar Wai's other films such as *Chungking Express*, and *Blueberry Nights* (2007) (his only US film so far) and consider to what extent they deal with similar themes.

Bibliography

Doyle, C. (1997) 'To the End of World'. *Sight and Sound* (May). BFI

Payne, R. M. 'Ways of Seeing Wild: The Cinema of Wong Kar-Wai'. *Jump Cut:* a review of contemporary media at http://www.ejumpcut.org

Wright, E. 'Wong Kar-Wai' at http://www.sensesofcinema.com/contents/directors/02/wong.html

Fight Club (Fincher, US, 1999)

Fight Club is a revealing film to study; its themes and reception make this an unusual and controversial film.

Production context

> 'Those idiots just green lit a $75m experimental movie.' (David Fincher)

> 'This is a seditious movie about blowing up people like Rupert Murdoch.' (Twentieth Century Fox executive)

(Both quoted in Waxman, 2005)

Figure 19.8 *Fight Club* (*Dir*: David Fincher, 1999).

The production context of *Fight Club* illustrates one of the paradoxes of Hollywood as an industry: the funding by global conglomerates of films which attack the capitalist, consumer culture of which they are a part. In the case of *Fight Club* this strange position was exacerbated by the fact that it was also unconventional in the use of style and structure: an 'experimental movie'.

ACTIVITY

Do you think *Fight Club* is an experimental film in its use of visual style and narrative structure? Does it conform to the conventions of Hollywood cinema in any way? Does it remind you of any other films you have seen?

This paradox of production isn't new in Hollywood. The studio system has always been characterised by competing interests: Hollywood as a business, film as an art form (and by extension filmmakers as artists). That *Fight Club* was funded (it was a big-budget, star-led, special effects production) and distributed also reveals the role of producers and studio executives who protect personal projects – rather than its being due to a single, obsessive auteur.

Themes and style

The themes of the film suggest some of the reasons for the controversy it caused:

- US society – and by extension the West – is represented as fake, superficial, consumerist, dehumanising.
- People no longer have authentic emotions but ersatz ones created through buying things.

This desensitised state is symbolised through the representation of life and death:

- Serious illness is packaged into support groups which are unable to deal with real, difficult emotions.
- The narrator's job as a risk assessor for a car company has reduced life and death to a formula.

The lack of authenticity in contemporary society (life is referred to as a 'copy of a copy') is also explored in the representation of masculinity:

- Men have been feminised as they no longer have their traditional roles in society – they are no longer 'real men'.
- Meaning in life can be found through the close bond with other men (rather than women – the film has been described as homoerotic) and the experiencing of physical pain.

MISOGYNY: misogyny is the hatred of women as a sexually defined group (rather than the hatred of a specific woman). According to David Fincher, Helena Bonham Carter initially turned down the role of Marla because the film is 'so misogynist. It's just awful' (Waxman, 2005).

ACTIVITY

Gender and ideology

What different attributes and characteristics are associated with masculinity and femininity in *Fight Club*? What does this suggest about the ideology of the film?

One of the most influential critics in the US at the time of the film's release – Roger Ebert – described the film as 'cheerfully fascist' and 'macho porn – the sex movie Hollywood has been moving toward for years, in which eroticism between the sexes is replaced by all-guy locker-room fights' (read the whole review at: http://rogerebert.suntimes.com).

ACTIVITY

Do you think *Fight Club* is a fascist film? What elements in the film do you think Ebert is referring to?

The other major point of attack for critics of the film was that it is misogynistic, something that Ebert also refers to.

ACTIVITY

- What is meant by the phrase 'the sex movie Hollywood has been heading toward for years'? What does this suggest about the representation of women in Hollywood films?
- Can you find any positive reviews from *Fight Club*'s initial release?

It is interesting to note how the critical evaluation of *Fight Club* has changed since its release – now it is commonly referred to as a classic of American cinema, dealing with difficult, important themes.

Reception

Fight Club 'opened to scandalised reviews and lousy box office'; the film provoked a level of controversy similar to *Natural Born Killers* (Oliver Stone, 1994) and *Clockwork Orange* (Stanley Kubrick, 1971). The main criticism of *Fight Club* on its release was that it was socially irresponsible, encouraging its audience to re-enact the violence seen on screen (the same accusations made against *Natural Born Killers*).

INFORMATION BOX – THE COLUMBINE SHOOTINGS

i

The reception of *Fight Club* has to be understood in the context of the Columbine shootings which led to widespread concerns about the link between youth violence and the media. *Fight Club* was released in the US just five months after the shootings.

In Colorado in April 1999, two male high school students killed twelve of their fellow pupils, a teacher and then themselves. In an attempt to explain why two teenagers would do something like this, many commentators, politicians and religious leaders argued that they were influenced by violent video games (Doom), music (Marilyn Manson) and films (*Natural Born Killers*).

ACTIVITY

The violence in *Fight Club* was no more explicit than many other films (particularly in the action genre) of the period which didn't provoke the same outrage.

■ What is it about the representation of violence in *Fight Club* which made it so disturbing?

AUDIENCE THEORY AND MEDIA EFFECTS: in media studies, psychology and sociology, media effects refers to a range of theories about the effect the media has on its audience. Many of the attacks on *Fight Club* are based on the hypodermic theory: the idea that the media injects the audience with a message that they are unable to resist, leading people to act in antisocial, violent ways. For an argument against this theory see David Gauntlett, 'Ten things wrong with the effects model' at http://www.theory.org.uk/effects.htm.

Regulation and censorship

In the UK *Fight Club* was passed with an 18 certificate but with cuts; these were of scenes described by Robin Duvall of the BBFC as dealing with pleasure in pain – sadism. The scenes with cuts included the narrator beating Angel Face to a pulp, saying afterwards, 'I wanted to destroy something beautiful'.

In Hollywood there was also concern that *Fight Club* would provoke the US government into tightening regulation in the film industry. *The Hollywood Reporter* (an influential industry newspaper) argued that '[*Fight Club*] will become Washington's poster child for what's wrong with Hollywood. . . . The film is exactly the kind of product that lawmakers should target for being socially irresponsible in a nation that has deteriorated to the point of Columbine' (Busch, 1999).

ACTIVITY

Director as auteur

Watch Fincher's earlier, more mainstream film *The Game* (1997); what similarities in themes and style can you identify with *Fight Club*?

Producer as auteur

Art Linson was the producer of *Fight Club*; look up his filmography on www.imdb.com. To get a clearer sense of the work of a Hollywood producer read Linson's book *What Just Happened?*, which includes material on the production of *Fight Club*.

Bibliography

Busch, A.M. (1999) 'Hollywood Will Take it on the Chin for Fox's Morally Repulsive Fight Club'. *Hollywood Reporter*, October

Ebert, R. (1999) '*Fight* Stresses Frightful Areas'. *Chicago Sun-Times*, 15 October

Linson, A. (2002) *What Just Happened?: Bitter Hollywood Tales From the Front Line*. Bloomsbury

Taubin, A. 'So Good it Hurts'. *Sight and Sound*. BFI, November

Waxman, S. (2005) *Rebels on the Backlot*. Harper Perennial

Talk to Her (Almodovar, Spain, 2002)

Figure 19.9 *Talk to Her* (Pedro Almodovar, Spain, 2002).

The subject matter of *Talk to Her* immediately suggests why it is a controversial and unsettling film.

The story focuses on a nurse, Benigno, who has devoted his life to caring for Alicia who is in a coma, performing the most intimate tasks of her care. Before the car accident which caused Alicia's coma, Benigno was obsessed with her, secretly watching her at her dance class and following her home. Benigno believes he has a relationship with Alicia in her comatose state, one which is 'better than a lot of marriages'. In a separate – but soon to be connected – story, Marco is in a relationship with Laura, a female matador. She is gored by a bull and, also in a coma, is nursed in the room next to Alicia's. Marco and Benigno become friends, but their attitudes to their patients are very different; Marco finds that he cannot bear to touch or talk to Laura, believing her to be brain dead.

Talk To Her was Almodovar's next film after *All About My Mother* (1997), his most critically and commercially successful film to date, with an accessible style and optimistic perspective. That contrast with the more abstract nature of *Talk to Her* was another reason for its mixed reception. Although the film differs in many ways from Almodovar's previous work it is interesting to note how it actually explores his recurring themes in a more sombre way.

Almodovar as auteur

The themes explored in Almodovar's films include:

- The fluidity of gender: masculinity and femininity are shown to be constructed rather than natural, and as such characters can choose different gender identities.
- Characters that are trapped by traditional expectations of gender are shown to be weak and are often destroyed by their need to conform.
- The ambiguity of sexual identity: characters in Almodovar's films are not defined by a discrete sexual identity; they may be gay or straight at different times.

In addition, the films are self-reflexive, foregrounding the nature of filmmaking; Jose Arroyo (2002) states that central to Almodovar's films is the exploration of how images are constructed and interpreted.

Themes: ambiguity and meaning

The problem of interpretation is a central theme in *Talk To Her* – for the characters and for the audience. Watching the film can be a disorientating experience as we are never completely sure what has happened, whether we should sympathise with the characters or be horrified by them; the director deliberately does not tell us. For example, the film opens with an avant-garde theatrical performance watched by the two central characters Marco and Benigno. Marco is visibly moved by the performance, it is the first of several occasions on which we see him cry, while Benigno looks at him with incomprehension at his reaction. Both reactions are authentic but neither is shown to be right or wrong by the director. This scene suggests the differing positions available for the viewer – identification with the characters or distance from them.

ACTIVITY

There are a number of different examples of performances in *Talk To Her*. List as many as you can; you should include all kinds of performance, not just theatre.

- What themes link these different scenes?
- How does the audience (on and off screen) react to the different performances?

Communication and silence

Unsurprisingly for a film called *Talk To Her*, communication is one of the main themes – surprisingly (or ironically) the main example of communication is between Begnino and Alicia. When Alicia was awake the two did not communicate; now she is in a coma Benigno believes they do.

ACTIVITY

- Note the different scenes of communication in the film; these may range from scenes of dialogue to the changing nature of relationships.
- How many of these examples deal with misunderstandings?

The narration of the film – the way in which the director organises the story events – is one of the key ways of communicating with the audience.

ACTIVITY

- *Talk to Her* has a complex narrative incorporating a linear and flash-back structure; produce a diagram or timeline of the film to indicate the periods which are left out of the screen time.
- What information does the director keep from the audience? What effect does this have on our interpretation of the film?

The shrinking lover

One of the main disruptions to the narrative flow is the silent film pastiche – a representation of the film which Benigno went to see because he knows that Alicia loves silent cinema. In an interview Almodovar stated that he used the film within a film 'to hide something that is going on in the film and something which the spectator should not see'.

ACTIVITY

- What do you think has been 'hidden' from the spectator during the film within a film?
- What events take place off screen elsewhere in the film?
- Does the audience know if Benigno raped Alicia?
- How does the type of narration used by Almodovar link to the themes of the film?

The experience of not knowing what happens in sections of the film is part of what defines *Talk to Her* as art cinema; unlike more mainstream films it does not direct the viewer in what they should think or feel.

ACTIVITY

Do you believe Benigno did rape Alicia? Whatever you decide about this will affect your understanding of the ending of the film. What is your interpretation of the meaning of the final scenes?

METAPHYSICS: *Talk to Her* has been described as a metaphysical film: Metaphysics is a branch of philosophy concerned with the nature of being and existence, discussing what it means to be alive. Metaphysical studies seek to explain elements of existence which are not easily understood in our everyday life. It is concerned with explaining the features of reality that exist beyond the physical world and our immediate senses. One of the ways in which this is explored in the film is through Benigno's belief that he can communicate with Alicia, that she is alive in a meaningful way.

ACTIVITY

- Almodovar's work is concerned with identity and the way in which characters can choose different identities at different times. This is often represented in the way that characters exchange identities; what examples of this can you see in the film?
- *Talk to Her* is concerned with the possibility of resurrection; watch some of Almodovar's other recent films (e.g. *Volver, All About My Mother*) and consider how this theme is explored in different ways.

Bibliography

Arroyo, J. (2000) 'The Constructedness of Gender in the Cinema of Almodovar' in Fleming (ed.) *Formations*. Manchester University Press

Mackenzie, S. (2002) 'All About my Father'. *Guardian*, 17 August, available at http://www.guardian.co.uk/film/2002/aug/17/features.weekend

Marsh, S. 'Pedro Almodovar' at http://www.sensesofcinema.com/index.html

Morvern Callar (Ramsey, UK, 2002)

Figure 19.10 *Morvern Callar* (Momentum/Alliance Atlantis/BBC/Company, 2002, *Dir*: Lynne Ramsay).

A resurgence of concern over national identity was growing through the 1980s and 1990s as was the demand for a Scottish Parliament, and with the birth of the Scottish Parliament came renewed efforts to support filmmaking that reflected a Scottish national identity (in all its forms). While filmmaking had been receiving support for some years in Scotland, the focus had been on trying to produce films generic enough to succeed in international markets, yet the concerns over the dilution of Scottish identity saw this focus change to encourage filmmakers to explore Scottishness in all its forms, including the undiluted accents found in both *Trainspotting* and more so in *Sweet Sixteen*. Not only was Scotland speaking its own cinematic language, it was also doing it in its own accents, as a clearer, twenty-first-century Scottish national identity began to emerge with a representative set of distinctive messages and values.

Lynne Ramsay's 2002 success *Morvern Callar* is illustrative of an emerging and changing national identity in its darkly comic tale of Morvern Callar (Samantha Morton), a 21-year-old small town supermarket checkout girl from western Scotland, who wakes on Christmas morning to find her writer boyfriend has committed suicide. In a moment of opportunism she decides to conceal his death, and pass off his unpublished novel as her own. While there is clear amorality on display, there is an almost nihilistic charm and innocence in Morvern's actions that make the spectator question where their own morals would have taken them in this situation.

Raiding her dead boyfriend's bank account, Morvern escapes the life that the small port town offers, taking her best friend Lanna (Kathleen McDermott) with her to Ibiza to live a life of clubbing and partying. While Lanna plays to the stereotype and is devoured by the night-life, Morvern moves away from the tourist areas and sets about selling the novel for an advance beyond her dreams (to a wonderfully sophisticated English woman – something which resonates in this very Scottish of films), one that will allow her to permanently escape her former life.

Grim and minimalist, this film is strangely compelling in presenting an existentialist, post-Thatcherite view of a new, young Scotland that shrugs off the despair of the past and grips opportunity by the throat. Morvern is detached from the moment her boyfriend dies at the start of the film, and seems to be looking down on the events she drifts through and into. The hardness of life has made her into a voyeur, unable to engage fully with her own life and accordingly unable to distinguish right from wrong. Indeed, the film becomes a metaphor for a post-Thatcherite Scotland, cursed by a hard past and a current weightlessness, seeking identity, seeking a new anchor point, and seeking to redefine itself in a new, youthful context.

Morvern is struck dumb and immobile by grief at finding her boyfriend's body, and there is an almost anti-narrative sense pervading the first twenty minutes of the film, where the audience comes to share in the agony of her inability to take action. When she does act, she divorces her actions through placing her Walkman earphones in her ears and turning up the volume. The music becomes a symbol of her distance. Indeed, at times, the film itself is strangely silent except for this music, and this only serves to emphasise the metaphorical and literal emptiness of Morvern's life. This emptiness, and distance, prevents the spectator from judging her actions and allows Morvern to remain a sympathetic, if fundamentally damaged, character. It is certainly a feature of Ramsay's assured direction that Morvern's emptiness and distance is contained and enveloped by a sense of perpetual motion that makes Morvern's emotional state seem all the more fragile in its internalised confusion and numbness.

The bleakness of Morvern's situation is mirrored in the *mise-en-scène* with the cold grey granite and the sallow shadow life that she sleepwalks through in Scotland, contrasted sharply with the rich heightened tonal palette of a sun-soaked, ecstasy-fuelled Spain where everything is tinged with light and where she also becomes soaked in colour.

Structurally the film is disjointed and accordingly difficult to engage with. However, the lengthy slow opening serves to position the spectator to feel the shock and pain of the contrast when Morvern goes to Spain. Without this, the spectator might not experience the nihilism that Morvern is feeling, and may miss Lynne Ramsay's subtle shifts of mood, in the same way that only through coming out of the darkness of a hangover can the 'feeling' of light and sound be experienced. The camera work, the sound design, the lighting, and, of course, Samantha Morton's incredibly delicate nuanced performance, all combine to support the narrative to emphasise the waking dream that Morvern cannot escape. Hers is the curse of those who throw off their past in the bid for a new future, only to find it is as empty and unfulfilling as that which they are trying to escape.

Thus there is a double irony in the fact that Lynne Ramsay in making this film is throwing off the past history of Scottish filmmaking, a history that would have prevented her from making this film in the first place. In her filmmaking she is redefining Scottish film and is presenting new representations of Scotland, creating a new identity for Scottish film while making a film about a detached and empty identity created by disconnecting with the past.

Morvern Callar is undoubtedly a complex film that creates more questions than it answers, yet it is a film that is wrapped in a magical realism, the psychological realism of the distressed and of the dispossessed, and it is in this that the film's strength and fascination lies.

Supporting Media

http://uk.youtube.com/watch?v=5gmbLGmjbpg&feature=related
Morvern Callar trailer

http://uk.youtube.com/watch?v=3WA56zQ-les
Christmas party scene from *Morvern Callar*

Act A larger unit of action that usually segments the story into a beginning, middle and end (or a variant on this providing five acts, seven acts and so on). The act is often defined by a change of fortune, either for the better or for the worse, and this is a change that signifies the end of one part of the story and the beginning of another.

Actualities A primitive form of early cinema that captured simple events such as trains arriving or leaving, public events, and simple activities (such as a baby's breakfast). They differ from documentary in that they are simply recordings with no underpinning agenda or intention to position an audience.

Allegory The use of symbolism to represent deeper meanings which are often moral or political.

Avant-garde Taken from military terminology, 'avant-garde' became an accepted term for describing art which was experimental, innovative and which challenged the artistic norms of the day. Although the term can be used to describe artists at any period since the beginning of the twentieth century onward, it specifically refers to a group of movements which developed during and after the First World War (1914–1918) in Europe. These movements included Futurism, Abstraction, Cubism and Dada.

Although routinely referred to as an avant-garde movement, the Surrealists were at odds with the aims of the more purely artistic movements – wanting to pursue social and political action as well.

Bollywood This term is a pun on the word 'Hollywood'; as with 'Hollywood', it refers not only to a place of film production (Mumbai, formerly Bombay) but to a style of filmmaking.

Camera obscura Effectively a pin-hole camera on a grand scale. A room was made light-tight, except for a small hole opened to the outside world, which would suddenly reveal a mirror image of the outside world, upside-down on the opposite wall. This was developed further as lenses and mirrors were invented, and now a corrected image can be seen. This is fundamental to the way a film camera works. There is an excellent *camera obscura* on the Royal Mile in Edinburgh, Scotland.

CGI (computer-generated images) This is obviously an interesting technological development in itself, but the most important aspect of these images for the industry is probably the way in which they have made animation a much cheaper, and therefore more profitable, possibility. Traditional animation involving the production of thousands of individual drawings was both time-consuming and expensive, and as a result few feature-length animations were made. From *Toy Story* (Lasseter, 1995) onward, full-length animations have become an important part of the commercial film business.

Chambara Effectively a subgenre of the jidaigeki films, in which sword fighting is the principal element. Most Samurai films fall into this subgenre. The term is also used to describe the sword play in any film and has been used to describe the gunfights in the yakuza movies.

Culture

1 The way in which forms of human activity and interaction are socially transmitted.
2 The way of life of a particular human community living at a specific time and in a particular place.

Deconstruction This theory challenges the assumption that a text has an unchanging, unified meaning that is true for all readers, and also the idea that the author is the source of any text's meaning. The approach suggests instead that there is a multiplicity of legitimate interpretations of a text.

Theories such as this, developed particularly during the 1970s, tended to emphasise the viewer's control over the creation of the film being watched. However, other theories have attempted to demonstrate how the spectator is fixed in place by the text (or by the system of values within the text) so that audiences are manipulated by filmmakers into seeing things, and therefore thinking, in certain ways.

The tension between concepts of the reader/spectator as on the one hand active and in control, and on the other as passive and a victim, lies at the heart of ideas regarding the experience of spectatorship, or the process that is taking place as we view films.

Documentary reconstruction Usually part of a documentary, where events are reconstructed for the camera, sometimes using the locations and people involved, and sometimes using sets and actors. In contemporary documentary such reconstruction is usually labelled as such, though early filmmakers were less concerned with the legitimacy of such approaches (Edison filmed some scenes for his documentaries on the Boer War at a New York golf-club, passing it off as the 'real').

Docu-soap Very much a television development, this type of documentary follows a set of characters through a series of events across a set of documentaries (usually a three-, six- or eight-part series). Their lives, opinions and emotional states are very much to the fore, with the surface subject of the documentary often reduced to the situation of backdrop. A long-running example of this (with worldwide spin-offs) is *Airline* (Granada/LWT, ITV, UK, 1999–2005).

Drama-documentary A type of documentary that dramatises an event (or series of events) and uses the techniques of the fiction film to construct the 'real'. Such documentaries may include 'voice of God narration' to lessen the demand on the dramatisation to explain complex underpinning issues. A good example of the drama-documentary comes in *The Somme* (Darlow Smithson Productions, Channel Four, UK, 2005, *Dir*: Carl Hindmarch).

Ethnological documentary A type of documentary that looks at the lives and culture of a particular group in a scientific or analytical fashion. This would include a wide range of films from many of the Nazi documentaries made about other races to 'prove' the entitlement of the Aryan race to be declared a 'master race', through to the television documentary series *A Child of Our Time* (BBC, UK, 2000–2006) that follows the developmental issues of a group of children born in the year 2000.

Expressionism This refers to the expression of the inner thoughts or emotions of the filmmaker or a character through the use of stylistic elements of film form. Thus distorted shapes within the set design might be used to suggest, in some sense, a warped or perverted perspective on the world, and heavy shadows might be used to suggest the presence of darker aspects of human nature. The performance of actors (along with their make-up and clothing) can also become heavily stylised in order to further suggest psychological states. Clearly such heavy stylisation that moves towards symbolism is in direct opposition to the use of film to give a sense of photographic realism.

(It may well be that of the German films you consider you will come to see only *The Cabinet of Dr Caligari* as being fully expressionistic.)

Fantasmagorie (or in English, the Phantasmagoria) A 'magic lantern' show where still images were rear-projected from a movable projector on to a translucent screen, producing a 'suggestion' of a moving image. Later refined with a number of simultaneous projections, the 'magic lantern' show was in many ways responsible for building an audience for moving images.

Fascism Fascism was a nationalistic political movement that first came into organised existence in 1919 as the 'Fasci di Combattimento' Party under Benito Mussolini, who, in 1924, became the fascist dictator of Italy ('Il Duce'). Opposed to a rising tide of post-First World War socialist and communist political approaches, fascism promoted the Italian state above the individual, the Italian race above all others, and the ordinary Italian above the intellectual. Mussolini waged war in the 1930s in Ethiopia, in Spain (supporting the fascist General Franco), and in Albania, and joined forces with Germany's Adolf Hitler in 1936, declaring war on Great Britain in 1940. Overthrown by his own government in 1943, Mussolini formed a new government under the Nazi occupiers in the north of Italy. He was executed by Italian partisans in 1945, and the Fascist Party was banned.

Focus film A film that forms the central focus of research or investigation. Such films should offer significant qualities in relation to an area of investigation, and it should be relatively easy to select key scenes from them to illustrate points relating to a particular context. It is worth considering not only the film as a text (the film itself) but also the film's context (the specific production context as well as the broader social/historic/political context). A focus film may be considered as a catalyst for an event or movement, and as a symptom of an industrial or social/political condition. Such films should form the basis of consideration of other related films – either those that share common elements, or those which offer clear contrast.

French Poetic Realism A forerunner of and influence on Italian Neo-realism, and itself influenced by the German Expressionist movement (see Chapter 9 on German and Soviet cinemas of the 1920s). Poetic Realism offered a 're-created realism' that was highly stylised and studio focused, concentrating on replicating the 'real' world through the *mise-en-scène* in the studio. Despite the re-created realism, this form of cinema was highly symbolic, implanting the narrative with objects and actions that were symbolic of the main (usually male) character's situation. Some of the principal filmmakers of this movement include Marcel Carné, Julien Duvivier and Jean Renoir.

Gendaigeki Films that are set in the contemporary period and deal with present issues and debates. These often deal with themes around family life and the changing nature of gender roles in postwar Japan.

Gender Refers to the social differences between men and women, girls and boys. These are the expectations that society has about men and women's roles and responsibilities. These gender expectations will change over time and will be different in different countries and among different cultures.

Ideology A set of beliefs and values by which an individual, a group or a whole society orders its understanding of the world. Each of us views the world in a particular way; we have beliefs about how society should be organised and what values should underpin everything that happens in society but not everybody shares our view of the world; that is to say they have a different ideological perspective on things.

Investigative documentary The most common type of documentary that introduces a 'problem' or question, which it then goes on to solve. Dramatic filmic techniques are often used to heighten the tension and draw the audience into the documentary world. Much television documentary follows this format.

Jidaigeki A genre which was originally based on Kabuki theatre, but which evolved to include any period drama film prior to Japan opening itself up to Western influence (pre-1868). Most of the Jidaigeki films come from the film-making traditions of the studios based in Kyoto.

Keiko-eiga A style of filmmaking which has a distinctive (often overt) left-wing political message, or political aim, and is usually framed in a contemporary setting.

Dismissively termed 'tendency films' by the Right, these films often reflected growing dissatisfaction with the nature of studio production, and the desire by many of a new breed of filmmaker to convey their own views on society.

Melodrama Intense, heavily emphasised, if not exaggerated emotional drama often revolving around the family-related trials and tribulations experienced by a central female character.

Mockumentary A fiction film that uses documentary form to suggest it is actually a documentary. Often comic in nature, the mockumentary can be so effective in using documentary form that audiences become convinced they are watching a true documentary (many people have fallen into this trap with *This is Spinal Tap* (Mainline/Embassy, US, 1984, *Dir*: Rob Reiner), which used a very familiar and convincing 'rockumentary' style to detail the life of fictional band 'Spinal Tap').

Montage Essentially this simply means to assemble a series of shots and so refers to the process of editing any film. Within the context of post-1917 Soviet cinema where the process of editing came to be so intensely linked to the creation of meaning, the term took on a slightly more specific use with the sequencing of shots being explored in especially intense ways (the common example given is the Odessa Steps sequence in *Battleship Potemkin*).

Narrative The story of the film, usually (at this time) told linearly and in chronological order. Film narrative involves not merely the story but the methods employed to make sense of that story, and a set of conventions (of shot, of screen direction, of editing) had to evolve so that a 'standardised' way of telling cinematic stories could evolve.

Naturalism The idea that through the close observation and realistic recording of human interaction we are able to get nearer to understanding the complexities of individual characters and the wider society. This began as a late nineteenth-century movement in theatre and the novel but has had a profound influence upon film where, for instance, acting has often been judged on the ability to reproduce the fine detail of human behaviour. This may be seen as an extreme form of realism.

Neo-realism A term first employed by Italian screenwriter Antonio Pietrangeli in 1943 when describing Visconti's *Ossessione* (a film he wrote the screenplay for).

Growing out of Italian fascist documentary production, and influenced by the French filmmaker Jean Renoir's poetic realism, this movement set out to use a documentary style; to use location shooting rather than studio re-creation; to show the reality of everyday life (dropping in and out of the narrative with little by way of explanation of histories or prediction of futures); to focus on social reality (poverty, unemployment, political/social unrest/change); to use 'natural' dialogue and non-professional actors to deliver it; and to avoid literary adaptation, instead using 'real' stories developed for the cinematic medium.

Using long takes, deep focus cinematography, largely natural light, handheld camerawork, and (in the original Italian movement) dubbed sound, the style was sparse, stark and documentary-like.

Playback singing A technique under which songs are pre-recorded by specialist singers allowing the actor to lip-synch the lyrics. Playback singers have an acclaimed role in the Bollywood film industry.

Plotting A story is 'plotted' by taking out the key elements, the parts of the story that have dramatic effect and can be visualised. This can be approached by writing down a single short sentence that sums up an element (which will become a scene) on a small card. These cards can then be laid out, reorganised, removed or added to, until a skeleton of the plotted narrative emerges.

Power The various forms of control some individuals and groups within society have over other individuals and groups.

Propaganda The purposeful manipulation of an audience's thoughts, behaviour, beliefs and attitudes, usually towards a common ideology. Filmmakers often use symbols, specifically charged dialogue, or carefully constructed visual sequences to 'position' an audience. The fascists believed film to be a powerful tool of propaganda, and ensured that all of their filmmakers were schooled in the techniques of propaganda.

Propaganda film A film made with the express intention (either by the filmmaker or by those commissioning the film) of persuading an audience of the validity of a particular viewpoint, and positioning them to share that viewpoint. Documentary works particularly effectively as a medium of propaganda due to its nature of representing the 'real' and in the audience's unquestioning belief in its depiction of 'truth'.

Governments (British, American, Soviet, Nazi German, fascist Italian, and Japanese, among many others) have used the power of documentary as a propaganda tool in order to shepherd their people into a particular belief or cause, and history shows that it has been an effective technique.

Proscenium arch The primitive cinema relied on a fixed camera position with everything happening within the single positioned frame. The audience were in the same position in relation to the action as they were in the theatre, with the action 'framed' by the theatrical 'arch' that rises from the stage (though the Lumière films are somewhat unique in usually seeking a diagonal angle to emphasise the depth of the scene). This differs from later early cinema, which, once editing and a range of shot sizes were developed, 'moved' the audience around the action, creating a much more dynamic effect on spectators who themselves were developing a greater sophistication within the medium.

Realism A cinematic style that attempts both to use filmmaking techniques to create the 'illusion of reality' (and thereby allows an audience to engage with the on-screen subject as 'real') and to shoot narratives that are representative of 'the real' without attempting to 'fix' a meaning on them (allowing the audience to 'read' a film's reality in a variety of ways according to their own view on the subject, and to what they see on screen).

Representation The variety of ways in which individuals and groups are displayed to audiences within the media and other cultural texts.

Scene A single unit of action within a film, usually defined by location. When a character moves out of one location and appears in another it is usually seen as a scene change (unless there is continuous on-screen movement between the scenes, in which case it is seen as a sectionalised scene, numbered 1a, 1b and so on). Scenes can be seconds long (a single shot of an eye at the sights of a rifle, for example) or lengthy, with conversations, entrances, exits and action dominating them.

Sequence A set of related scenes will build into a sequence, where they become a larger unit of story. Sequences may follow a task or an action (such as the defusing of a bomb, or a chase) intercut with some related scenes (the bomb-maker travelling to the airport, or a freight train heading towards a level crossing), or may be structured around a set of scenes with a common element running through them.

Sex Refers to the biological differences between men and women. Sex is fixed and does not change over time; it is the same across countries and across cultures, while gender is often different.

Shomingeki A genre of (principally) comic drama films that deal with the lives of the middle class, and the difficulties presented by corporate life. Such films offer clear criticism of the nature of postwar Japanese culture, through the gentle mocking of characters who have been industrialised.

Spectacle The 'camera-trickery' of early cinema that initially excited and has led to this period being termed a 'cinema of attractions'. Of course this use of spectacle developed the audience's sense of cinema not merely as a visual medium but as one that provoked sensation (of being run over, of exploding, of going to the moon). As primitive cinema underwent its transformation, it was recognised that the audience needed more than spectacle alone – spectacle had to be carried by emotional involvement, by strong stories and identifiable characters, for it to continue to be a key element of cinematic expression.

Spectator Technically this term is most correctly associated with a psycho-analytical approach to film which focuses upon the relationship of the individual to film. The approach suggests that in following the narrative certain subject positions are constructed for the viewer to occupy; men, for example, might iden-tify with the male hero and women with the female protagonist hoping to achieve marriage. It was brought to prominence by feminist film theory in the 1970s which saw the dominant positions offered for the viewer by classical Hollywood films as being essentially 'masculine'.

Surrealism An art movement based on the unexpected and shocking juxta-position of unrelated images.

Synoptic This word is related to the word 'synopsis', and literally means 'of, or relating to a summary'. In this instance it is used to point towards the nature of the FM4 Varieties of Film Experience as bringing relevant elements of the learning from the other units at AS and A2 to bear on a single film, and to suggest that this earlier learning has a clear place here.

Synthesising learning At AS level there was a clear and strong focus on the construction of meaning and emotion, and on the relationship between producers and audiences. This was defined through the application of macro and micro techniques, and dealt with issues of how spectators made meaning from an extract, and through the examination of British and American film through their producers, audiences and broader contexts.

At A2, the learning developed across two units and a range of topics is brought together and synthesised to approach a research project (that may have been stimulated by study of AS level units) and a practical creative project where meaning and emotion may be explored within a 'live' context of producer and audience.

The significant factor here is in focusing learning undertaken down to these two projects, applying knowledge and skills in a practical research or constructional way.

Vampire films These movies stretch back to at least the silent *Nosferatu* (Murnau, 1922) and feature female as well as male vampires. The most interesting discussions around these films involve issues to do with gender, sexuality and power. It is possible to see both male and female vampires as reflecting male desire and/or being connected to misogynistic attitudes. On the other hand, female vampires do put the woman in a position of power.

Voyeurism and film A voyeur is a person who gains sexual pleasure or satisfaction from watching others (although it can also refer to an extreme interest in scandal or tragic events), while remaining hidden. While film theorists have used the concept to explain our enjoyment of watching films, filmmakers have also used it as a theme in their work. The most celebrated example of this is Hitchcock whose film *Rear Window* (1953) makes explicit the pleasures of spying on others.

The infamous scene in *Reservoir Dogs* (Tarantino, 1992), when Mr Blonde tortures his hostage, may also be read as an exploration of the voyeuristic impulse. Tarantino explicitly moves the camera away from the most horrific scene, asking the spectator to examine their reaction – disappointment? Wanting to see?

White telephone films Under the fascist dictator Benito Mussolini, filmmaking came under state control. Mussolini dictated that Italian film must show Italy in a positive light, and should compete directly with film being produced in Hollywood. This led to the production of films set in the decadence of grand hotels, swish nightclubs and the first-class lounges of ocean liners, reflecting the similar decadence prevailing in 1930s Hollywood musicals and screwball comedies. The height of extravagance at the time was to have a white telephone (telephones were usually black), and this became the symbol of these films and their Art Deco *mise-en-scène*. The films were largely lightweight comedies, musicals and easily resolved dramas (most often set in the glow of Roman history, in the greatness of a fascist future, or in the sophistication of an urban reflection of America), offering an idealised view of Italy far removed from its peasant economy.

Yakuza The Japanese gangster film. This genre deals directly with the young, organised criminal gangs that became established in urban Japan in the 1960s, and through highly stylised ultra-violence reflect key sociological divides in the postwar image of Japan.

WEB RESOURCES

www2.tky.3web.ne.jp/~adk/kurosawa/J-AKpage.html
Akira Kurosawa database

www.articlemagazine.com/articlesp99/drothbarbody.html
The Cinema of Revolution by Daniel Rothbart – detailed exploration of Pontecorvo and *The Battle of Algiers*

www.bbfc.co.uk
The British Board of Film Classification

www.bfi.org.uk
The British Film Institute

www.carleton.edu/curricular/MEDA/classes/media110/Voigt/paper5.html
Essay on Neo-realism

www.cjr.org
Up-to-date information on who owns what in the media entertainments industry

www.cyberfilmschool.com
Cyber Film School: Pro-end DV filmmaking site

www.disney.co.uk *or* disney.go.com
www.earlycinema.com
A host of great information, biographies, timelines and so on with a focus on early cinema

http://easyweb.easynet.co.uk/~s-herbert/momiwelcome.htm
The unofficial MOMI (Museum of the Moving Image) site. Cannot be bettered for a detailed and informative look at early cinema

www.errolmorris.com
Errol Morris official site

http://festival.sundance.org
The official website for the Sundance Film Festival, including interviews with directors, short films and details of forthcoming events

www.filmsite.org

www.gpc.peachnet.edu/~jriggs/film1301/notes10.htm
Study guide for Neo-realism

www.greencine.com
Megan Ratner's article on Neo-realism

www.inblackandwhite.com
Useful overview of key Italian Neo-realist films and filmmakers

www.imdb.co.uk
The Internet Movie database; a fantastic resource, includes filmographies of early cinema filmmakers

www.institut-lumière.org/english/frames.html
The official French site dedicated to the Lumière brothers

http://inventors.about.com/library/inventors/blmotionpictures.htm
History of the motion picture – full of biographies, company case studies and information.

www.jmdb.ne.jp/
Japanese movie database

www.michaelmoore.com
Michael Moore official site

www.movie-reviews.colossus.net
Movie review site

www.newscorp.com

www.nickbroomfield.com/home.html
Nick Broomfield official site

http://pears.lib.ohio-state.edu/Markus/Welcome.html
Kinema Club site – good academic papers and reference material

www.screenonline.org.uk
BFI's ScreenOnline archive – excellent articles, biographies, and resources on diverse subjects

www.script-o-rama.com
Script and screenwriting site

www.slamdance.com
The official website for the Slamdance Film Festival, with interviews with directors, short films and details of forthcoming programmes

www.sony.net

www.supersizeme.com
Official website for the film *Supersize Me* with details on Morgan Spurlock

www.timewarner.com

http://website.lineone.net/~luke.mckernan/Links.htm
Early cinema gateway, listing links to various useful sites

BIBLIOGRAPHY

Abrams, N., Bell, I. and Udris, J. (2001) *Studying Film*. London: Hodder Arnold

Aitken, I. (1988) *The Documentary Film Movement: An Anthology*. Edinburgh: Edinburgh University Press

Anderson, J. and Richie, D. (1993) *The Japanese Film*. Princeton: Princeton University Press

Baliol, T. (1985) *The American Film Industry*. Wisconsin: University of Wisconsin Press

Barnes, J. (1998) *The Beginnings of the Cinema in England, 1894–1901*. Exeter: University of Exeter Press

Barnouw, E. (1993) Documentary: *A History of the Non-fiction Film*. Oxford: Oxford University Press

Bassinger, J. (1993) *A Woman's View: How Hollywood Spoke to Women 1930–1960*. London: Random House

Biskind, P. (2004) *Down and Dirty Pictures: Miramax, Sundance and the Rise of Independent Film*. London: Bloomsbury

Block, B. (2001) *The Visual Story*. London: Focal Press

Bondanella, P. (1993a) *Italian Cinema: From Neorealism to the Present*. London: Continuum

Bondanella, P. (1993b) *The Films of Roberto Rossellini*. Cambridge: Cambridge University Press

Bordwell, D. (1994) *Ozu and the Politics of Cinema*. Princeton: Princeton University Press

Bordwell, D. and Thompson, K. (eds.) (1997) *Film Art: An Introduction*. New York: McGraw Hill

Bordwell, D. and Thompson, K. (2003) *Film History: An Introduction*. New York: McGraw Hill

Bruzzi, S. (2000) *New Documentary: a Critical Introduction*. London: Routledge

Buckland, W. (2000) *Teach Yourself Film Studies*. London: Hodder & Stoughton

Catterall, A. and Wells, S. (2001) *Your Face Here: British Cult Movies Since the Sixties*. London: Fourth Estate

Chanan, M. (1995) *The Dream That Kicks: The Prehistory and Early Years of Cinema in Britain*. London: Routledge

Christie, I. (1995) *The Last Machine*. London: British Film Institute

Clayton, J. (1993) *Journalism for Beginners*. London: Piatkus

Cook, P. (ed.) (1999) *The Cinema Book*. London: BFI

Corrigan, T. (1997) *A Short Guide to Writing About Film*. Harlow: Longman

Cousins, M. (2004) *The Story of Film*. London: Pavillion

Davies, S.P. (2001) *A–Z of Cult Films and Film-makers*. London: B.T. Batsford

Dyer, R. (1979) *Stars*. London: BFI

Gaffney, F. (2008) *Screenwriting*. Auteur

Gamm, K. (2004) *Teaching World Cinema*. London: BFI

Gledhill, C. and Williams, L. (eds) (2000) *Reinventing Film Studies*. London: Arnold

Grant, B.K. (ed.) (2004) *Planks of Reason: Essays on the Horror Film*. Lanham, MD: Scarecrow Press

Hardy, F. (ed.) (1966) *Grierson on Documentary*. London: Faber

Hayward, S. (2000) *Cinema Studies: The Key Concepts*. Abingdon: Routledge

Hill, A. (1997) *Shocking Entertainment: Viewer Response to Violent Movies*. Luton: University of Luton Press

Hill, J. and Church-Gibson, P. (eds) (1998) *Oxford Guide to Film Studies*. Oxford: Oxford University Press

Hollows, J. and Jancovich, M. (eds) (1995) *Approaches to Popular Film*. Manchester: Manchester University Press

Hunter, L. (1994) *Screenwriting*. Hale

Izod, J. and Kilborn, R. (eds) (2000) *From Grierson to Docusoap: Breaking the Boundaries*. Luton: University of Luton Press

Katz, S. (1991) *Film Directing Shot by Shot*. Wiese

Kolker, R. (1983) *The Altering Eye*. Oxford: Oxford University Press

Lacey, N. (2005) *Introduction to Film*. Basingstoke: Palgrave Macmillan

Levy, E. (1994) *Cinema of Outsiders*. New York: NYU Press

Liehm, M. (1984) *Passion and Defiance: Film in Italy from 1942 to the Present*. Berkeley: University of California Press

Marcus, M. (1986) *Italian Film in the Light of Neorealism*. Princeton: Princeton University Press

Medved, M. (1992) *Hollywood vs America: Culture and the War on Traditional Values*. London: HarperCollins

Neale, S. (ed.) (1998) *Contemporary Hollywood Cinema*. London: Routledge

Nelmes, J. (ed.) (1999) *An Introduction to Film Studies*. Abingdon: Routledge

Owen, A. (2003) *Story and Character: Interviews with British Screenwriters*. London: Bloomsbury

Parkinson, D. (1995) *History of Film*. London and New York: Thames and Hudson

Penley, C. (ed.) (1988) *Feminism and Film Theory*. London: Routledge & Kegan Paul

Phillips, P. (2000) *Understanding Film Texts: Meaning and Experience*. London: BFI

Phillips, W.H. (2005) *Film: An Introduction*. Boston: Bedford/StMartin's

Rabinger, M. (1989) *Directing: Film Techniques and Aesthetics*. London: Focal Press

Richie, D. (1980) *Japanese Cinema: An Introduction*. Hong Kong: Oxford University Press

Robinson, D. (1998) *From Peep Show to Palace. The Birth of American Film*. University Presses of California, Columbia and Princeton

Rocchio, V. (1999) *Cinema of Anxiety: A Psychoanalysis of Italian Neorealism*. Texas: University of Texas Press

Rudin, R. and Ibbotson, T. (2002) *An Introduction to Journalism*. Oxford: Focal Press

Shipman, D. (1995) *Cinema: The First Hundred Years*. London: Weidenfeld & Nicolson

Slocum, D. (2001) *Violence and American Cinema*. London: Routledge

Stacey, J. (1994) *Star Gazing, Hollywood Cinema and Female Spectatorship*. London: Routledge

Vermilye, J. (1994) *Great Italian Films*. Secaucus, NJ: Citadel Press

Vincendeau, G. (ed.) (1996) *The Companion to French Cinema*. London: BFI

Weisser, Y. and Weisser, T. (1998) *Japanese Cinema – The Essential Handbook 4th Edition*, Vital Books

Williams, C. (ed.) (1990) *Realism and the Cinema*. London: Routledge

Yoshimoto, M. (2000) *Kurosawa*. Durham, NC: Duke University Press

INDEX

À Bout de Souffle (*Breathless*) 229, 233–7, 238, 240–1
À nous la liberté 391
À Propos de Nice (*On the Subject of Nice*) 319
Aazmi, Shabana 85
The ABC of Cinematography 301
abstract ('absolute') film 350, 362
Abstraction 188, 426
Abu-Hassad, Hany 73
accented cinema 107
accessing experimental film 361
Acres, Birt 295, 296
action 57; background 61; key 61
action descriptors 61, 62
actors, non-professional 204, 205, 215, 216, 217, 218, 400
acts 56, 426
actualities 9, 294–5, 297, 298, 300, 302, 315, 316, 317–19, 328, 426
Adams, Randall Dale 332
Adamson, Andrew 36
adventure film 197
advertising 11, 12, 354; experimental film 351; television 9, 11, 371
An Affair to Remember 149
Africa 220
L'Age d'or 184, 187, 188, 193
Agence-France-Presse 108
Agostini, Philippe 393
Ahmadinejad, Mahmoud 103
AIDS 159
Airline 331
Akhtar, Farhan 80, 94
Albania 213, 428
L'albero degli zoccoli (*The Tree of Wooden Clogs*) 201, 209–13
Alfie 44

Algeria 258
Alice 184, 197, 198–200
alienation theory 359–60
All About Eve 274, 275
All About My Mother 268–9, 270, 274–6, 278–9, 280, 281, 419
All Over Me 35
allegory 283, 412, 426
Allen, Kevin 33
Almodovar, Pedro 76, 268, 269, 274, 419–23
alternative films 354; *see also* experimental film
Althusser, Louis 253
Les Amants du Pont Neuf 34
amateur aesthetic 113
American cinema: Direct Cinema movement 332, 338–9; documentaries 316, 327, 338–40, 341; early cinema 291, 295, 297, 302, 303–10, 312, 386–91; experimental 362, 414; gothic 40–2; Japanese film influences 132–3; Neo-realist 202, 219; new queer cinema 277; single film critical studies 394–8, 401–6, 413–18; and War Industries Board 312; *see also* Hollywood
American History X 365, 377, 379
Amin, Shimit 83
Amores Perros 145, 151, 251
anarchism 186
And There Came a Man 209
Anderson, Lindsay 337
Andreotti, Giulio 226
Andrew, G. 110
animation 10–11, 12, 19, 31, 36, 99, 300; Iranian cinema 99, 107–9
antisocial behaviour 377, 379, 417

Apocalypse Now 36
Après le Bal 299
Araki, Greg 277
Arau, Alfonso 144, 150
Arbuckle, Fatty 308
Argentina 311
Ariel Awards 148, 152
Armour of God 247
Arquette, Rosanna 274
Arrancà la vida (*Tear this Heart Out*) 145, 159–60
Arriaga, Guillermo 151
Arrivé d'un Train en Gare de La Ciotat 294
L'Arroseur arrosé 297
Arroyo, Jose 420
Art Deco 215, 433
Art Theatre Guild (ATG) 136
Asano, Shiro 126
Asoka 80
Astruc, Alexander 232
'atmos' sound 54
Attack on a China Mission 298, 318
attitude, characters 58–9
Auden, W.H. 321, 323, 360
audience: active 115–16, 174, 378; defined 49, 50; demand 180, 295; documentaries 53, 63, 74–5; early cinema 294, 300, 301, 308, 369; emotional response 75, 301, 364–81; and experimental film 75, 190, 353, 360; identification 7–8, 234, 242, 271, 272–3, 396; ideology 18–19; Iranian cinema 100; manipulation 214; and media effects model 417; New Wave cinema 242; passive 115, 378; presentation 42–3, 45; target 365; *see also* spectators/spectatorship
audience theory 115, 417
Australia 294
auteur 25, 31, 34, 114, 125, 196, 395–6, 418; collaborative 31; institutional 31; producer as 418
auteur theory 231–2, 241, 395
authored documentary 340–1
automatic writing 185, 186, 190
avant-garde 188, 334, 354, 426; *see also* experimental film

Babareza, Mahmoud 108
Babel 145, 151–2, 157–8

Babylon 35
Bachchan, Amitabh 85, 87
background, action 61
Bad ma ra khahad bord (*The Wind Will Carry Us*) 202
BAFTAs 151
Baggot, King 308
Bahrani, Ramin 202, 223
Baiss, B. 40
Bakshi, Anand 88
I Bambini Ci Guardano (*The Children are Watching Us*) 203
Bamforth, James 297
Banionis, Donatas 407
Bara, Theda 308
Barbaro, Umberto 213
Barjatya, Sooraj R. 80
Barrymore, Drew 307
Barrymore, Lionel 307
Barthes, Roland 253
Basse, Wilfred 319
Bassinger, Jeanine 279
Batalla en el Cielo (*Battle in Heaven*) 145, 153–5
La Battaglia di Algeri (*The Battle of Algiers*) 202, 218, 222, 223, 399–401
Battleship Potemkin 163, 165, 166, 169, 170, 321, 430
Bayona, Juan Antonio 145
Bazin, André 4–5, 15
BBC 330, 340
behaviour, characters 58–9, 190
Behind the Rent Strike 333
beliefs 17, 19, 251
Belle de Jour 191
Belmondo, Jean-Paul 132, 241
Bend it Like Beckham 35, 120
benshi 126
Berlin: der Sinfonie der Grosstadt (*Berlin: Symphony of the City*) 318
Bertolucci, Bernardo 36, 132, 196
Besson, Luc 34
A Better Tomorrow 247
Bhaji On the Beach 35
biblical epics 298, 307, 308
The Bicycle Thieves 201, 205–9, 216, 217–18, 221, 223
Big Fish 197
The Big Shave 365, 371
The Big Swallow 298
Bigelow, Kathryn 35

Biggie and Tupac 333
Binoche, Juliet 34
Biograph 305, 306–7, 308, 324
Bioscope Expeditions 318
Birth of a Nation 309, 310, 365, 377
The Biter Bit 297
Black Panthers 403
The Black Pirate 36
The Blackboard Jungle 405
Blackboards 99
Blanchett, Cate 151, 157
blasphemy 117
Blasseti, Alesandro 217
Blaxploitation movies 32, 402
Blier, Bertrand 196
blockbusters 112
Bloody Sunday 173
Blueberry Nights 413
Boer War 324, 330
Bogart, Humphrey 240–1
Bollywood 72, 79–98, 426; comedy 80, 88,
    96; fantasy and reality 92–3; language
    81, 82, 85; melodrama 91–2, 96; mixed
    genre, use of 80; music 80, 83, 84, 85,
    95–6; presence and absence in 97–8;
    star system 93–4; themes 80, 91, 96–7
Bombay *see* Mumbai
Bombay Talkies 85
Bondarchuk, Natalya 407
Bonham Carter, Helena 415
books 39, 40
Boorman, John 130
Boquet, Carole 191
Borowik, Wlodzimierz 337
Bose, Rahul 85
Le Boulevard du Crime (*The Boulevard of
    Crime*) 392
Bowling for Columbine 339–40
Brando, Marlon 338
Brazil 202, 219, 220, 259–67, 311
Breathless 229, 233–7, 238, 240–1
Brecht, Bertolt 359–60
Breton, André 186
Brighton School 297–8
Britain 169, 193, 246, 311
British cinema 12, 423–5; documentaries
    318, 320–3, 327, 330, 332, 337; early
    cinema 294, 295, 296–8, 301–2, 312;
    Free Cinema movement 332, 337;
    industry 189; new queer cinema 277;
    Social Realism 219, 337

British Film Institute (BFI) 103, 337
British-Indian film 35
Britten, Benjamin 321, 323
Brooks, Richard 405
Broomfield, Nick 333
Browning, Tod 365, 372, 373
Brugger, Pieter Jan 243
Buckland, W. 395
buddy movies 274
The Buena Vista 339
Bullet Boy 35
Bullet in the Head 247
Bunraku puppet theatre 140
Buñuel, Luis 13, 184, 187, 191–7, 345,
    349, 351–3
Burton, Tim 36, 40–2, 197
Busch, A.M. 418
Bush, George W. 103

The Cabinet of Dr Caligari 51, 163, 165,
    172, 175–82, 345, 349, 350
Cabria 310
Cahiers du Cinema 231–2, 395
Cain, James M. 217
Caine, Michael 44
Calcutta 84, 86
Calder, Alexander 362
camera: chronophotographic 290;
    experimental film 357–8; fixed 113;
    handheld 234, 401; home-movie 296;
    kinetic 296; movement 54; moving
    shots 297; New Wave film 237, 244;
    pinhole 4, 289, 426
camera obscura 289, 426
'Le Camera Stylo' ('The Camera Writes')
    232
camp aesthetic 278, 280–1
Cannes Film Festival 107, 152, 156, 210,
    336, 401
capitalism 168, 170, 171
Capra, Frank 327
Carax, Louis 34
Cardone, J.S. 35
Carné, Marcel 76, 203, 392–4, 429
Caro, Marc 197
Carrasco, Salvador 144
Carrey, Jim 187
Carroll, Lewis 198
Casino 34
Casino Royale 51
Casler, Herman 306

Cassavetes, John 202
caste system, India 82
The Castle of Otranto (Walpole) 197
catalogue item numbers 43
catalogue of research 29–30, 38–42, 45
Catholic Church 193, 196, 211, 220, 221
Cavalcanti, Alberto 319, 321, 323, 327,
    337, 387
La Caverne Maudite 299
celluloid film 291, 293, 296
Cendrillon 299
censorship 25, 349, 379, 418; Buñuel 193;
    Indian film 86; Iranian film 100, 104,
    105, 106, 116–17; Japanese film 128,
    133, 137; self- 185
Central Office of Information 321–2, 327
Centro de Capacitacíon Cinematográfica
    (CCC) 156
Centro Do Brazil (*Central Station*) 202
Centro Experimentale Di Cinematographia
    213, 225
Centro Universitario de Estudios
    Cinematográficos (CUEC) 156
Chabrol, Claude 231
Chadha, Gurinder 25
'chain' drama 311
Chak De India (*Go For It*) 83
chambara 125, 132, 133, 427
Chan, Fruit 246
Chan, Jackie 247
Chandra, Tanuja 89
Chandran, Ravi K. 94
Channel Four 341
Chaplin, Charlie 76, 167, 307, 308, 309,
    386–91
characters 38, 58–9; attitude 58–9;
    behaviour 58–9, 190; idealised 272;
    identification with 7–8, 234, 242, 271,
    272–3, 396; motivation 190; names 61;
    Soviet cinema 171, 172; Surrealist film
    190, 191
chase films 298, 308
Chiang Kai-shek 325
chick flicks 278
Un Chien Andalou 13, 184, 187, 189, 190,
    193, 345, 349–50, 351–3, 369, 370,
    372
A Child of Our Time 330, 428
children 169–70, 173
Children of Men 151
China 229, 246, 247, 294, 311

A Chinese Ghost Story 27
Chinese-Japanese war 325 325
Ching Siu-Tung 247
Chocolat 34
Chop Shop 202, 223
Chopra, Aditya 80, 89
Chopra, Pamela 89
Chopra, Yash 79, 88, 89
chronophotographic camera 291
Chungking Express 229, 242, 244–6, 413
Churchill, Joan 333
Cimino, Michael 35
cine clubs 319
Cinecittà studios 214, 215, 225
Cinema Deraciner 159
Cinema du Look 146, 155
Cinema du Papa 233, 237
cinema of exile 100, 102, 106, 107–9
cinema of the humble 218, 219
Cinema Novo 219, 220
cinéma vérité movement 332
cinématographe 293, 294, 299, 303
cinematographers 54, 62
cinematography 38, 349
Cinevillagio (The Film Village) 215
La Ciociara (*Two Women*) 204
The Circus 387
Citizen Kane 395
City of God 251, 252, 253, 259–67
City Lights 388
City of Lost Children 197
'City Symphony' films 318, 319, 357
civil rights movement 402–3
Clair, René 391
class 19, 164–5, 171–2, 221
classification systems 379; Iran 105
Clavell, James 405
The Clearing 243
Clockwork Orange 416
Clooney, George 273
Close Up 102
close-ups 113, 297
closure 234
Cocteau, Jean 185
Cold War 127, 219
collaborative auteur 31
collaborative production 136
colonialism: British 311; French 258–9
colour film techniques 36
Columbine shootings 417
Comando Vermelho 265

comedy 1, 126; Bollywood 80, 88, 96; early 387; Italian cinema 204; Japanese cinema 125, 136; Mexican cinema 159; screwball 215; shorts 308; slapstick 126, 187, 188; Soviet cinema 165
Commedia all'Italiana 226
commentaries 30
communication 345–6, 421
communism 34, 127, 133, 168, 213, 225, 226
Communist Party 186
Como agua para chocolate (*Like Water for Chocolate*) 144, 150
composition 54
compromise 52–3
computer-generated images (CGI) 10–11, 36, 112, 427
concentration camps 327, 336
conferences 41
conflict 73, 253–4
constructs, films as 348–9
content 369–77
continuity: of action 297; in narrative 234
continuity editing 188, 189, 190, 191, 234–5, 298, 331–2
Coppola, Francis Ford 36, 128
The Corbett-Fitzsimmons Fight 295
costume drama 159
counter-cultures 253
The Craft 40
Crash 243
Crawford, Joan 278, 279
creative projects 24, 26–7, 47–68; aims and context 49, 50–2, 65; options 48; reflective analysis 49, 65–7; top tips 67–8
Crichton, Charles 34
crime 187
critical reflection 78
Cronos 152, 159
Crouching Tiger Hidden Dragon 247
Crowe, Russell 377
Crown Film Unit 327
The Crow 40
Crowther, Bosley 393
The Crying Game 365, 377
Cuarón, Alfonso 144, 145, 150–1
Cuba 220, 226
Cubism 188, 426
cultural context 17–18, 62, 251, 252; Bollywood 81–2, 83

cultural studies 25, 31–2, 34–5, 37
culture 252–3, 427
Curtis, Richard 243
Curtis, Tony 405

da Silva Quadros, Janio 265
Dada movement 188, 426
Dagover, Lil 175
Daguerre, Louis 290
Daiei Studios 133, 134, 137
Dali, Salvador 13, 184, 186, 187, 351
dance *see* song-and-dance
Dancer in the Dark 350
Danzón 144, 152
Davar, Shiamak 89
Davis, Bette 274, 278, 279
The Day the Earth Stood Still 34
The Day I Became a Woman 99–100, 268–9, 281–4
De Niro, Robert 31, 36, 371
de Santis, Giuseppe 201
de Sica, Vittorio 128, 201, 204–9, 214, 215, 216, 221–2, 223, 225
de Tavira, Jose Mari 160
Dead of Night 243
Decla-Bioscop 180
deconstruction 378, 427
The Deer Hunter 35
The Defiant Ones 405
Del Rio, Dolores 147
del Toro, Benicio 151
del Toro, Guillermo 145, 152, 159
Delon, Alain 132
DeMille, Cecil B. 308
Démolition d'un mur 297
Deneuve, Catherine 191
Denmark 311, 312
Depp, Johnny 273
The Derby 295
Deren, Maya 185, 345, 351, 353
deselected material 41–2
Deslaw, Eugene 319
Desperately Seeking Susan 274
dialogue 48, 59–62, 62; natural 204
Dibb, Saul 35
Dickson, W. K. L. 291, 305, 306, 317, 324
diegetic sound 112, 234
Dietrich, Marlene 374
digital exhibition 33
Dil Chahta Hai (*The Heart Desires*) 79–80, 94–8

Dil to Pagal Hai (*The Heart is Crazy*) 79, 88–94, 97
Dilwale Dulhaniya Le Jayenge (*The One With a True Heart Will Win the Bride*) 80, 83
Direct Cinema movement 332, 338–9
directing 48
director of photographer *see* cinematographers
directors 54, 62; Sami 32
disbelief, suspension of 238, 239
discontinuity editing 235, 236
The Discreet Charm of the Bourgeoisie 191
dissolves 190, 299
distribution 32, 33, 106; German films 180; state control of (Iran) 100
Dixit, Madhuri 83, 88, 93
docu-soap 330, 427–8
documentaries 1, 9, 10, 12, 19, 31, 271, 315–43, 331, 337; audience 53, 63, 74–5; authored 340–1; city 318, 319, 357; contemporary resurgence 339–40; editing 329, 331–2; ethnological 316, 330, 428;
expository mode 331; form or style 63, 329–35; interactive mode 332–3, 340; investigative 330, 429; Italian Fascist 202, 203, 213, 214, 215, 225; Japan 126, 141; observational mode 331–2; personal 336, 337, 340; propaganda 214, 225, 324–8, 331, 336; and the real 316, 318, 319, 324, 328–9, 331, 341; reconstruction 330, 427; reflexive mode 334–5; sound 293, 331, 338; spoof 12; step outline 26, 48, 62–5; techniques 112–13
documentary-makers mindset 53
documentary style 172, 175, 204
Don't Look Back 338
Dorani, Bezhad 223
double exposure 299
Douglas, Gordon 405
Douglas, Michael 339
Downfall 35, 37
Doyle, Christopher 410
Dracula (Stoker) 197
drama-documentary 330, 428
dreams 14, 185, 189, 196, 197
Dreams That Money Can Buy 345, 362
Drew, Robert 338

Dreyer, Carl 311
Drifters 320, 321
drugs 264
dubbing 54, 55
Duchamp, Marcel 362
duty as theme, Bollywood 91, 96–7
Duvall, Robin 418
Duvivier, Julien 203, 429
DVD, Iran 100, 103
Dylan, Bob 338

Ealing Studios 31, 34
early cinema 6, 289–313, 369
Eastman, George 290, 291, 293, 305
Eastman Kodak 305
Easy Street 388
Ebert, R. 110, 416
economic context 77
economic power 253
Ecstacy 35
Edinburgh Film Festival 103
Edison, Thomas Alva 291, 292, 296, 297, 302, 303, 305, 317, 330
editing 349; continuity 188, 189, 190, 191, 234–5, 298, 331–2; discontinuity 235, 236; documentaries 329, 331–2; elliptical 234, 236; experimental film 350, 356; New Wave 234; parallel 301, 302; Soviet cinema 164, 165, 166, 174, 356; Surrealist film 188, 190, 191
editors 54
education 200
Edward Scissorhands 40, 197
Egypt 294
1860 217
Eisenstein, Sergei 146, 155, 164, 165, 167, 170–4, 321, 356
Elite Squad 265, 266
elliptical editing 234, 236
emotional response 75, 301, 364–81
Empire 350
Empire Marketing Board 321
empowering women 74, 99–100, 268–85
Enduring Love 33
Les Enfants du Paradis (*Children of Paradise*) 76, 392–4
The English Patient 34
epics 226, 298, 307, 308, 309–10
equality, gender 269, 270
Ernst, Max 362

El espinanzo del Diablo (*The Devil's Backbone*) 152
Essanay 305, 307
Ethiopia 213, 428
ethnicity 25, 32, 35, 251, 257
ethnological films 316, 330, 428
European cinema 132, 146, 155
Every Day Except Christmas 337
exhibition 32
exile genre *see* cinema of exile
'the exotique' 295
expanded film/video 75, 344–63, 373
experimental film 11, 12, 14, 31, 344–63, 372, 414; accessing 361; audience and 75, 190, 353, 360; camera 357–8; editing 350; Iranian cinema 100; narrative 350; performance and movement in 349–50; *see also* Expressionism; German cinema; New Wave; Soviet cinema; Surrealism
Experimental Film Fund 337
Expressionism 50, 126, 155, 164, 165, 189, 203, 349, 428
Ey Iran 120

Face Off 247
fade to black 234
Fahrenheit 9/11 8, 339–40
Fairbanks, Douglas 309
fairy-tales 197, 298
family as theme: Bollywood 80, 91, 96–7; Japanese cinema 125
fans and fandom 365–6, 379–60
Fantasmagorie 289, 290, 428
fantasy 197, 198–200, 297; Bollywood 92–3
Farewell My Concubine 413
'Fascist Trilogy' 215
Fascists/Fascism 202, 203, 206, 213, 215, 219, 224, 325, 377, 428
La Fée aux choux 298
Feher, Friedrich 175
feminine/femininity 270, 271, 393–4, 415, 420
feminism 269
feminist film theory 8, 269, 270–3, 274, 278
Festen 229
festival films, Iranian 107, 110
fictional narrative 9, 12, 13, 14–15, 19, 112, 113, 125

The Fifth Element 34
Fight Club 76, 413–18
Film Centre 321
film industry 25, 32; early 292–312; funding 32, 100, 106, 414; Japanese 126–7, 133–6; regulation *see* regulation
film noir 16, 52, 65–7, 132
film schools: Iran 284; Italy 213, 225; Mexico 155–6, 161
film speed 293
film theory 14–15
film types 8–11
filmmakers, mindset 52–3
finance *see* funding
Fincher, David 76, 413–18
First World War 163–4, 178, 311–12, 324
'fitas cantatas' 311
Fitzhamon, Lewin 301
Flaherty, Robert 315, 316, 320, 321, 327, 329
flashbacks 243–4
Fleisher, Richard 128
Flemming, Andrew 40
Flemming, Victor 36
Fletcher, John 337
Flowers and Trees 36
'fly-on-the-wall' observation 172
focus films 29, 31, 33, 37, 38, 429
Fog of War: Eleven Lessons From the Life of Robert S McNamara 333
Fonda, Jane 359, 361
Ford Motor Company 337
Fordism 389
The Foresaken 35
form 369–71; Japanese cinema 126, 137–40; and theme, link between 397
Forrest Gump 35
The Four Hundred Million 325
Four Rooms 243
fourth wall 235
Fox Pictures 307
Fox Talbot, William Henry 290
Fox, William 305, 307
France 180, 189, 193, 254–9, 345, 349–50, 351–3; Cinema Deraciner 159; Cinema du Look 146, 155; colonialism 258–9; documentaries 319, 332, 335, 336; early cinema 292–4, 297, 298–300, 303, 310, 311–12; experimental film 345, 349–50, 351–3, 359–61; *see also* New Wave

immigration 259; Neo-realism 202; New Wave (*nouvelle vague*) 100, 126, 132, 135, 139, 155, 229, 230, 231–42; poetic realism 203–4, 392–4, 429; racism 259; surrealism 187, 188, 189, 191–7
Franco, General 213, 325, 428
Franjou, Georges 336, 337
Frankenheimer, John 130
Frankenstein (Shelley) 197
Frankfurt School 115
Freaks 365, 372, 373
Frears, Stephen 365
Fred Ott's Sneeze 317
Free Cinema movement 332, 337
freedom 194
French language 259
French revolution 194
Freud, Sigmund 185
From Dusk Till Dawn 35
funding 32, 100, 106, 414
Futurism 188, 426

The Game 418
Gandhi, Indira 86–7
Gangs of New York 225
gangster films 28, 34, 246; *see also* yakuza
García Bernal, Gael 151
Garibaldi, Giuseppe 217
Gates of Heaven 332
Gatti, Marcello 401
Gaumont 298, 310
Gauntlett, David 417
Gav (The Cow) 102
gendaigeki 125, 126, 129, 133, 141, 429
gender 7–8, 14, 19, 158, 221, 251, 415, 429; as performance 270–1, 283; projects 25, 31, 32, 34, 35; representation of 119–20, 261, 268–85, 405–6; and sex, distinguished 270
gender equality 269, 270
gender identity 270
gender relations, Iranian cinema 104, 114, 116, 117
gender roles, Japanese cinema 125, 127, 141
General Film Company 305, 307
generational conflict 120, 141
genre 8, 349, 397–8; German cinema 180–1; Japanese cinema 125, 136,

141; Mexican cinema 145, 159; mixed, Bollywood 80; postmodernism and 279; projects 24–5, 40–2; surrealism 180–1
genre theory 115
German cinema 34–5, 37, 73, 163–6, 175–82, 189, 345, 347–8, 362; distribution abroad 180; documentaries 318, 326–7, 328, 330; early film 310–11, 312; Expressionism 50, 126, 164, 180–2, 190, 203, 349, 350; genre 180–1; historical context 163–4; narrative structure 180–1; New Wave 230; themes 164–5
Germania Anno Zero (Germany Year Zero) 73, 216
Germany 34–5, 37, 134, 213
ghost stories 246, 247
Il Giardino del Finzi-Continis (The Garden of the Finzi-Continis) 204
Gibbons, Cedric 36
Gibson, Mel 225
Giménez Cacho, Daniel 159
Gish, Lilian 307, 308, 310
Go Fish 35, 277
Godard, Jean-Luc 155, 229, 231, 232–41, 244, 245, 345, 349, 359–61, 395
Godzilla franchise 136
Golden Lion Award 129
Gone With the Wind 36
Gonzales, Isamar 223
González Iñárritu, Alejandros 145, 151–6, 157–8, 251
good and evil 90
The Good Shepherd 36
Goodfellas 34
Gorin, Jean-Pierre 359
Gothic film 40–2, 197–8
Goulart, Joao Bechoir Marques 220, 265
government *see* state
Gowariker, Ashutosh 80, 83
Goya 193
GPO Film Unit 321, 322
Grandma's Reading Glass 298
Grant, Cary 218
The Great Train Robbery 302
Greater New York Rental Company 305
Greece 213
Greengrass, Paul 173
Grierson, John 315, 316, 320, 321–3
Griffith, D. W. 307, 309, 310, 377
Guazzoni, Enrico 310

Guess Who's Coming to Dinner 405
Guy-Blanché, Alice 298

Haggiag, Brahim 218
Haggis, Paul 243
La Haine 251, 252, 253, 254–9, 264, 267
Halliwell's Film and Video Guide 39, 377
Hallström, Lasse 34
Hamburger Hill 35
Hamer, Robert 34
Hanson, John 202
Happy Together 76, 409–13
Harry Potter and the Prisoner of Azkaban 151
Haskell, Molly 270
Haslem, Wendy 41
Haynes, Todd 277
Hays Code 35
Hayward, S. 197
Hepworth, Cecil 300, 301–2
Hernández, Marco 153
Hero 247
The Hidden Half 106
Hindi language 80, 81
Hindmarch, Carl 330, 428
Hirani, Rajkumar 85
Hirshbiegel, Oliver 35
historical context 17–18, 82, 83, 253; Brazilian cinema 265; French cinema 258–9; German/Soviet cinema 163–4; Iranian cinema 101–3; Japanese cinema 126–7
historical films 298, 308, 310–11
Hitchcock, Alfred 76, 189, 273, 365, 394–8, 433
Hitler, Adolf 213, 326, 428
The Hobbit 152
Holi festival 95
Hollywood 3, 12, 80, 128; birth of 307–10; comedies 215; film language 271–2; funding 414; and Italian film 215, 219, 226; and Marxist theory 115; and Mexican cinema 146–7, 150, 151; musicals 215; narrative structure 171; and New Wave cinema 230; realism and 239; standard 170–1; style 189, 271–2
The Hollywood Reporter 418
L'Homme Blanc (*The White Man*) 392
Un homme de têtes 299
L'Homme-orchestre 299–300

homosexuality 281, 393–4, 412–13
Hong Kong 244–7, 409–13
Hood, Gavin 251
Hopper, Jerry 36
horror films 35, 145, 159, 180–1, 187, 190, 197–8, 226, 368
Hubert, Roger 393
Hughes, Howard 36
Hum Aapke Hain Koun! (What Do I Mean to You?) 80
hypodermic theory 417

ICAIC 226
ICI 322
idealisation 272
identification 7–8, 234, 242, 271, 272–3, 396
identified issue 49, 50, 65
identity 423; gender 270; national 203, 219, 411–12, 424; repressed 198
ideology 16–17, 18–19, 171, 251, 252, 276, 415, 429
Ieri, Oggi, Domani (*Yesterday, Today, Tomorrow*) 204
Ifans, Rhys 33
illusion 2–3, 4, 7
image studies 270–1
imitation of life 239–41
The Immigrant 388
immigration, France 259
Imperial Relations Trust 321
improvisation 185
In the Heat of the Night 405
Inagaki, Hiroshi 130
Iñárritu *see* González Iñárritu, Alejandros
Ince, Thomas 307, 308
Incident at Clovelly Cottage 296
independent film 354; America 307; Japan 125, 134, 136
India: caste system 82; independence 86; language 80–1, 82, 85; marriage 84, 89; partition 86; politics 86–7; religion 82, 86; society and culture 81–2; women, role of 89
Indian cinema 84–6, 311; Neo-realism 86, 202; *see also* Bollywood; British-Indian film
industrialisation 303–7
industry *see* film industry
institutional auteur 31
institutional framework 25, 32, 35–6

Instituto Luce 214, 225
Instituto Mexicano de Cinematografía
    (IMCINE) 147, 148, 161
interactive documentary form 332–3,
    340
interactivity 345–6
international film styles 73
internet 39, 41, 294, 341
Intolerance 309–10
investigative documentaries 330, 429
The Ipcress File 44
Iqbal 83
Iran: Islamic culture 104, 105–6, 107;
    Ministry of Culture and Arts (MCA)
    102; political history 101–3; religion
    105–6, 116
Iranian cinema 72, 99–123, 268, 281–4;
    accented 107; audience 100;
    censorship/regulation 100, 104, 105,
    106, 116–17; cinema of exile 100, 102,
    106, 107–9; conventions of 122;
    experimental 100; festival films
    (art house) 107, 110; funding 100;
    gender/gender relations 104, 114, 116,
    117, 119–20; generational conflict 120;
    history 101–3; nationalism and
    patriotism 120; Neo-realism 202; and
    new technology 100; New Wave 100,
    102; and politics/political background
    101–3; state and 100, 104; themes
    116, 119–20; Western influences 116;
    women and 99–100, 102, 104, 114,
    117, 122
irising 234
Islamic society 104, 105–6, 107
Italian cinema: documentaries 202, 203,
    213, 214, 215, 225; early cinema 310,
    312; epics 310; and Hollywood 215,
    219, 226; newsreels 213, 215, 225;
    White Telephone 214, 215, 225, 433;
    see also Italian Neo-realism
The Italian Job 44
Italian Neo-realism 86, 126, 155, 201–28,
    399–401; criticism of social and
    political institutions 203, 221–4; and
    other national cinemas 202, 203,
    219–20; political context of 211,
    213–15; social context of 206, 215;
    style 210, 216, 217–18
Italy 189
Ivens, Joris 319, 325, 327

Jackson, Peter 152, 197
Jagmagia, Kassim 94
Janowitz, Hans 175, 178, 181
Japanese cinema 72, 124–43, 294; and
    American film, influence on 132–3;
    censorship 128, 133, 137;
    documentaries 126, 141; early 311; film
    form 126, 137–40; gender roles 125,
    127, 141; genres 125, 136, 141;
    historical background 126–7;
    independent production 125, 134, 136;
    industry 126–7, 133–6; New Wave 125,
    134, 135–6, 139, 140; political context
    126, 140–1; politics 125; production
    contexts 126; social context 126,
    140–1; themes 125, 137; western/
    European influences 126, 132; women
    and 137, 141
Japón (*Japan*) 145
Le Jardinier et le petit espiegle 297
Jarmusch, Jim 413
Jennings, Humphrey 321, 327
Jenson, Vicky 36
La Jetée 345, 350, 351, 353–4
Jeunet, Jean-Pierre 155, 197
Jewison, Norman 405
Jews 259
jidaigeki 125, 126–7, 128, 129, 132, 133,
    140, 141, 429
Jodhaa Akbar 80
Johar, Karan 80
Johnny Gaddar (*Johnny Traitor*) 85
Johnstone, Claire 271
Jordan, 365, 377
Judith of Bethulia 307
Jules et Jim 229
Julien, Isaac 277
jump cuts 235, 236, 244

kabuki theatre 125
Kagemusha 128
Kaige, Chen 413
Kalem Picture Company 305, 307
Kalin, Tom 277
Kapadia, Dimple 94
Kapo 223
Kapoor, Karisma 88
Kapoor, Pankaj 85
Kapoor, Shahid 83
Kassovitz, Mathieu 251, 254, 259
Kaufman, Boris 319, 327

Kaufman, Denis *see* Vertov, Dziga
Kaufman, Mikhail 355
Kaufman, Phillip 34
Kaye, Tony 365, 377
Keaton, Buster 187
keiko-eigai 125, 135, 141, 429–30
Kennedy, John F. 338
Kent International Film Festival 339
key action 61
Keystone Cops 187, 307, 308
Khan, Aamir 83, 85, 94
Khan, Amjad 85
Khan, Farah 89
Khan, Irfan 85
Khan, Saif Ali 94
Khan, Shahrukh 83, 85, 88, 93
Khanna, Akshaye 94
Khatami, Mohamad 103
Kher, Kirron 85
Khomeini, Ayatollah 102
Khvato, Vassili 167
Kiarostami, Abbas 99, 100, 102, 103, 107,
    109–17, 202, 223
Kill Bill, Vol.1 8–9, 10
Kimiai, Masoud 102
Kind Hearts and Coronets 34
Kinematograph Company Ltd 298, 318
kinetic camera 296
kinetic lantern 296
kinetograph 291
kinetoscope 291–2, 296, 297, 306
King, Martin Luther 402–3
Kings of the Road 35, 37
Kino Pravda 318, 319
Kinoks film group 358
Kismet (*Fate*) 86
kitchen sink dramas 337
knowledge and skills audit 77
Kodak 291, 305
Koi no katamichi kippu (*One-way Ticket
    of Love*) 135
Koopman, Elias 306
Korean War 127, 133
Koroshi no rakuin (*Branded to Kill*) 132
Kracauer, Siegfried 177
Kramer, Stanley 34, 405
Krauss, Werner 175, 182
Kubrik, Stanley 365, 375, 416
Kuch Kuch Hota Hai (*Something
    Happens*) 80
Kukunoor, Nagesh 83

Kulishov effect 316
Kulkarni, Sonali 94
Kumar, Akshay 85, 88
kung fu films 246, 247
Kurosawa, Akira 124, 126, 127, 128, 130,
    137
Kurosawa, Heigo 128
Kurt and Courtney 333
Kwan, Stanley 413

El laberinto del fauno (*Pan's Labyrinth*)
    145, 152
Lacey, Nick 65
Ladri di Biciclette (*The Bicycle Thieves*)
    201, 205–9, 216, 217–18, 221, 223
Laemmle, Carl 307
Lan Yu 413
Lang, Fritz 73, 164, 345, 347, 390
language 6–7, 74, 271–2, 346–8;
    Bollywood 81; early film 300, 301–2;
    French 259; New Wave cinema 230,
    232, 241, 242, 245; shared 346–7;
    visual 346–7
Lasseter, John 11, 36
Last Year at Marienbad 185, 244
The Lavender Hill Mob 34
Lawrence, Florence 307, 308
le Vigan, Robert 392
*The Leader, His Driver and the Driver's
    Wife* 333
Leaving Jerusalem by Railway 295
Lee, Ang 247, 413
Left Wing Book Club 322
Leger, Fernand 362
Leigh, Mike 112
Lenin, Vladimir 324
Leon 34
Let Him Have It 365, 375
Levi Strauss, Claude 397
Life of an American Fireman 302
lighting 54, 61; Neo-realist 210, 216, 217
Lilies of the Field 405
Lin, Brigitte 246
Linah De Passe (*Line of Passage*) 73
Linklater, Richard 197
Linson, Art 418
'live' sound 54
The Living End 277
Livingstone, Jenny 35
Lloyd, Harold 308
Loach, Ken 10, 112, 365

location shooting: experimental film 358; German film 165; Neo-realism 204, 210, 216, 217; New Wave 234
Loera, Durn 147
Lola 152
London Film Society 321
Look At Britain Series 337
Looking For Langston 277
Loose Change 341
Lord of the Rings 152, 197
Los Angeles School of Black Independent Filmmakers 219
Love Actually 243
Lubin Studios 305
Lucas, George 128
Luhrman, Baz 18
Lumière brothers 6, 9, 292–4, 297, 298–9, 317–18

McCarey, Leo 149
McDermott, Kathleen 424
MacDonald, Kevin 339
Machaty, Gustav 35
Mackendrick, Alexander 34
McNeice, Louis 321, 323
macro issues 38, 385
Made in Hong Kong 246
Madonna 274
Madras 80, 84
magazine reviews 39
magazines 40–1
Maggiorani, Lamberto 207, 218
magic lantern 4, 290
The Magnificent Seven 128
Magritte, René 186
Mahabharata 84
Mahadevan, Shankar 94
Makhmalbaf, Marzieh 100
Makhmalbaf, Moshen 99, 102, 103, 105, 284
Makhmalbaf, Samira 99, 284
Makhmalbaf Film House 284
Malcolm X 403
male gaze 271–4
Man with a Movie Camera 345, 355–8
The Man in the White Suit 34
Marey, Étienne-Jules 290–1, 293
Margules, Ludwig 151
El Mariachi 144
Marker, Chris 335, 336, 345, 350, 351, 353–4

Marley, Bob 256
marriage, India 84, 89
martial arts films 28, 246, 247
Martinique 258
Marvin, Henry 306
Marxism 115, 167, 168, 253
Mary Jane's Mishap, or Don't Fool with Parafin 298
masculine/masculinity 141, 393–4, 415, 420
The Mask 187
masking 234
master scene scripts 48, 60
Matthews, C. 40
Matuszewski, Boleshaw 315
Mayer, Carl 175, 178, 181
Maysles, Albert and David 338
Meadows, Shane 112
Mean Streets 34
meaning 16, 23, 31, 33, 329, 335, 345–6, 348, 348–9, 353, 378, 385
Medak, Peter 365, 375
media effect model 417
Meet Marlon Brando 338
Mehra, Rakensh Omprakash 83
Mehrjui, Dariush 102
Meirelles, Fernando 159, 251, 265
Meisel, Edmund 318
Méliès, George 298–300
melodrama 278, 430; Bollywood 80, 91–2, 96; defined 92
Memento 243
memory 14
Mendonsa, Loy 94
La Mer 294
Meshes of the Afternoon 185, 345, 351, 353
Meshkini, Marziyeh 268, 269, 283, 284
messages 38
metaphysics 422
Metropolis 73, 163, 164, 345, 347–8, 390
Mexican Academy of the Cinematic Arts 156
Mexican Academy of Film 148, 152
Mexican cinema 72, 144–61, 220; early 311; European influences 146, 155; film schools 155–6, 161; genres 145, 159; 'golden age' 147, 150; historical background 146–7; and Hollywood 146–7, 150, 151; internationalisation of 156–8; neo-realist influence 146, 155;

and the state 147, 148; themes 146, 158–9
Michell, Roger 33, 34
micro issues 38, 385
mid-shots 113
Mifune, Toshiro 129–30
Mil nibes de paz cercan el cielo, amor, jams acabrs de ser amor (*A Thousand Clouds of Peace Fence the Sky, Love, Your Being Will Never End*) 145
Milani, Tahmeni 106
Mimic 152
mindset 52–3
Ming Liang-Tsai 246
Minghella, Anthony 34
Miraculo a Milano (*Miracle in Milan*) 201, 216, 221–2
Miro, Joan 186
Mirren, Helen 243
mise-en-scène 38, 61; experimental films 180, 349; French cinema 298; German cinema 180; Italian cinema 215, 217, 310; Japanese cinema 138; Poetic Realism 203; Spanish cinema 274
Mishimawho, Yokio 141
misogyny 14, 247, 415
Mission Impossible 2 247
Mix, Tom 308
Miyazaki, Hayao 197
Mizoguchi, Kenji 137, 138
Moana 315
mockumentary 331, 430
Modern Times 76, 386–91
modernism 133, 158
monster films 136
montage 189, 316, 318, 430; Soviet 164, 165, 174, 190, 356
Montand, Yves 359
mood 61
The Mood For Love 410
Moore, Michael 8, 339–40, 341
Morocco 365, 374
Morris, Errol 332–3
Morton, Samantha 424, 425
Morvern Callar 76, 423–5
Motion Picture Patents Company (MPPC) 305, 307
motivated cutting 190
Moulin Rouge 18
Muhkerjee, Rani 86
multiculturalism 257

multiple exposure 318
multiple-superimposition 300, 318
Mulvey, Laura 271
Mulvey, M. 110
Mumbai (Bombay) 80, 81, 84, 86
Munich 32
Munna Bhai 85
Murnau, Friedrich 165, 189
Mushkadiz, Anapola 154
music, Indian film 80, 83, 84, 85, 86
music videos 351, 354
musicals 215
Mussolini, Benito 206, 213, 215, 225, 428, 433
mutoscope 306
Mutual/Reliance-Majestic 309
Muybridge, Eadweard 290
My Beautiful Laundrette 365
My Own Private Idaho 277
My Son the Fanatic 35

Nanook of the North 316, 329
Napoleonic wars 193
narcissism 272
narration 55; 'voice of God' 330, 331, 335, 428
narrative 7, 8, 300, 301, 349, 430; experimental film 350; fictional 9, 12, 13, 14–15, 19, 112, 113, 125
narrative dissonance 56
narrative structure 38, 397–8; German film 180–1; Iranian cinema 110, 114; New Wave cinema 242–5; Surrealist film 195–6
narrative theory 232
Nation Film Board of Canada 321, 327
National Cinema 31, 72–3, 106–7, 192; definition of 100; Neo-realism and 202, 203, 219–20
National Democratic Front Party, Mexico 147
National Film Theatre (London) 337
National Front, France 259
national identity 203, 219, 411–12, 424
nationalisation, Japanese film industry 126
nationalism 120
nationhood 107
Natural Born Killers 416
naturalism 15, 430
La Nave Bianca (*Hospital Ship*) 215

Nazis 206, 213, 215, 219, 225, 326–7, 328, 330, 336, 428
Neale, Steve 65
Near Dark 35
Nelson, Ralph 405
Neo-realism 73, 86, 146, 155, 202, 430; *see also* Italian Neo-realism
Nestor 307
Netherlands 319
New Mexican cinema *see* Mexican cinema
new queer cinema 277
New Theatres (Calcutta) 85
New Wave 73, 115, 189, 229–49; audience 242; Chinese cinema 247; French (*nouvelle vague*) 100, 126, 132, 135, 139, 155, 229, 230, 231–42; German 230; and Hollywood 20; Hong Kong cinema 244–7; Iranian 100, 102; Japanese 125, 134, 135–6, 139, 140; language 230, 232, 241, 242, 245; narrative structure 242–5; and new technology 237
New York Stories 243
newsreels 213, 215, 225, 303, 308
Newton, Huey P. 405
Nichols, Bill 330
nickelodeons 303–5, 308
Niépce, Nicéphore 290
Night Mail 321, 322, 323
Nihon no yuru to kiri (*Night and Fog in Japan*) 124, 135, 139
Nikita 34
Nikkatsu Studios 132, 133, 134, 136
Nilsson, Rob 202
Nkosi Sikelei' iAfrika 120
Nolan, Christopher 243
non-diegetic sound 112, 113, 234
Noorani, Ehsaan 94
Nordisk company 311, 312
North by Northwest 398
The Northern Lights 202
Northern Photographic Works 296
Norton, Edward 377
Nosferatu 13, 163, 165, 178, 180, 181, 187
Notebook on Cities and Clothes 334
Notting Hill 33
nouvelle vague *see* New Wave
Novaro, María 144, 145, 152, 155
Novo Cine Mexicano *see* Mexican cinema

Nuit et Brouillard (*Night and Fog*) 336
Nuremberg trials 327

O Dreamland 337
Oberhausen Manifesto 20
observational documentary form 331–2
Offside 99, 105, 117, 118–22
Ohayô (*Good Morning*) 139
Okamoto, Kihachi 130
Olmi, Ermanno 201, 209–13
Olympische Spiele (*Olympia*) 326–7
On the Beach 34
On the Bowery 337
Once Were Warriors 365, 377
One Day in September 339
Operation Barbarossa 327
Operetta tanuki goten (*Princess Racoon*) 132
El Orfanato (*The Orphanage*) 145, 156, 158
Ornaghi, Luigi 212
Orphée 185
Oscars 107, 151–2, 204, 205, 223, 333, 401
Oshima, Nagisa 124, 134–5, 136, 139
Ossessione (*Obsession*) 201, 203, 214, 217, 430
La Otra Conquista (*The Other Conquest*) 144
The Outlaw 36
Ové, Horace 35
Ozu, Yasujiro 124, 138–9, 141

Padilha, Jose 265, 266
Pakistan 86
Palestine 294
Panahi, Jafar 99, 117
Paradise Now 73
Paragraf Zero (*Paragraph Zero*) 337
parallel editing 301, 302
Paramount Pictures 307
Paris is Burning 35
Parker, Albert 36
Parks, Gordon 402
Partido Revolucionario Institucional (PRI) 147, 150, 160
The Passion of the Christ 225
Pastrone, Giovanni 310
Pathé 293, 298, 303, 310, 311, 312
Pathé-Méliès 305
Pather Panchali 202, 223–4

Paths of Glory 365, 375
patriotism 120
Paul, R. W. 295, 296–7, 299
Pedro de Andrade, Joaquim 220
'peephole' devices 4
Penn, Sean 151
Pennebaker, D.A. 338
Pereira dos Santos, Nelson 220
The Perfect Vagina 341
performance: experimental film 349–50;
    gender as 270–1, 283
Perry, J. 403
Persepolis 99, 107–9
personal documentary 336, 337, 340
Pet Detective films 187
Phantasmagorie 289, 290, 428
The Phantom of Liberty 184, 191–7,
    197
'The phantom ride' 295
photographic gun 291–2
photography 84, 290
Pickford, Mary 307, 309
Pierrot le Fou 244
Pietrangeli, Antonio 203, 430
pinku eigo 132
Pirates of the Caribbean 58, 197
Pisutoro Opera (*Pistol Opera*) 132
Pitt, Brad 151, 157, 158, 273
Plan 9 from Outer Space 34
Planet of the Apes 197
Platoon 35
playback singing 85, 431
plotting 56–7, 114, 431
poetic realism 203–4, 392–4, 429
point-of-view shots 297, 396
Poison 277
Poitier, Sidney 405
Polanco, Alejandro 223
polemic 232
police 259, 264
Police Story 247
political context 82, 252; Brazilian cinema
    265; French cinema 258–9; Indian
    cinema 83, 86–7; Iranian cinema 101–3,
    121; Japanese cinema 126, 140–1;
    Mexican cinema 147; Neo-realism 211,
    213–15, 220
political institutions, neo-Realist criticism
    of 203, 221–4
political power 253
political studies 25, 31–2, 34–5, 37

political views 16, 19; extreme 377;
    Japanese cinema 125; Mexican cinema
    159; Soviet cinema 167–9, 170–2;
    Surrealism 185–6, 199–200
la politique des auteurs 231, 232, 395
Pommer, Erich 180
Pontecorvo, Gillo 76, 202, 218, 222, 223,
    399–401
pop art 131
pornography 132, 136
La Porta del Cielo (*Gate to Heaven*) 204
Porter, Edwin S. 300, 302
portmanteau film 243
post-production 54, 55, 112; censorship
    (Iran) 105
The Postman Always Rings Twice (Cain)
    217
postmodernism 270, 279
Il Posto (*The Job*) 209
poverty 73
power 14, 73, 253–4, 431
Prabhat Studios 85
Prasad, Udayan 35
pre-production 55; censorship (Iran) 105
presence and absence, Bollywood films
    97–8
presentation scripts 30, 42–5
Pressure 35
Primary 338
producers: as auteur 416; ideology 18–19
production 55; collaborative 136;
    independent *see* independent film;
    projects 26, 32, 48
production companies 32
production contexts, Japanese cinema
    126
professional practice 47, 49
Project Proposal Form 28–9
propaganda 174, 214, 225, 312, 324–8,
    331, 336, 431
Propp, Vladimir 397
proscenium arch 294, 431
Proyas, Alex 40
Psycheck 247
Psycho 365, 372, 373, 397, 398
psychoanalytical approach 7–8; *see also*
    unconscious
psychology 177, 179
'pull-down' mechanism 291
pull focus 297
Pulp Fiction 243

Qaisar (Caesar) 102
queer, as a term 277
The Quiet American 44
Quo Vadis? 310

Rabiger, Michael 66
race/racism 19, 259, 377, 402–6
Raghavan, Sriram 85
Raining Stones 10
Raja Harishchandra (King Harishchandra) 84
Ramsey, Lynne 76, 423–5
Ran 128
Rang De Basanti (Paint It Saffron) 83
Rashomon 124, 127, 128, 129, 130, 137, 141
ratings system, Iran 185
Ray, Man 319, 362
Ray, Satyajit 202, 223–4
realism 4–5, 8, 12, 15, 111–12, 146, 165, 202–3, 219, 431; and imitation of life 239–41; see also Neo-realism; Poetic Realism
the real 2, 4, 9, 75, 92, 93, 179, 202, 217, 348; documentaries and 316, 318, 319, 324, 328–9, 331, 341
Rear Window 273, 397, 433
Redford, Robert 243, 277
reflective analysis 49, 65–7
reflexive cinema 274–5
reflexive documentary mode 334–5
Regen (Rain) 319
regulation 25, 32, 349, 379, 418; Iran 100, 104, 105, 106, 116–17; see also censorship
Rehman, A.R. 85
Reimann, Walter 175, 181
Reiner, Rob 331, 430
Reisz, Karel 337
religion 212; India 82, 86; Iran 105–6, 116
Renoir, Auguste 241
Renoir, Jean 155, 203, 429, 430
Le Repas de Bébé 293, 294
representation 32, 254, 394, 431; of gender 119–20, 261, 268–85, 405–6; of women 16, 102, 104, 261, 268–85, 405–6
Rescued 301
research: primary 30, 39; secondary 30, 39

research skills 25
Reservoir Dogs 273, 365, 370, 373, 433
Resnais, Alain 135, 185, 244, 335, 336
responsibility as theme, Bollywood 91, 96–7
reversal technique 195, 196
reviews 39
Rey, Fernando 191
Reygadas, Carlos 145, 153–5
Rhythmus 21/Rhythmus 23 362
Richardson, Tony 337
Richter, Hans 345, 362
Riefenstahl, Leni 31, 325, 326–7, 328
Rine Que Les Heures (Nothing But Time) 319
Riso Amaro (Bitter Rice) 201
Ritchie, Guy 28
Ritha, Paul 321
ritual 158
The River 246
Robert, Étienne Gaspar 289
Robinson, D. 391
Rocco e i Suoi Fratelli (Rocco and His Brothers) 201, 226
Rocha, Glauber 220
RocknRolla 28
Rodgers, Lisa 340–1
Rodriguez, Robert 35, 144
Rogosin, Lionel 337
Rohrig, Walter 175, 181
Rokudenashi (The Good For Nothing) 135
roles 49, 50
Roma, Città Aperta (Rome, Open City) 201, 215, 217, 221, 400
roman poruno 136
Romper Stomper 365, 377, 379
Ronin 130
Roshan, Hrithik 83
Rossellini, Roberto 73, 201, 214, 215, 216, 217, 219, 224, 225, 400
Rosso, Franco 35
Rough Sea at Dover 295
Run Lola Run 35, 37
Rushdie, Salman 102
rushes 55
Russia 310–11, 312; see also Soviet cinema
Russian revolution 163, 167, 169, 311, 324
Ruttman, Walther 318, 319

Saadi, Jacef 218
Saikaku Ichidai Onna (*The Life of Oharu*)
 124, 137–8
Salisbury, Mark 42
Salles, Walter 73, 202
Sami directors 32
Samurai films 125, 127, 128, 129, 130,
 132, 137, 427
San Francisco 325
Le Sang des Bêtes (*Blood of the Beasts*)
 336, 337
Sans Soleil (*Sunless*) 335
Sanshiro Sugata 128
Santa Fe Film Festival 150
Sarris, Andrew 395
satellite television 100, 103
satire 194, 196
Satrapi, Mariane 99, 107
Savage Grace 277
scenes 38, 56, 61, 432
Schuzou River 229, 246
Schwarzenegger, Arnold 280
sci-fi 18, 34, 159, 197, 406–8
Sciuscia (*Shoeshine*) 205, 223
Scorcese, Martin 31, 34, 128, 225, 238,
 365, 371
Scotland 423–5
Scott, Ridley 413
screenplays 48, 55–62
screenwriters mindset 53
screenwriting projects 26
scripts 57–62; layout 60–1; master scene
 48, 60; presentation 30, 42–5; short
 film 48
Second World War 206, 259, 327
Seig des Glaubens (*Victory of Faith*) 326
Seishun zankoku monogatari (*Cruel Story
 of Youth*) 134–5
self-censorship 185
self-reflexive cinema 236–7
Selig 305, 307
Selznick, David O. 217
Senegal 258
Sennett, Mack 307
sequences 56, 432; extended 48
Serrano, Antonio 144
sex 432; and gender, distinguished 270
Sexo, pudor y lágrimas (*Sex, Shame, and
 Tears*) 144
sexual content 369, 376–7
sexual relationships 117, 159, 405–6

sexuality 14, 19, 32, 412–13, 420
Shadows 202
Shaft 402
Shah, Naseeruddin 85
shaped masks 297
Sharma, Konkona Sen 85
Shell Film Unit 321, 322
Shelley, Mary 197
The Sheltering Sky 36
Shichi-nin no Samurai (*Seven Samurai*)
 128
Shinju ten no Amijima (*Double Suicide*)
 124, 139–40, 141
Shinko Studios 133
Shinoda, Masahiro 124, 139–40
Shintoho ('New Toho') Studios 134
The Shipping News 34
Shirin 103
Shochiku Studios 132, 133, 134, 136
shocking cinema 369–78
Sholay 85
shomingeki 125, 138, 432
short films 31, 48, 308; scripts 48
Shoulder Arms 388
Shrek 36, 197
Sichel, Alex 35
Sight and Sound 39, 395
silent film 6, 126, 187, 189, 234, 387
Sin dejar huella (*Leaving No Trace*) 145,
 152
Singapore 246
Singer, Bryan 380
Singh, Manmohan 88
Singh, Uttam 88
'singing films' 311
single film critical study 31, 76, 385–425
Sippy, Ramesh 85
Sivan, Santosh 80
skills and knowledge audit 77
Slacker Uprising 341
Slackers 197
slapstick 126, 187, 188
Sleepy Hollow 36
Slow, percy 301
'slug line' 61
Small Scale Research Project 24–5, 27,
 28–46, 48
Smith, Albert E. 324
Smith, George Albert 297–8
Smith, J. 40
Sneider, Roberto 145, 159–60

soap operas 278
social context 17–18, 77, 251; Bollywood 81–2, 83; Brazilian cinema 265; French cinema 258–258–9; Japanese cinema 126, 140–1; Neo-realism 206, 215, 220
social institutions: neo-Realist criticism of 203, 221–4; power relations within 253–4
Social Realism 219, 337
social studies 25, 31–2, 34–5, 37
socialism 213
Solaris 76, 406–8
Sólo con tu pareja (*Love in a Time of Hysteria*) 144, 148–9, 151
The Somme 330, 428
song-and-dance, Indian film 80, 84, 85, 86, 95–6
Sontag, Susan 281
Sortie des Ouvriers de l'Usine Lumière (*Workers Leaving a Factory*) 292, 293, 317–18
sound 55, 61, 349; 'atmos' 54; diegetic 112, 234; documentaries 331, 337; 'live' 54; Neo-Realism 210; New Wave 234; non-diegetic 112, 113, 234; surround 33; synchronised 293, 331, 338
sound effects 54
sound recordists 54
soundtrack 54
South Africa 120
South Korea 246, 247
Soviet cinema 73, 163–75, 213, 323, 345, 355–8, 406–8; characters 171, 172; documentaries 318, 324; editing 164, 165, 166, 174, 356; historical context 163–4; politics 167–9, 170–2; themes 164–5
Soviet montage 164, 165, 174, 190, 356
space-time manipulation 5, 14, 299
spaghetti westerns 226
Spain 194, 213
Spanish-American war (1898) 324
Spanish cinema 193, 268–9, 270, 274–6, 278–9, 280, 281, 419–23, 428
Spanish Civil War 325
The Spanish Earth 325
special effects 55, 297
specialist studies 73–4
spectacle 301, 432

spectators/spectatorship 7–8, 74–6, 77, 78, 127, 432; *see also* audience
spectatorship topics 74–5
Spielberg, Steven 32, 130
Spirited Away 197
spiritual realism 219
split-screen cinematography 299
Spurlock, Morgan 8, 340, 341
Stacey, Jackie 274
Staiola, Enzo 207
Stallone, Sylvester 280
Stanislavsky technique 31
star system, Bollywood 93–4
star/performer 24, 31, 33–4; birth of 308–9; types, female 279–80
state 32, 196; Iran 100, 104; Mexico 147, 148; Neo-realist criticism of 221–2
Sternberg, Josef von 365, 374
Stoker, Bram 197
Stone, Admiral 224
Stone, Oliver 35, 416
Stop Thief! 298
storytelling 5, 9, 10, 19, 56
Strand Film Unit 321
Stranger Than Paradise 413
Strike 163, 165, 166, 167–75, 356
Sturges, John 128
stylisation 165
subconscious 13, 197, 198
subcultures 252–3
Subway 34
Sundance Film Festival 152, 156, 277
Supersize Me 9, 340
supporting films 33
Surrealism 5, 13, 14, 73, 184–200, 185–6, 283, 351, 432; as art movement 186; audience and 190; Buñuel and 13, 184, 187, 191–7, 351–3; characteristics 188–90; and fantasy film 197, 198–200; narrative structure 195–6; politics 185–6, 199–200
surround sound 33
Suzuki, Seijun 124, 131, 132
Svankmajer, Jan 184, 196–7, 198
Svilova, Elizaveta 355
Swades (*Homeland*) 83
Sweet Sixteen 365, 424
Sweet Sweetback's Baadasssss Song 76, 365, 376, 401–6
Swoon 277
synchronised sound 293, 331, 338

synoptic dimension 71–2, 432
synthesising learning 433

Taare Zameen Par (Stars on Earth) 83
Taiwan 246
Talancón, Ana Claudia 159
Talk To Her 76, 419–23
Tamahori, 365, 377
Taniguchi, Senkichi 130
Tarantino, Quentin 8, 10, 133, 238, 243, 273, 365, 370, 433
Tarkovsky, Andrei 76, 406–8
Tarzan and His Mate 36
Taxi Driver 365, 371, 373
Taylorism 389
'tear-jerkers' 278
technology 1–3, 25, 32–3, 36, 100, 237
Televisa 151
television 136, 146, 147, 339; advertising 9, 11, 371; satellite 100, 103
Il Tempo Si e Fermato (Time Stood Still) 209
10 99, 109–16, 122
tendency films 125
Terreblanche, Eugene 333
text 37–8
textual analysis 235
That Obscure Object of Desire 184, 191
theatre: Bunraku puppet 140; kabuki 125
theatrograph 296
Thelma and Louise 413
themes: Bollywood 80, 91, 96–7; and form, link between 397; Iranian cinema 116, 119–20; Japanese cinema 125, 137; Mexican cinema 146, 158–9; Soviet/German cinema 164–5
There's Something About Mary 339
Theroux, Louis 340
They Call Me MISTER Tibbs! 405
The Thin Blue Line 332
The Third of May, 1808 (Goya) 193
This is Spinal Tap 331, 430
Thomas, Daniela 73
thrillers 159, 397–8
Through the Olive Groves 99
A Time of Love 103
time-space manipulation 5, 14, 299
timelines 30, 55
Tisse, Edouard 167
Titicut Folies 338

titles 55
To Sir, With Love 405
Todo Sobre mi Madre see All About My Mother
Todorov, Tzvetan 397
Toei ('Eastern Film Company') Studios 134, 136
Toho Studios 133, 134, 136
Tokyo Monogatari (Tokyo Story) 124, 138, 141
Tokyo Nagaremono (Tokyo Drifter) 124, 131, 132–3
Le Tombeau d'Alexandre (The Last Bolshevik) 335
Tora! Tora! Tora! 128
Toro no O Fumo Otokatachi (They Who Step on the Tiger's Tail) 128
Toronto Film Festival 148
Touching the Void 339
Tout va bien 345, 349, 359–61
Toy Story 11, 36
Toy Story 2 36
Trainspotting 424
The Tramp 387, 388
travelogues 315
The Tree of Wooden Clogs 201, 209–13
'trick' photography 299
Triumph des Willens (Triump of the Will) 31, 325, 326, 328
Troche, Rose 35, 277
Tropa de Elite (Elite Squad) 266, 267
Truffaut, François 229, 231, 395
The Truman Show 197
truth 9, 127, 318, 324, 407
Tsotsi 251
Tsumasaburo, Brando 134
Twentieth Century Fox 307, 380
21 Grams 151, 157
Twin Town 33
Tykwer, Tom 35

Umberto D 216
The Unbearable Lightness of Being 34
unconscious 185, 189, 190, 197
underground films 354
United Artists 309
United States see American cinema; Hollywood
Universal Pictures 307
unreal 1, 5
'Unseen World' series 318

Urban, Charles 301, 318
urban stories 73

values 17, 19, 38, 251
vampire films 13–14, 433
Van Peebles, Melvin 76, 365, 401–6
Van Sant, Gus 277
Vargas, Getulio 220
Veer-Zaara 85
Veidt, Conrad 175, 182
Venice Film Festival 129, 138, 223, 401
Vertigo 76, 394–8
Vertov, Dziga 14, 318, 319, 324, 345,
    355–6, 358
video 33, 48, 54–5; expanded 75, 344–63,
    372; music 351, 354
La Vie et la Passion de Jesus Christ
    298
Vietnam 258
Vietnam War 35
vignettes 211
Vigo, Jean 319, 391
Vinterberg, Thomas 229
violence 369–76, 417
Viridiana 193
Visconti, Luchino 201, 203, 214, 217, 226,
    430
visualisation 62
Vitagraph 305, 307, 324
Vitti, Monica 191
'voice of God' narration 330, 331, 335,
    428
voicing 311
von Trier, Lars 350
Le Voyage à travers l'impossible 300
La Voyage dans la Lune 300
voyeurism 272, 273, 373, 397, 433

Walpole, Horace 197
war films 274
'war on terror' 194
Warhol, Andy 350
Warm, Hermann 175, 181
Watt, Harry 321, 323, 327
Watts, Naomi 151
We are the Lambeth Boys 337
Weary Willie and the Gardener 297
The Wedding Banquet 413
Wedgewood, Thomas 290
Welles, Orson 147, 395
Wenders, Wim 35, 37, 334, 339

Western influences 116, 126
westerns 32, 126, 132, 145, 226, 274,
    306, 308
Weston, Judith 151
White Telephone films 214, 215, 225,
    433
Who Cares? 333
Why We Fight series 327
Wiene, Robert 165, 175, 345, 349
wildtracks 54
Williamson, James A. 297–8, 318
The Wind Will Carry Us 223
Wise, Robert 34
Wiseman, Frederick 338
A Woman of Paris 388
woman's film 278–80
women 13–14; empowering 74, 99–100,
    268–85; Indian society 89; Iranian
    cinema/society 99–100, 102, 104, 114,
    117, 122; Japanese cinema 137, 141;
    Mexican cinema 158; representation of
    16, 104, 137, 261, 268–85, 405–6;
    see also mysogyny
Wong Kar Wai 76, 229, 245, 246,
    409–13
Woo, John 247
Wood, Ed 34
Wood, Robert 332
Wood, Robin 395
World Cinema 72, 79, 126, 162, 192,
    203
Worley, D. 403
Wright, Basil 321, 323, 327
Wright, Geoffrey 365, 377

X-Men 380

Y to mam también (And Your Mother Too)
    145, 151
yakuza 125, 132, 136, 141, 434
Yamamoto, Kajiro 128, 130
Yamamoto, Yohji 334
*Yang + Yin: Gender in the Chinese
    Cinema* 413
Ye Lou 229, 246
Yoldore Tenshi (Drunken Angel) 128
Yoshida, Yoshishige 135
Young Soul Rebels 277

Zavattini, Cesare 204, 205
Zecca, Ferdinand 298

Zemeckis, Robert 35
Zero de Conduite 391
Zhang Yimou 247
Zinta, Preity 94

Zoetrope Studies 36
Zoopraxioscope 290
Zukor, Adolph 307
Zulu 44

Related titles from Routledge

AS Film Studies: The Essential Introduction

Sarah Casey Benyahia, Freddie Gaffney, John White

AS Film Studies: The Essential Introduction gives students the confidence to tackle every part of the WJEC AS level Film Studies course. The authors, who have wide ranging experience as teachers, examiners and authors, introduce students step by step, to the skills involved in the study of film. The second edition follows the new WJEC syllabus for 2008 teaching onwards and has a companion website with additional chapters and resources for students and teachers that can be found at **http://routledge.tandf.co.uk/textbooks/ 9780415454339**. Individual chapters address the following key areas, amongst others:

- British stars – Ewan McGregor
- Genre – Horror
- British Production – Working Title
- Social-Political Study – Living with Crime
- US Film – Westerns
- Film form
- Spectatorship
- The practical application of learning

Specifically designed to be user friendly, the second edition of *AS Film Studies: The Essential Introduction* has a new text design to make the book easy to follow, includes more than 100 colour photographs and is jam packed with features such as:

- Case studies relevant to the 2008 specification
- Activities on films like *Little Miss Sunshine*, *Pirates of the Caribbean* & *The Descent*
- Key terms
- Example exam questions
- Suggestions for further reading and website resources

Matched to the new WJEC specification, *AS Film Studies: The Essential Introduction* covers everything students need to study as part of the course.

ISBN 13: 978–0–415–45433–9 (pbk)
ISBN 13: 978–0–203–87162–1 (ebk)

Available at all good bookshops
For ordering and further information please visit:
www.routledge.com

Related titles from Routledge

Film Studies: The Essential Resource

Peter Bennett, Andrew Hickman, Peter Wall

Film Studies: The Essential Resource is a collection
of resource material for all those studying film at
university and pre-university level. The Resource
brings together a wide variety of material ranging
from academic articles; advertisements; websites;
interviews with directors and actors; magazines and
newspapers.

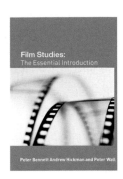

Individual sections address:

- Codes – examines the language of film, production,
  narrative and canon.

- Concepts – considers genre, the auteur, stars and realism.

- Contexts – covers themes of textual analysis, theoretical perspectives,
  industry and audience.

- Cinemas – investigates Hollywood, British cinema, national cinemas and
  alternative takes.

With each extract introduced and contextualized by the editors, and
suggestions for further activities and further reading included, *Film
Studies: The Essential Resource* is the perfect resource to kick-start
students' autonomy.

ISBN: 978–0–415–36567–3 (hbk)
ISBN: 978–0–415–36568–0 (pbk)

Available at all good bookshops
For ordering and further information please visit:
www.routledge.com

Related titles from Routledge

Film: The Essential Study Guide

Edited by Ruth Doughty and Deborah Shaw

Providing a key resource to new students, *Film: The Essential Study Guide* introduces all the skills needed to succeed on a film studies course.

This succinct, accessible guide covers key topics such as:

- Using the library
- Online research and resources
- Viewing skills
- How to watch and study foreign language films
- Essay writing
- Presentation skills
- Referencing and plagiarism
- Practical Filmmaking

Including exercises and examples, *Film: The Essential Study Guide* helps film students understand how study skills are applicable to their learning and gives them the tools to flourish in their degree.

ISBN 13: 978–0–415–43700–4 (pbk)
ISBN 13: 978–0–203–00292–6 (ebk)

Available at all good bookshops
For ordering and further information please visit:
www.routledge.com

Related titles from Routledge

Film Studies: The Basics

Amy Villarejo

Film Studies: The Basics is an engaging and accessible introduction that explores the intricacies of the film world to show how anyone can gain a broader understanding and a more pleasurable experience of film. Addressing general questions about why and how to study film, topics discussed include:

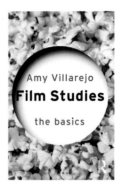

- the history, technology and art of the cinema

- the movie industry, from Hollywood to Bollywood

- who does what on a film set

- theories of stardom, genre and film-making

Including illustrations and examples from an international range of films drawn from over a century of movie-making and a glossary of terms for ease of reference, this is a must-have guide for any film student or fan.

ISBN 13: 978–0–415–36138–5 (hbk)
ISBN 13: 978–0–415–36139–2 (pbk)
ISBN 13: 978–0–203–01203–1 (ebk)

Available at all good bookshops
For ordering and further information please visit:
www.routledge.com

Related titles from Routledge

Cinema Studies: the Key Concepts

3rd edition

Susan Hayward

Ranging from Bollywood superstar Amitabh Bachchan to Quentin Tarantino, from auteur theory to the Hollywood blockbuster, *Cinema Studies: the Key Concepts* has firmly established itself as the essential guide for anyone interested in film. Now fully revised and updated for its third edition, the book includes new topical entries such as:

- Action movies
- Art direction
- Blockbusters
- Bollywood
- Exploitation cinema
- Female masquerade.

Providing accessible and authoritative coverage of a comprehensive range of genres, movements, theories and production terms, this is a must-have guide to a fascinating area of study and arguably the greatest art form of modern times.

ISBN 13: 978–0–415–36781–3 (hbk)
ISBN 13: 978–0–415–36782–0 (pbk)
ISBN 13: 978–0–203–02021–0 (ebk)

Available at all good bookshops
For ordering and further information please visit:
www.routledge.com

Related titles from Routledge

Fifty Key British Films

Edited by Sarah Barrow and John White

This book, the latest in the successful Key Guides series, provides a chance to delve into fifty British films considered a true reflection of the times. With case studies from the 1930s heyday of cinema right up to the present day, this chronologically ordered volume includes coverage of:

- The Ladykillers

- The 39 Steps

- A Hard Day's Night

- The Full Monty

- A Clockwork Orange

- The Wicker Man.

In *Fifty Key British Films*, Britain's best known talent, such as Loach, Hitchcock, Powell, Reed and Kubrick are scrutinised for their outstanding ability to articulate the issues of the time from key standpoints. This is essential reading for anyone interested in film and the increasing relevance of the British film industry on the international scene.

ISBN13: 978–0–415–43329–7 (hbk)
ISBN13: 978–0–415–43330–3 (pbk)
ISBN13: 978–0–203–93041–0 (ebk)

Available at all good bookshops
For ordering and further information please visit
www.routledge.com

Related titles from Routledge

AS Media Studies: The Essential Introduction for AQA

Third edition

Philip Rayner and Peter Wall

AS Media Studies: The Essential Introduction for AQA is fully revised for the 2008 specification with full colour throughout, over 100 images, new case studies and examples. The authors introduce students step by step to the skills of reading media texts, and address key concepts such as genre, representation, media institutions and media audiences as well as taking students through the tasks expected of them to pass the AQA AS Media Studies exam. The book is supplemented with a companion website at www.asmediastudies.co.uk featuring additional activities and resources, further new case studies, clear instructions on producing different media, quizzes and tests.

Areas covered include:

■ an introduction to studying the media

■ the key concepts across print, broadcast and e-media

■ media institutions

■ audiences and the media

■ case studies such as *Heroes*, *Nuts*, and the *Daily Mail*

■ guided textual analysis of real media on the website and within the book

■ research and how to do it

■ a production guide and how to respond to a brief

AS Media Studies: The Essential Introduction for AQA clearly guides students through the course and gives them the tips they need to become proficient media producers as well as media analysts.

ISBN13: 978–0–415–44823–9 (pbk)

Available at all good bookshops
For ordering and further information please visit:
www.routledge.com